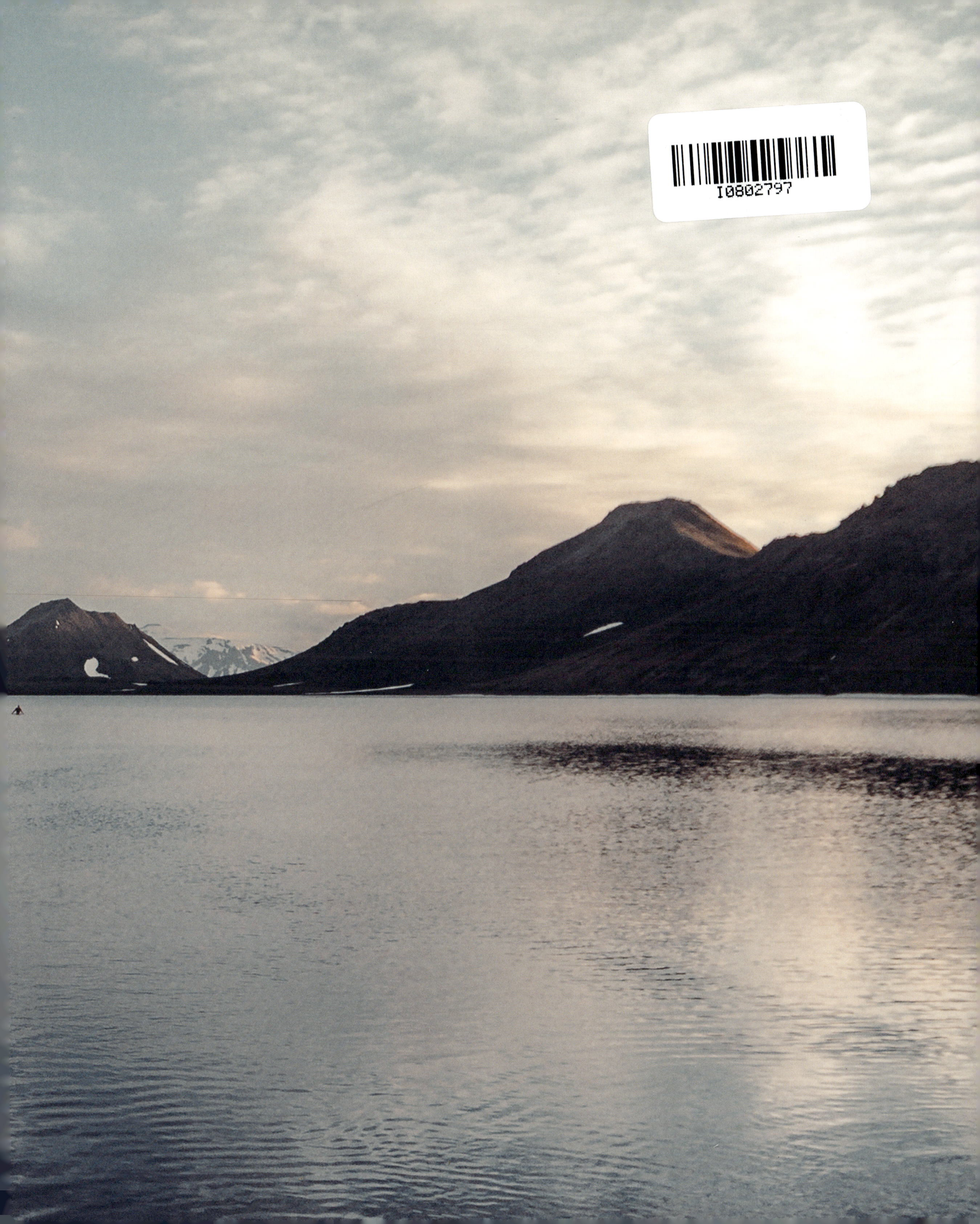

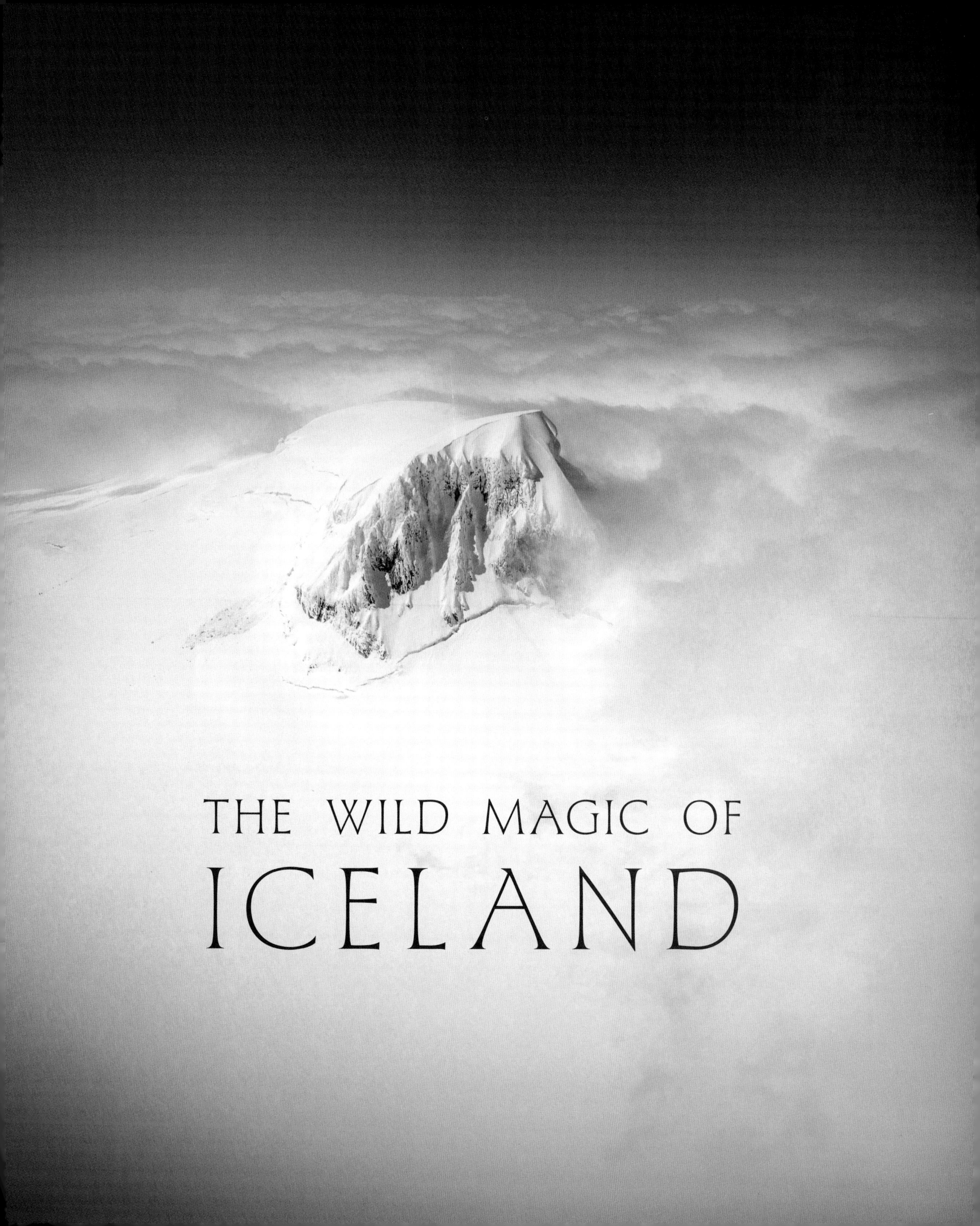

THE WILD MAGIC OF ICELAND

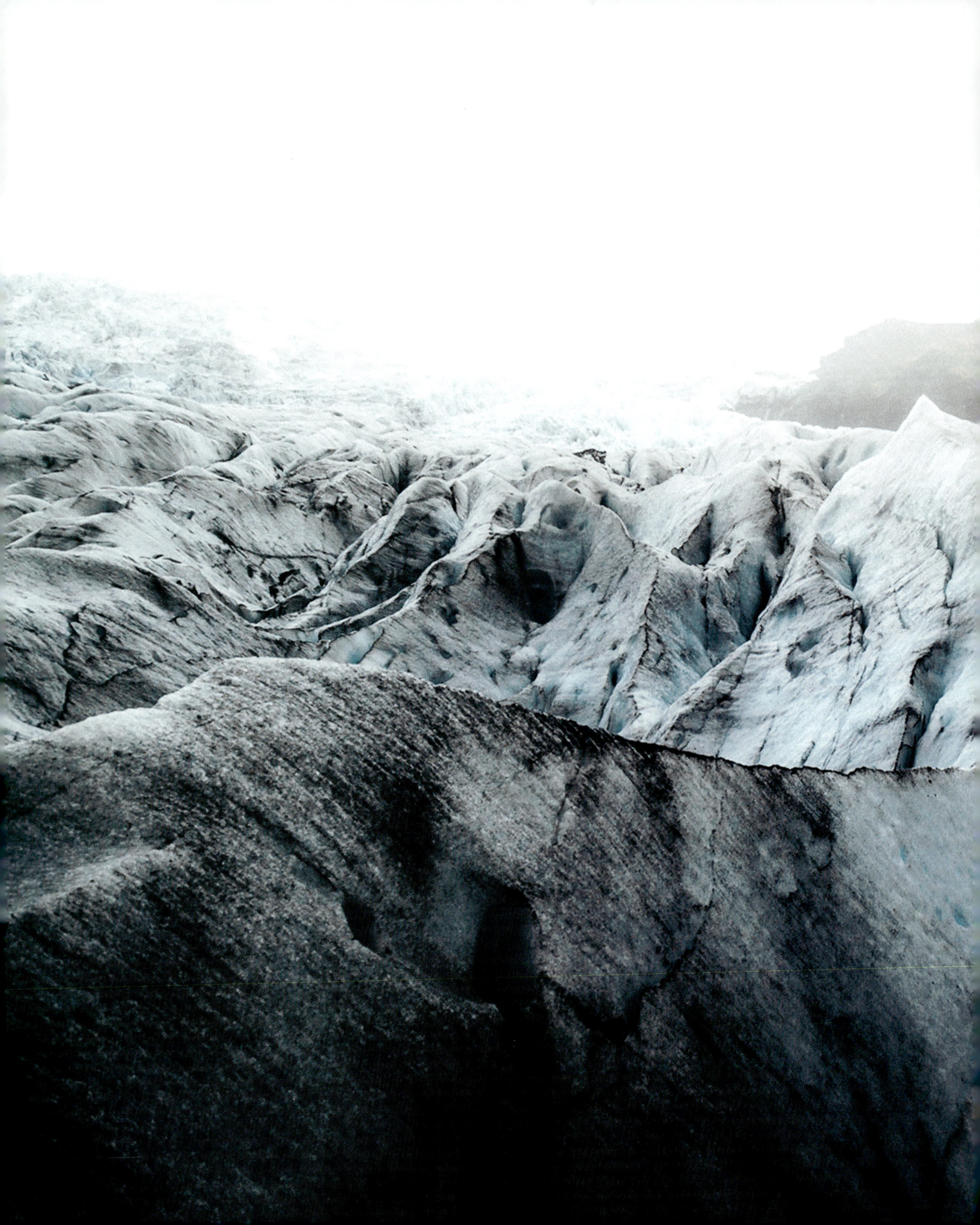

THE WILD MAGIC OF ICELAND

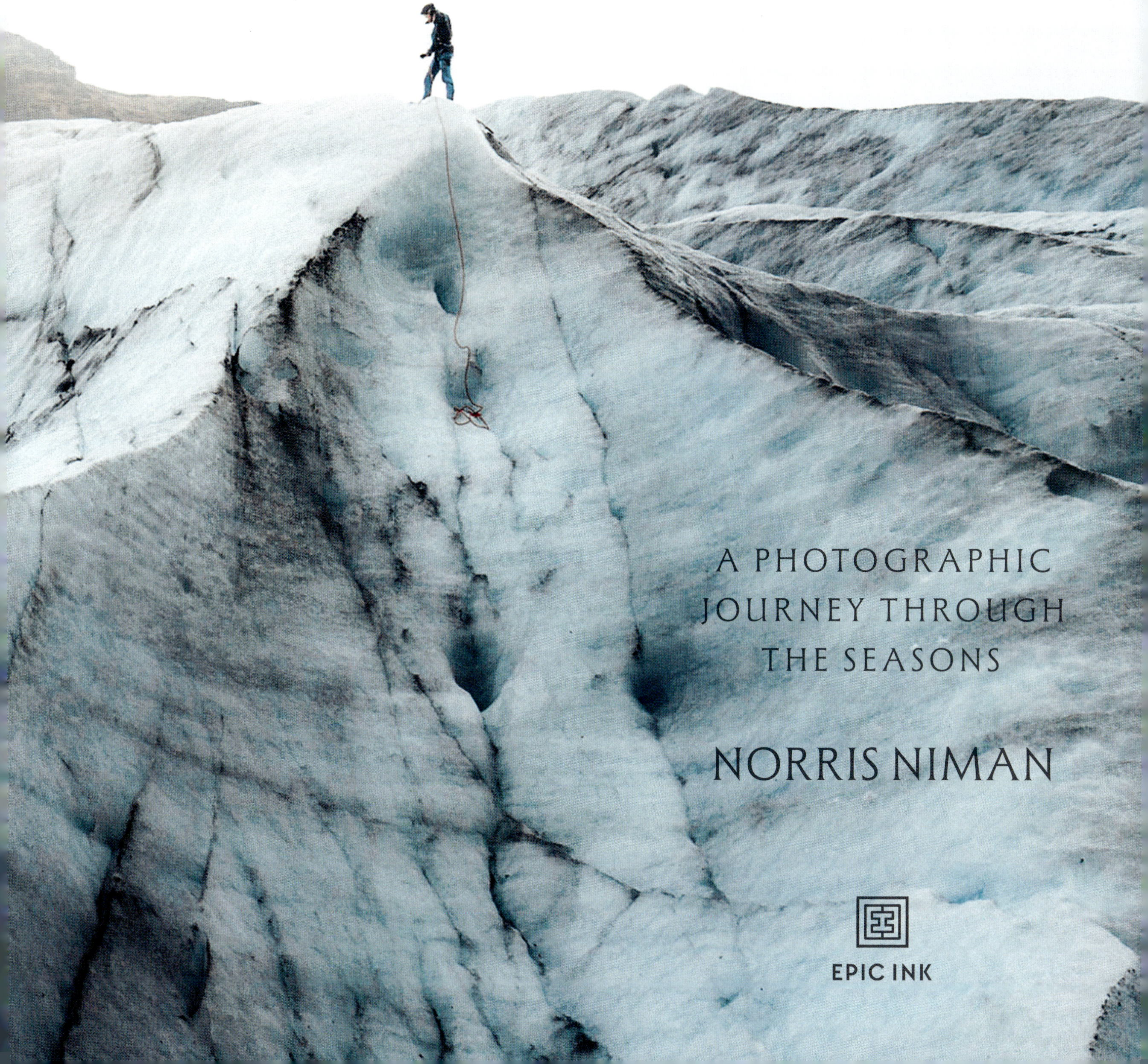

A PHOTOGRAPHIC JOURNEY THROUGH THE SEASONS

NORRIS NIMAN

EPIC INK

CONTENTS

Introduction
7

THE DEEP INHALE
JANUARY AND FEBRUARY
11

THE AWKWARD THAW
MARCH AND APRIL
51

THE GRAND AWAKENING OF EVERYTHING
MAY AND JUNE
91

MIDNIGHT SUN PARTY FOREVER

JULY AND AUGUST

131

THE SOFT DRAMA OF RETREAT

SEPTEMBER AND OCTOBER

171

THE QUIET COLLAPSE INWARDS

NOVEMBER AND DECEMBER

211

Gear List 251

Acknowledgments 252

About the Author 255

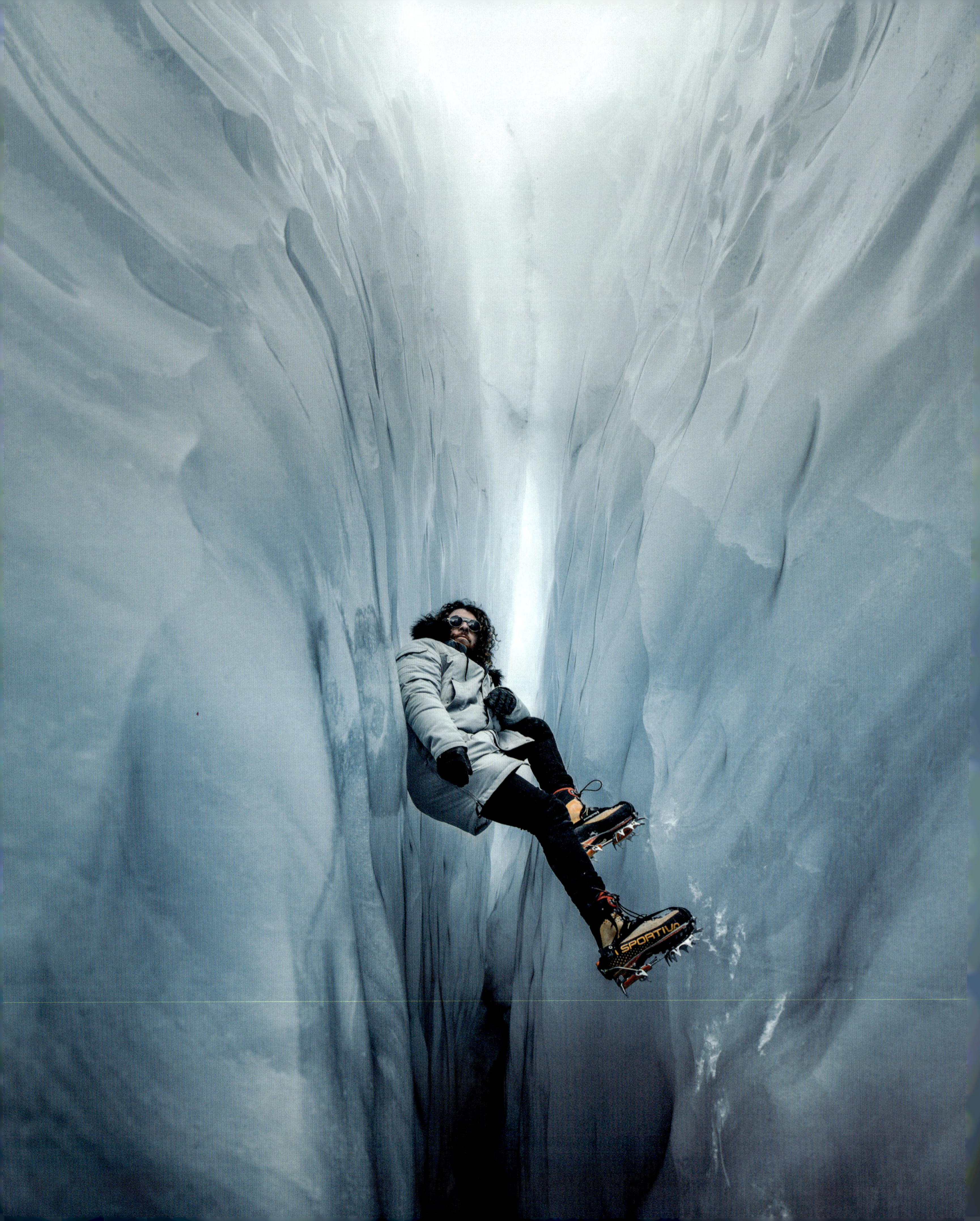

INTRODUCTION

In the old Norse culture, there were only two seasons: *Vetr*, winter, and *Sumar*, not winter.

It's hard to call anything "summer" in Iceland; it never gets all that warm, and we are situated pretty far north of where true summer takes place. But after a long slumber through the endless darkness of the deep winter, the blazing perpetual light of July and August ushers in a completely different era, a season that can definitely be considered "not winter."

Here in the far north, we follow the light—and it changes everything. There is no tidy everyday balance throughout the year, just full surrender to the big waves of seasonal extremes. You either learn to ride them or they ride you.

The darkest winter is a form of social and psychological semi-hibernation. Some say it's horrible and move away as soon as they can, but if embraced, it holds immense power. The people turn inwards, strengthen close connections, and recharge for when the light returns. And as it does, the whole island explodes on a newfound wave of energy, more potent for having been missed. Everything happens all the time. Then the light fades again and, in that quiet descent, the year exhales. Time to digest the intensity of the last light-filled marathon before the next wave crashes in.

Life here is taken day by day. It doesn't follow plans, it follows the weather—and the weather here is very Icelandic. The volcanoes don't care about your flight. The floods don't care about your hiking plans. And the landslides and avalanches just want to ride fast and far, no matter what's in their way.

So people here learn to adapt—to shift, adjust, reroute, and find joy in the new version of the day. There's even a saying: *Þetta reddast*. It kinda means "Hakuna Matata," or "it'll work out." (Yeah, every guide will say this on your first tour, but I *am* a guide.)

We don't say þetta reddast in a passive, fingers-crossed kind of way. More like a shrug, a laugh, and a determination to make something good out of whatever the island throws at you. And it works every time.

I am constantly amazed by humanity's resilience against the elements here in Iceland. It has taken a bunch of generations of suffering, effort, failure, and death to get this far and to be able to thrive here with relative ease.

Here, you need to shred all your desires to demonstrate any power over the elements. Don't demand any respect or any authority, and don't try to tame the weather. Just submit and you'll be fine.

And keep in mind: The light is only temporary. At some point, the darkness takes it all again.

HEYO, I'M NORRIS

To understand the photos in this book, you probably need to understand how someone ends up willingly freezing their fingers off for a decade.

I have been living and shooting in Iceland since 2015. I was only going to be here for three months, but I got stuck. In a good way. Possibly the best way. (I tried to leave once for a long weekend of two years, but I realized that the rest of the world wasn't better.)

It's not just the landscape that keeps me here. It's the wild, weird, wonderful people I keep accidentally sharing it with.

When you spend enough time in Iceland, you keep bumping into people. And not just in town! The real community moments happen out in the oddest, most remote places. I'll run into friends hanging off a glacier, ankle-deep in Icelandic powder, or next to the latest eruption, holding a marshmallow on a stick that's clearly too short to reach the lava from a safe distance. It's almost expected now that I'll pass someone in the middle of nowhere and think, *Of course, it's you.*

The people who end up in places like this are wired for wonder, physically and emotionally. They are just north of normal. They chase beauty without needing a reason. They have space within them for humanity and generosity. Winter is always coming, and we have to stick together to make it through—so the people here do.

I originally came here from Sweden to work as a scuba diving and snorkeling guide. Then I fell in love with showing people amazing things, so I became a glacier guide, then a trekking guide, a mountain guide, then an everything else guide, too. Discovering these mysterious lands was like filling in a blank map, and it brought me way too much excitement to leave Iceland. And wherever I went, I always brought my camera.

I quickly found myself at the center of a big boom of photographers realizing that Iceland was an island built especially for them. I had a camera, and I wasn't going to leave just because winter was coming. So, while I was guiding all the professional photographers coming in, I also got to start shooting these places professionally myself. While guiding countless photo tours, I absorbed more than I taught, turning every rock around to look at all of the angles. I have been here a decade now, having chosen this crazy island as my permanent home.

There are places that change you. I know, because Iceland has changed me. These places have an extra dimension of magic that you enter and experience while you're there. You arrive and leave a different person, with more understanding, empathy, and respect for a life that's only possible in one particular place. And no matter how hard you try to share the magic of these places in stories, it is almost impossible to recreate more than a fragment of it.

The magic of Iceland can't be fully captured or conveyed—but it shows up pretty well on camera.

So, let us begin.

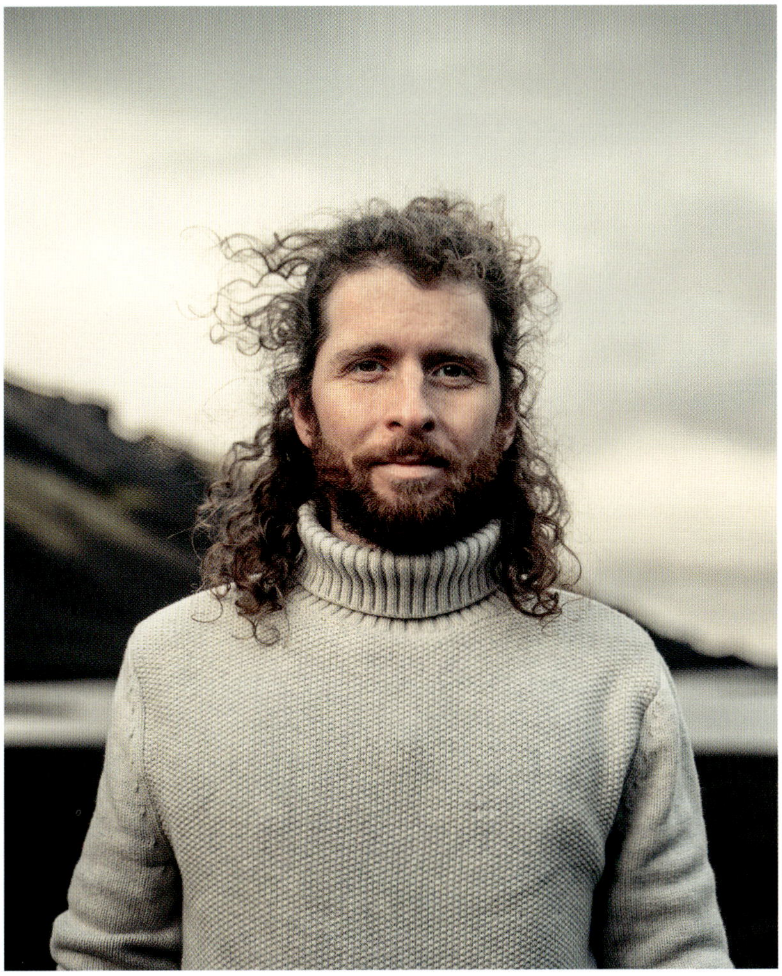

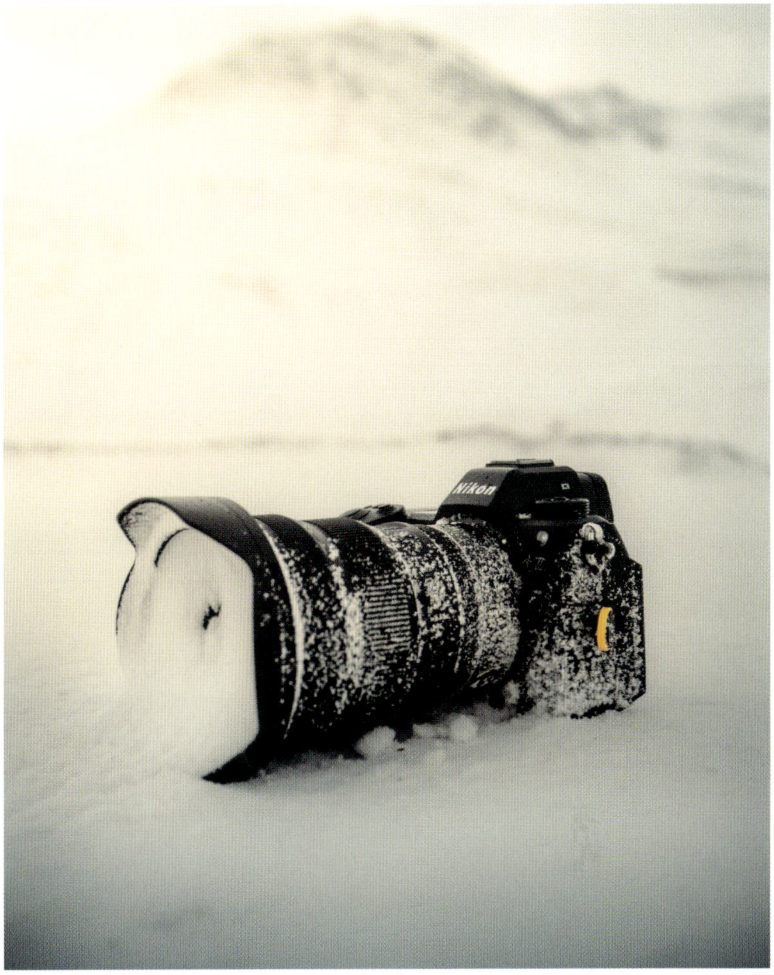
Nikon

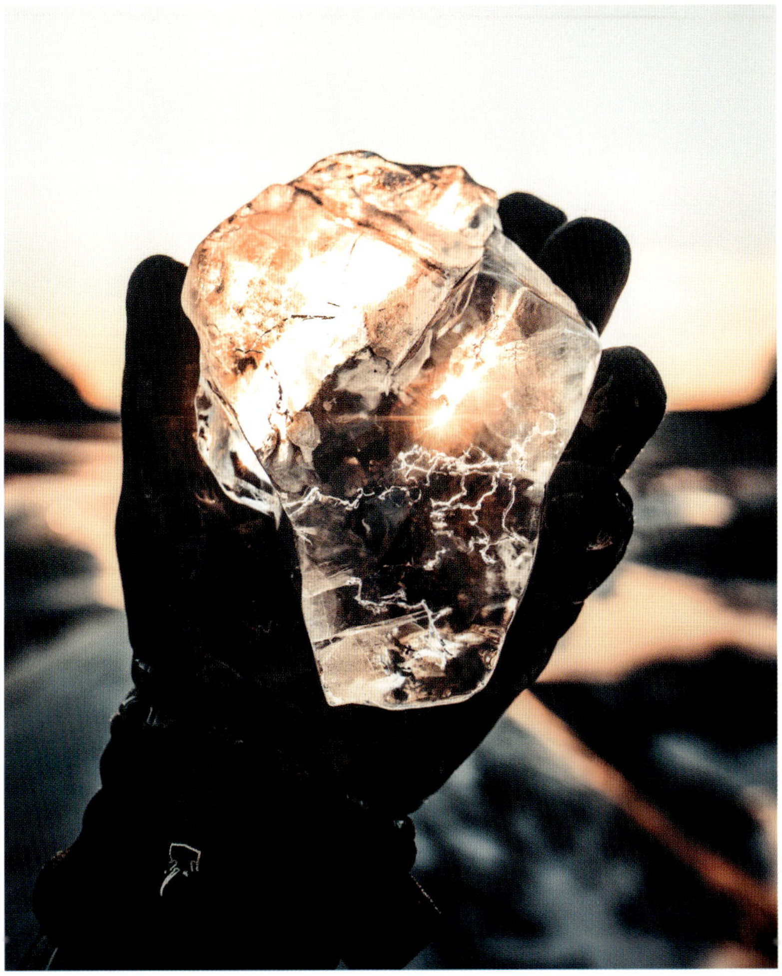

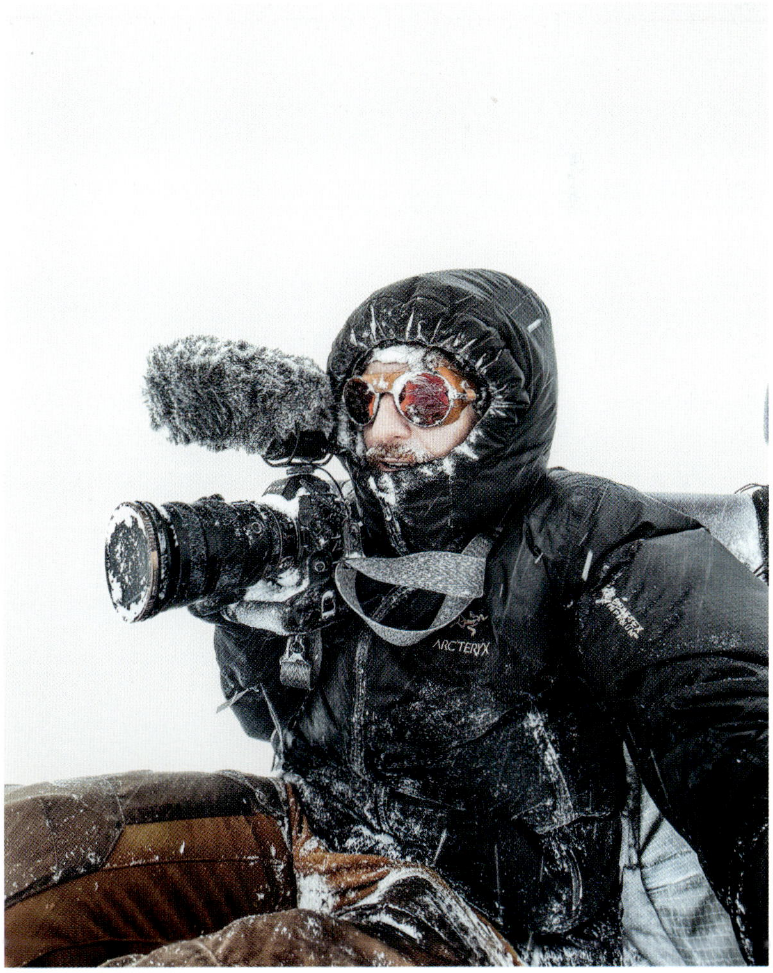
ARC'TERYX

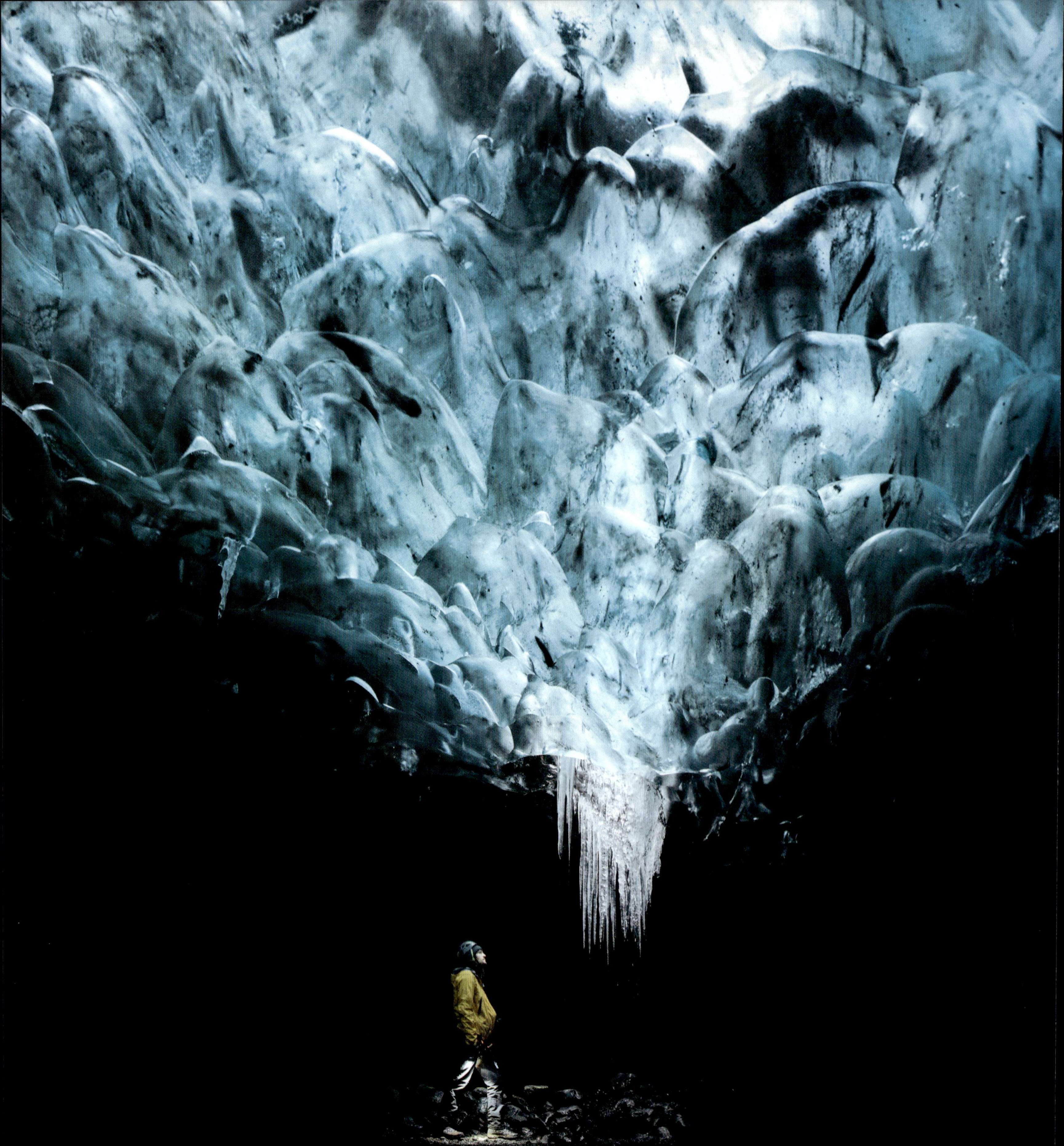

THE DEEP INHALE

January and February

Total darkness hangs on. Glaciers sleep.

The northern lights whisper behind the clouds.

Fewer words are used, and they're shortened.

Batteries die quickly. Time is a suggestion.

The night might seem bottomless. Especially when you're in the middle of it and it won't end for another month. But the night is actually tiny. Almost the entire rest of the universe is bright. Our perceived night is only a microscopic cone of darkness in a grand sea of light, like a grain of salt blocking candlelight on a dining table. But we spend so much of our lives inside it.

Here in the north—for a good part of the year—we're dancing just on the edge of Earth's shadow. Winter becomes a gravitational force. Streets are empty. No one is awake in the morning, and the ones who are stay in bed. It gets light just before noon, but the sun doesn't rise above the mountains. We just have to imagine its glow in the reflection of the snow.

Looking north out to sea you'll see the gradient of the planet's shadow. It goes from bright pink at the top, to deeper and darker purples until it turns to blue and blends into the ocean.

There's a quiet knowing shared by those who stay through this. A kind of emotional handshake. No one talks about how hard it gets, but we all feel it. We stay because we know that some things can only be earned in the dark. The darker the cold, the more warmth it draws out of the people. We gather closer and carry each other through.

Everything slows down. It's hard to leave the house in the dark. You put on five layers to go to the store and forget what you needed the second you step out. The wind blows your words sideways as your eyelashes freeze together. And somehow, you get used to it.

This is a time that holds a lot of silence and calm. It looks like nothing is moving, but everything is. Mosses storing sunlight. Rivers tunneling under the ice. People recalibrating their souls behind fogged-up windows. Winter is not dead, it's just when life turns inward. And everything is resting and recovering from the last season of light. There might be another one of those coming, but for now it feels too far off to even imagine. In our hibernation, the sun's warmth has been long forgotten. Only a soft echo of how it felt remains.

The slow silence is never truly empty either. It is filled with abandoned memories and new hopes. The darkness opens up a path for those small thoughts to flow in. The ones that don't come out of hiding in the intense noise of brightness. Only when you have made ample space do they come to follow along in your footsteps as you crunch through the snow. Those small, elusive thoughts come out to help you grow through this season of introspection.

There is plenty of time to breathe deeply, and to walk with them.

◂◂ VATNAJÖKULL

My suit is made out of gore-tex. I carry an axe to work. Rope keeps me safe and the hope that the volcanoes won't erupt makes every day a bit more exciting. This was my office for years. No matter how much of a photographer I become, I will forever be a glacier guide.

▸ VATNAJÖKULL II

It's in the darkest of times when it's easiest to hear the beating heart of the glacier. This is merely the opening of its digestive system, but we can already feel its rhythm.

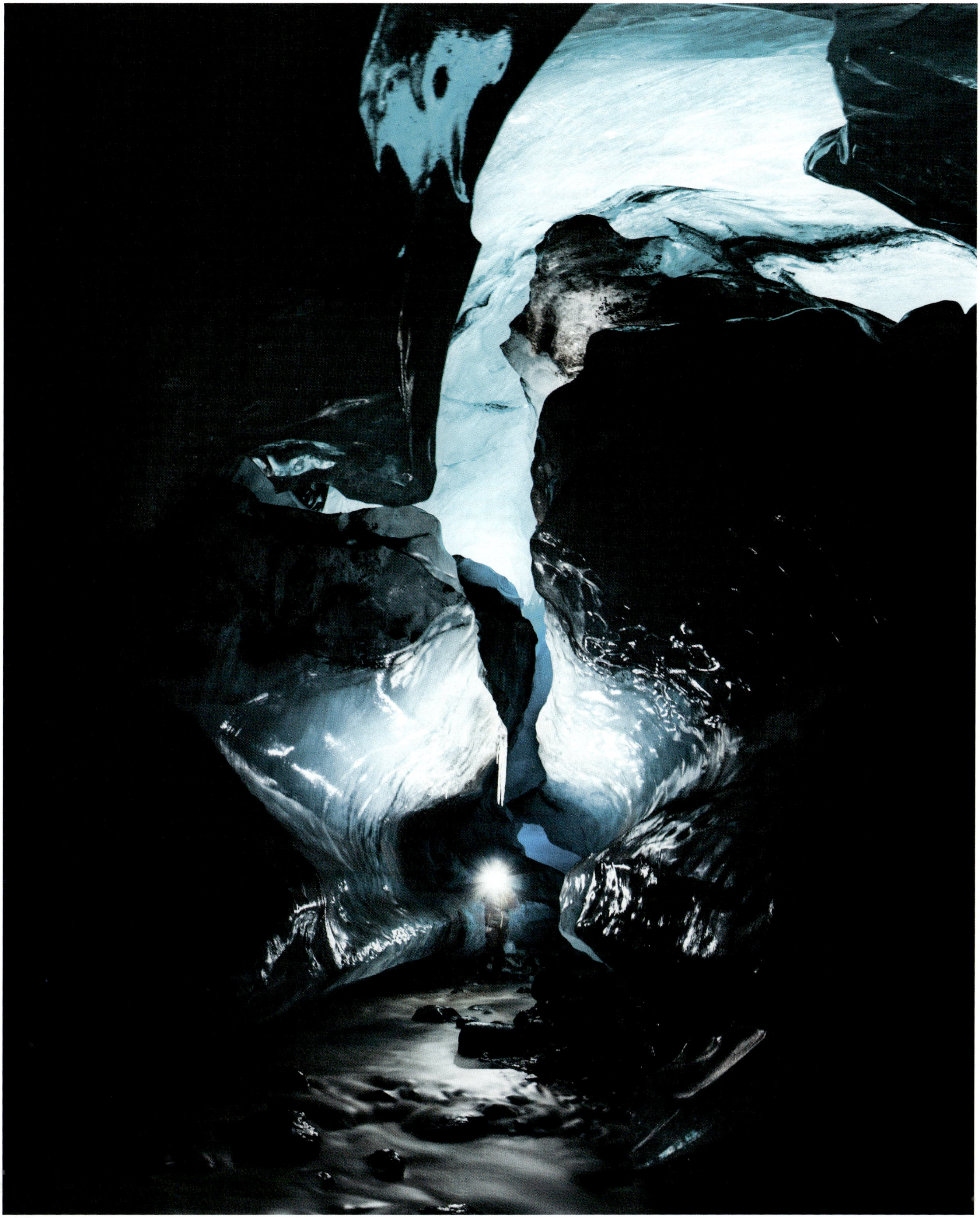

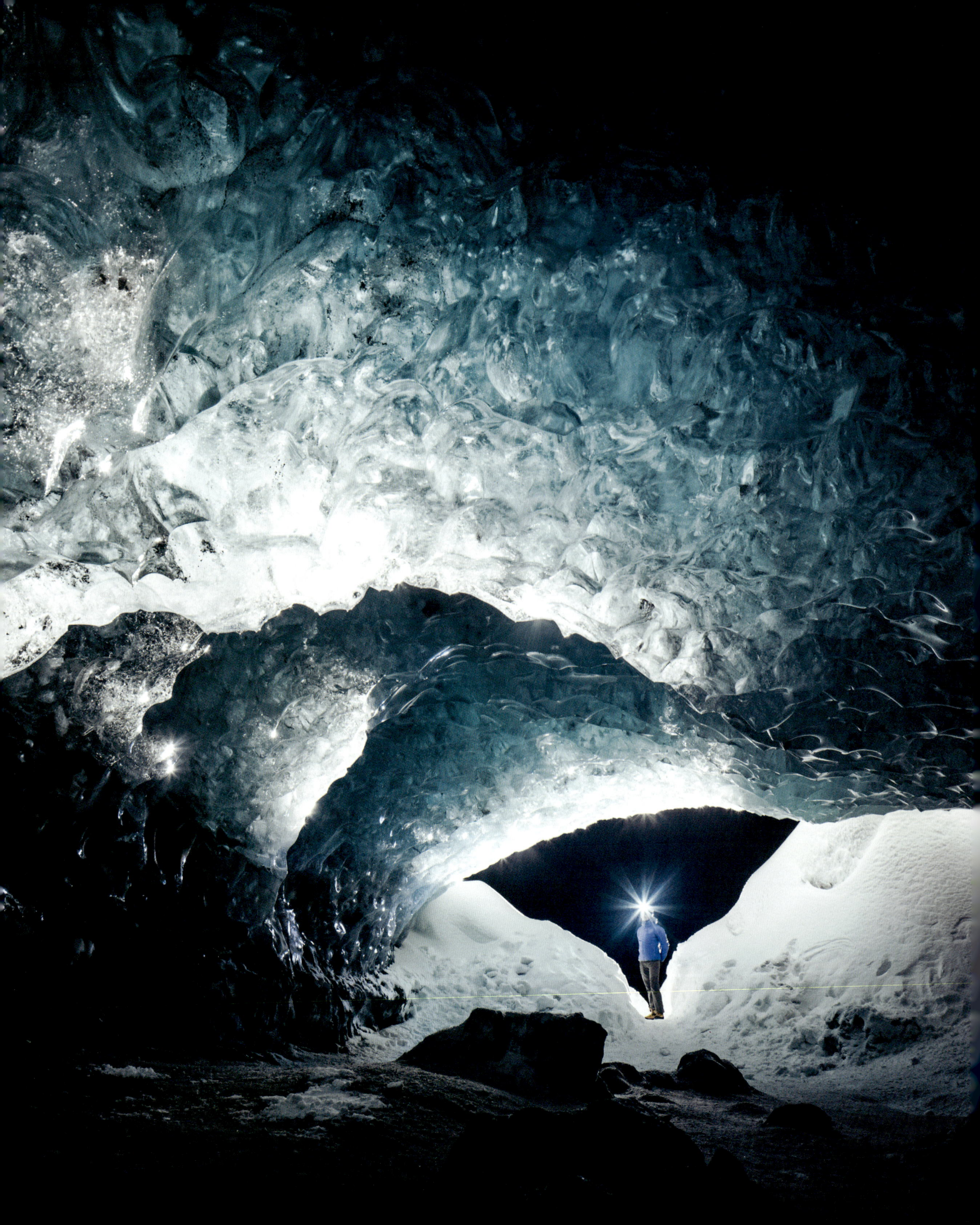

VATNAJÖKULL III

Some holes like to be frozen. We found one of them hanging out in the dark afternoon of deep winter.

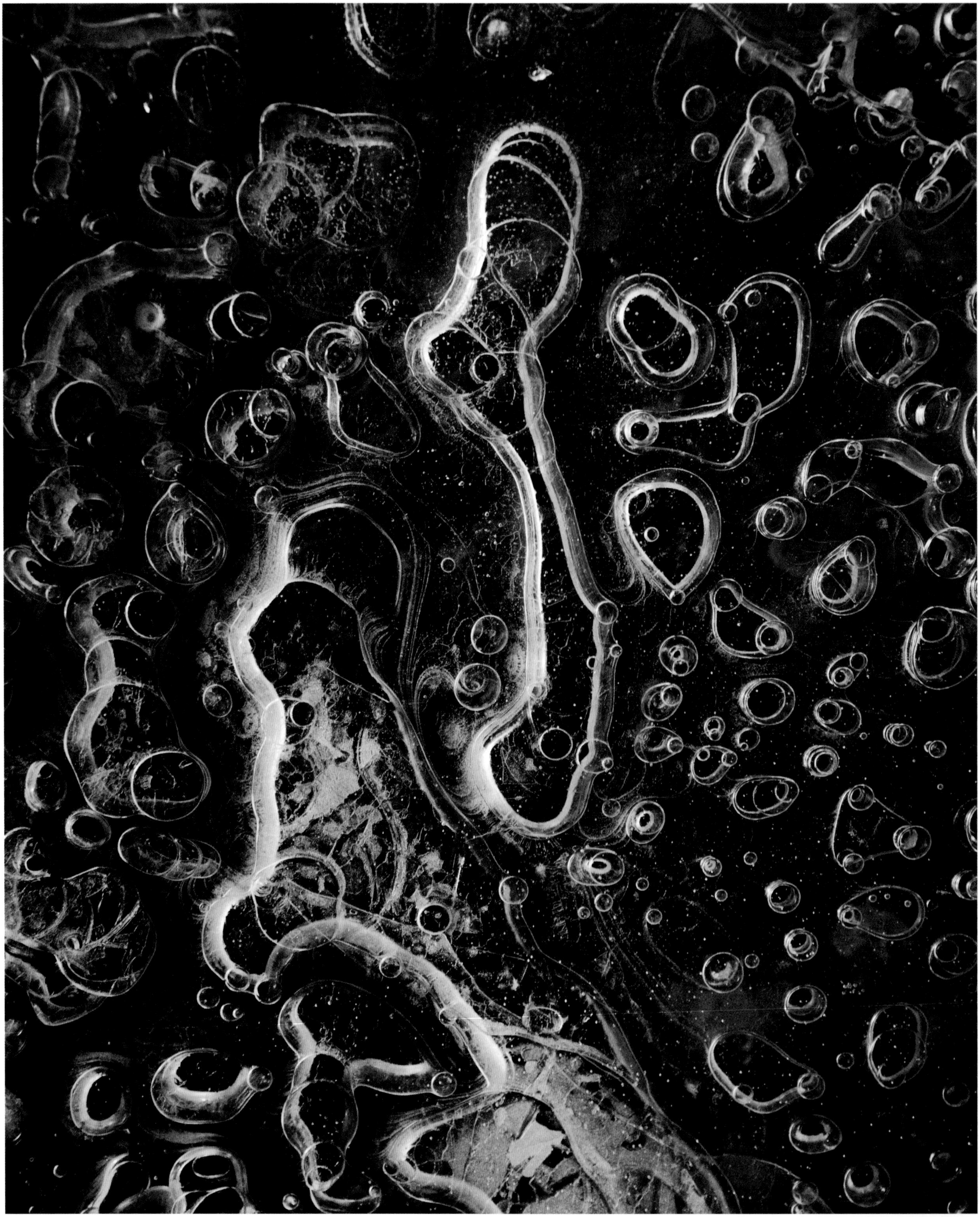

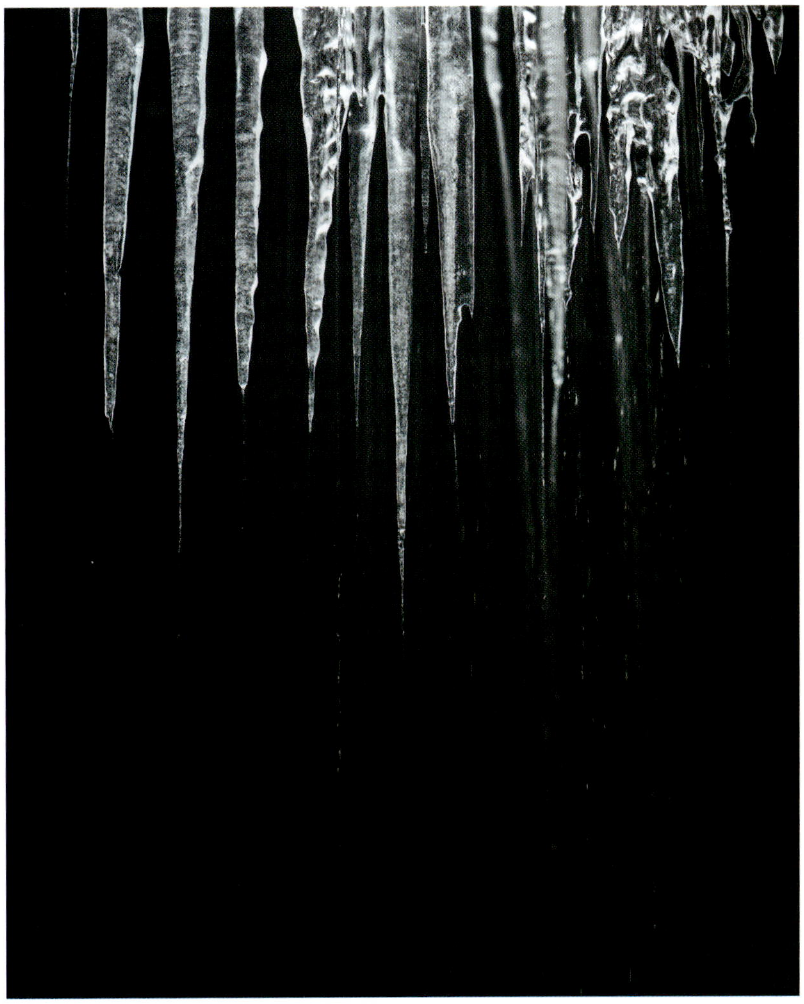

◂ FJALLSJÖKULL

Ancient air that could be as old as the breath of the Vikings, frozen in time inside the glacier.

▴ VATNAJÖKULL IV

Ice often cries in the dark, when it thinks no one is there to see. But sometimes we are there, just not usually to comfort it. We take our photos, then leave the ice to mourn the retreating winter.

▸▸ BORGARFJÖRÐUR EYSTRI

A lump of wild mountains came down to the Arctic Ocean for a drink.

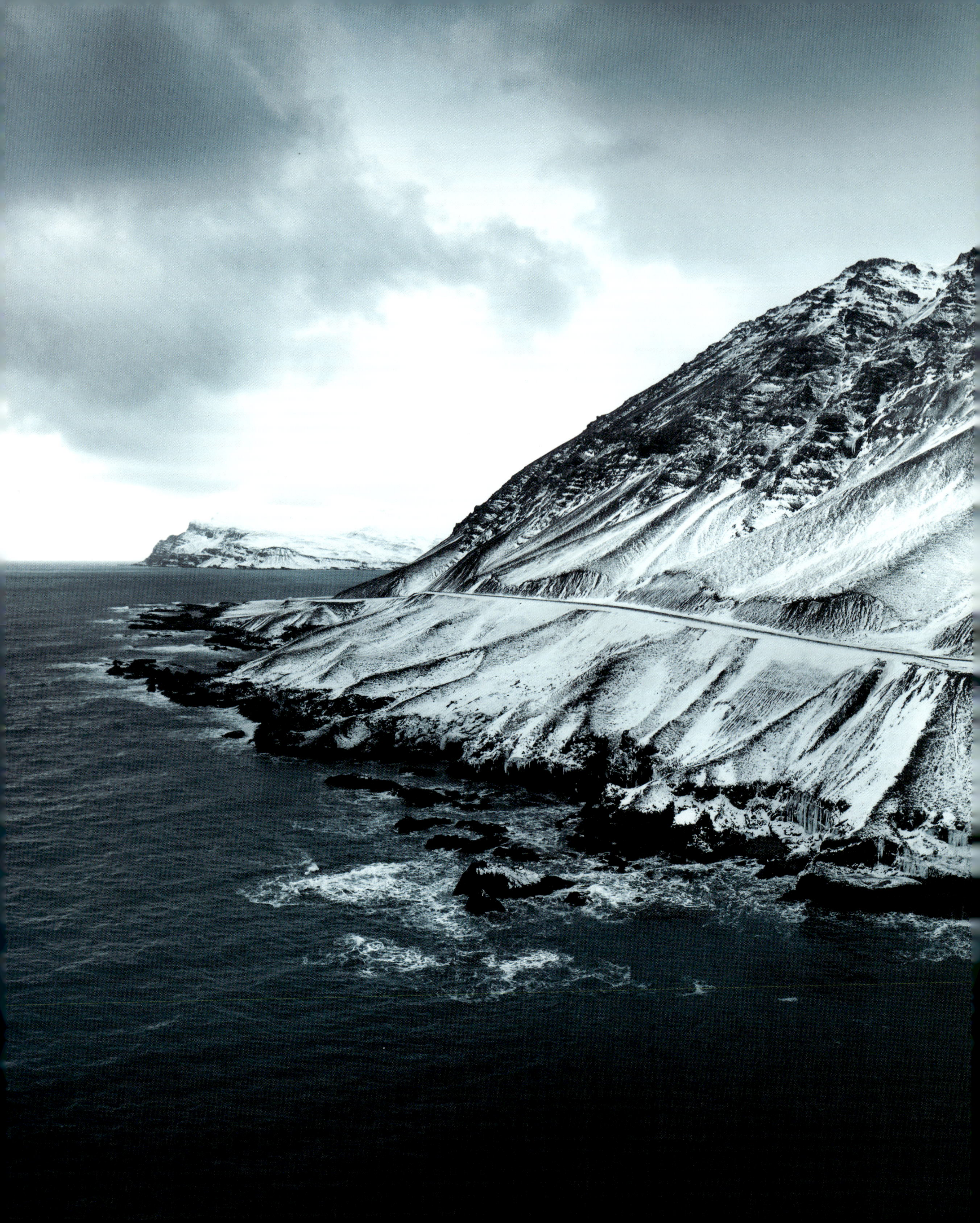

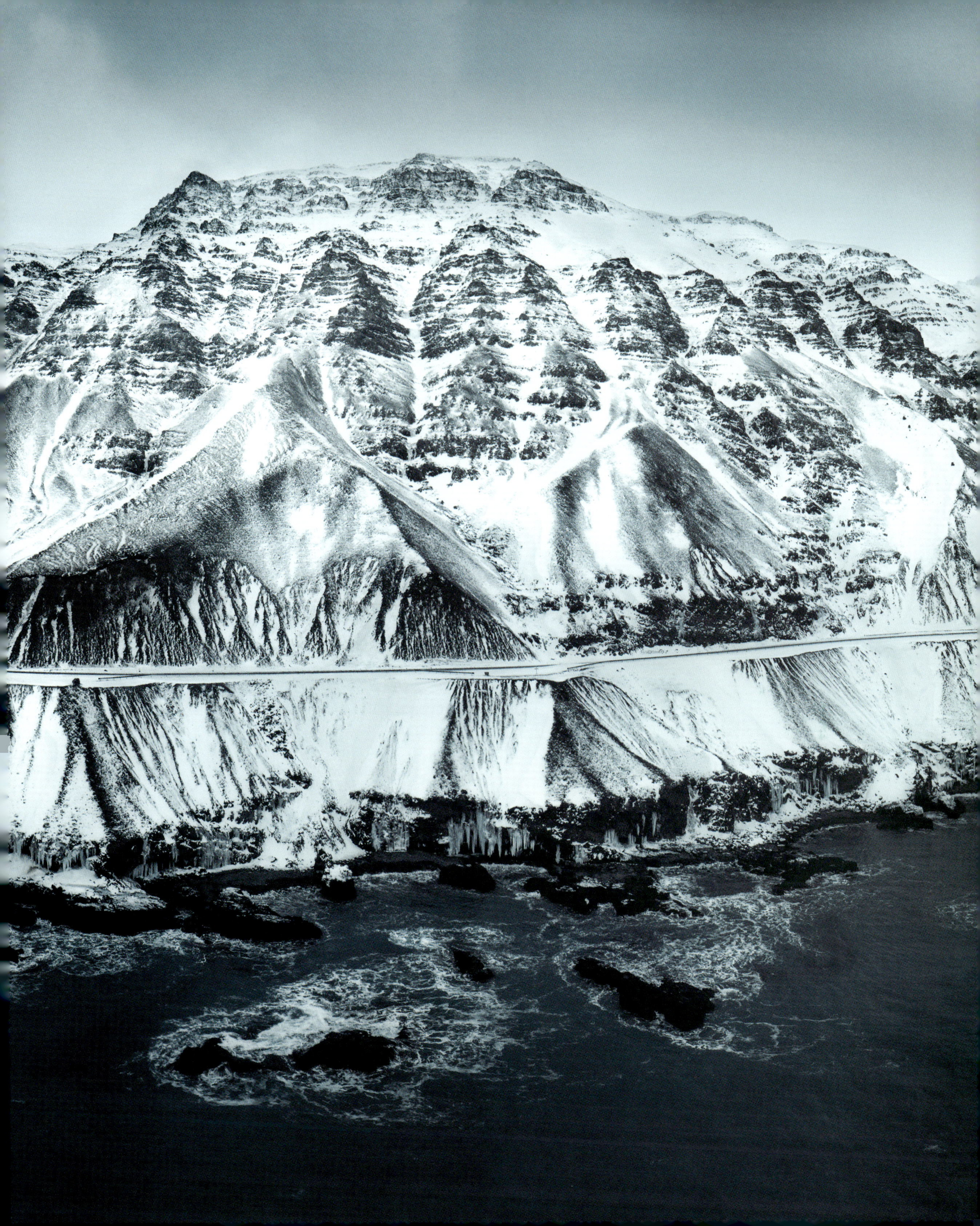

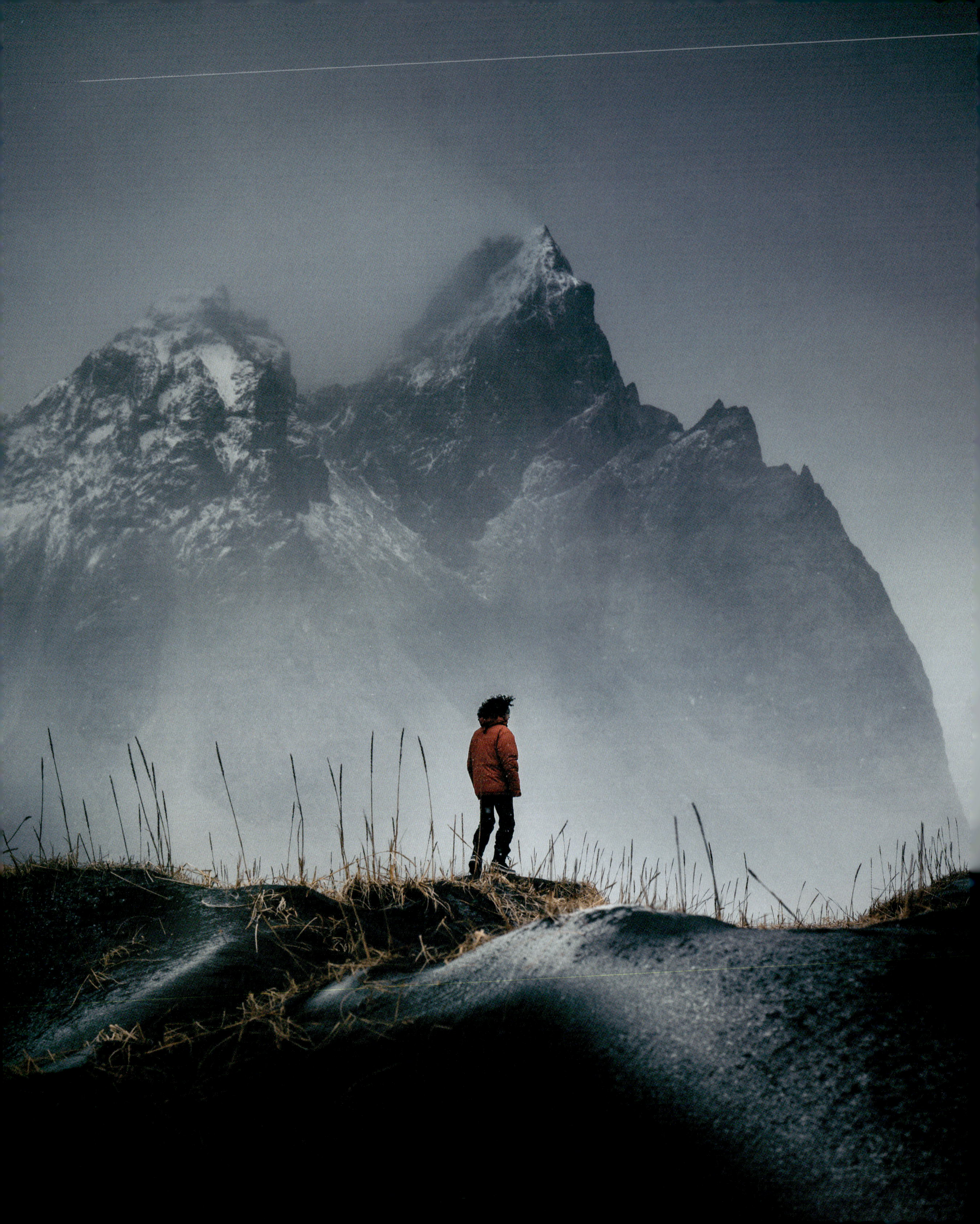

◂ VESTRAHORN

A great place to watch time blowing by.

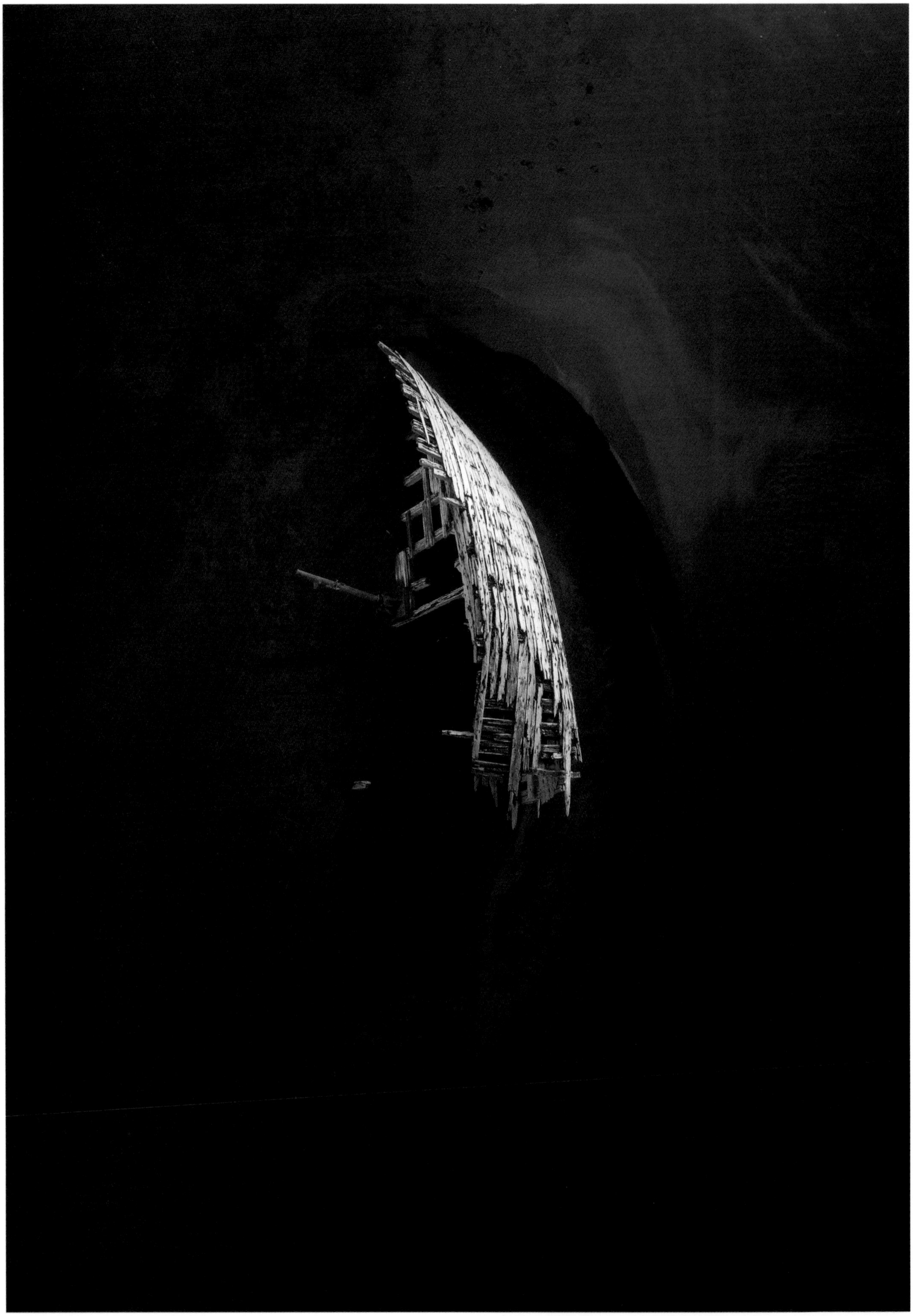

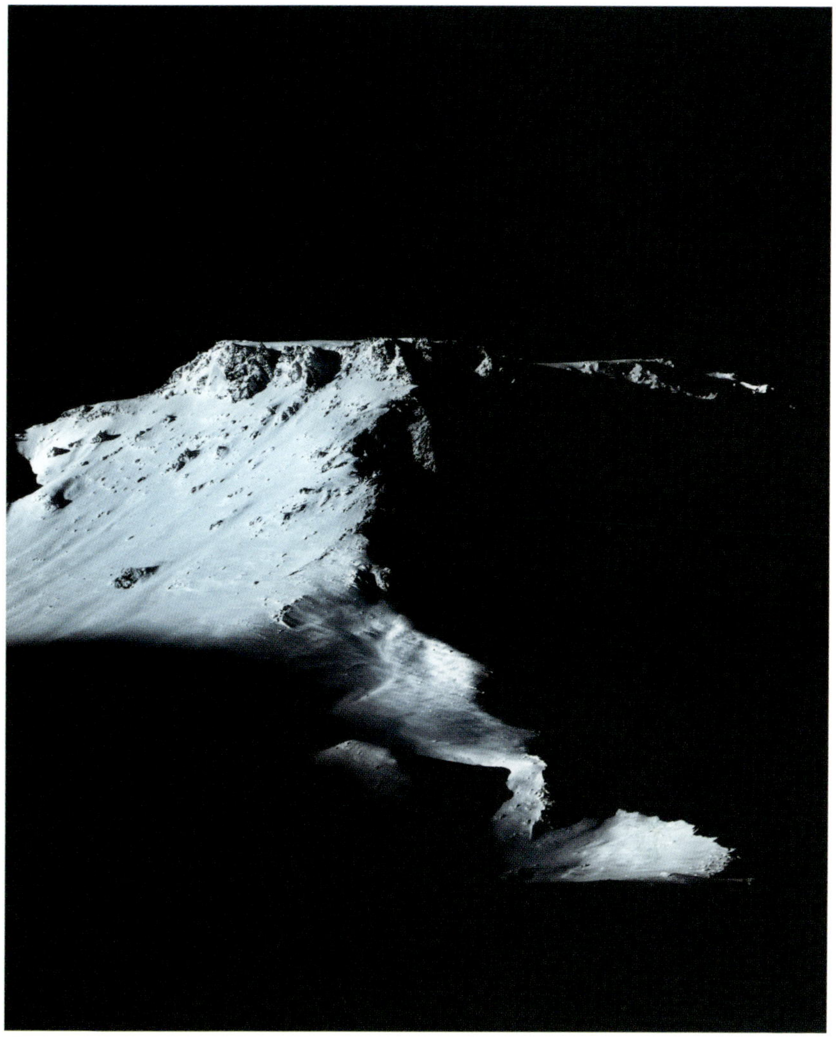

◂ NOT THE SEA

When the Vikings first arrived here, they tried to explore Iceland by boat. They forgot that it's a landmass consisting of land. It even says so in its name.

▴ THE PEAKS OF ICELAND

Visible once a month, because even in Iceland the bad weather takes a break every now and then.

▸ INGÓLFSHÖFÐI

A lot of nothing with a little bit of something.

▾ THE DESERT OF ASH

I found a horse that found meaning in a bunch of nothing, so I took a photo of it and now it has even more meaning.

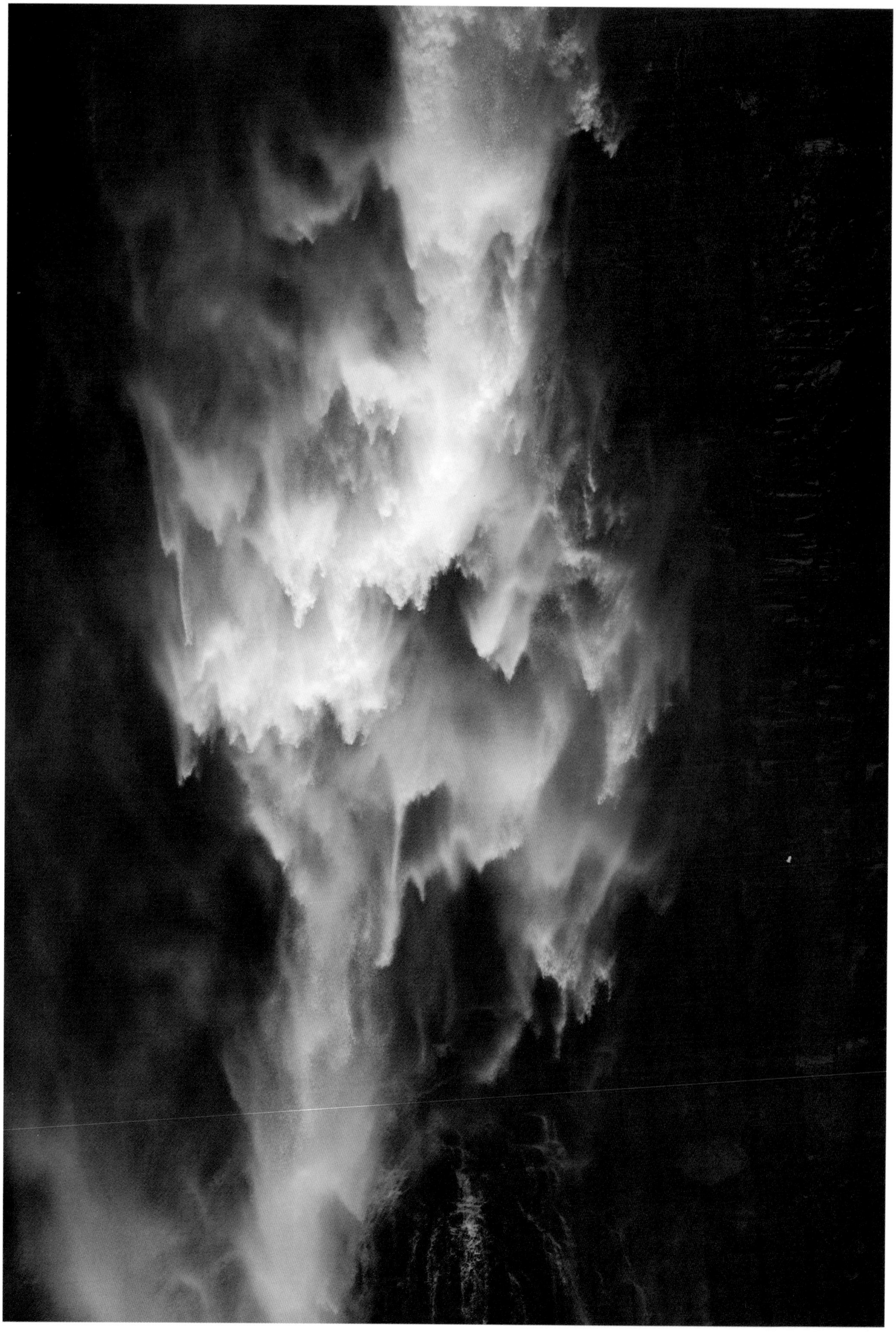

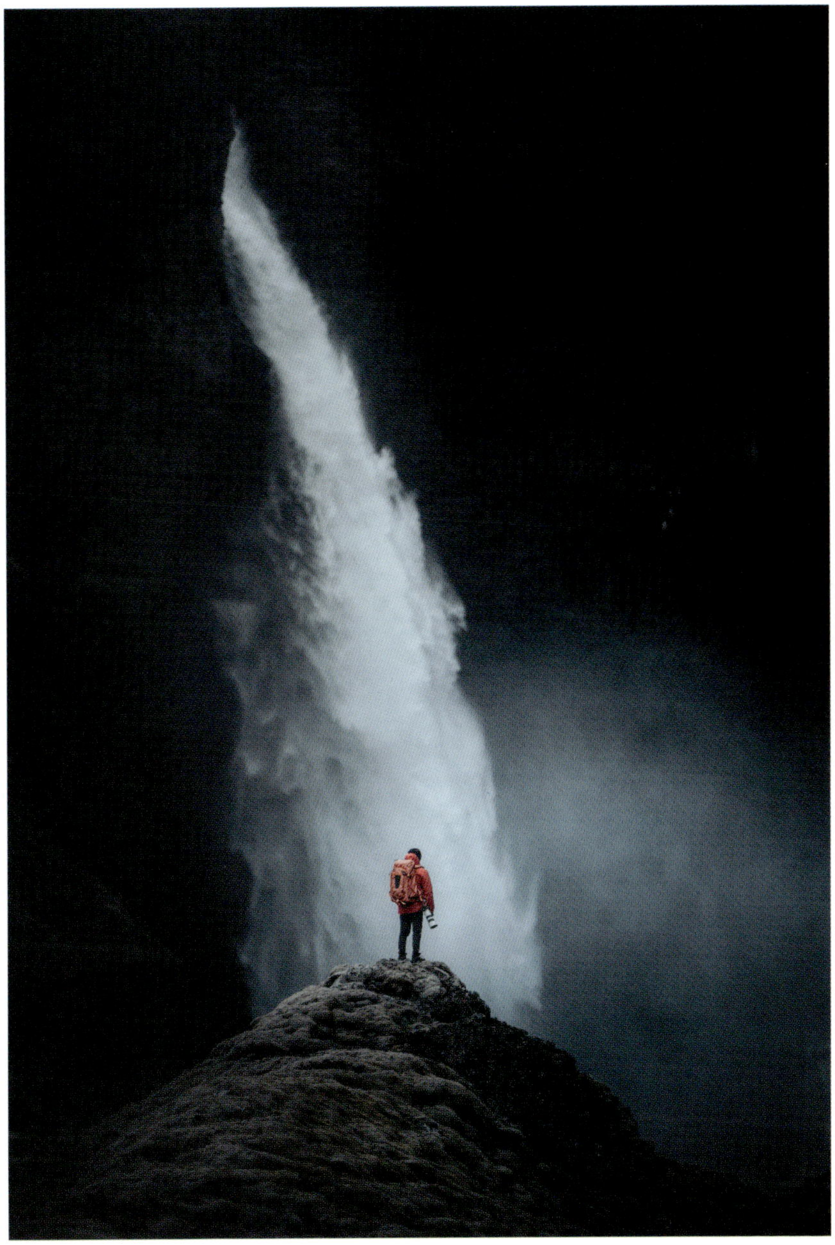

◂ ONE OF THOSE WET PLACES

Iceland is where waterfalls are manufactured and shipped to the rest of the world.

▴ HÁIFOSS

Once I walked out into nowhereness to watch water throw itself over a cliff. The water smiled when it saw me coming. After all these years, it was finally appreciated for its falling. It promised never to stop. Until it runs out.

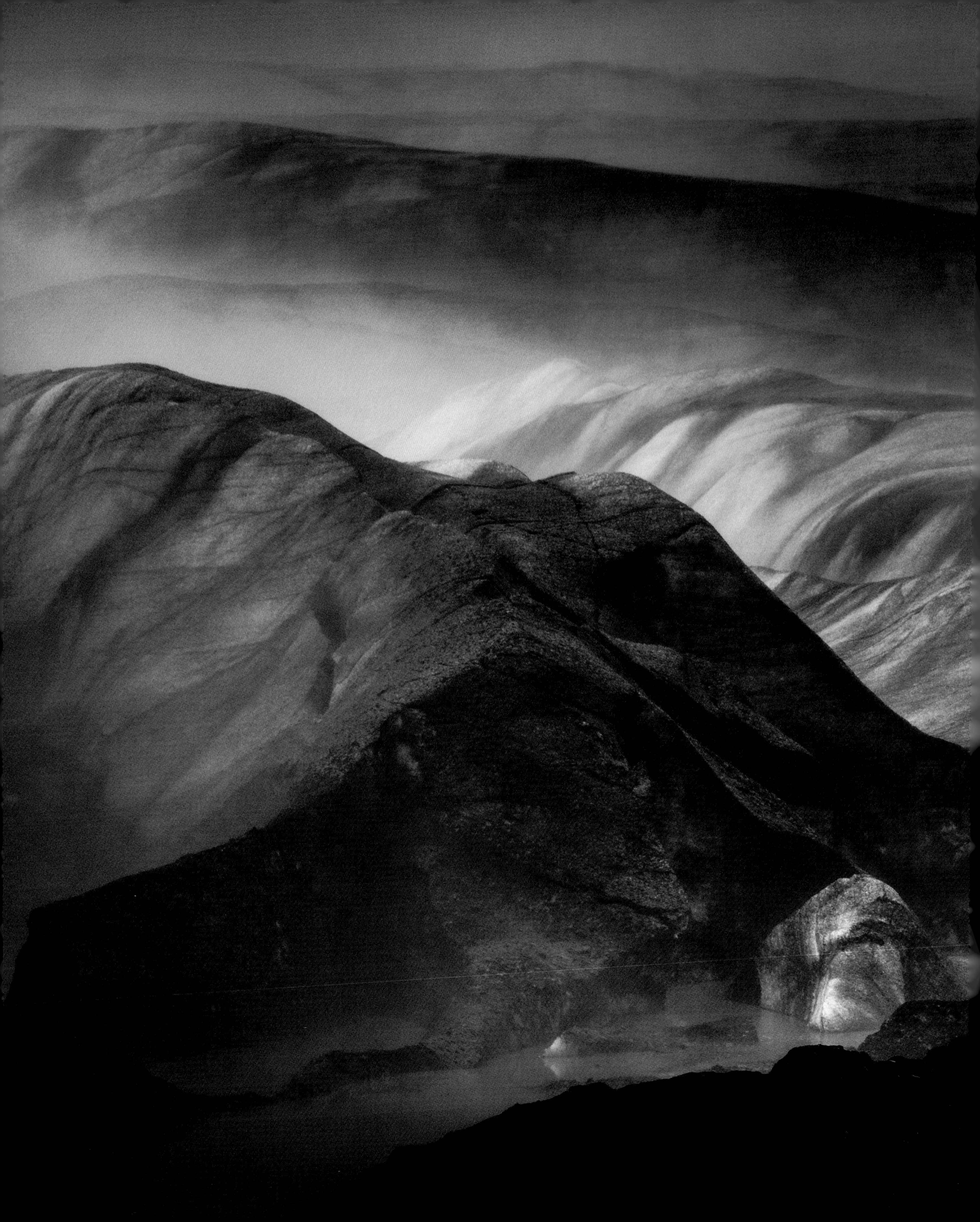

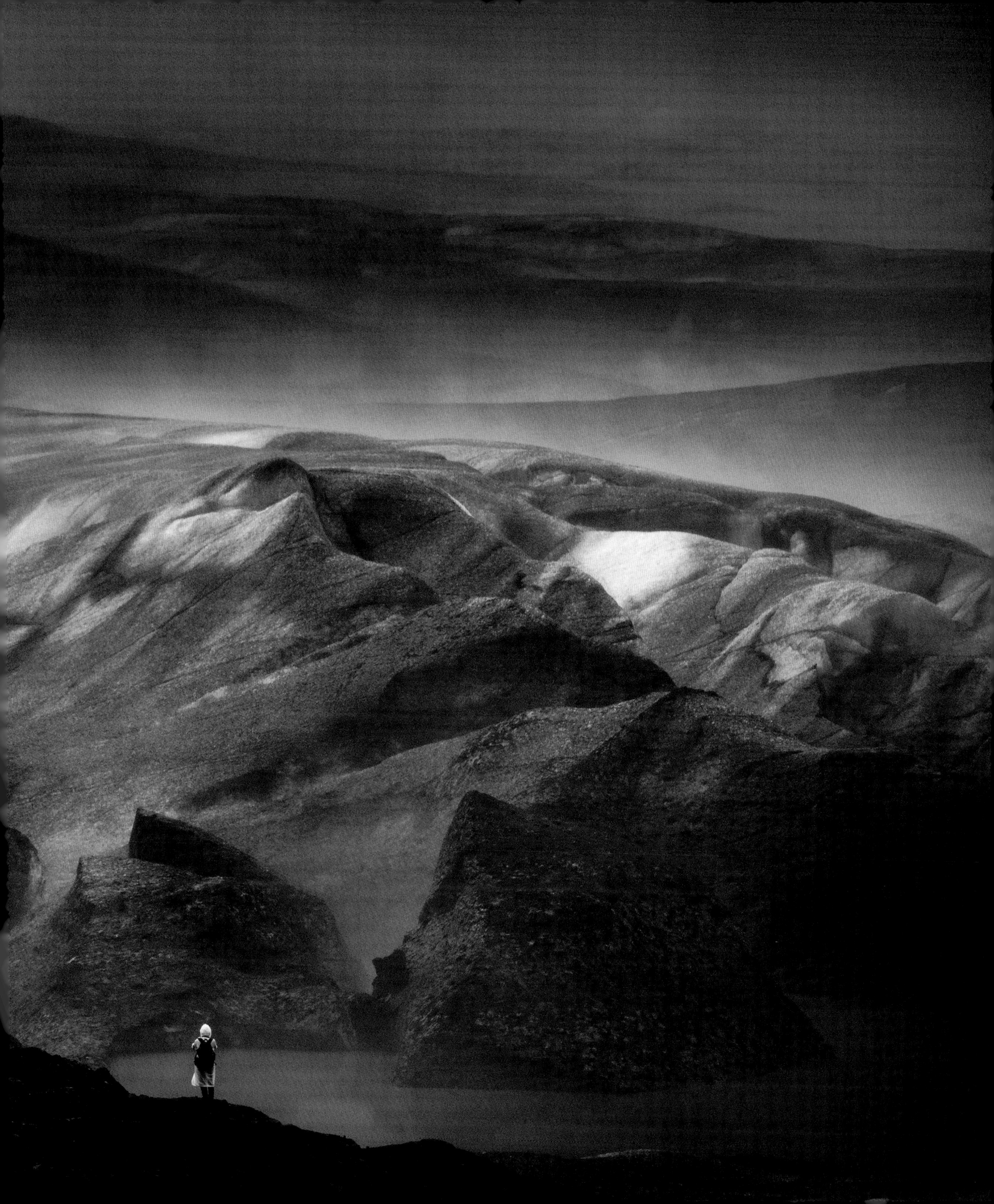

◂◂ VATNAJÖKULL V

Iceland is all about water. There's water shooting up, a lot more water coming down, water blowing sideways, always in your face, cold compressed blue water, hot water, really hot water, steam, fog, an insane number of clouds, powder, hail—as well as canyons, fjords, and mountains, all carved by water. And Icelandic tomatoes. (Because they taste like water, too.)

It's the sheer force of this water that makes this island so special. After all, almost nothing grows here, and the weather is usually horrible in comparison to anywhere else. But it's different here—and that difference makes it more beautiful. More powerful. The naked landscape can't hide any of it. This power is visible everywhere on this little rock in the ocean. You can see it all around you. You can feel it, too, if you get too close.

▸ VESTRAHORN II

A gang of mountains moved far north so they could hide in the dark all winter and scare people when it gets bright again.

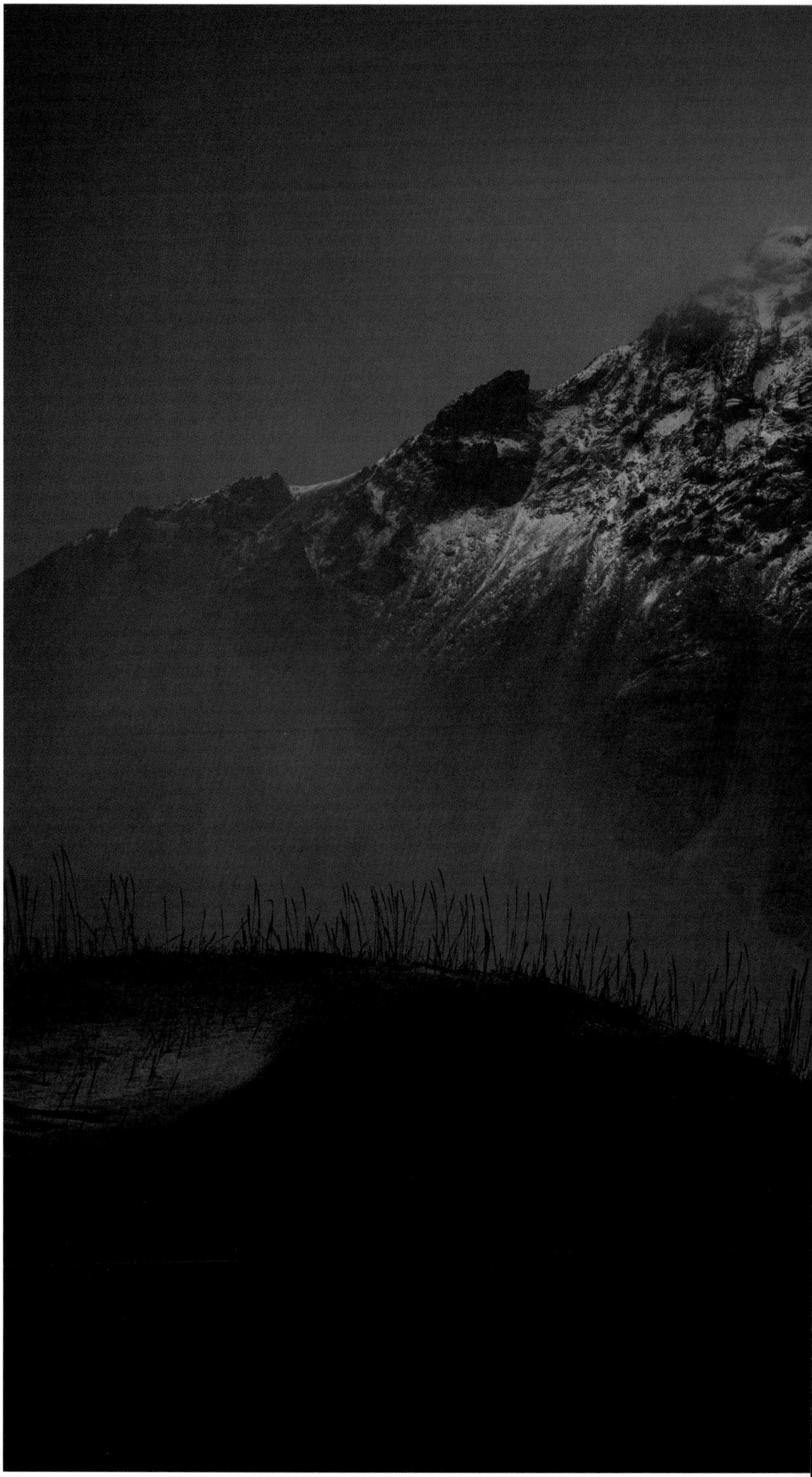

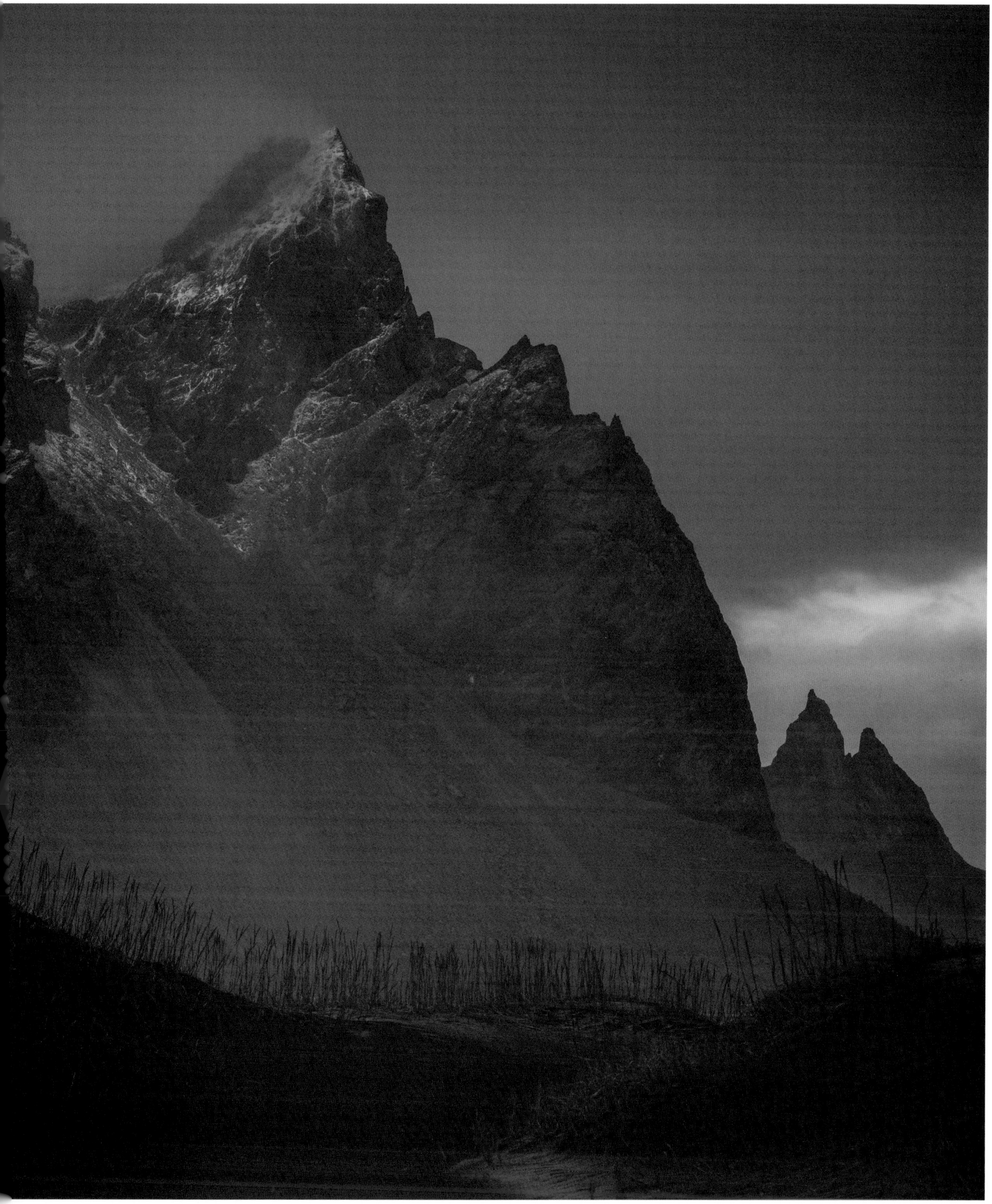

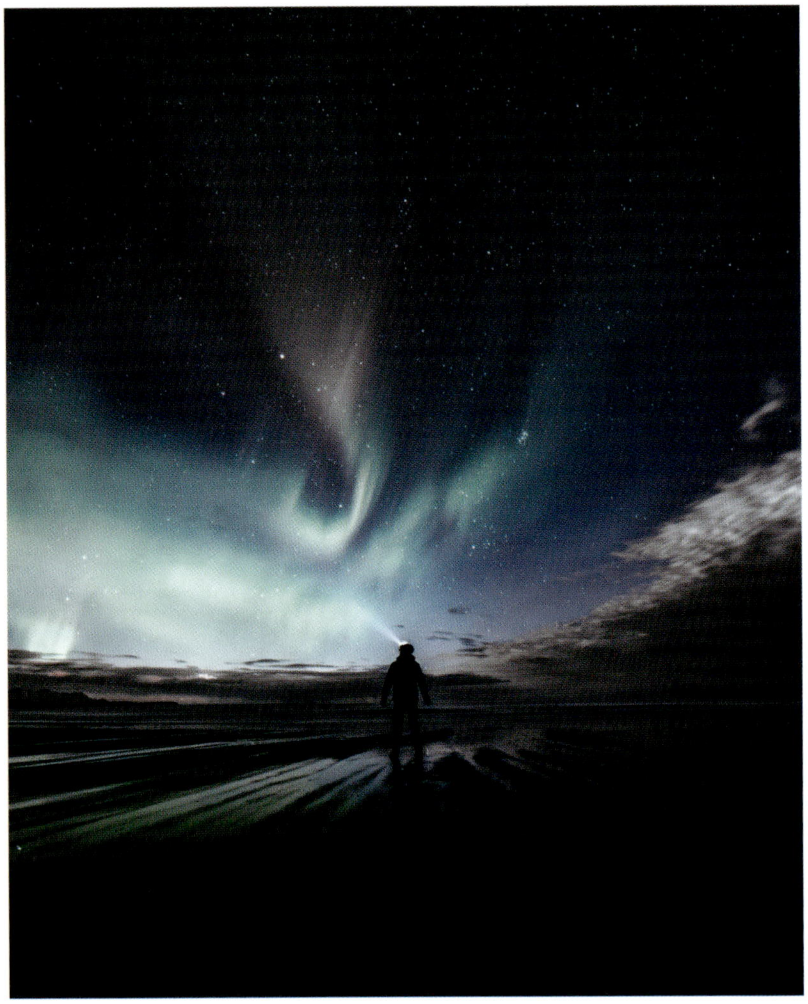

▲ SOMEWHERE IN THE SKY

If you open your mind too much it might fill the sky with colors.

➤ VESTRAHORN III

It's hard to shoot the northern lights. Not just because of the darkness, the cold, and the rarity of their appearance, but mainly because when they're worth shooting, they just look too good for anyone to be staring at a camera screen.

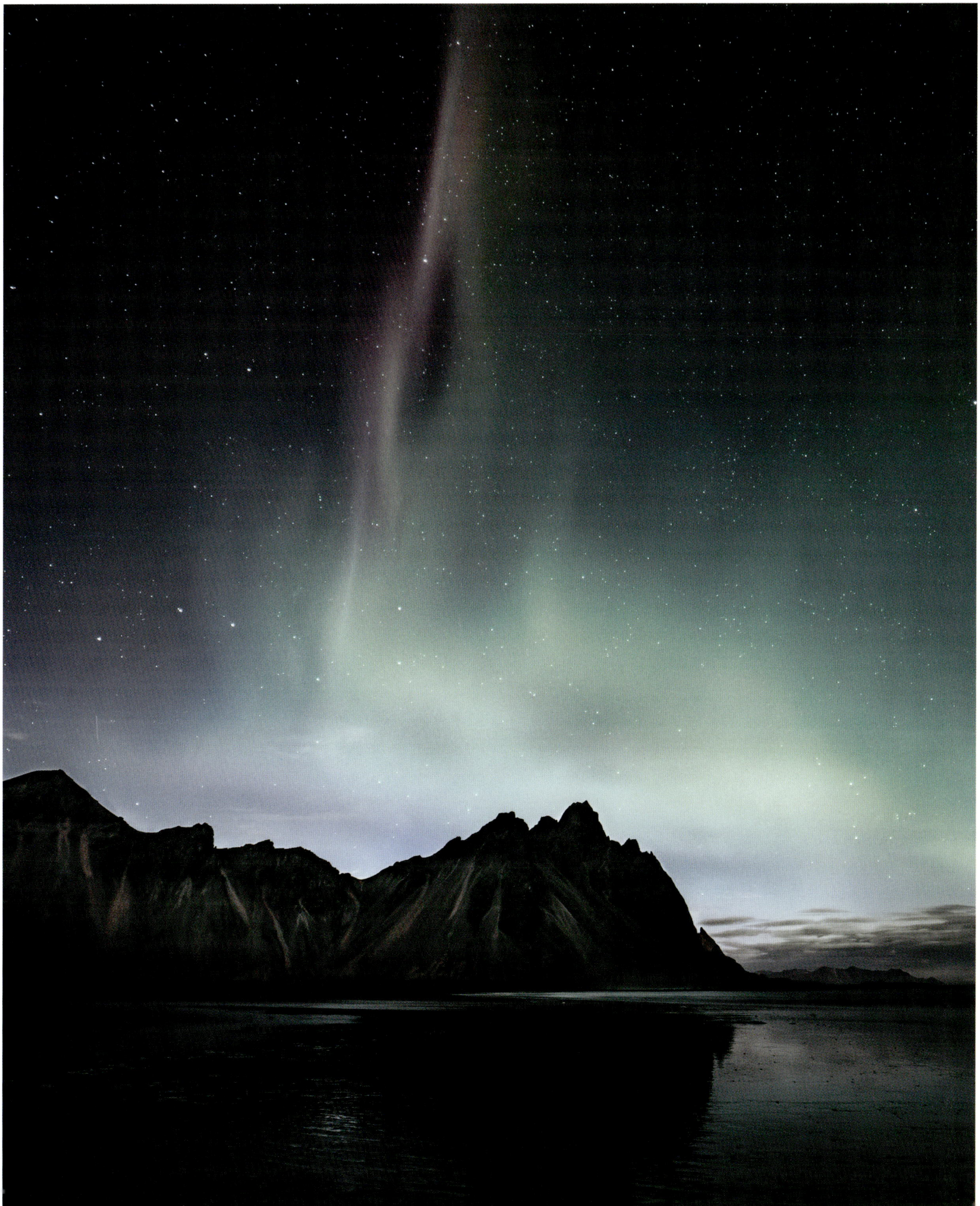

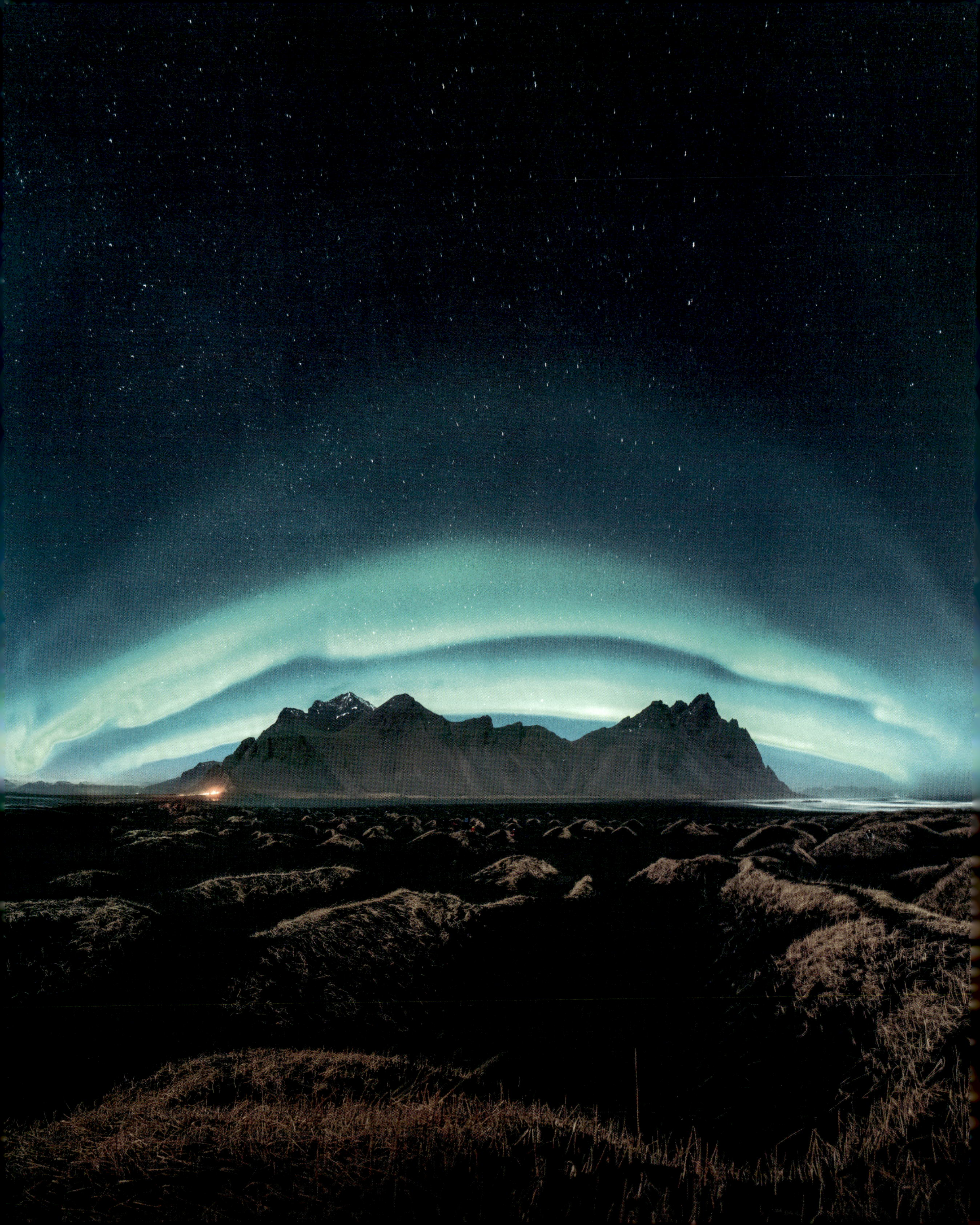

◂ VESTRAHORN IV

It took me nine years of long freezing nights in the darkness to get this shot. The sky knows when it's most appropriate to start the dance, and it only does so when everything aligns. It's worth the wait, every time.

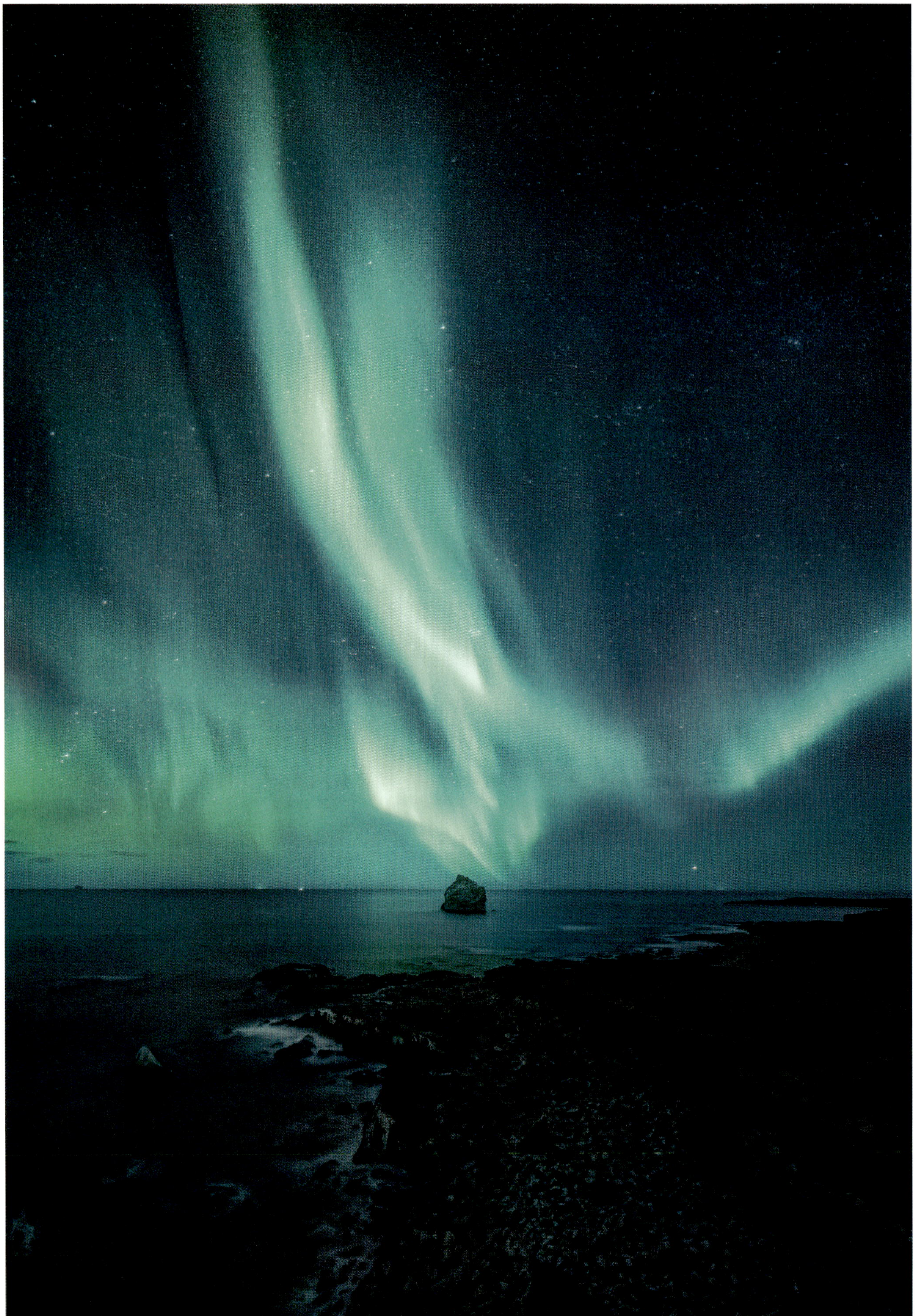

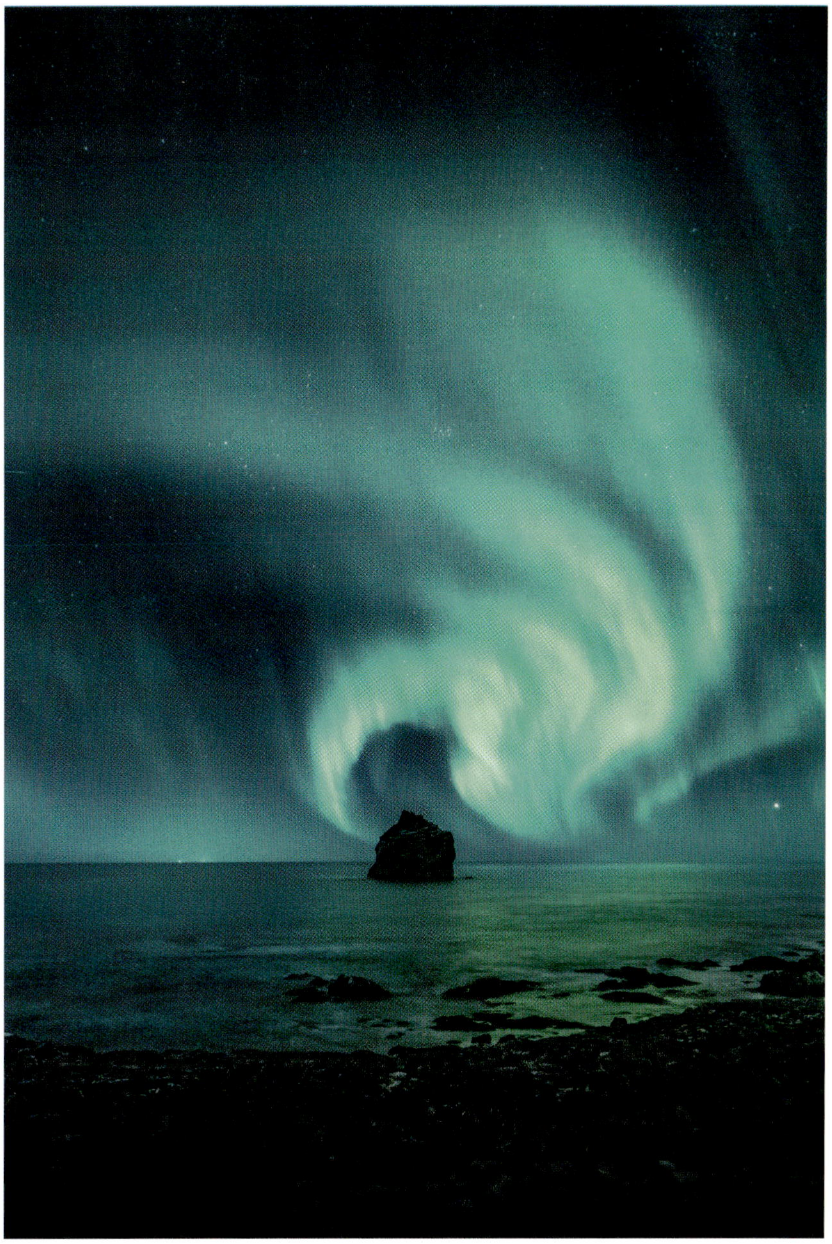

◀▲ REYKJANESVITI I & II

The sky can get lonely in its darkness. One time it came down to ask a rock for a dance.

▶▶ VESTRAHORN V

Once again the sky came down for a dance, and it caught the mountains drinking straight from the ocean once again.

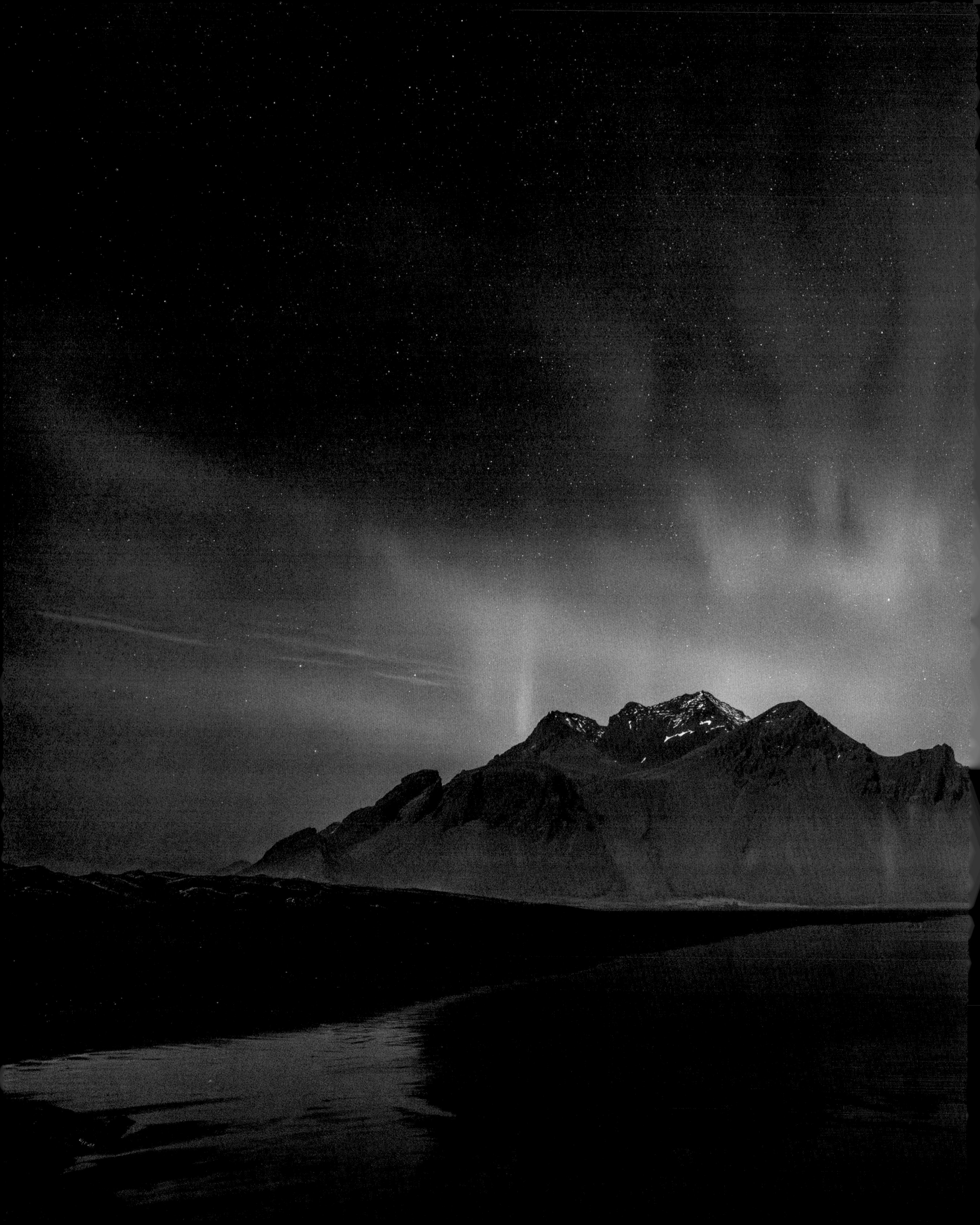

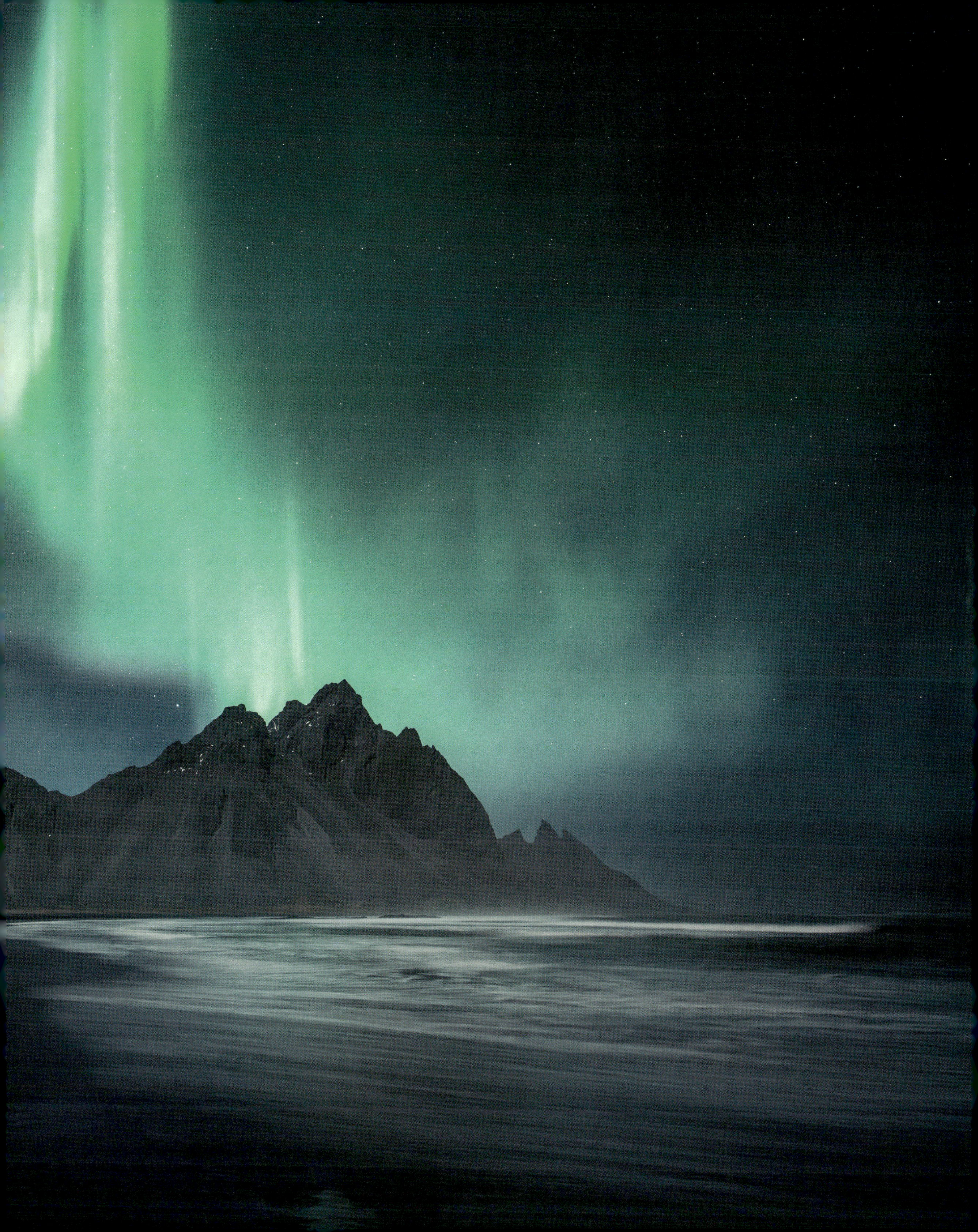

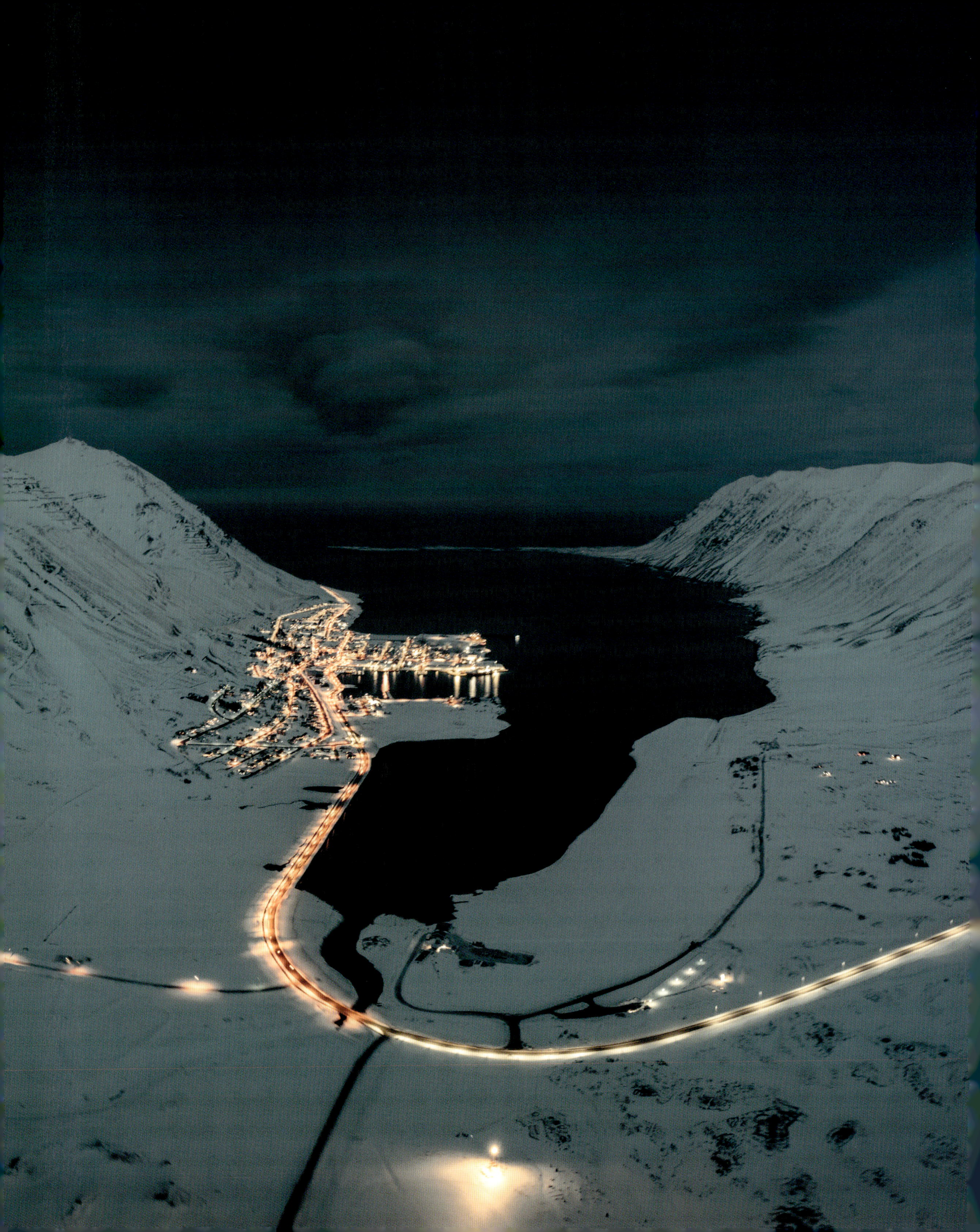

◂ SIGLUFJÖRÐUR

A wild town that put itself in the wildest of places. I first came to Siglufjörður in 2016, just after the Vikings had re-discovered this hidden place. I knew right away that it was special. A small fjord closed off from the rest of the world, where even the sun can't reach for the darkest parts of the year. But it shines in the heart of the people, and in the atmosphere around it. Coming here is like entering a fairytale. It's a place to heal and grow, to put the mountains on your shoulder and become one with the sea.

▸▸ SIGLUFJÖRÐUR II

This place is far away from almost everything else in the world and far away from everyone else, too. But it's close to where I am sitting, writing this book; my fiancée is painting our kitchen; close to where our first baby will take her first steps, and to where we just bought our first big human box to shelter in when it's too stormy to be outside.

It's so close, I even took this photo from our patio, with all the mountains looking down on me. I'll be heading up to be with them soon. And that's why we moved here. To this tiny town that somehow is much bigger than it is.

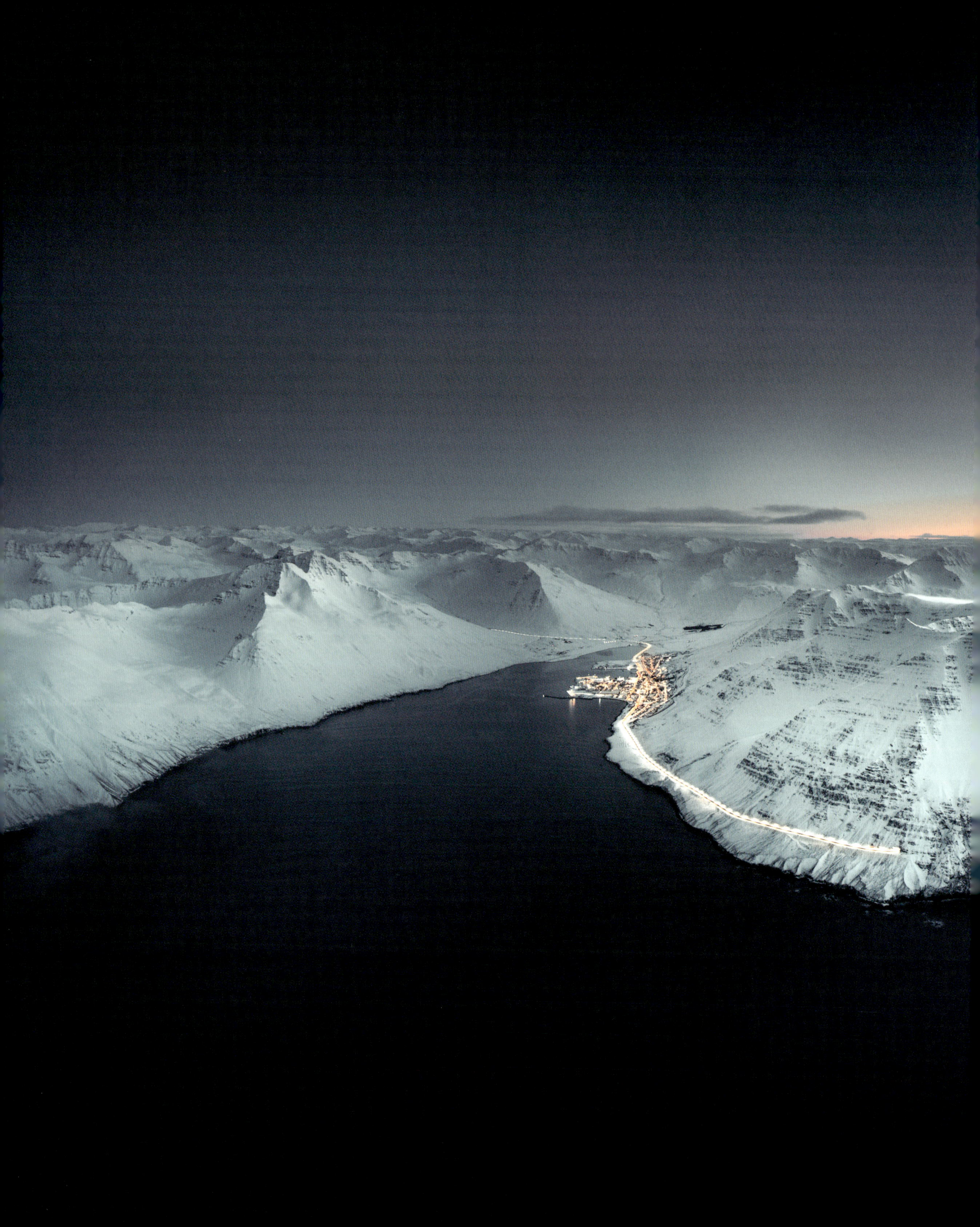

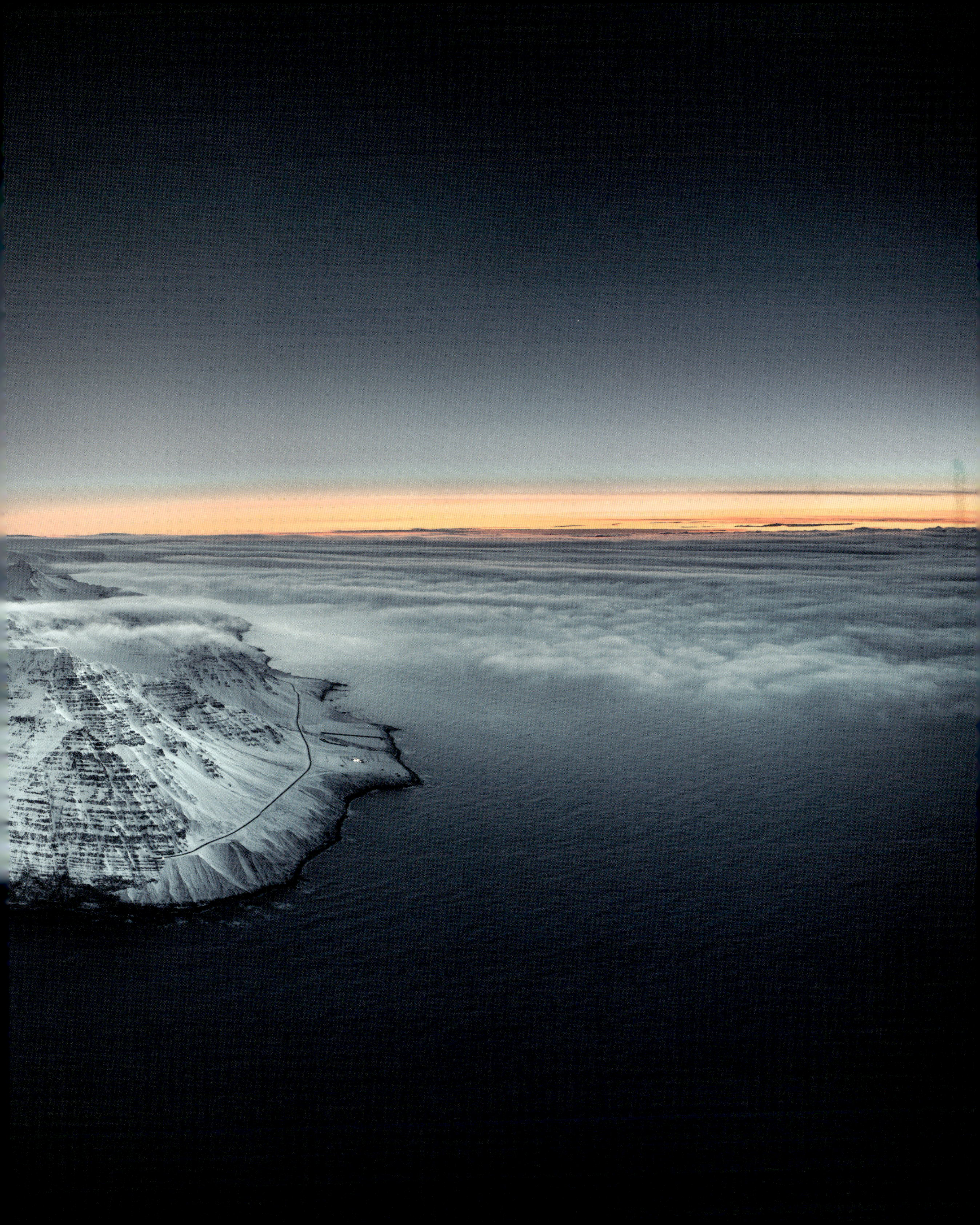

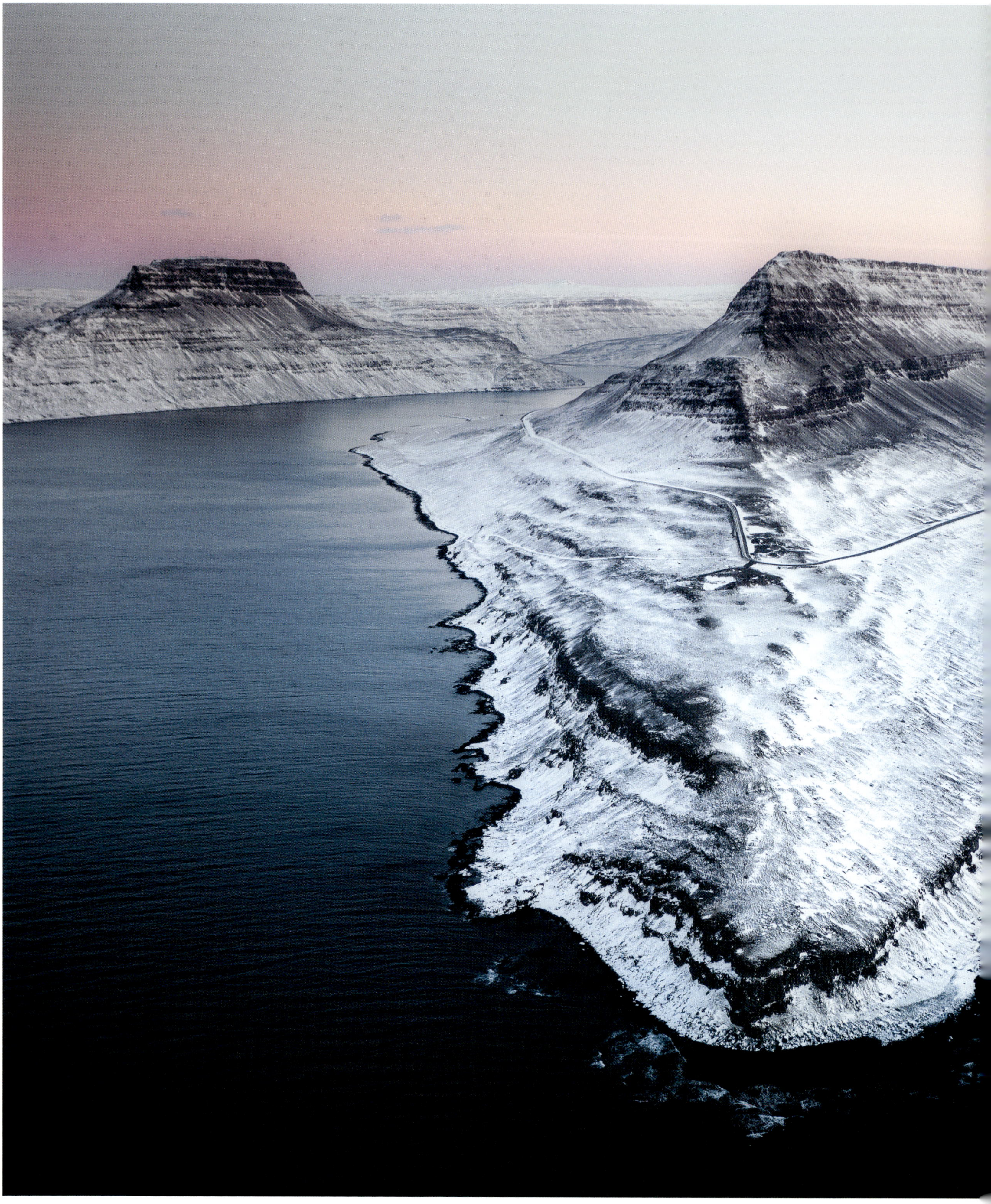

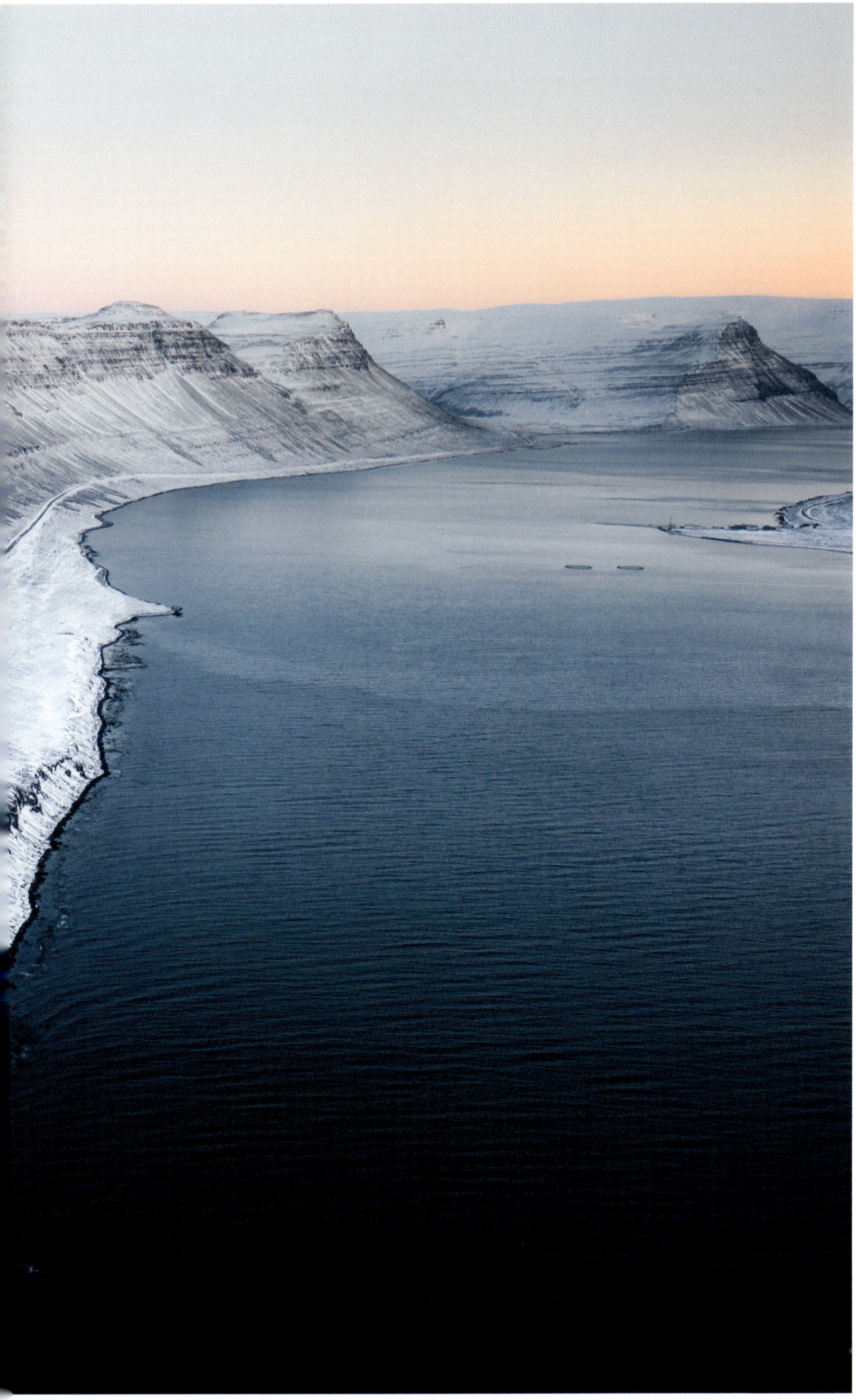

◂ EYRARFJALL

A mountain stretches out its tongue, trying to give the camera a lick. It's probably never tasted camera before. It tastes like memory cards and imagination.

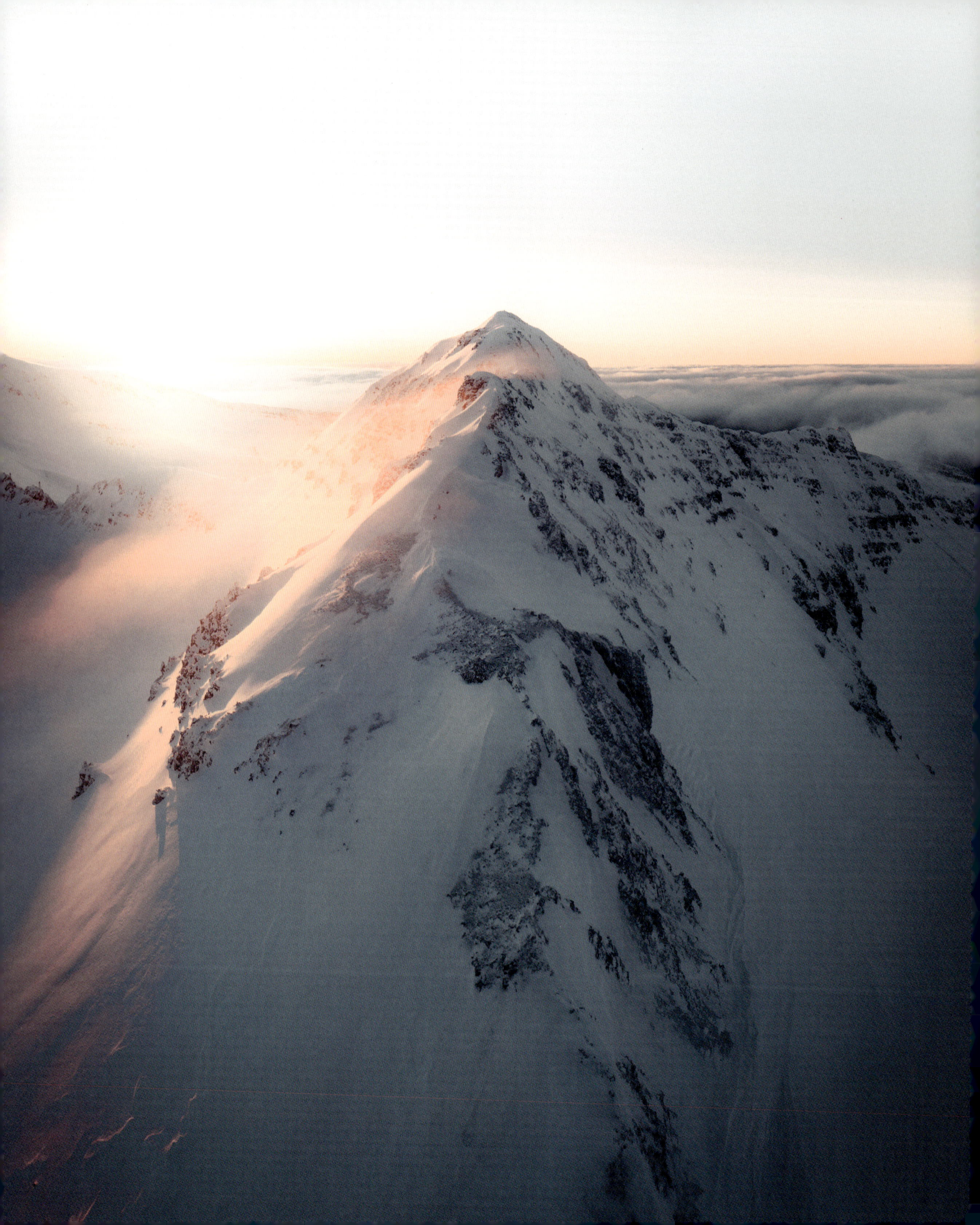

◂ TORFNAFJALLSHÚFA

This mountain wanted to be the tallest, so it would be the first to see the sunrise.

▸▸ SNÆFELLSNES

Watching the waters try to take over the lands, just to be pulled back by gravity every time they make an advance. Classic Earth stuff.

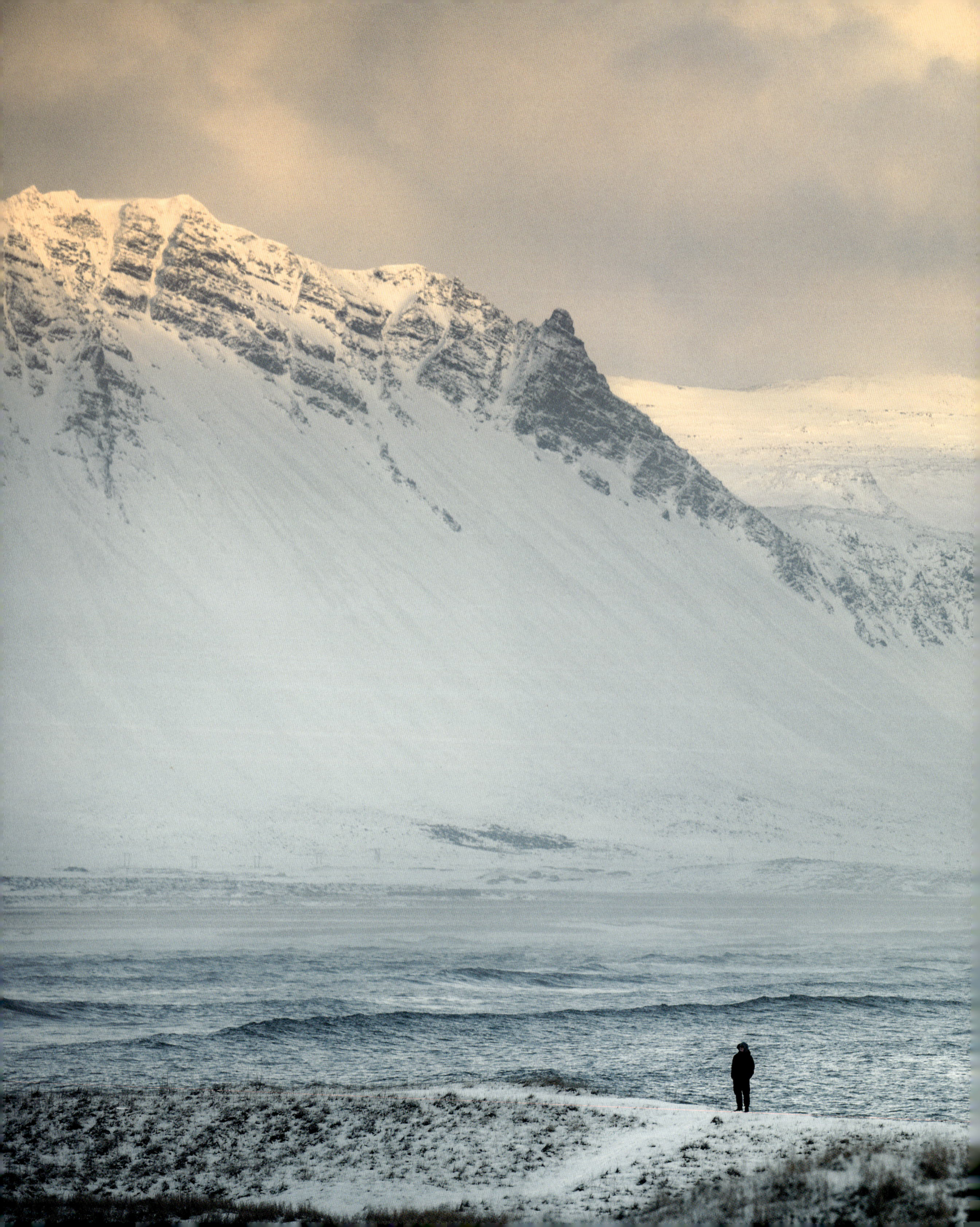

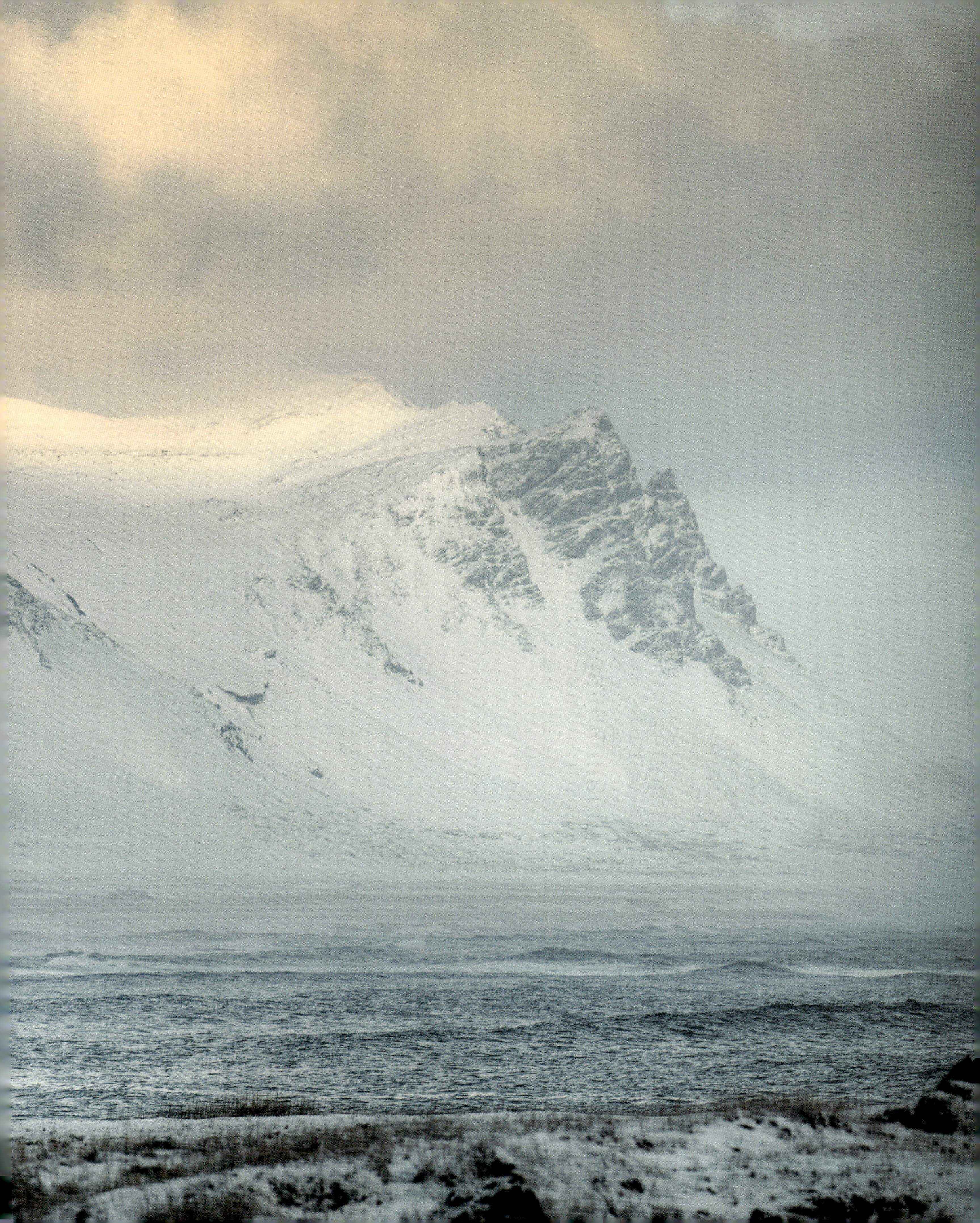

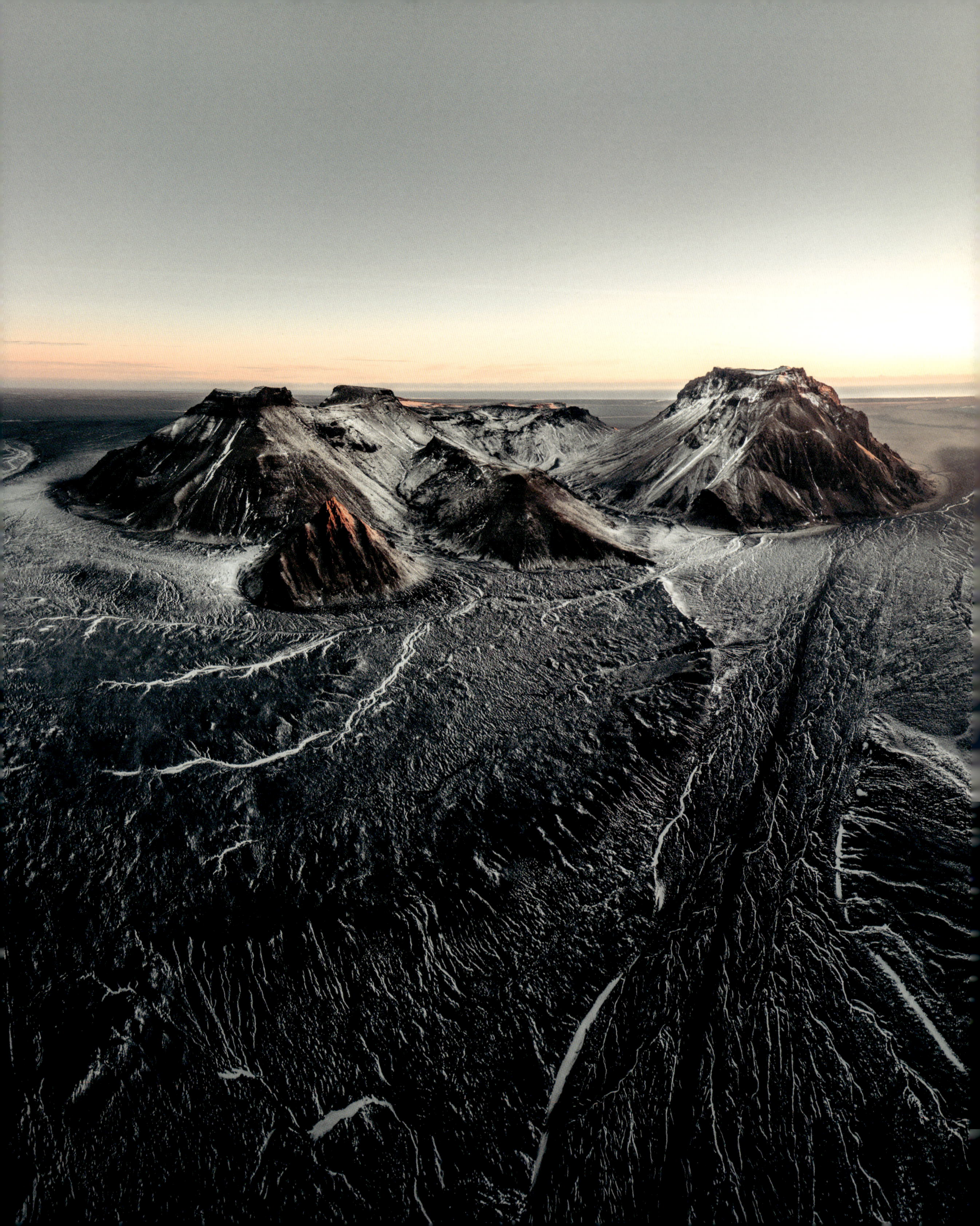

THE AWKWARD THAW

March and April

Light stumbles back, like a baby horse learning to walk on shaky legs. Snow pretends to leave just to come back with all its friends again. Everything tries. Not everything succeeds just yet.

Everything is brighter when it's covered in snow, even the darkness that stays so still it's almost invisible. The days already feel long enough if you don't wake up too early. And when you do wake up, it's time to go outside.

With return of the light, we also get contrast back. Those mountain peaks don't seem so hostile anymore. It's high time to dust off your winter hobbies. Layer up like an onion, put skins on your skis, pick a big pile of rocks and start climbing, setting a tempo that gets you to strip down to a t-shirt. (This is the way to simulate a tropical vacation in your Icelandic backyard.) When you reach the peak, scream its name at the top of your lungs to assert your presence and aliveness, and then scurry down as fast as possible before it gets dark again.

Some members of the emerging population still have a pale blue tint to their skin, marking the ones that stayed in Iceland through the winter. Many wear sunglasses now, even on the cloudiest days. But they meet. The streets are not empty anymore, and everyone runs into each other, sharing what they've gone through and helping pick each other back up.

Iceland is a very social place compared to the rest of Scandinavia. Although social-distancing-disguised-as-ample-personal-space still runs deep in the Viking blood, interaction here is important—even if it's just a "jæja" to break the silence every ten minutes in an otherwise quiet room full of people staring awkwardly at each other. Like an acknowledgment that everything is still in order and shall continue to be for the next ten minutes.

Everyone knows that more winters are coming, and coming for all of us. The long history of battling the elements and clinging to survival, day by day, carves a place for humanity in the hearts of the people here. They are helpful and caring, and they stick together, overlooking small differences and never taking things too seriously. They know that if we don't work together, we'll all freeze.

Here, you have the freedom to be you, whatever that means. You don't have to bury your real self to survive. You can just live. And even thrive.

◂◂ KURL AND THE OTHER PEAKS

Trying to survive a winter of solitude, these hills seek each other's company.

▸ MORSÁRJÖKULL

A glacier pretending to be a waterfall.

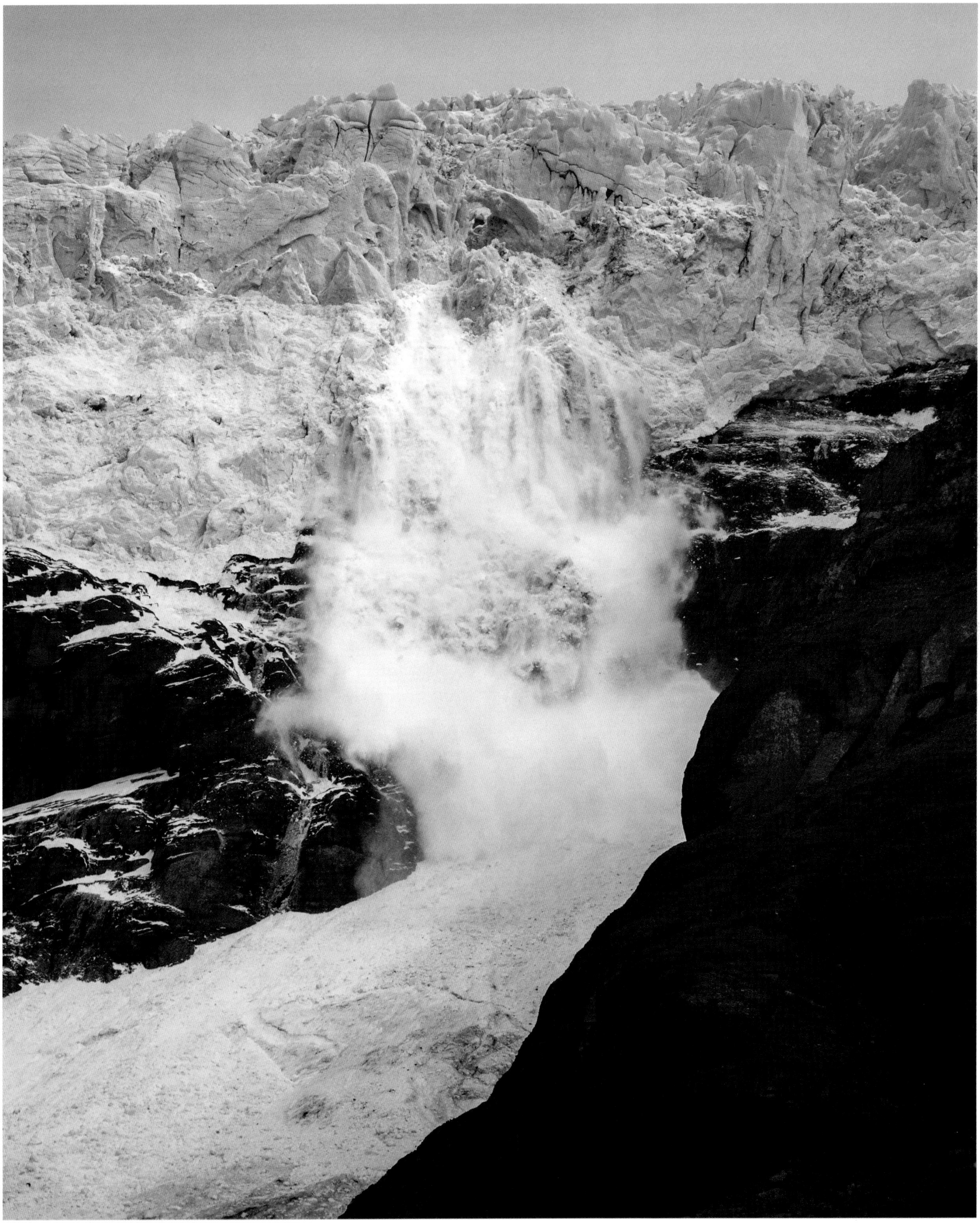

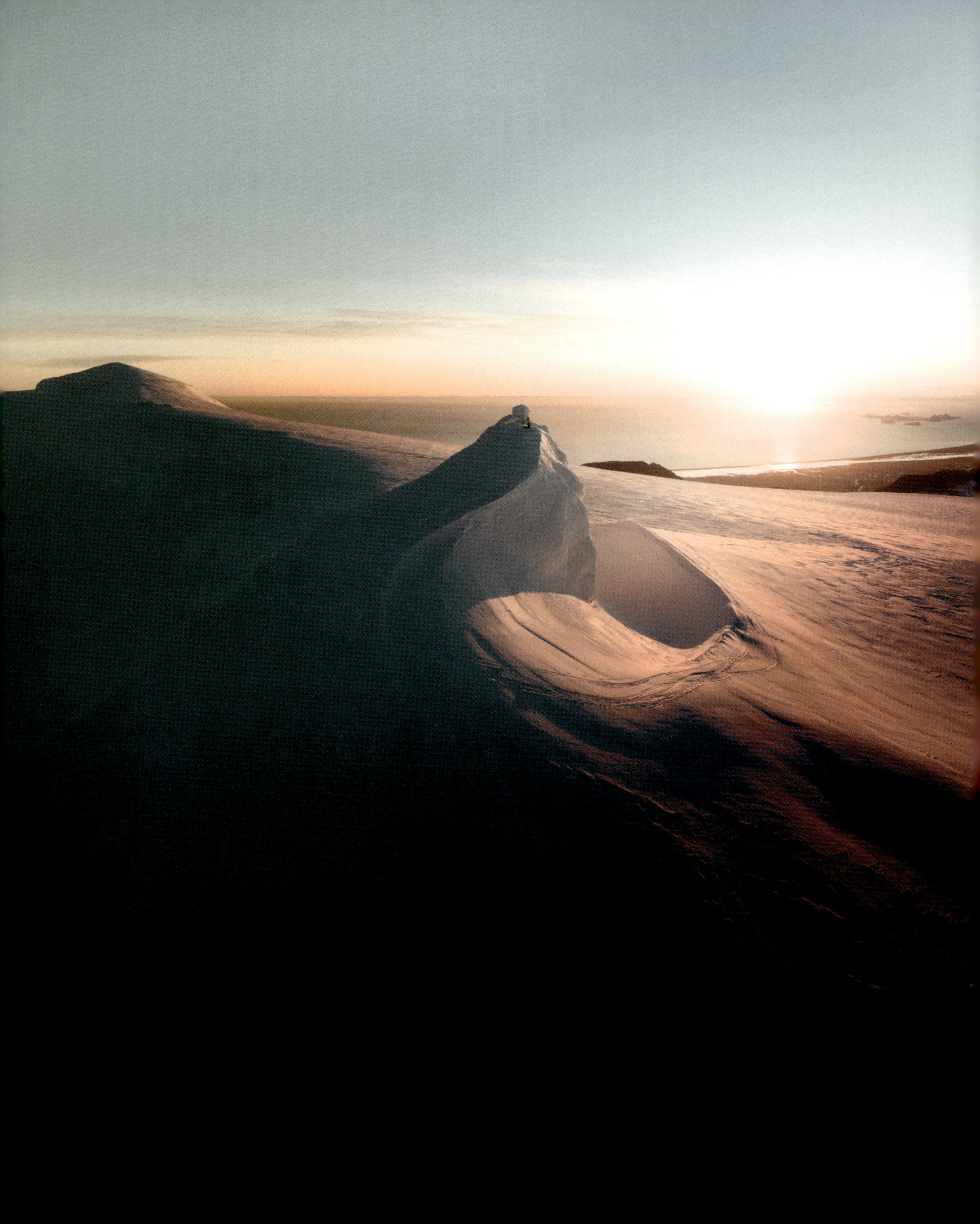

◂ EYJAFJALLAJÖKULL

Iceland is one giant melting ice cream cake, from the glaciers to the coast. And this is the best time of year to climb that ice cream—and taste it, too.

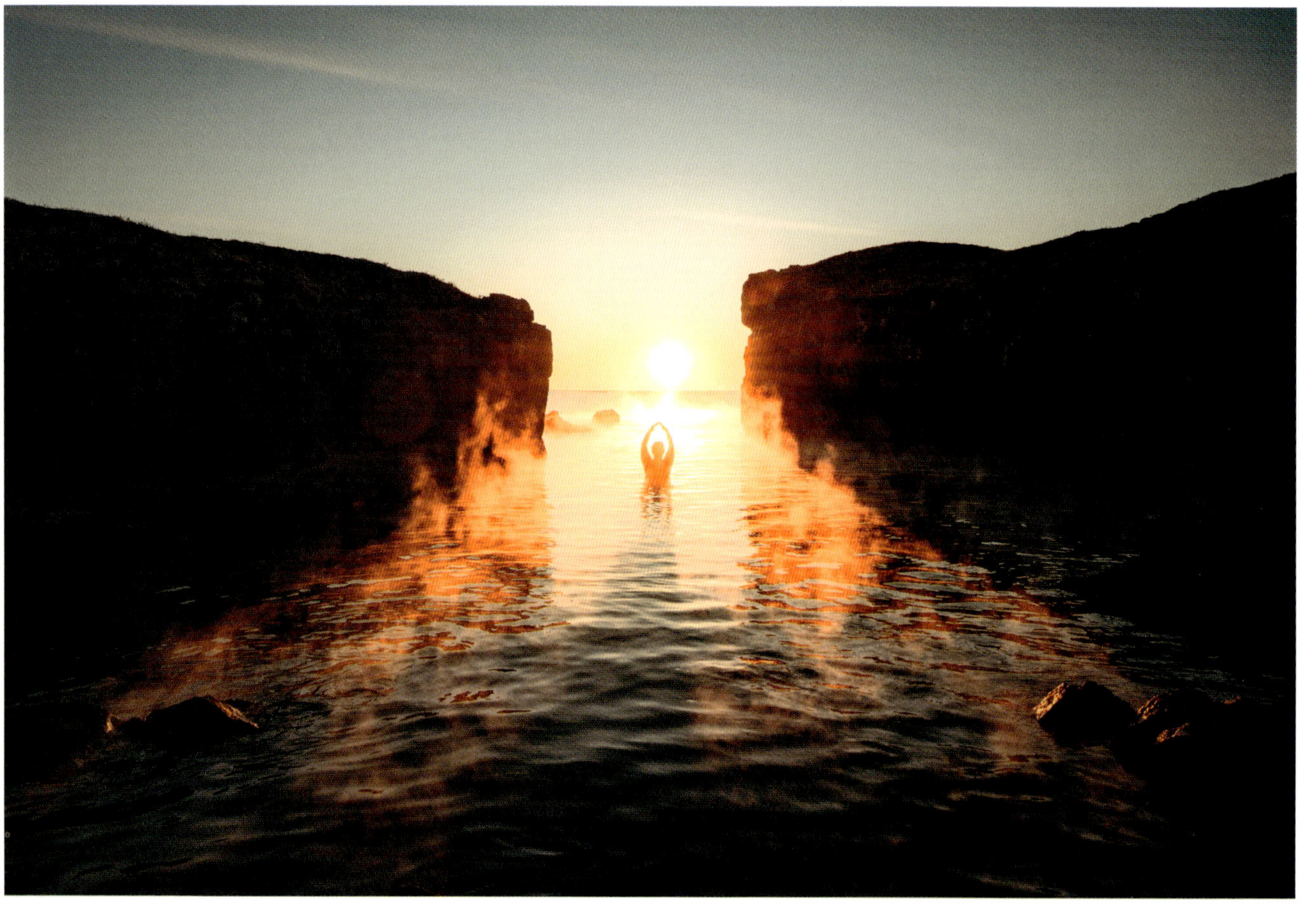

▲ ONE OF THE HOT PLACES

Welcoming back the sun can be an emotional process. After so much darkness, you start to forget what its warming power feels like. And even though that power is still months away from returning to full force, now that the sun has started reaching up over the clouds on the horizon you can get to know it once again.

▶ VESTRAHORN VI

Emerging from their own reflections, these young mountains are hoping to grow tall one day and reach all the way to the snowy skies. Until then, they're hanging out on one of the best-looking beaches out there. The sun on this particular evening dipped below the clouds of a passing storm just for a minute before saying goodbye for the day, turning the landscape into a masterpiece of a painting.

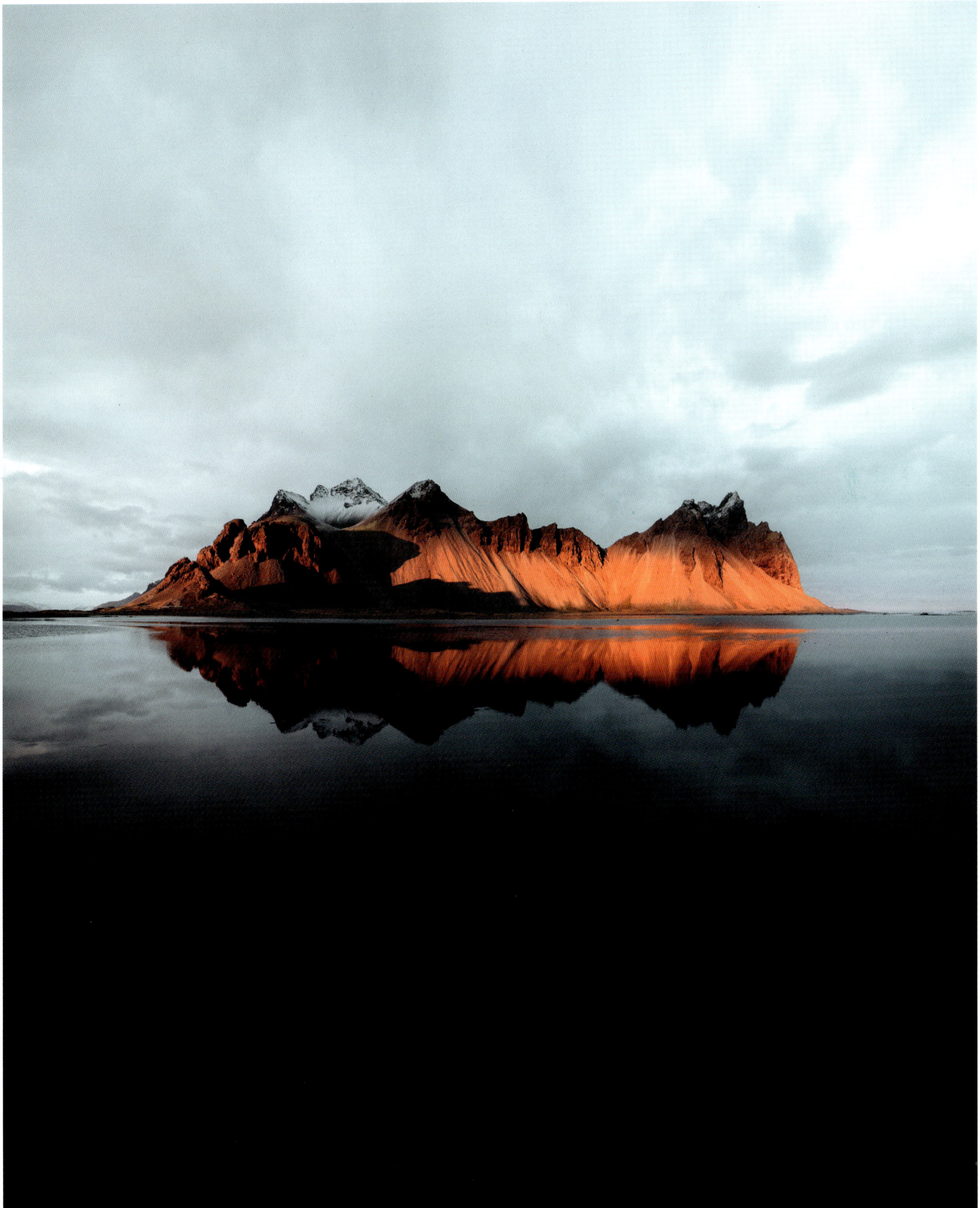

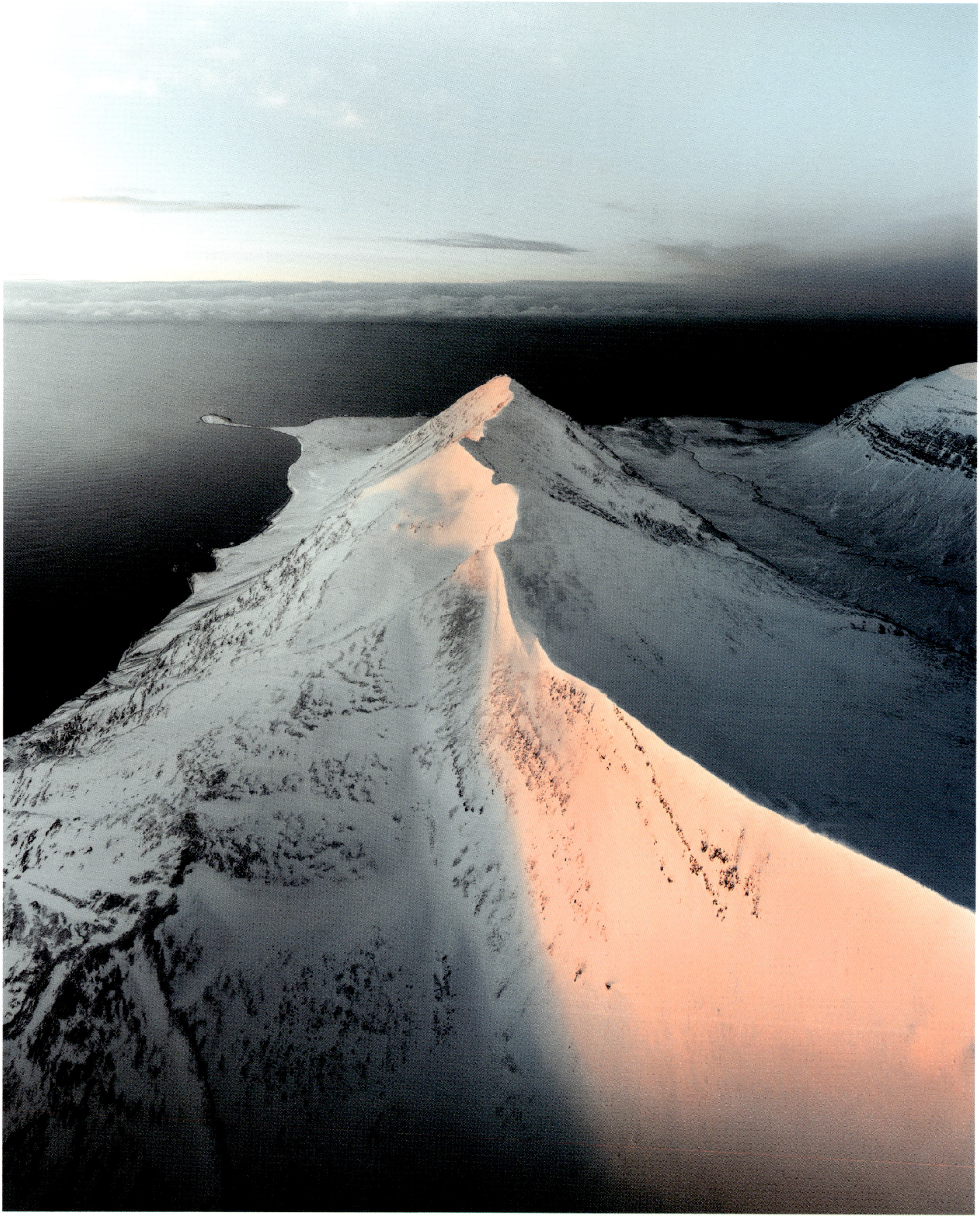

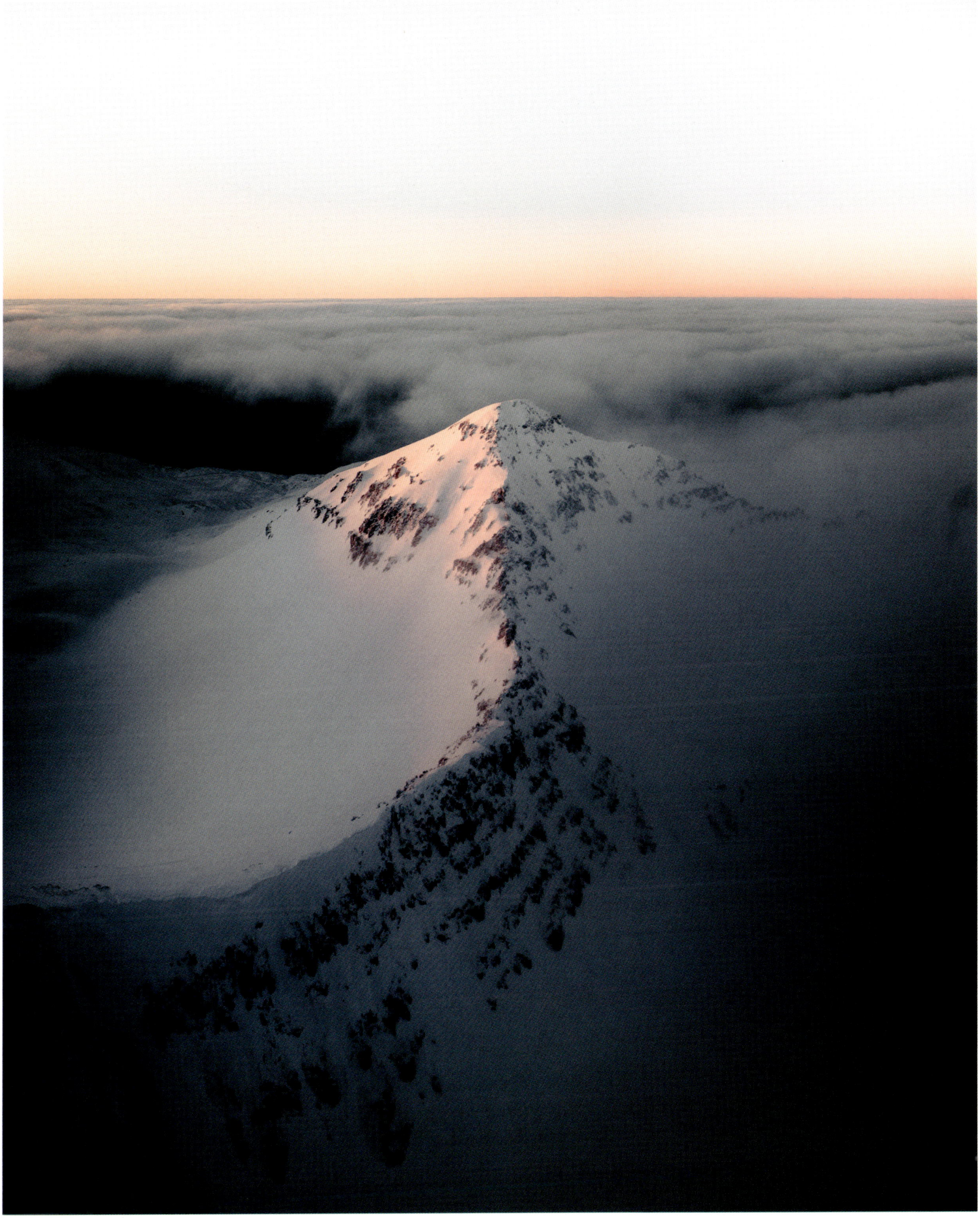

◂◂ DAGMÁLAHNJÚKUR (L)

Trying to stretch its way as far north as possible to maximize its chance of being dressed in snow, this mountain has gotten pretty far.

◂◂ ILLVIÐRISHNJÚKUR (R)

Dressed up in winter and keeping an eye out for incoming weather, this giant pile of rocks is here to watch over everything that's shorter than it is.

▸ VESTRAHORN VII

Although it's a very stormy place, people still come here to get away from the noise.

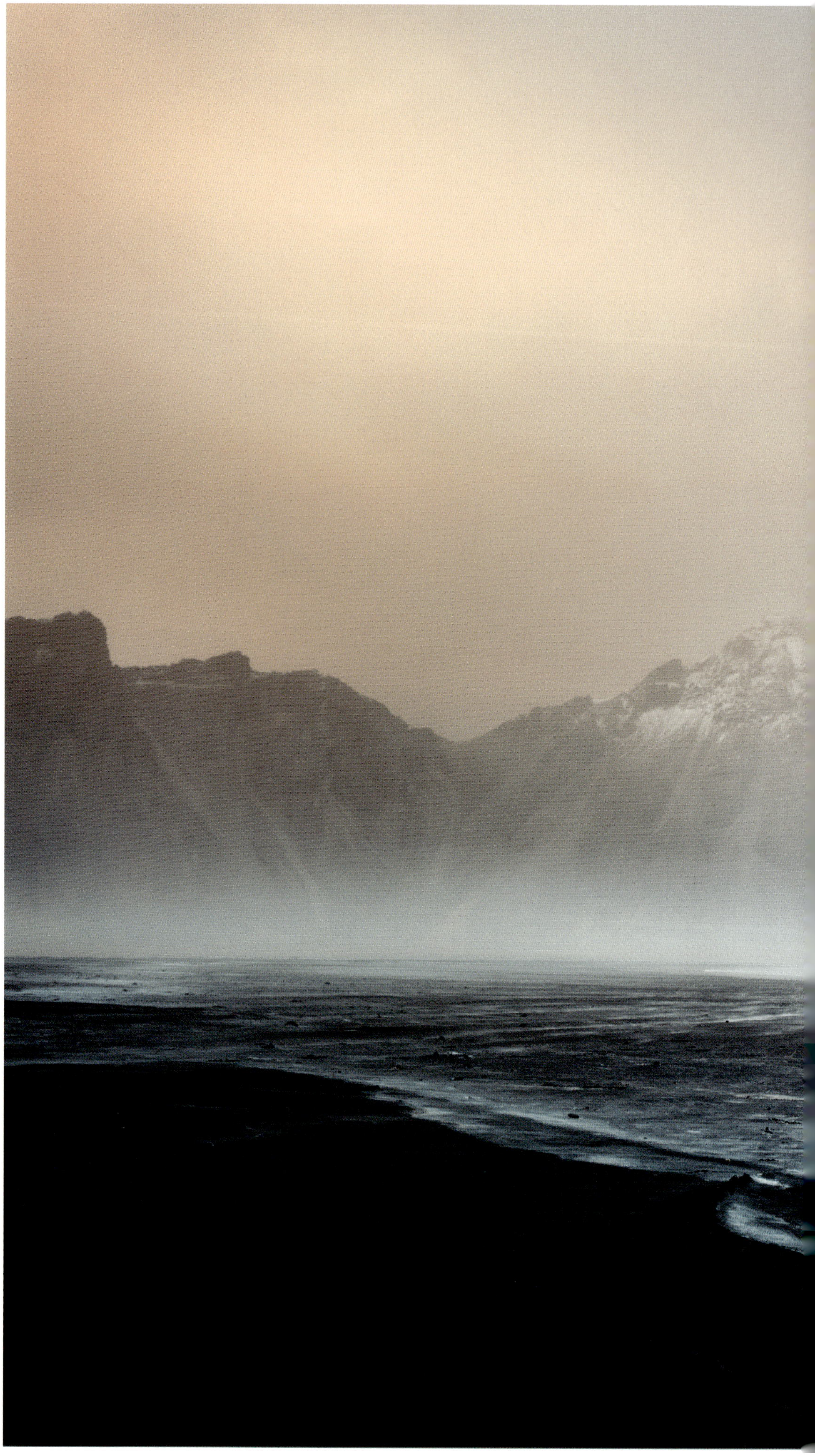

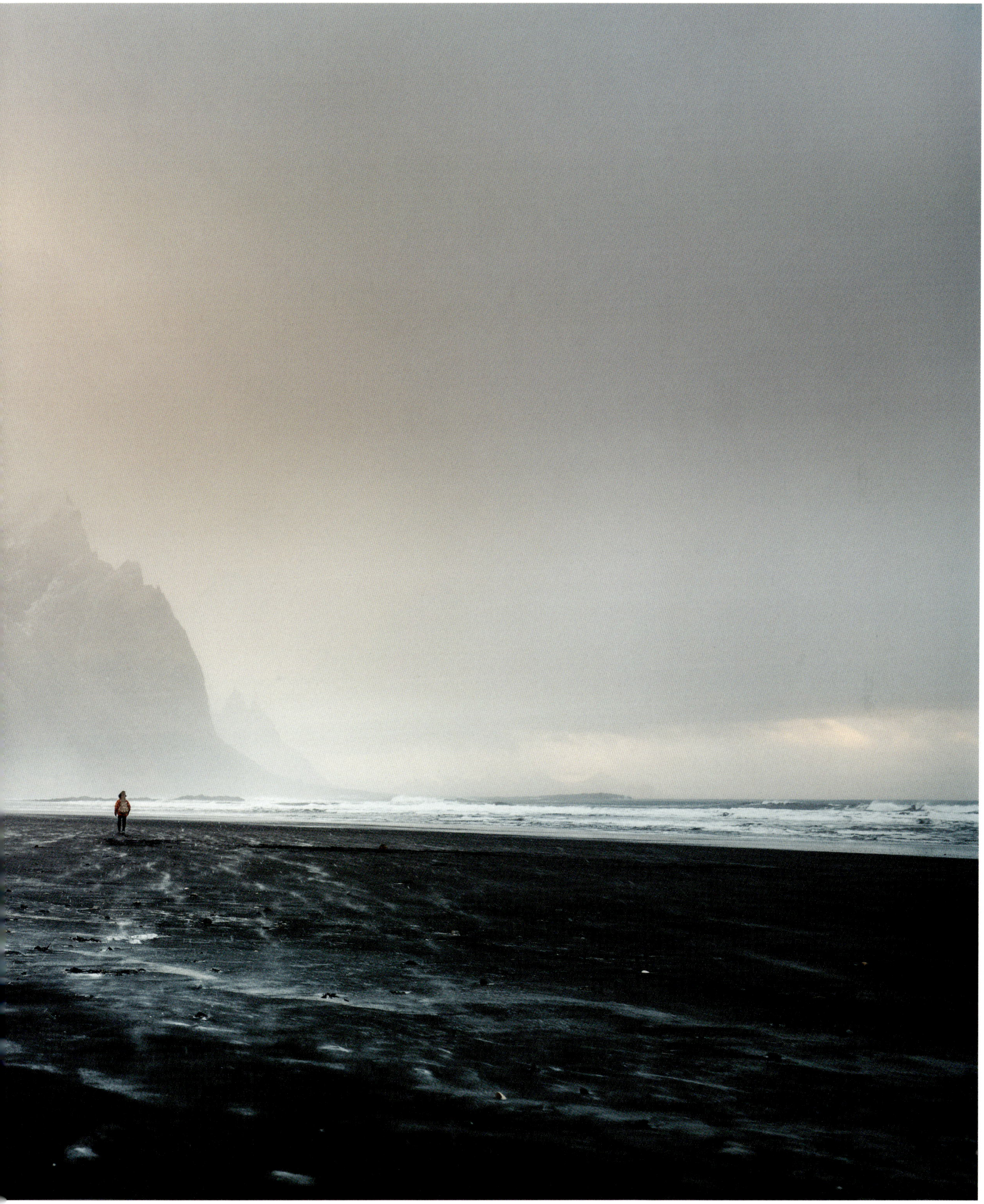

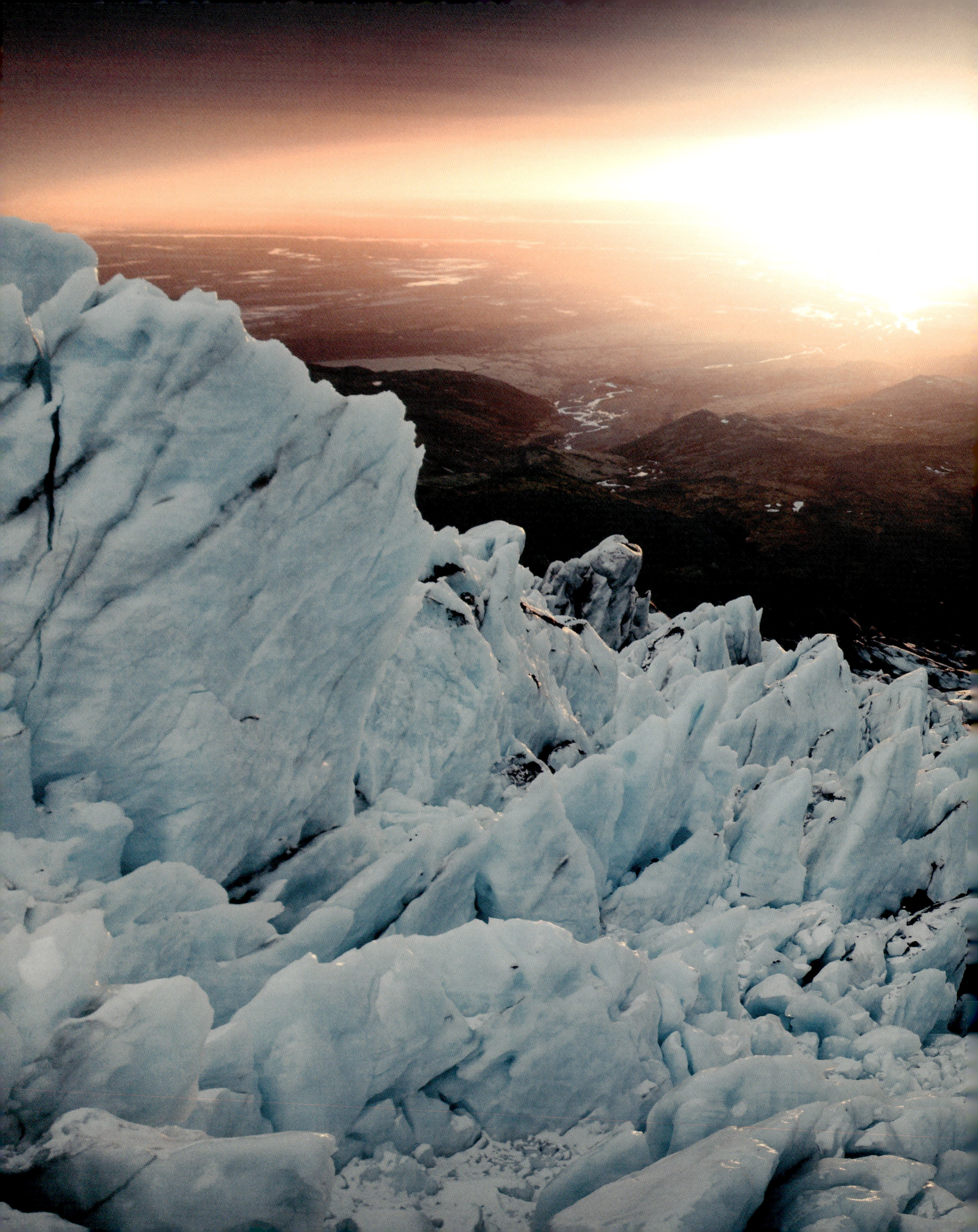

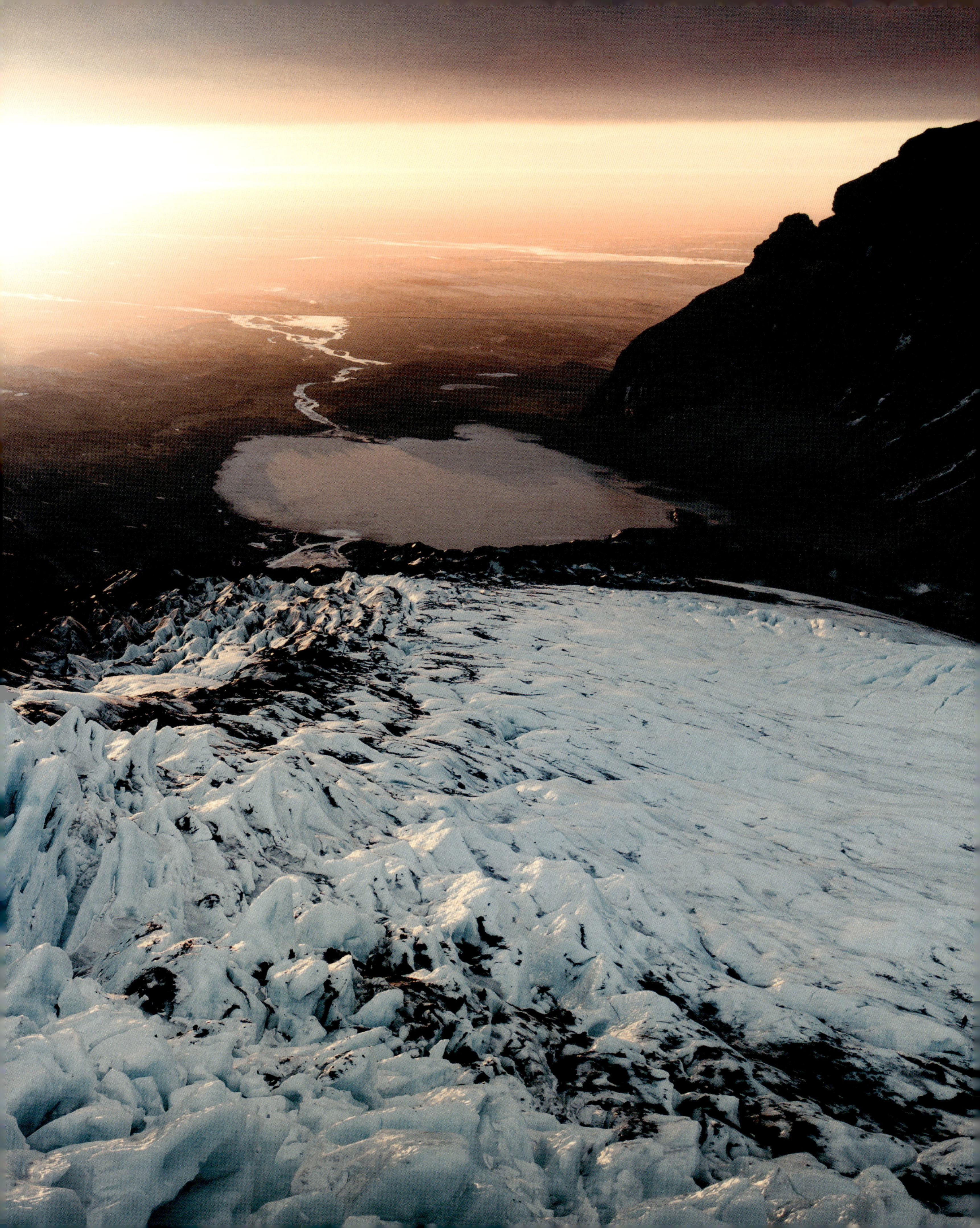

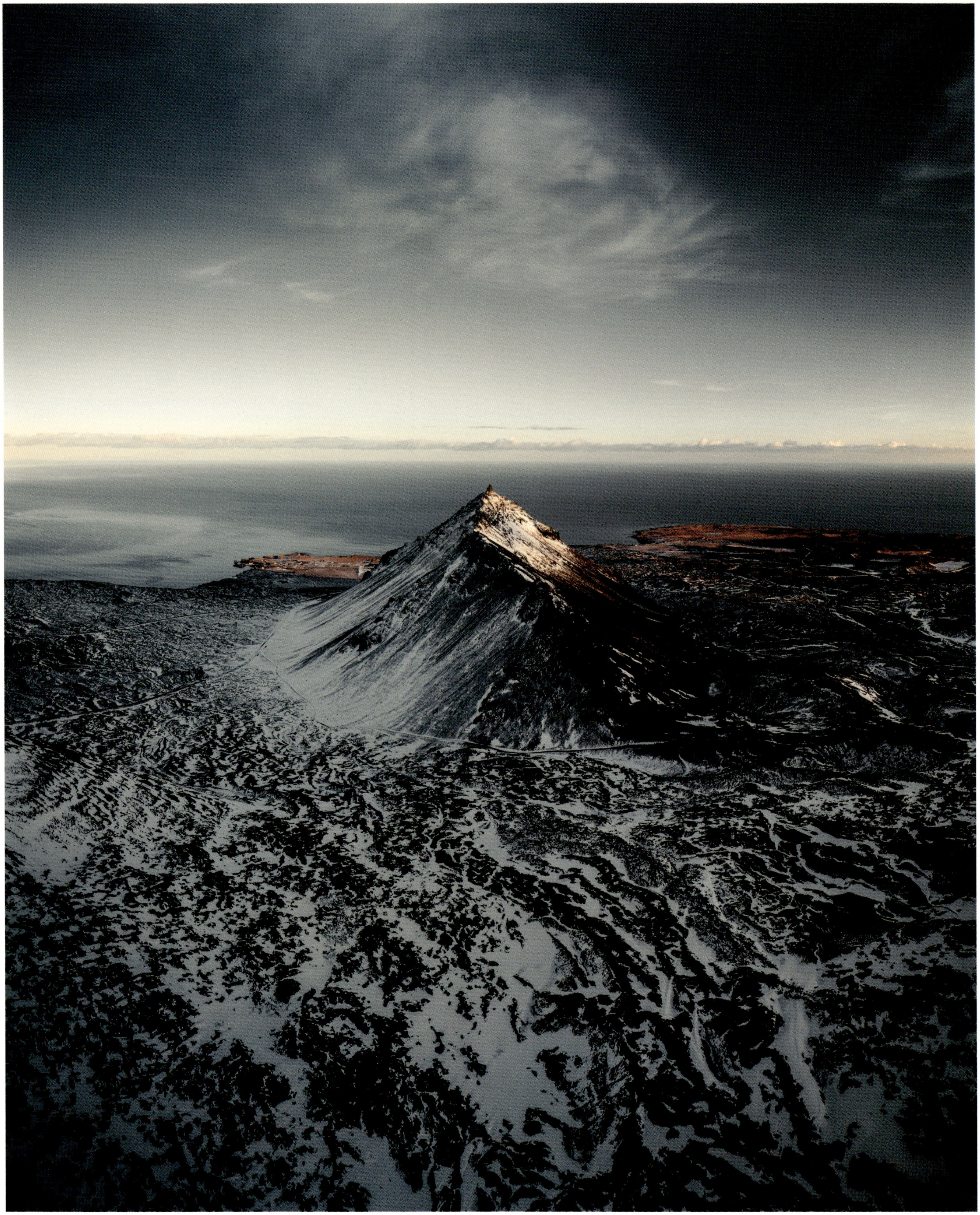

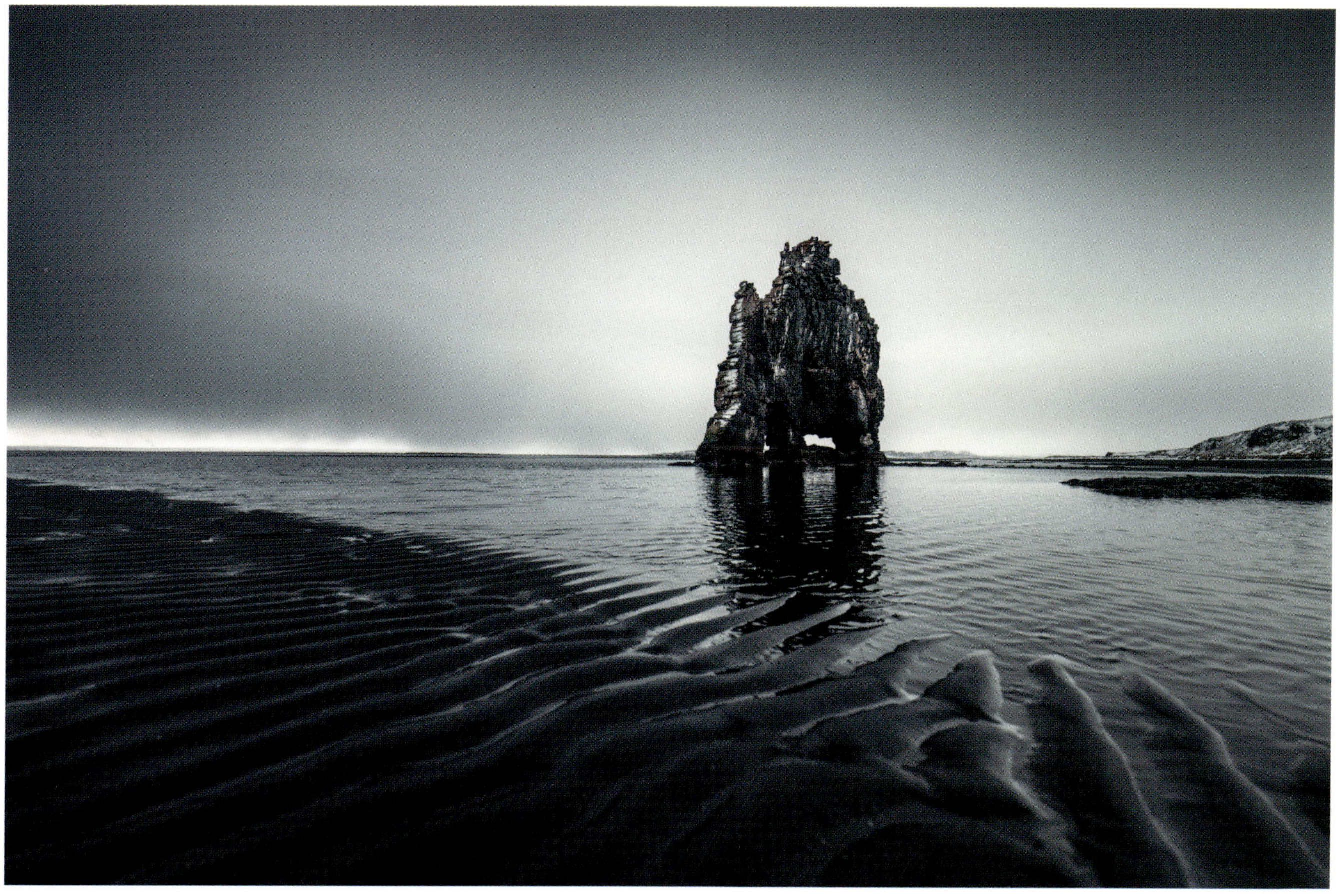

◂◂ FALLJÖKULL

A horde of ice slowly migrating towards warmer latitudes. Little do they know that they will never make it there in solid form.

◂ STAPAFELL

A landscape tried to reinvent its local flatness by growing a cone. Photo taken from a much larger cone.

▴ HVITSERKUR

A trollophantosaurus came down from some imaginary realm for a drink. It loved the great Icelandic water so much it decided to stay and drink it forever.

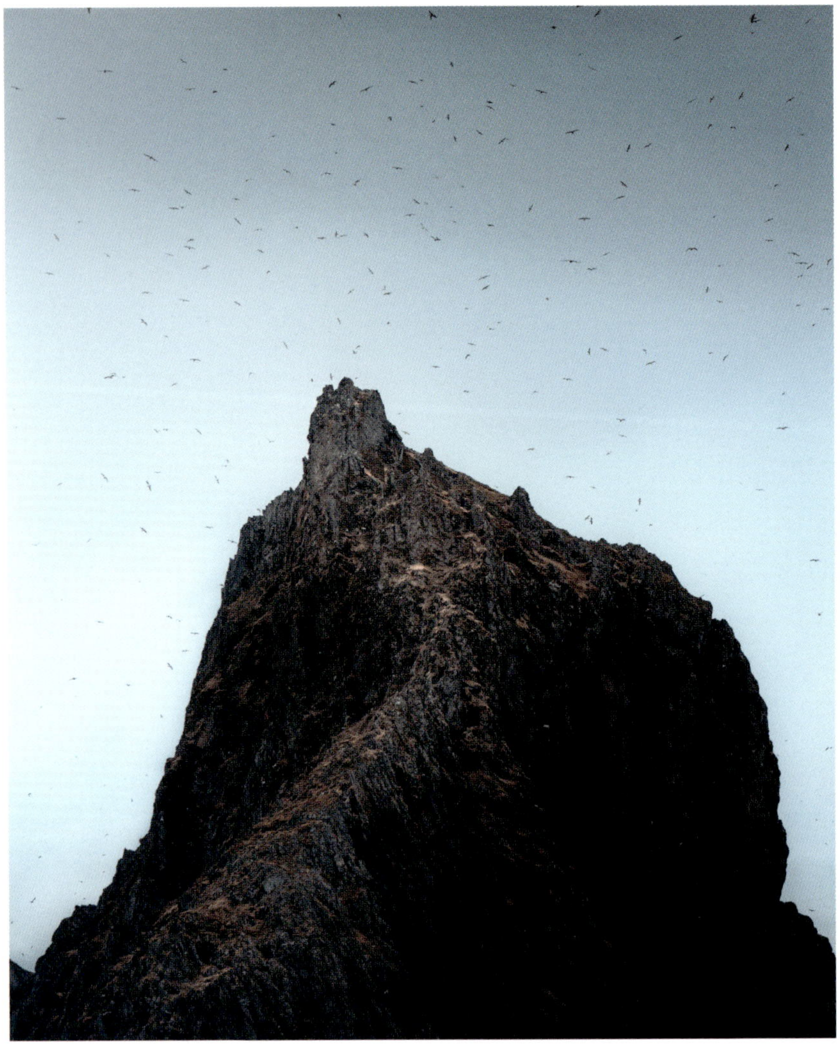

▲ EYSTRAHORN

Just a rock. But because it's the tip of a much larger and taller pile of rocks, it's special.

➤ GRAFARKIRKJA

An old church came down to the river to shave its hairy roof.

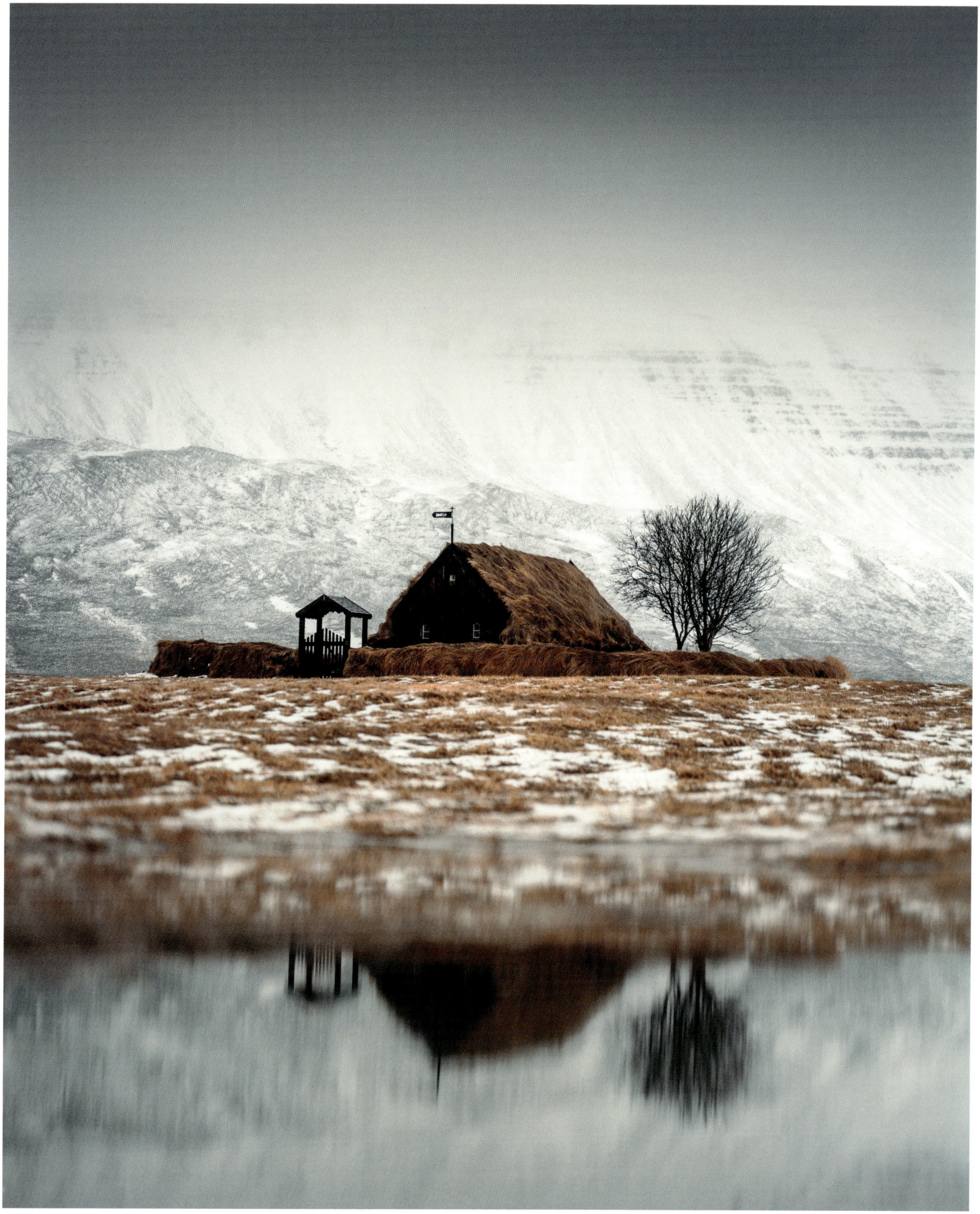

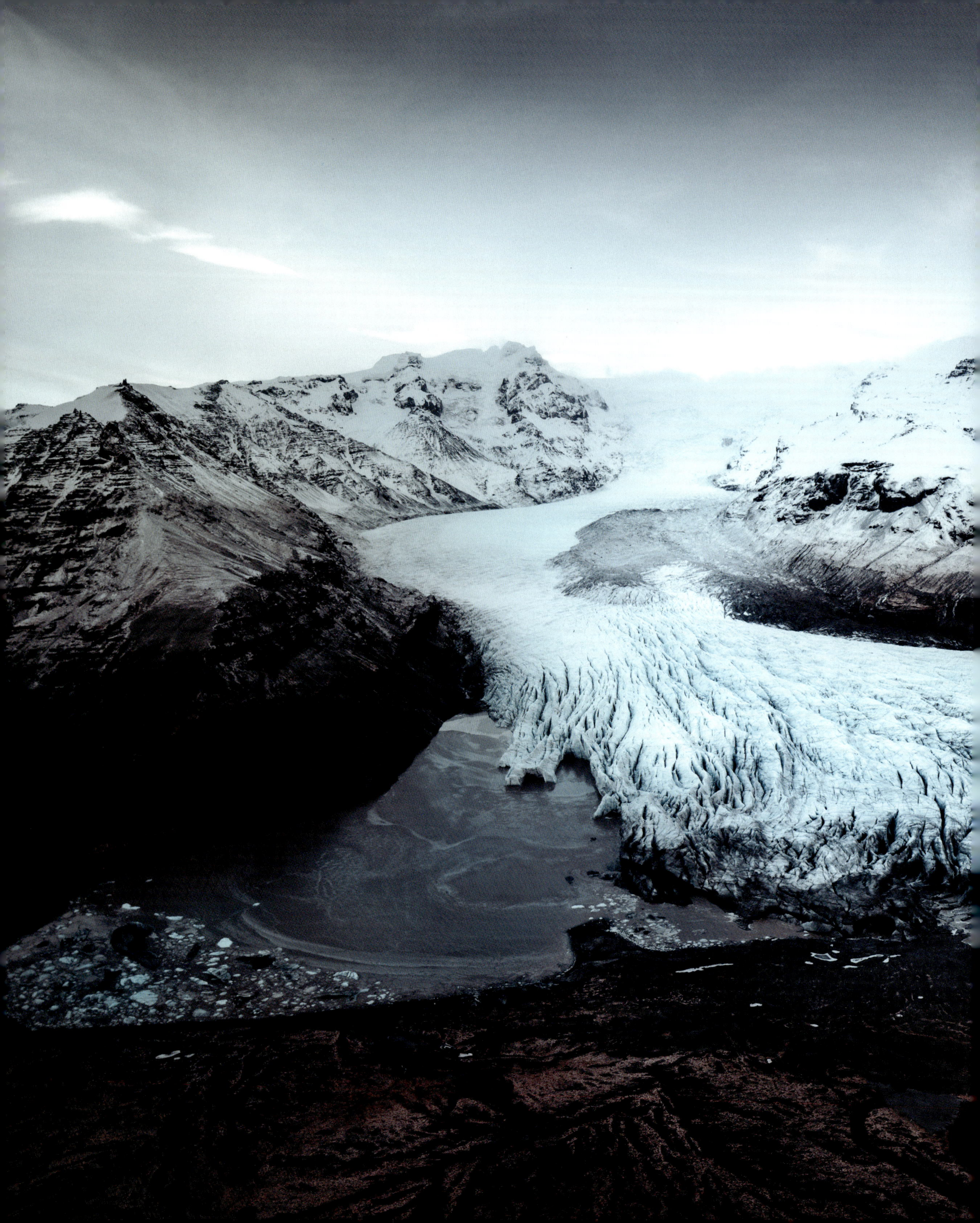

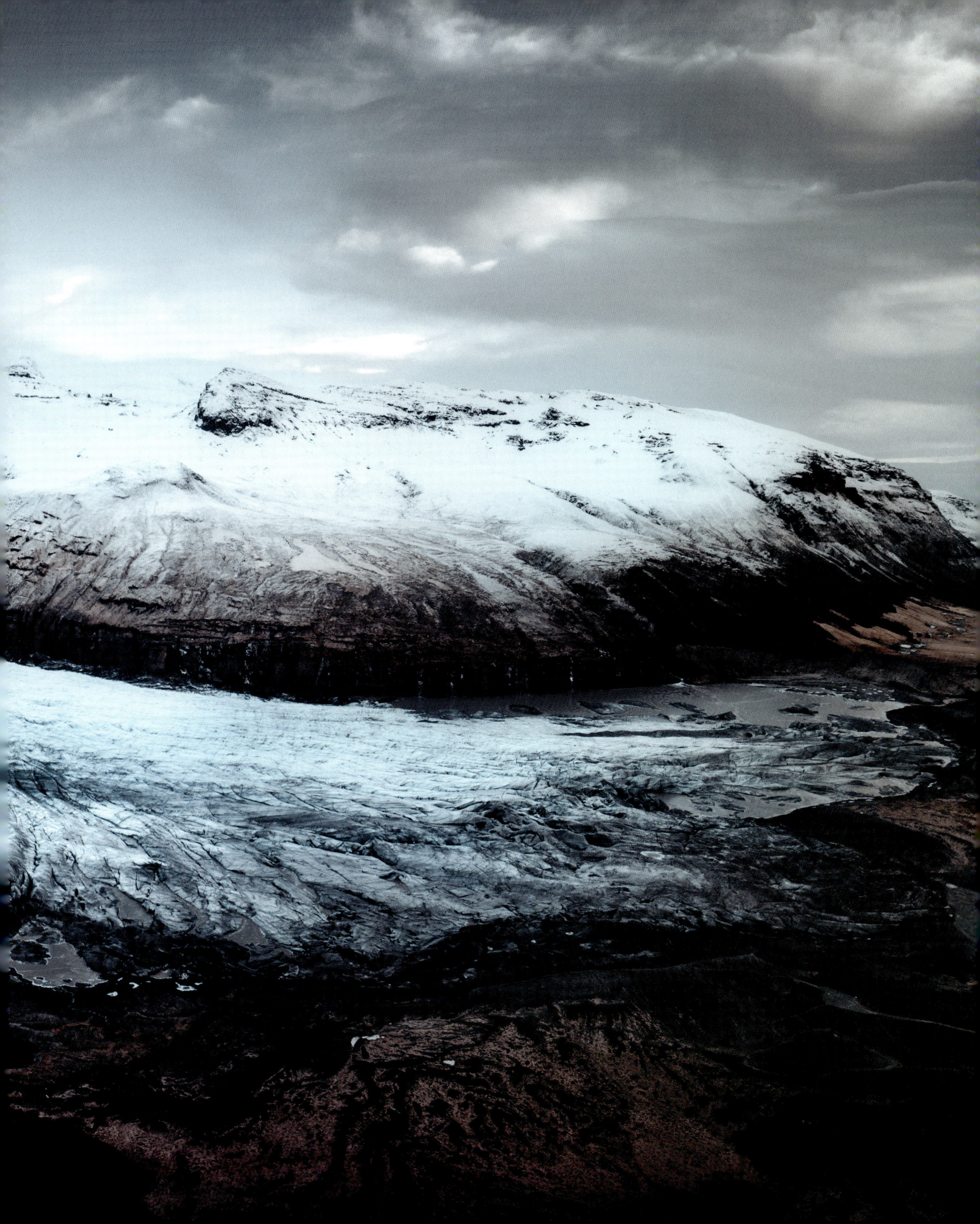

◂◂ SVINAFELLSJÖKULL

You might not recognize it, but you've probably seen this glacier before in movies. It has appeared as another planet, another world, a dramatic backshot, "north of the Wall," and, most commonly, as a stand in for the tallest mountain in the world.

▸ TINDFJALLAJÖKULL

Step one: Go to beautiful location. Step two: Wait for extreme cold. Step three: Climb higher because that's even colder. Step four: Take photo.

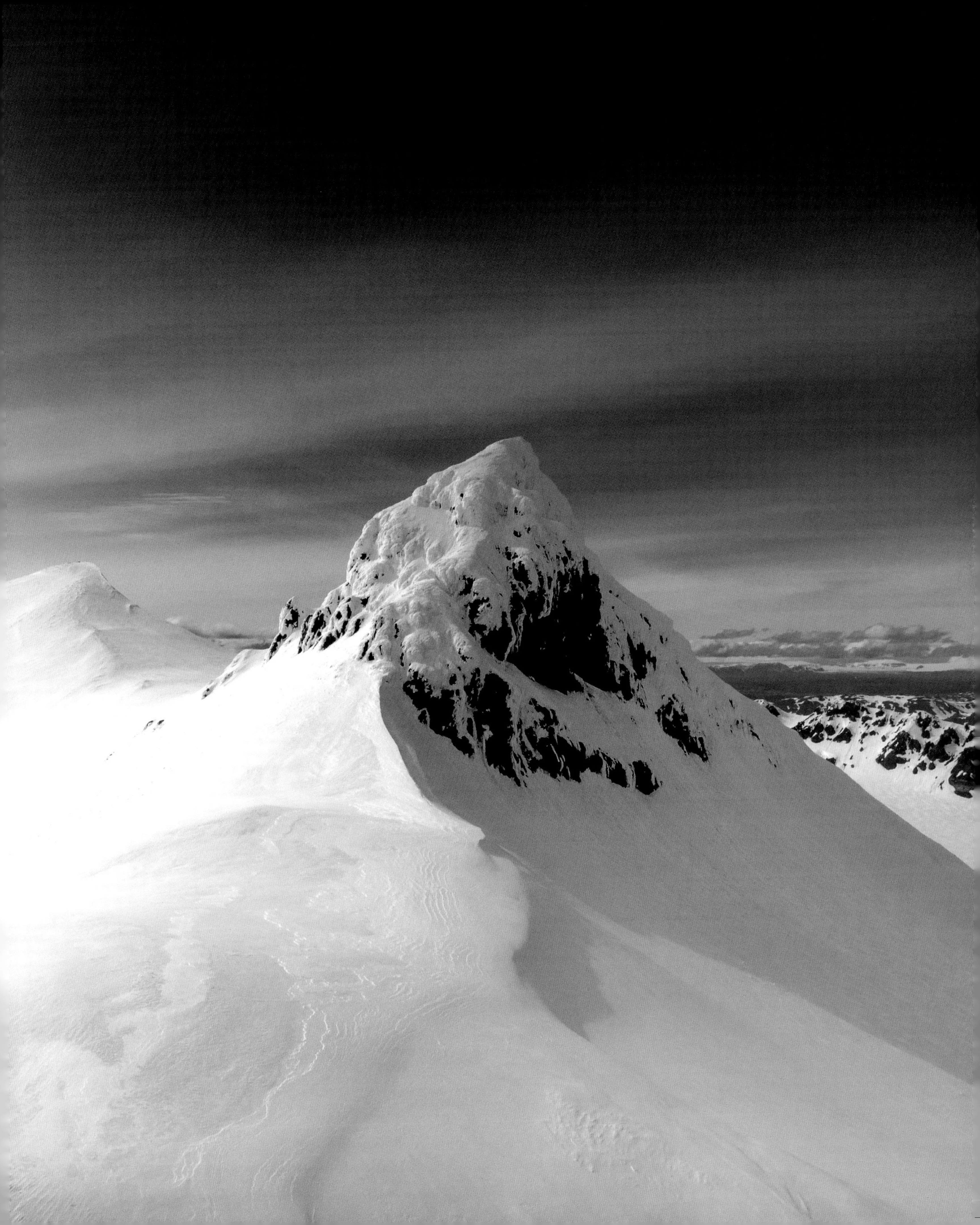

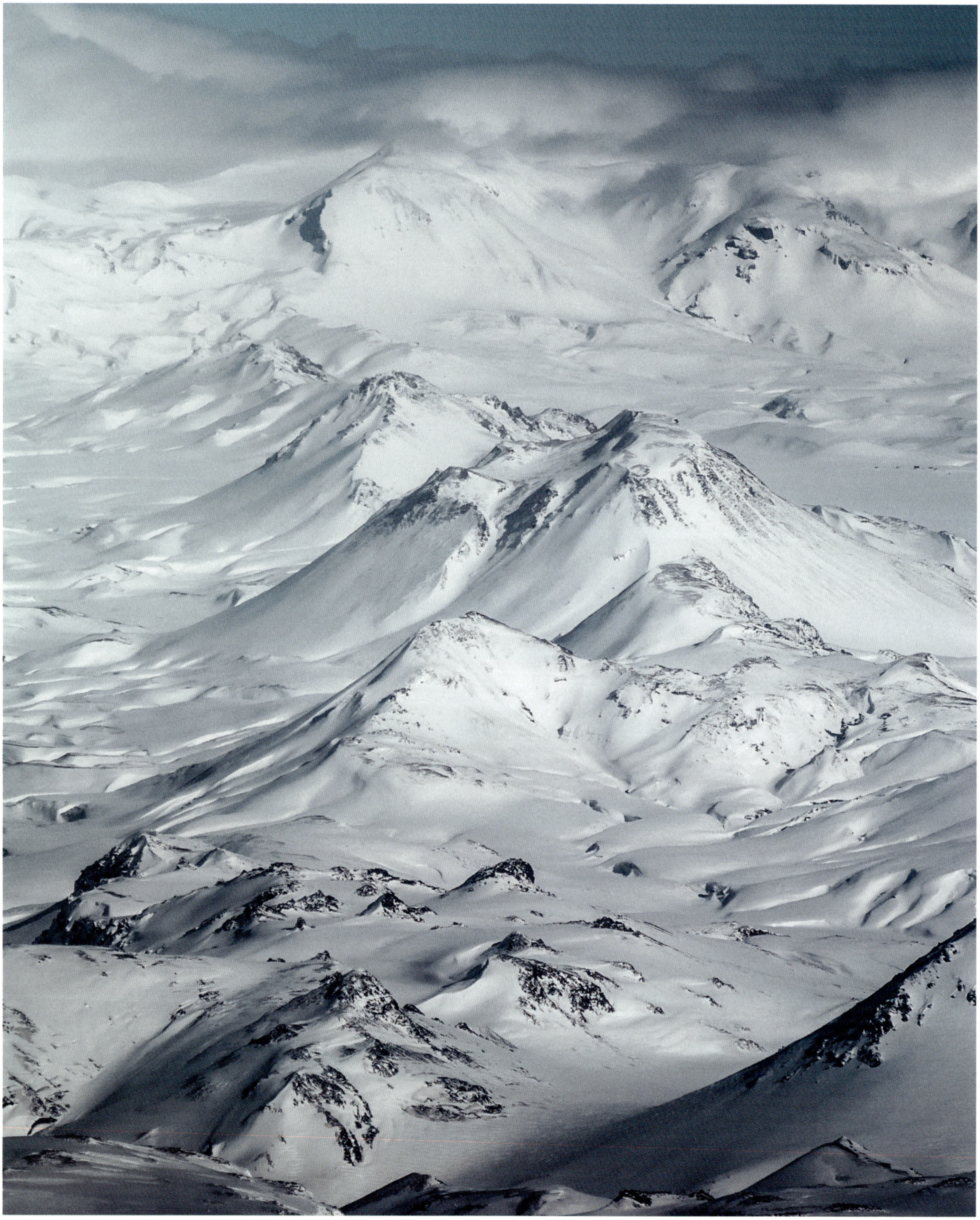

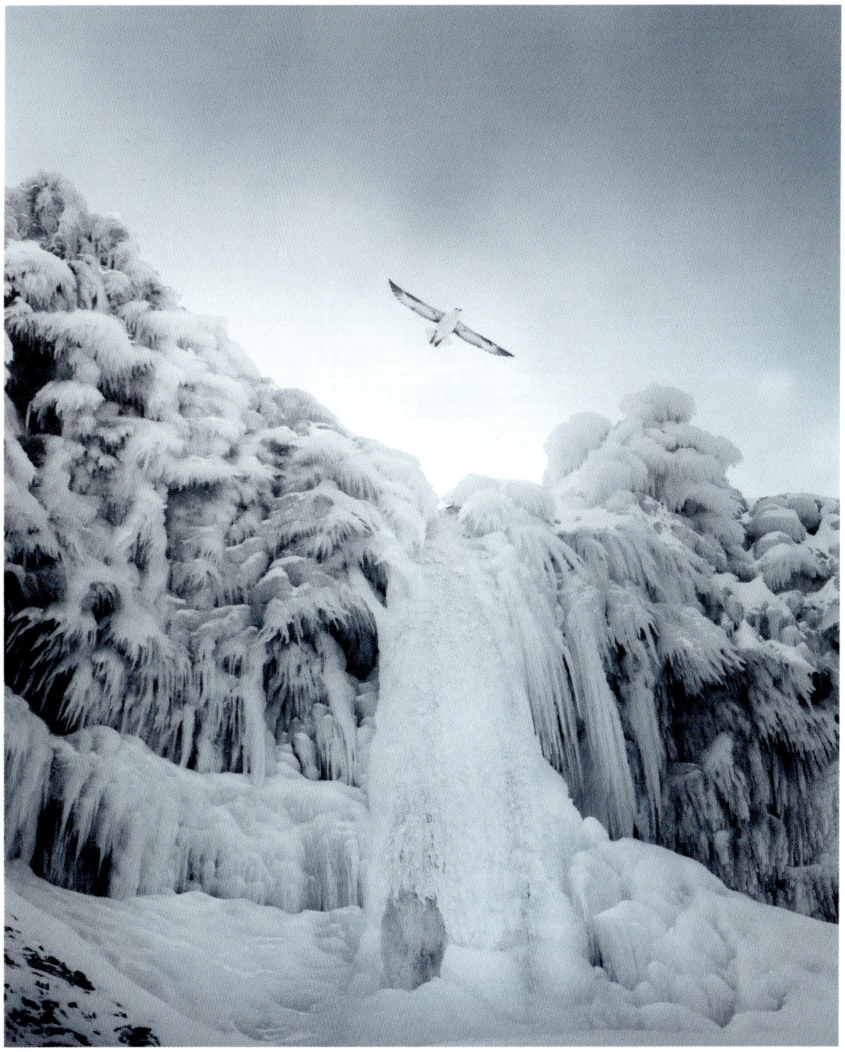

◂ TINDFJALLAJÖKULL II

Looking down at everything that seemed tall many steps ago.

▴ ONE OF THOSE 10,000 WATERFALLS

Some Icelandic waterfalls have teeth. And this one feeds on little birds.

▸▸ HVANNADALSHNJÚKUR

Went for a walk up Iceland's highest peak to see how it felt to be the tallest person on this island. After a sixteen-hour journey up above the clouds, I had to turn back right under the tip of the top. The risks of crossing the last crevasses weren't worth it this time. The drone made it up there, though.

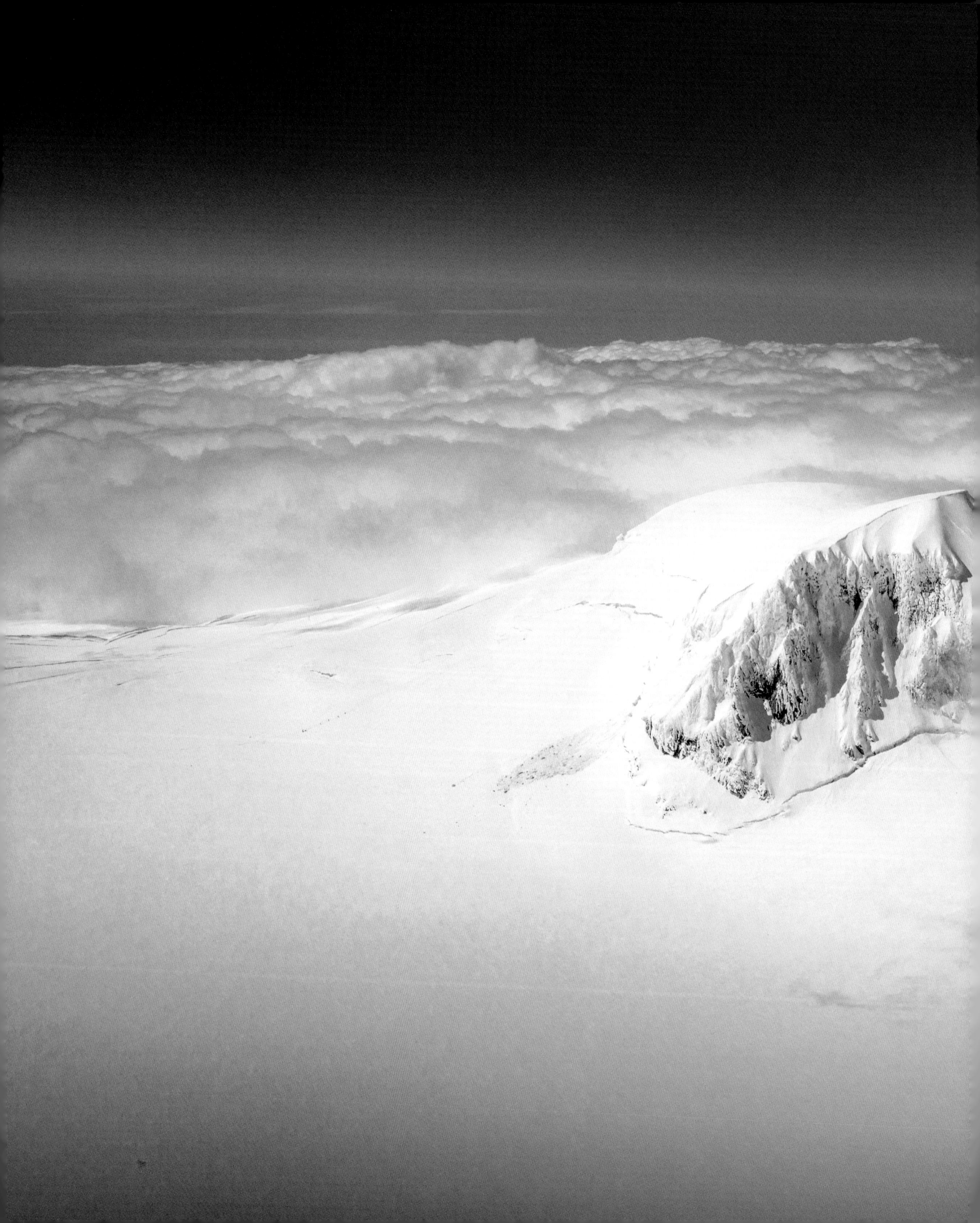

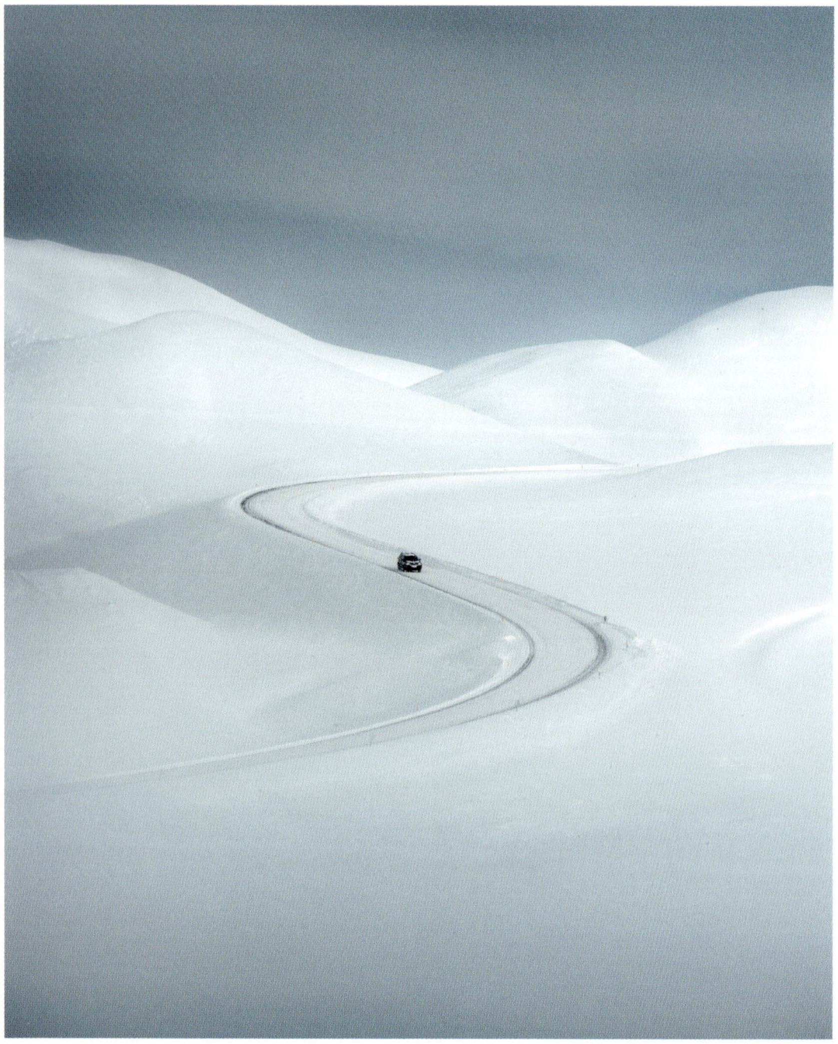

▲ MÝVATN

Sometimes it helps to have something human-made in these photos, otherwise thought and interpretation can get lost in trying to translate these views, and the world stops making sense.

► EYJAFJÖRÐUR

Cabins are just roofs with too many walls that block the views.

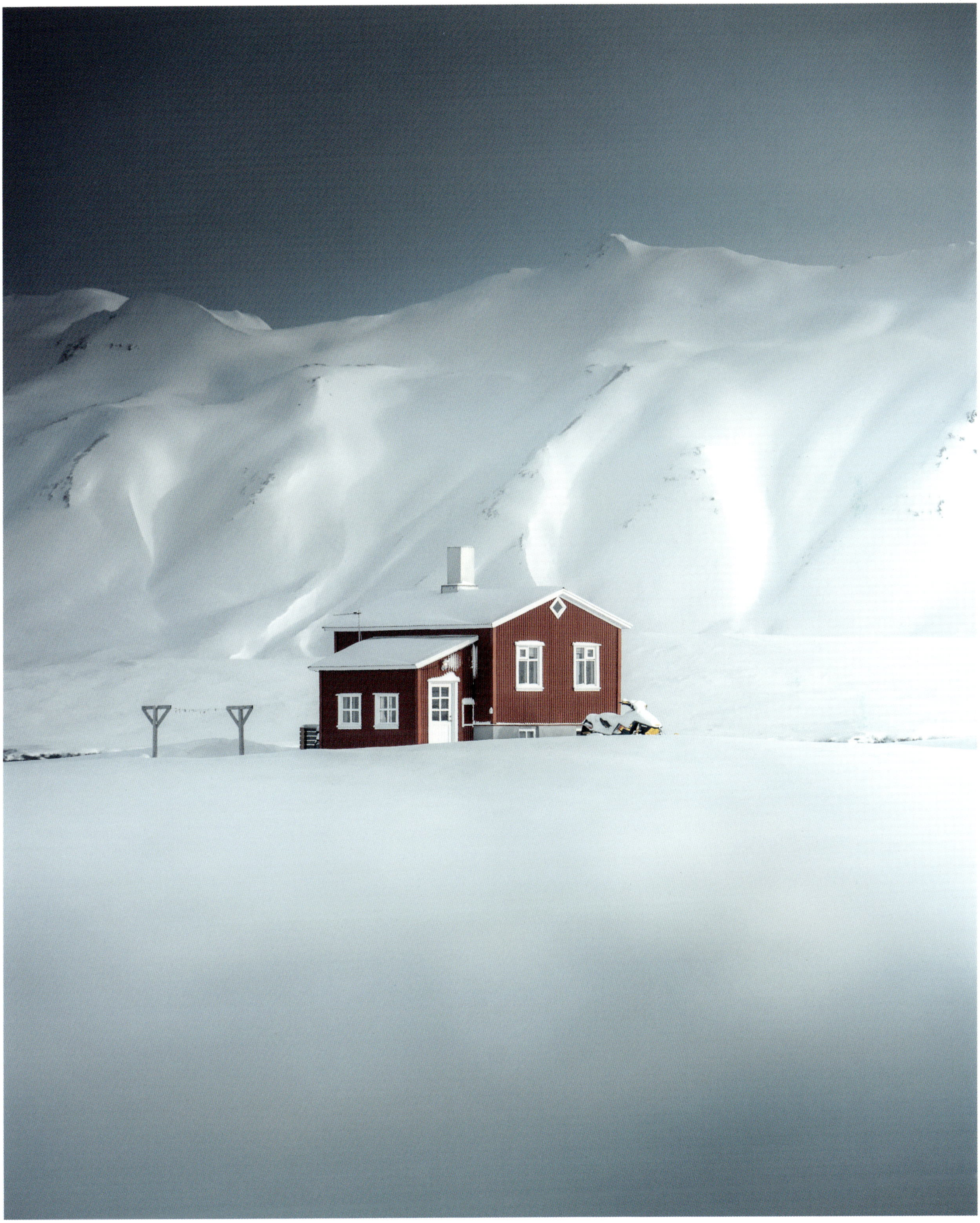

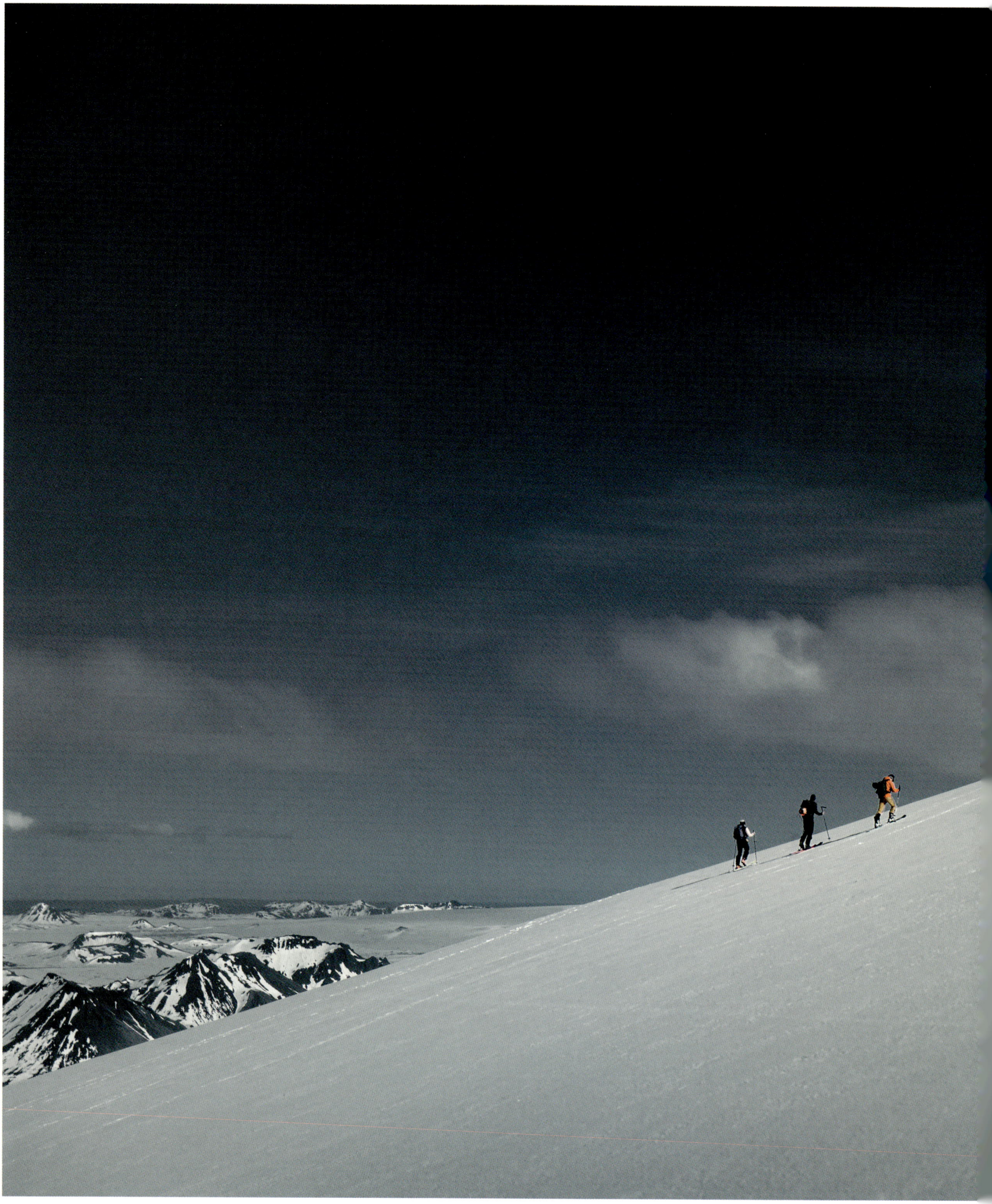

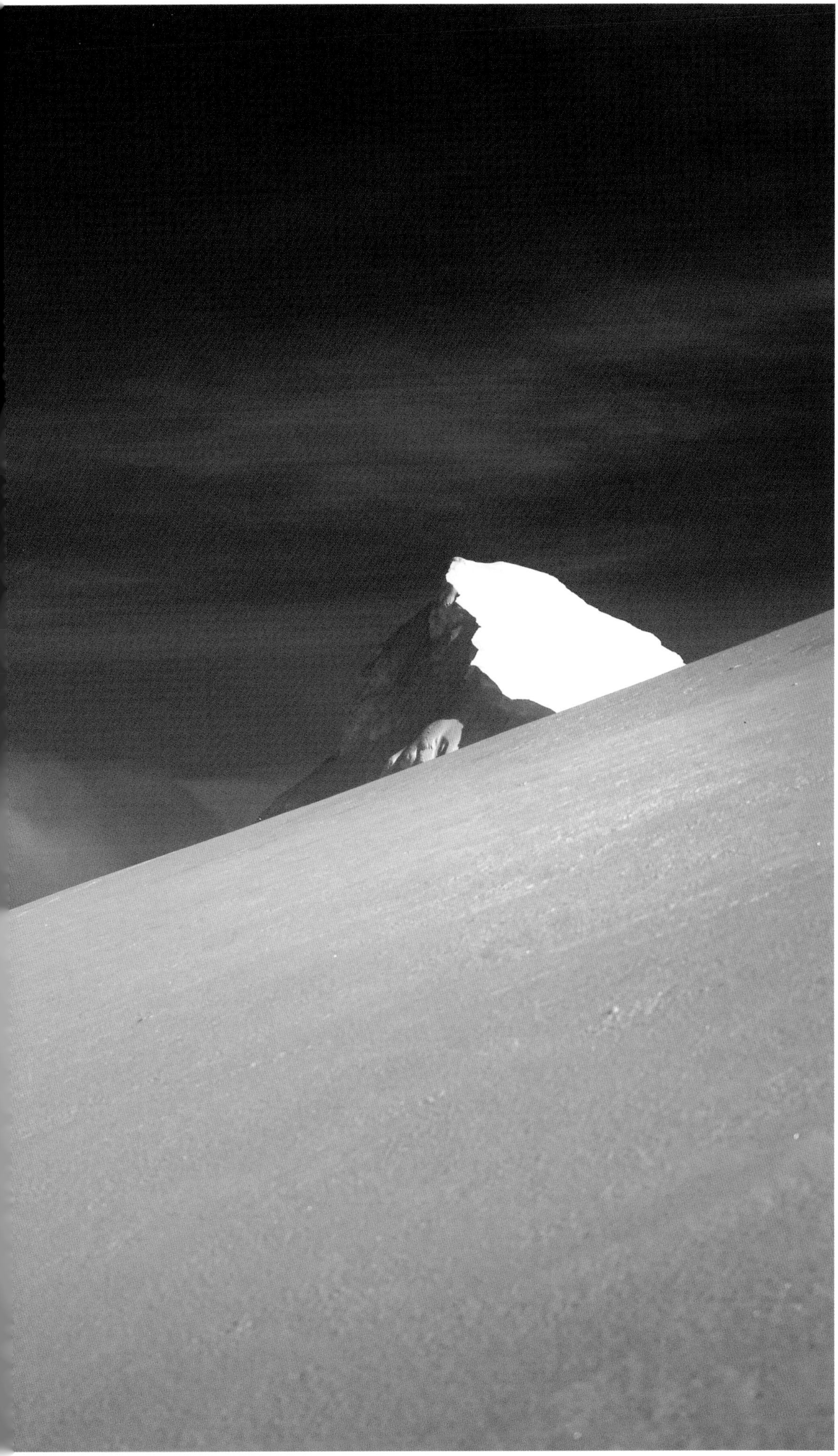

◂ TINDFJALLAJÖKULL III

Sometimes the north is so far north that you have to climb closer to the sun to actually see it.

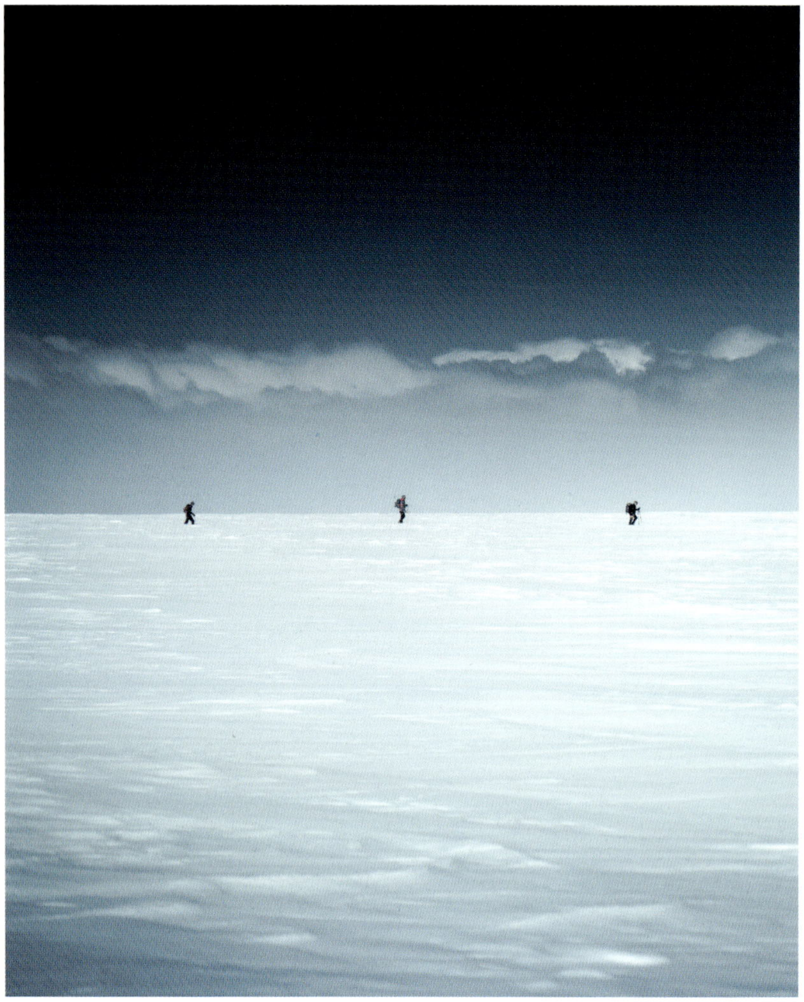

▲ HVANNADALSHNJÚKUR II

Lost in the middle of nothing.

➤ HVANNADALSHNJÚKUR III

Far above summer, heading to the peak of Iceland.

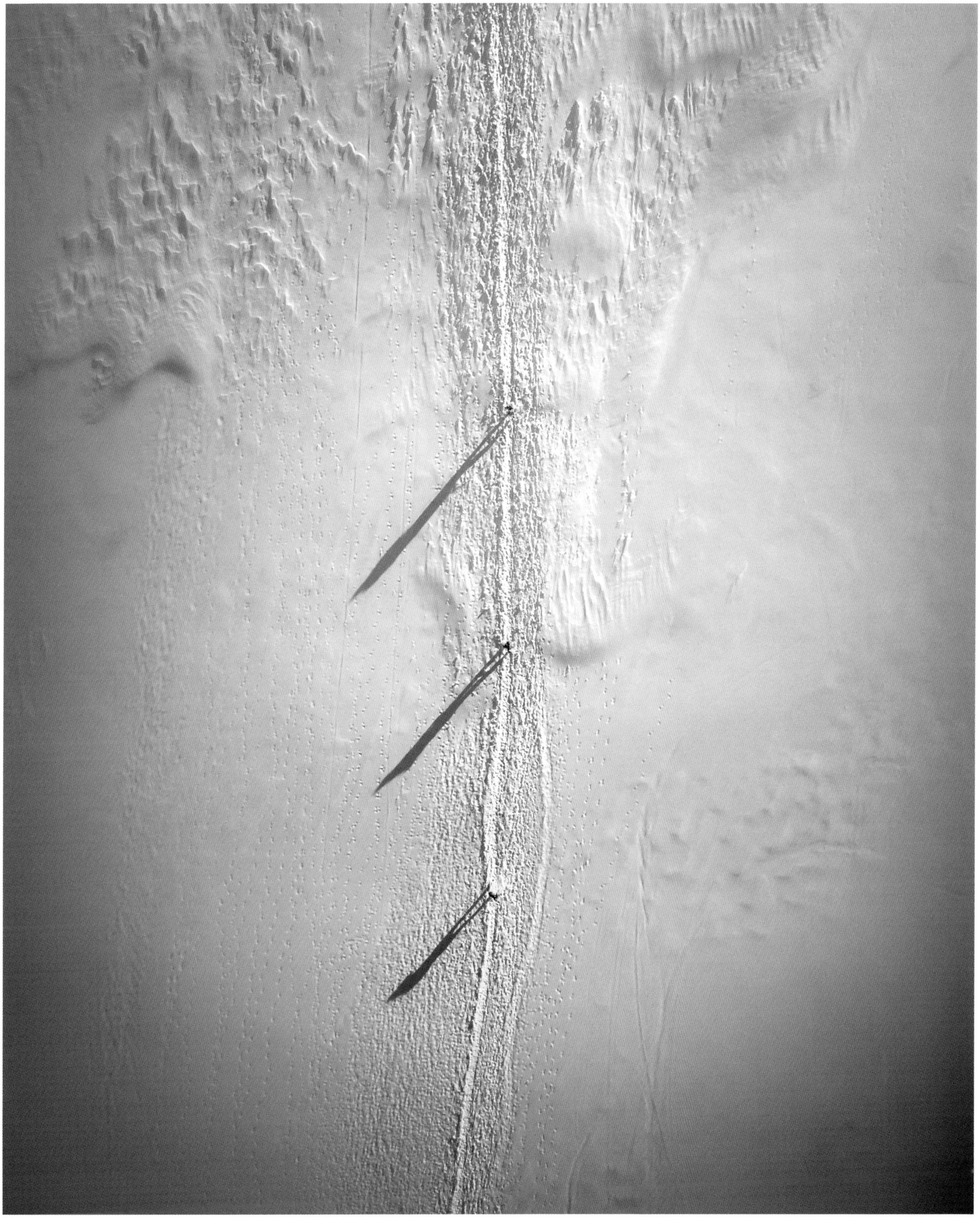

➤ SVINAFELLSJÖKULL II

A glacier that grew teeth so it can chew on the tourists that fall into it.

➤➤ FALLJÖKULL II

Vikings built these glaciers by freezing their own tears so they would have enough party ice for their mead.

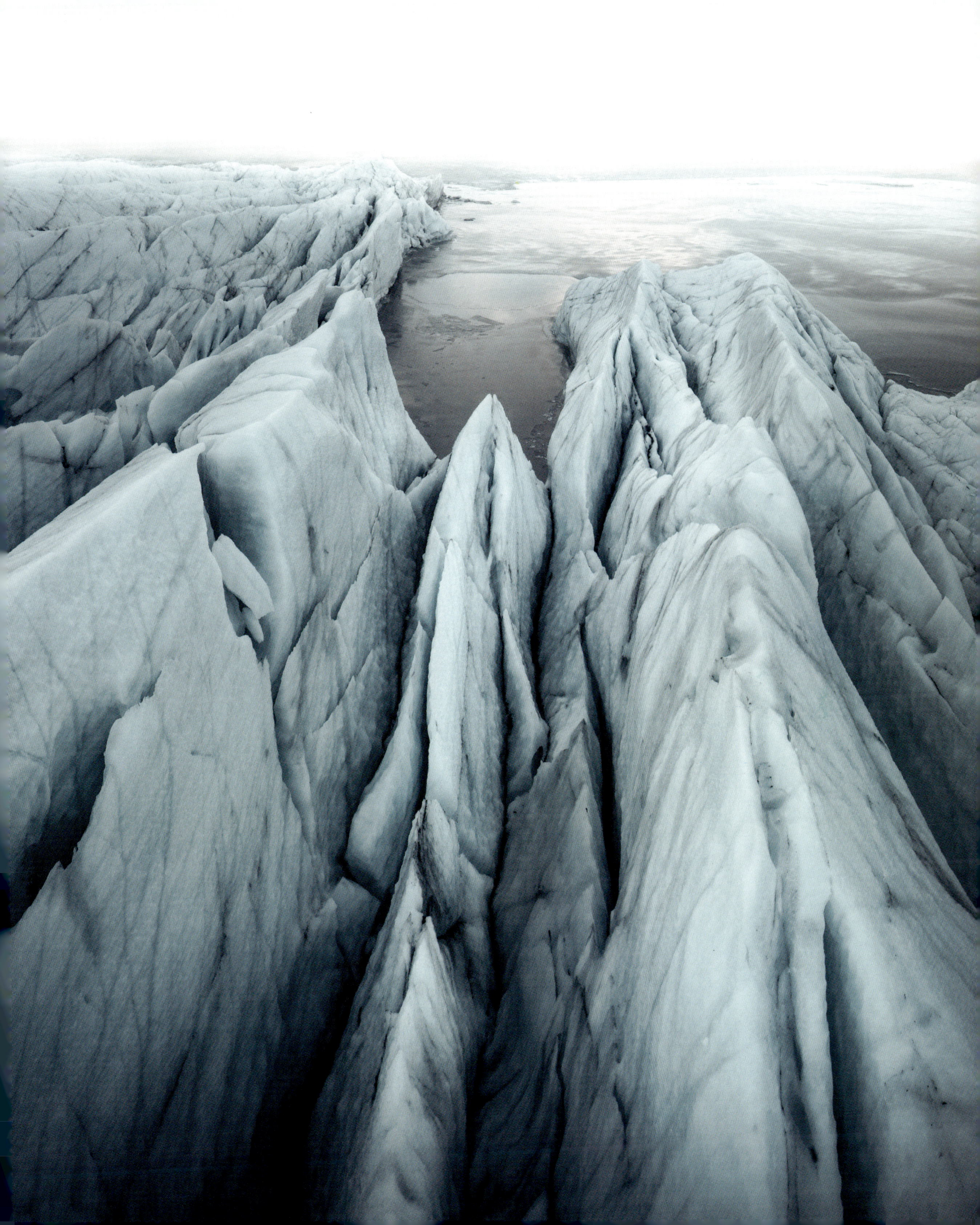

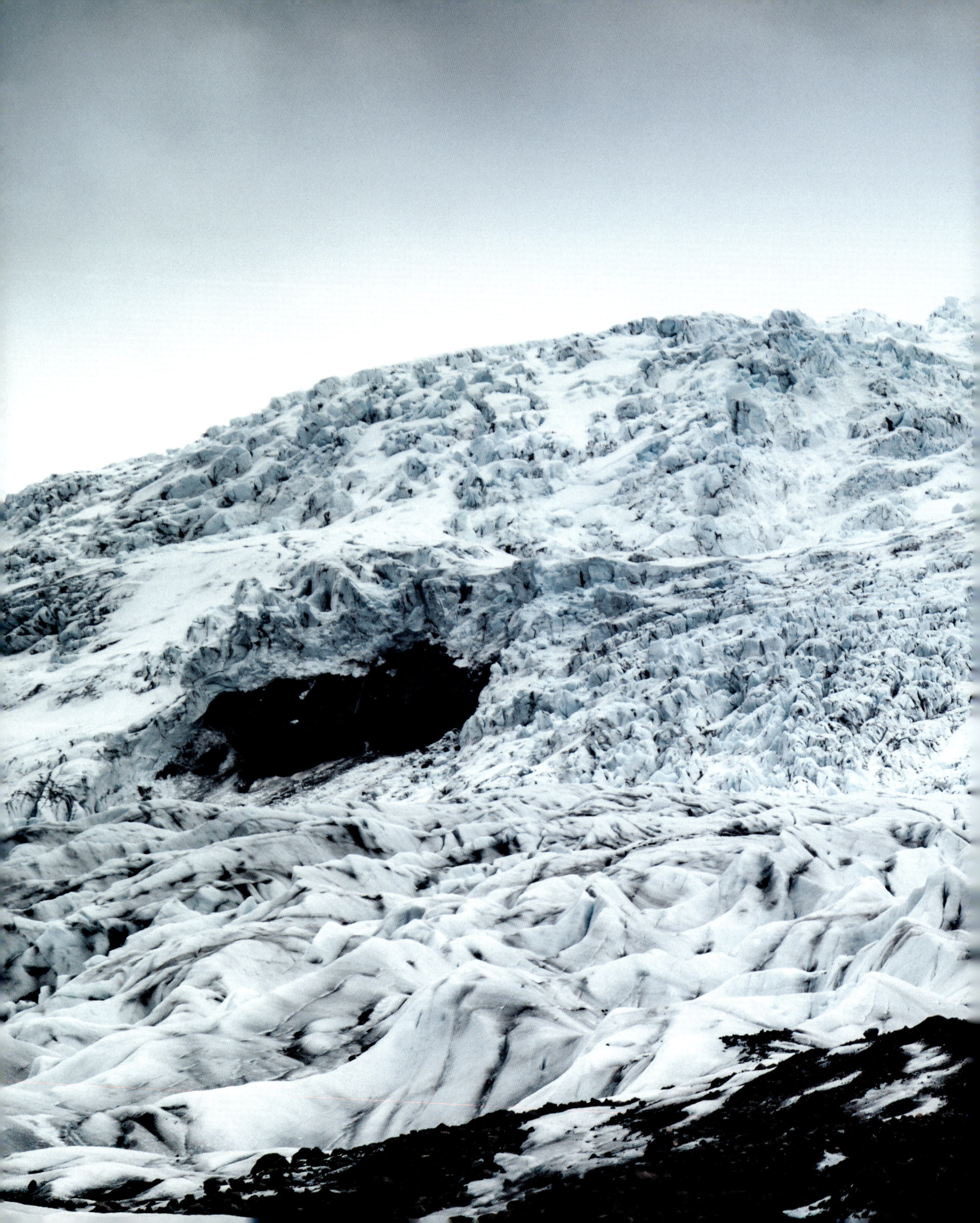

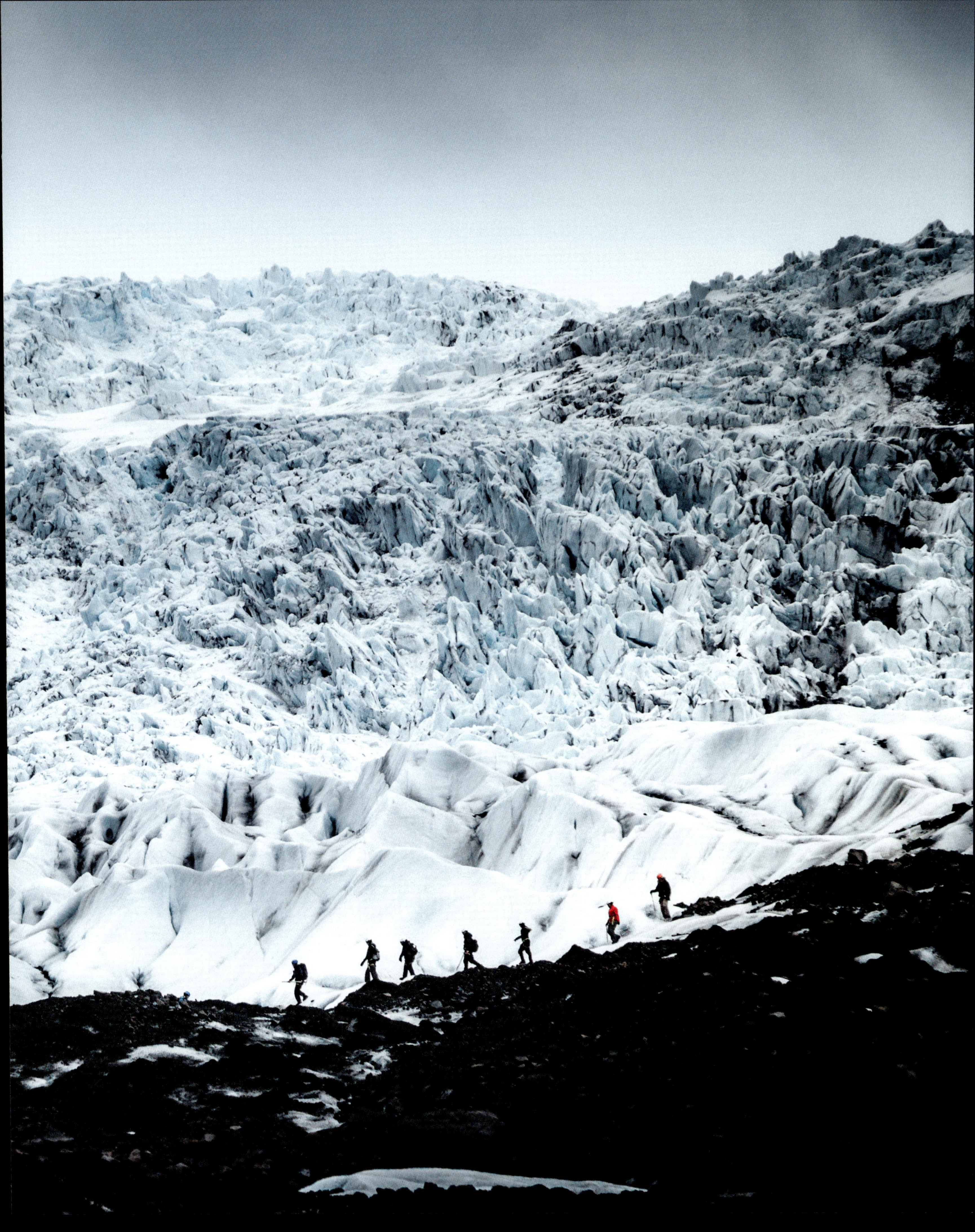

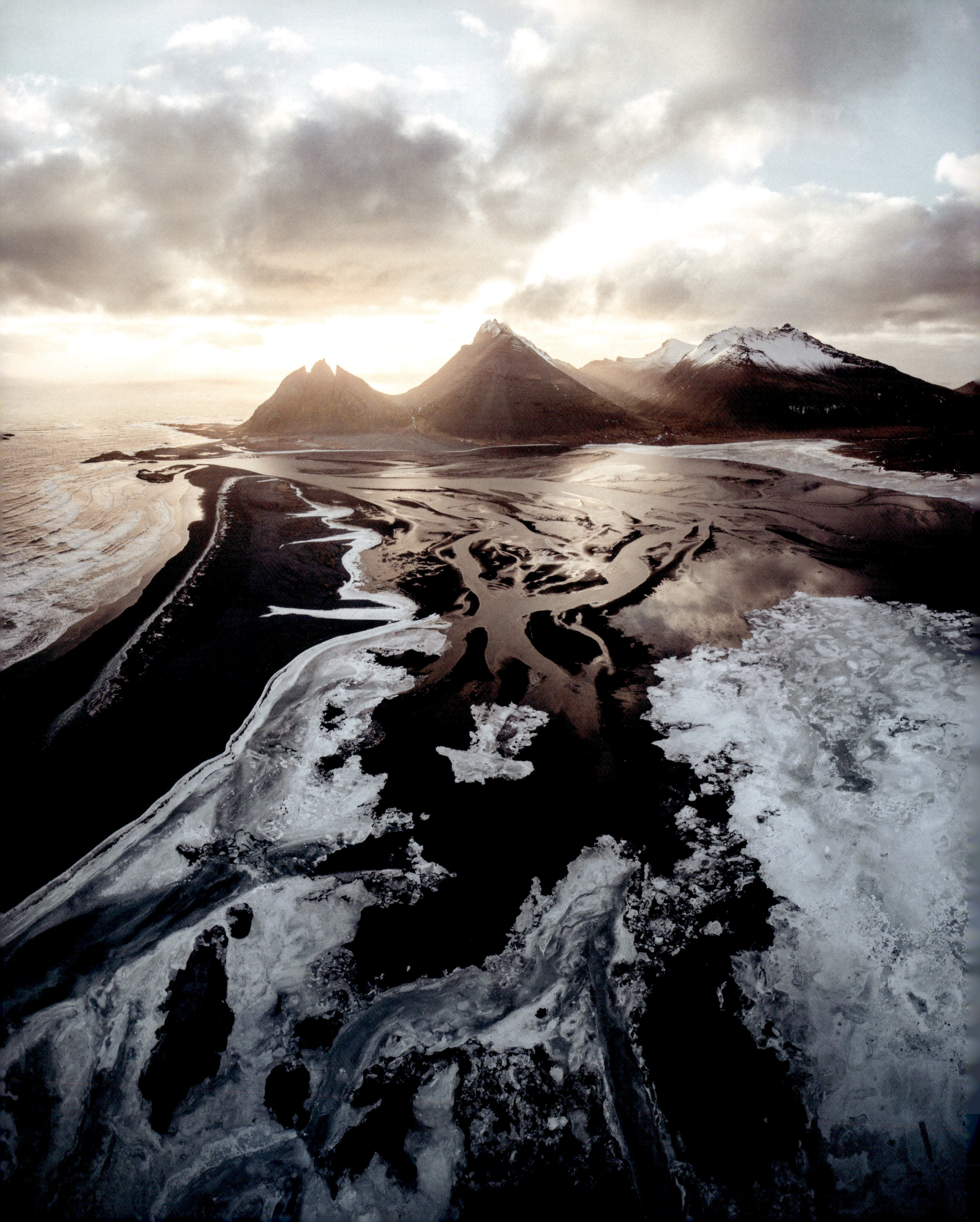

◂ HVALNESFJARA

Glacial waters on their way to the sea, telling the coastal mountains about life inland and everything they're missing.

▸▸ EYSTRAHORN II

Some landscapes grow horns to defend themselves from the falling sky above.

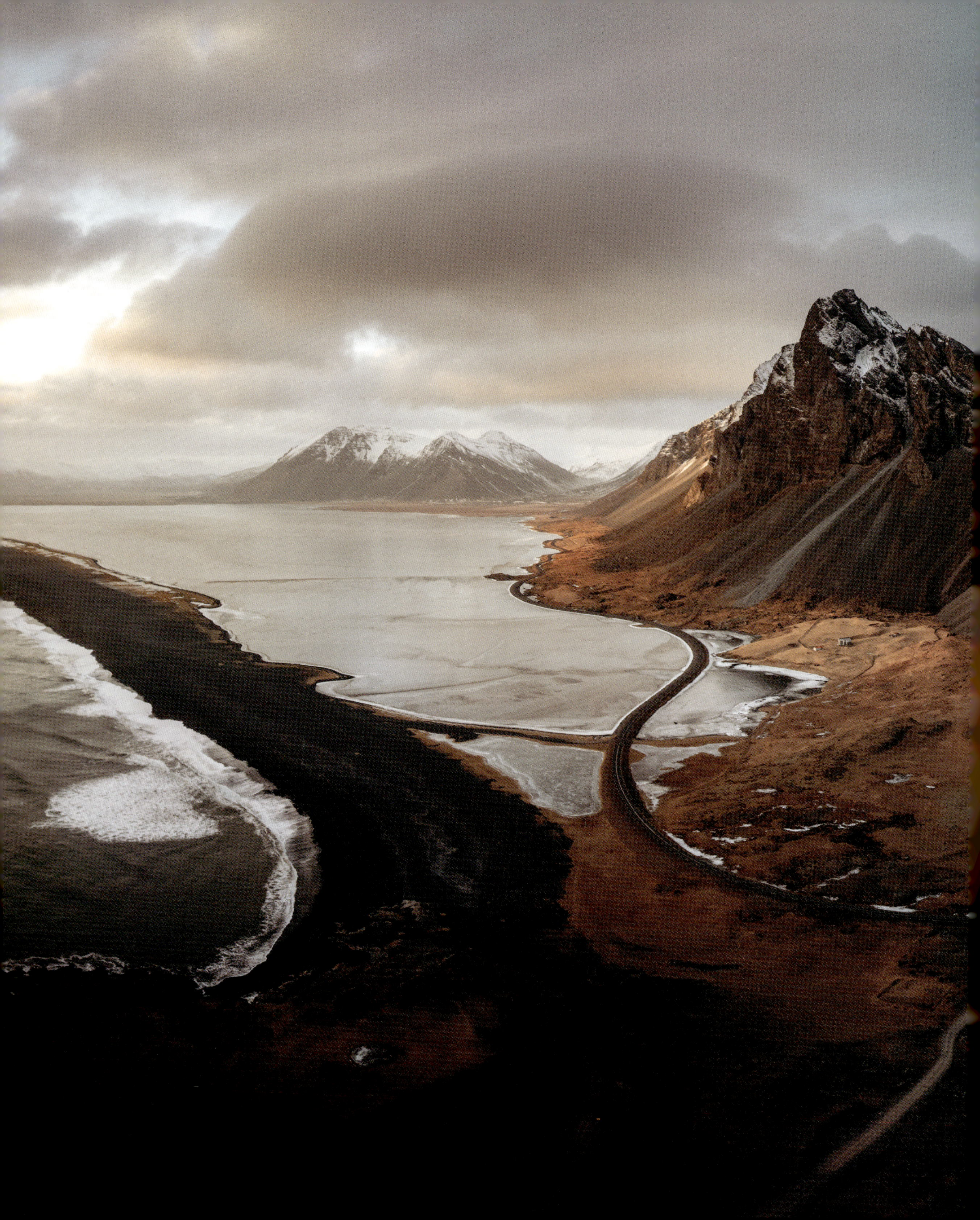

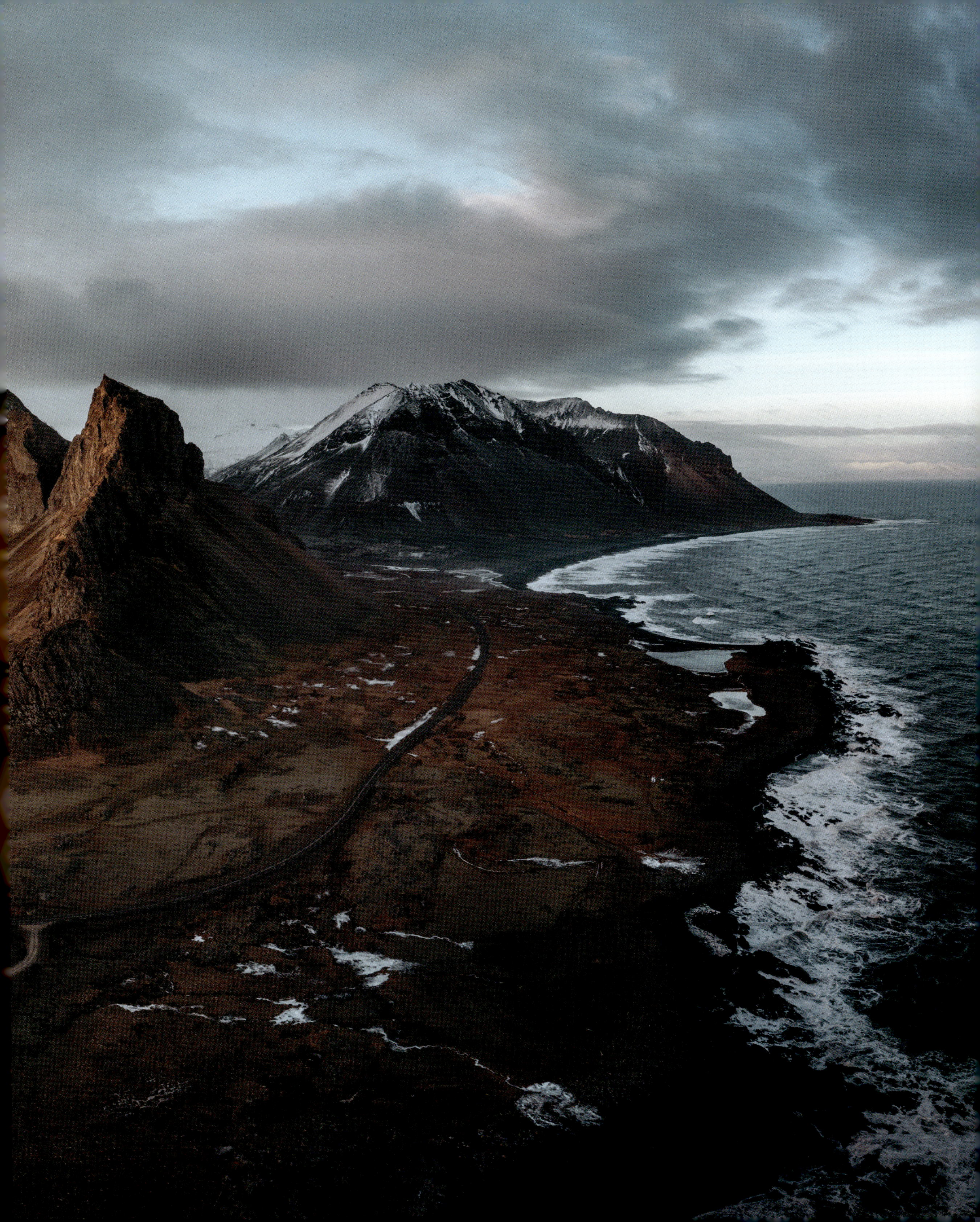

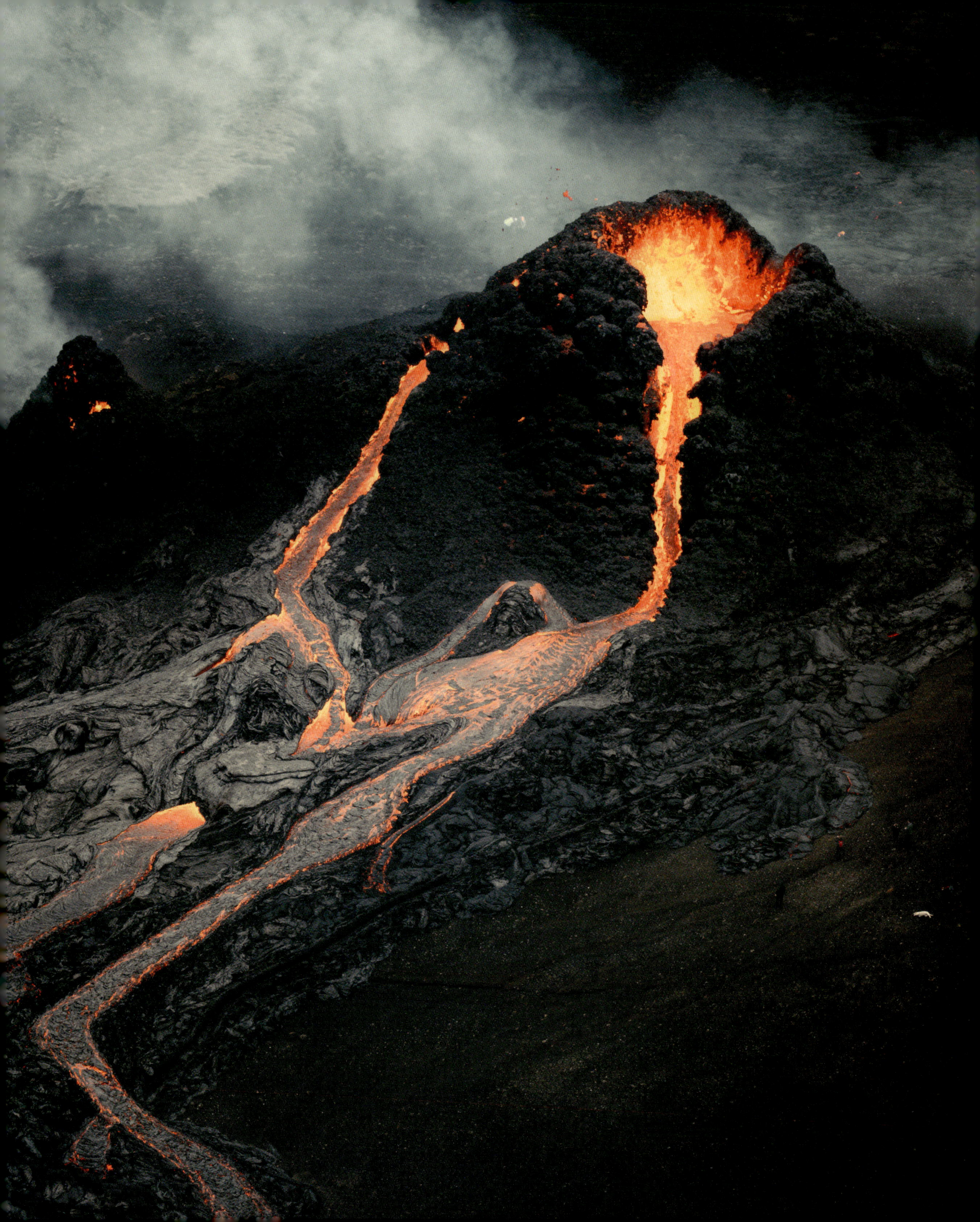

THE GRAND AWAKENING OF EVERYTHING

May and June

The air smells of life, a smell we forgot to miss until now.
The ground is soggy, confused, and overwhelmed.
If you step on it, you'll make it worse.
Everything is waking up, even the things that should
probably stay asleep. At least the sun forgets to leave.

The auroras are fading and the stars on the northern side of the horizon are already gone. They say it's the first day of summer in Iceland, but that's never been a real thing here. But at least it's becoming "not winter," at last.

The animals love this, and they stumble out to see it before realizing they've been starving all winter. Soon they start screaming for food.

Landscapes are waking up, and people rediscover the color green (mainly from photos of other, normal places). It takes a long time for Iceland to regain its full colors. But in the meantime, the sun begins to radiate with a glimpse of power and there's a universal desire to pretend that it's warm. After all, the weather *looks* warm through the window. It's even called "Gluggaveður," or *window weather*. Crowds of people sit lightly clad on the still-dead grass and shiver together, no one wanting to give up first and put on a sweater.

You can feel the natural forces coming alive again, both above and below. The energy that was frozen midmotion is now released. Sometimes the inside of Iceland spills out this time of year, providing a sort of Viking bonfire. It has become an almost annual ritual. People come to experience their raw emotions as close as possible to the glowing lava.

There are fewer and fewer wrong turns left to take. The only place still inaccessible is the highlands, the interior of Iceland. No one lives there in the winter, so no one knows what's going on there—but everyone agrees that it needs a few more months to sort itself out.

Take the headlamp and a few of the layers out of the backpack. It's better to travel light and stay on your toes for this next bit.

◂◂ GELDINGADALUR

Eruption, day one.

The first time I flew out over the lava with The Volcano Pilot, Haddi, I didn't know which of the two was more legendary. Even though this was the most remarkable experience of my life to this day, it's the people I shared it with, especially Haddi, that I remember, cherish, and will forever miss the most. The shared moment meant more than a volcano ever could.

▸ FAGRADALSFJALL

The 'cano has made a pretty big mess by now. I remember circling the whole lava field in an hour on foot. More recently we tried with electric mountain bikes and only got halfway around it. Still got a pretty great view, though!

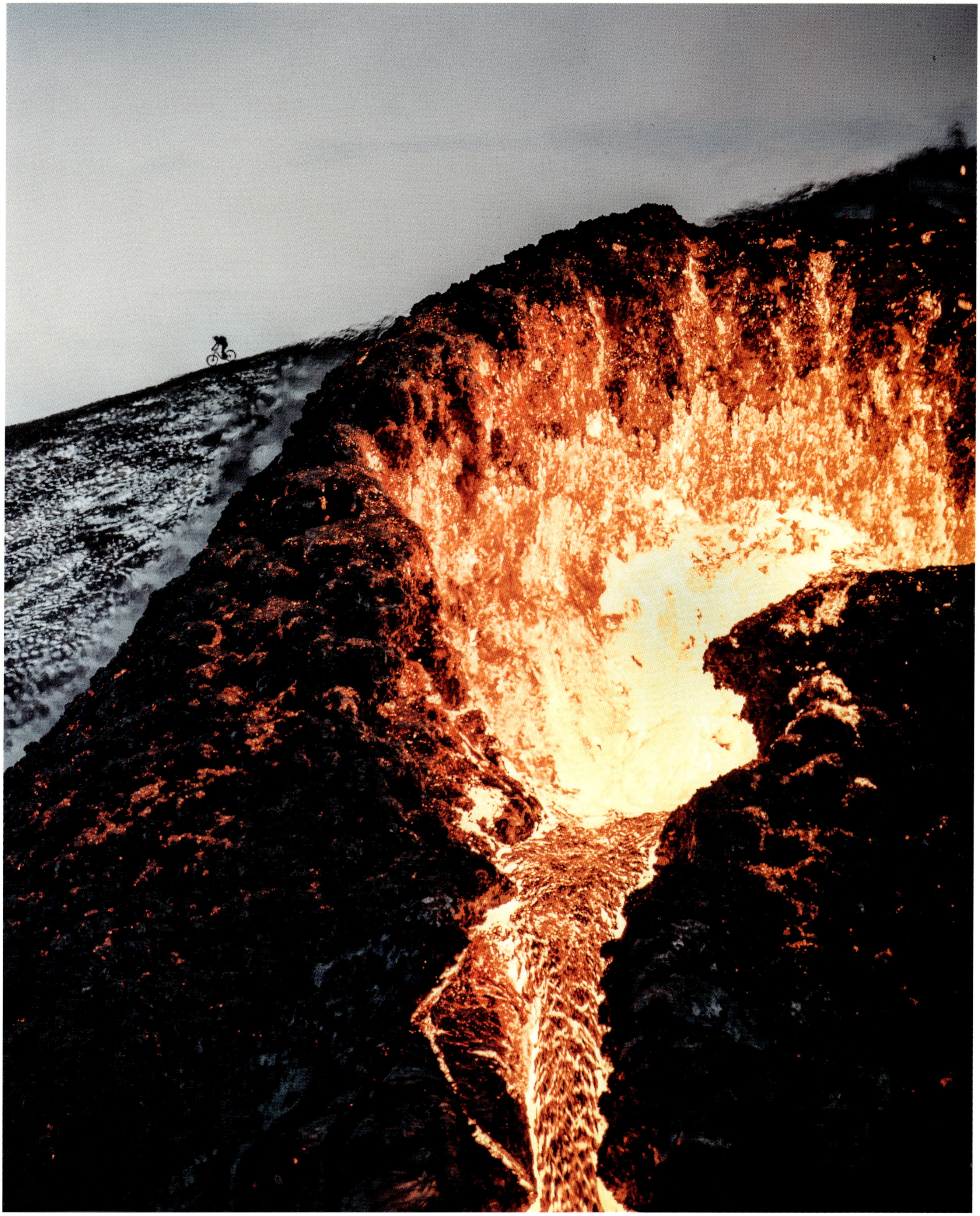

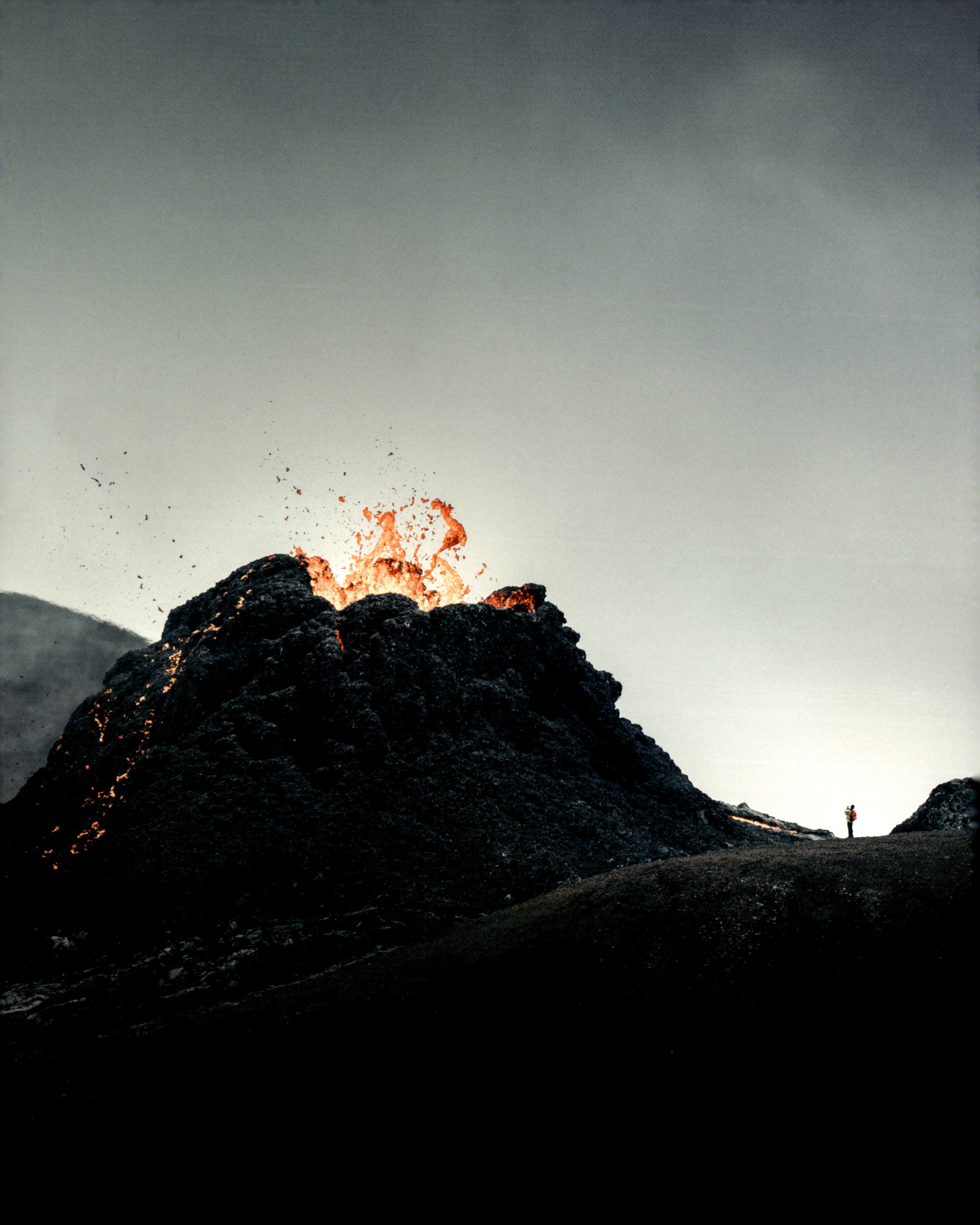

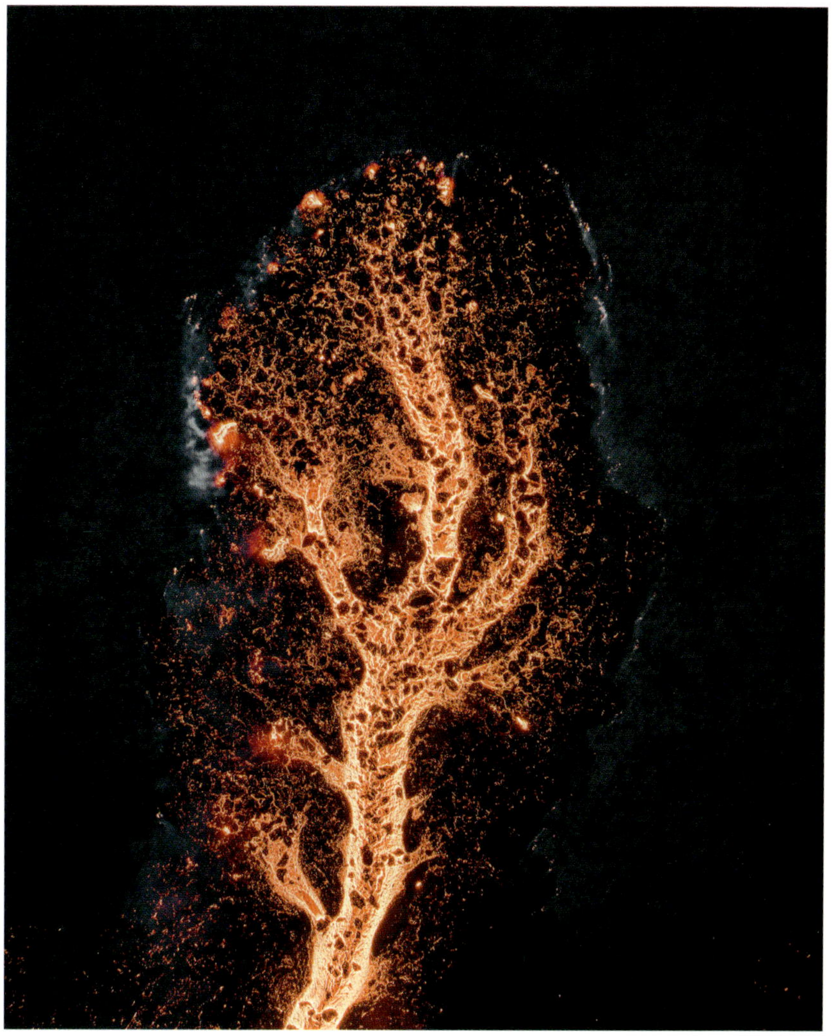

◂ GELDINGADALUR II

The police were already on location when I arrived at this eruption. I snapped this shot and asked if I was allowed to go up there. They said that it's everyone's land and they couldn't really stop anyone from going anywhere–but if anyone was going to die today, it would be the people up there. So, up I went.

▴ LITLI-HRÚTUR

It's probably trying to communicate with us.

▸▸ FAGRADALSFJALL II (L)

No wonder the Vikings believed in all sorts of crazy things. Look at what this land can do!

▸▸ FAGRADALSFJALL III (R)

A dying ember left behind. It will soon be dark here, with the only heat streaming from the depths below. Until it all stops, just to start again.

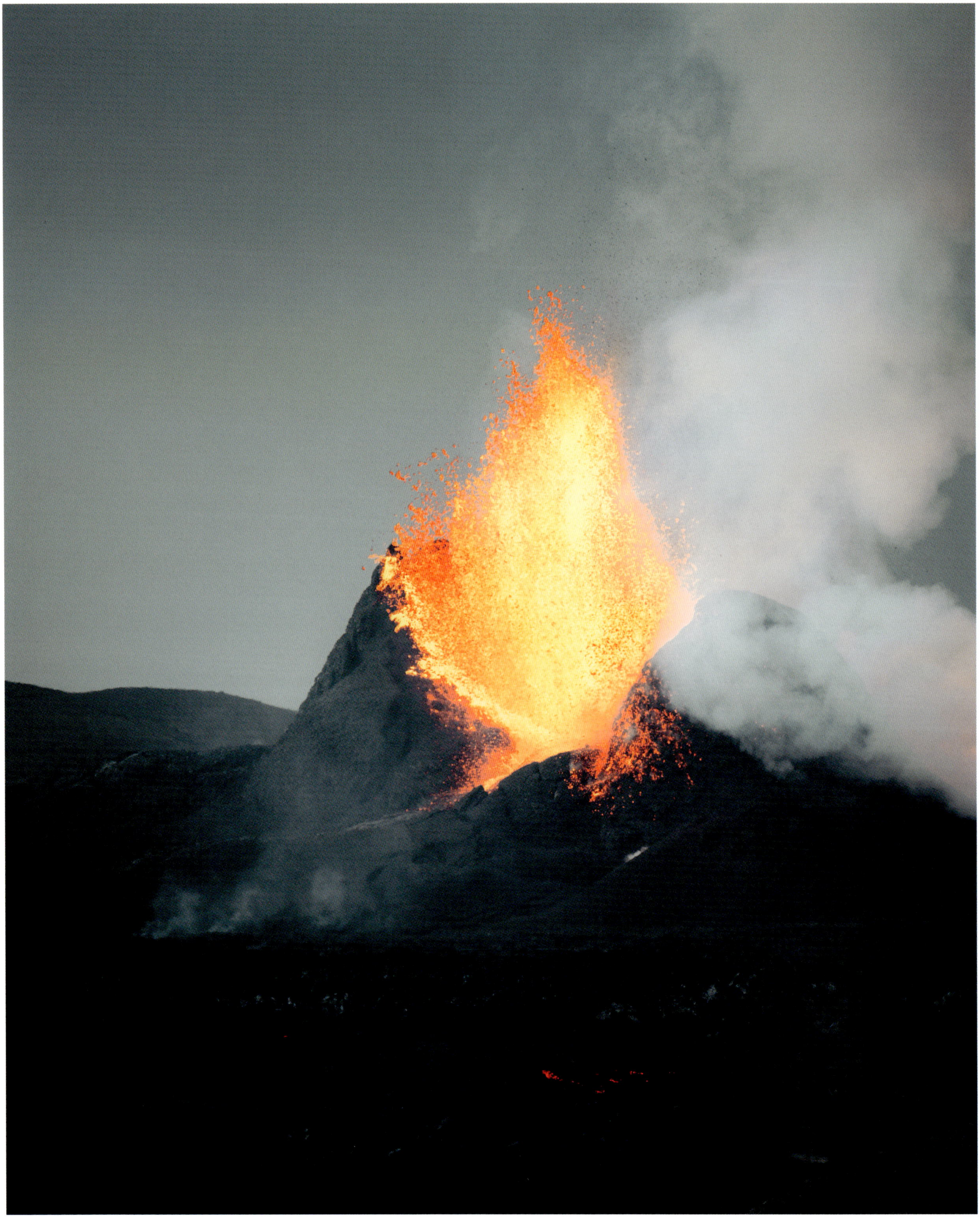

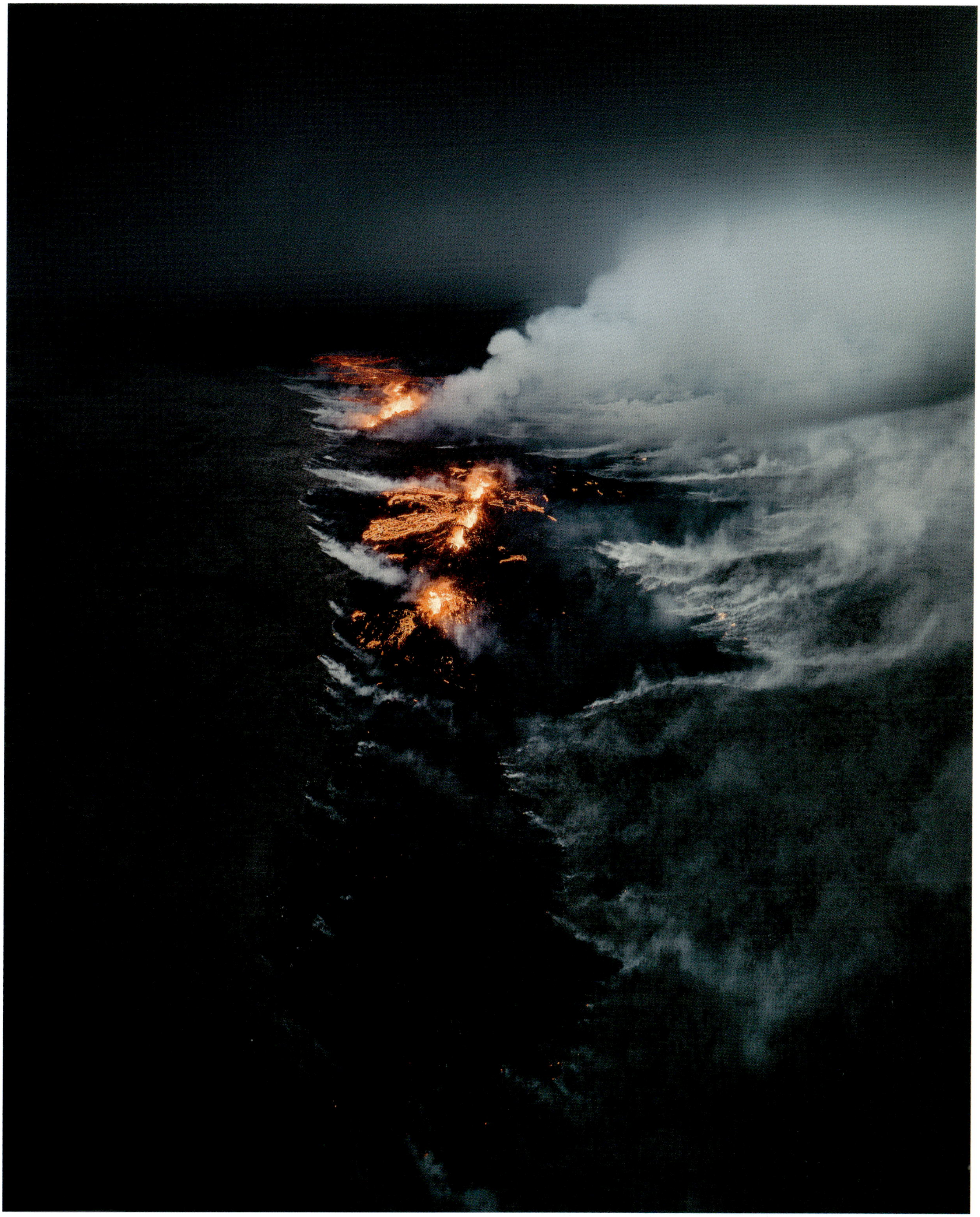

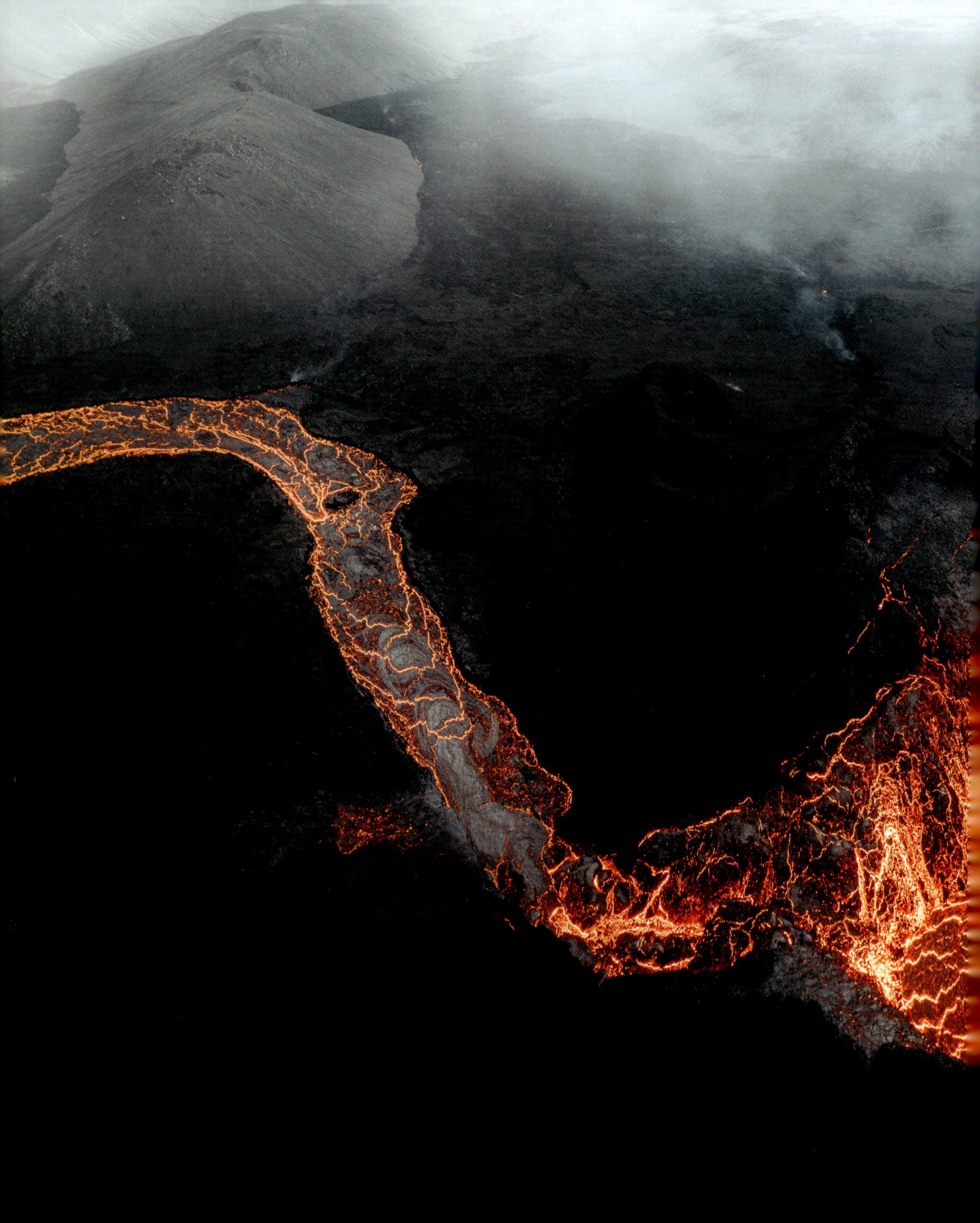

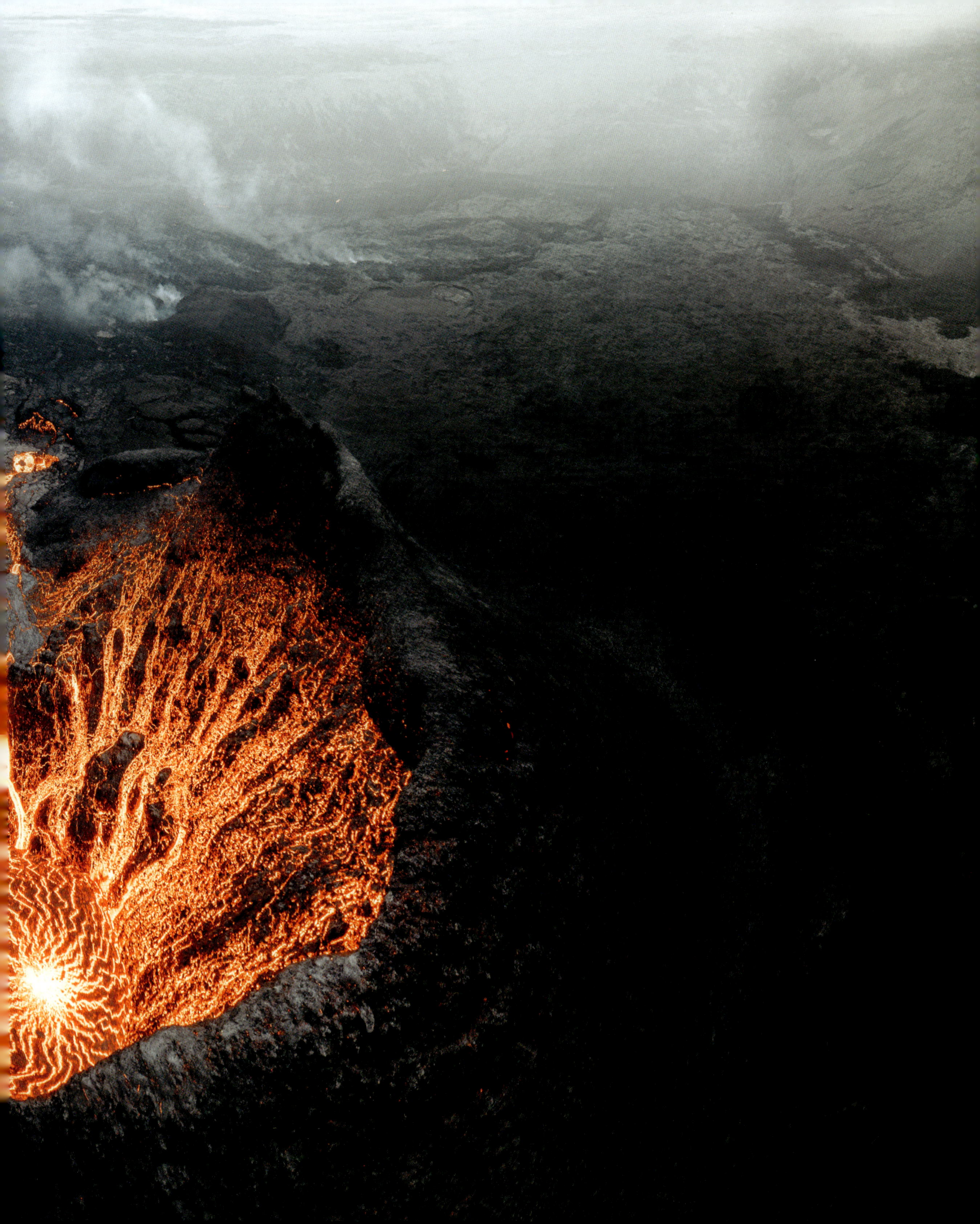

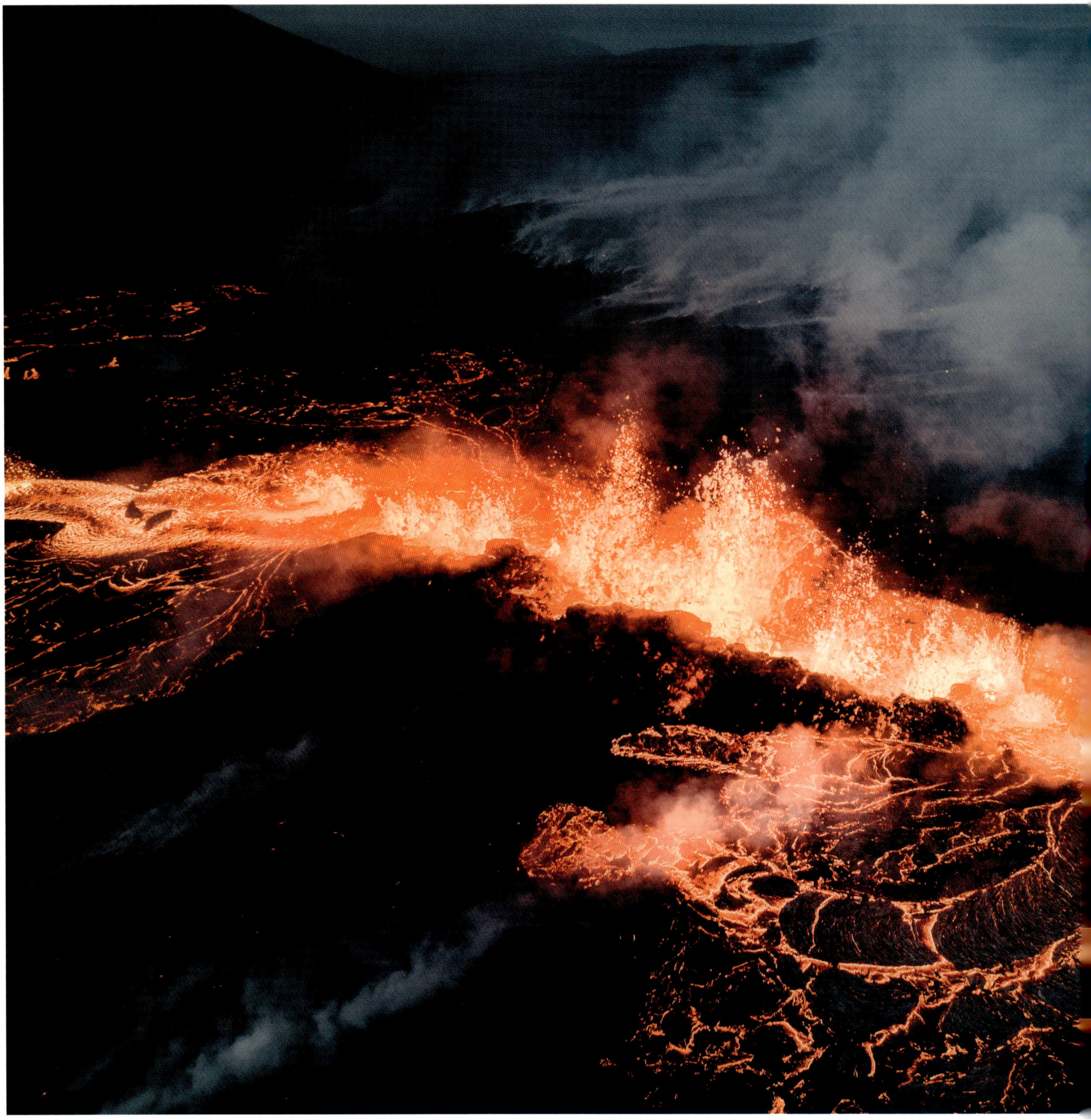

FAGRADALSFJALL IV

The Icelandic ground is in its teenage years, relatively speaking, and it's getting pretty rebellious these days.

LITLI-HRÚTUR II

'Cano goes blub blub
Lava goes woo
Earth spits fire
Just for you

FAGRADALSFJALL V

From my field notes: "Today is my tenth time visiting the volcano. I've watched it grow up, shot 10,000 photos, melted my drone a little, met old friends I haven't seen in years and found plenty of new ones. It's a volcano for the people. And it doesn't seem like it will stop anytime soon."

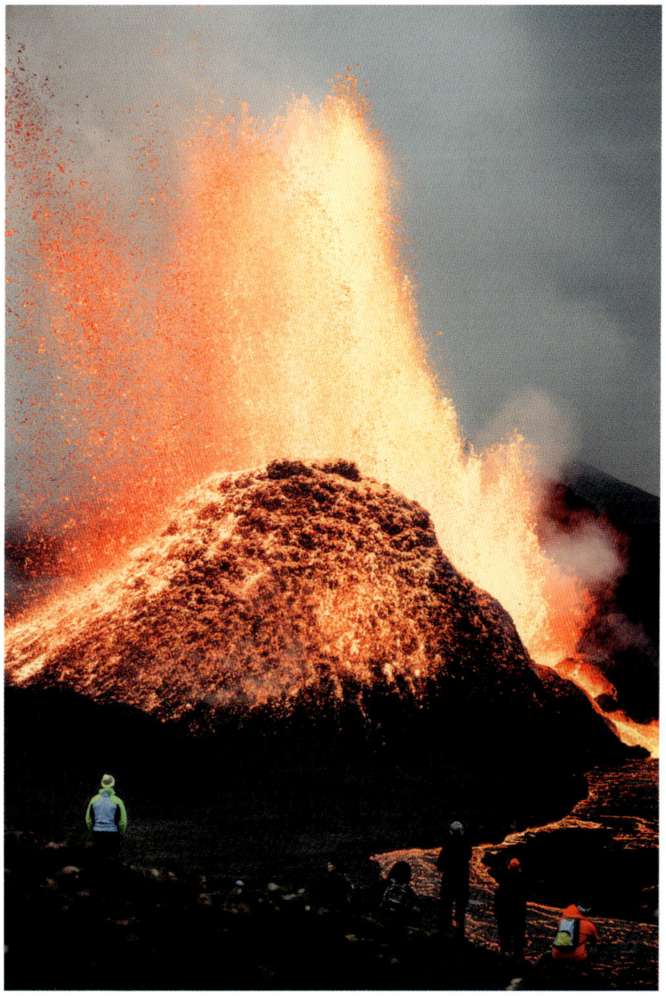

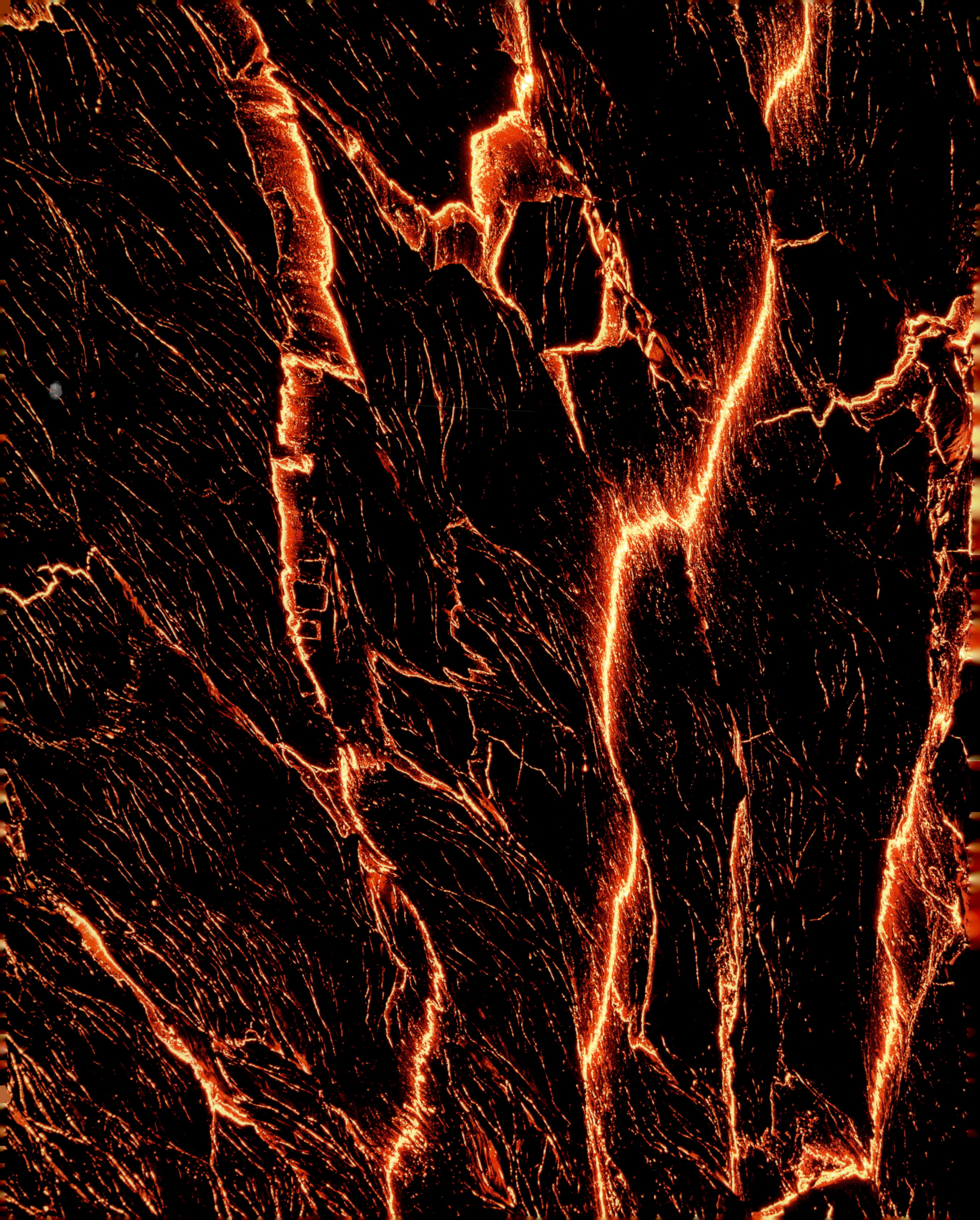

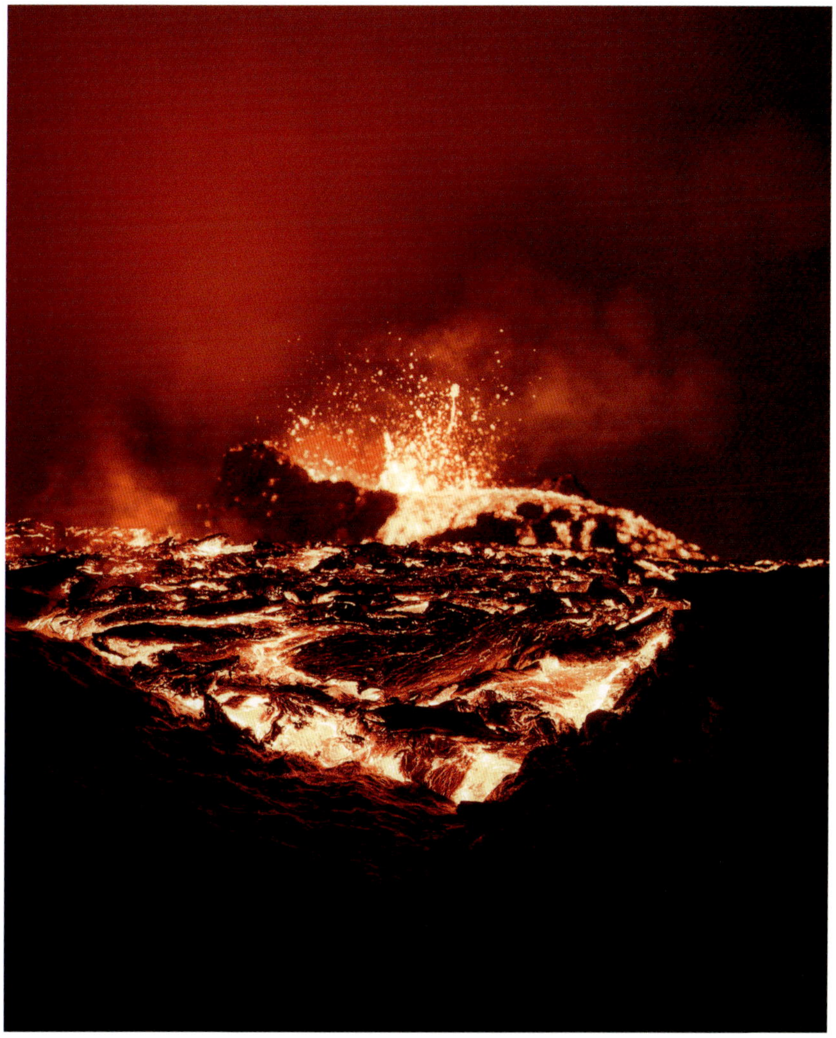

◂ LITLI-HRÚTUR III

Patterns draw drones in closer, melting them like flies into pure fire.

▴ FAGRADALSFJALL VI

The last photo ever taken of this piece of foreground.

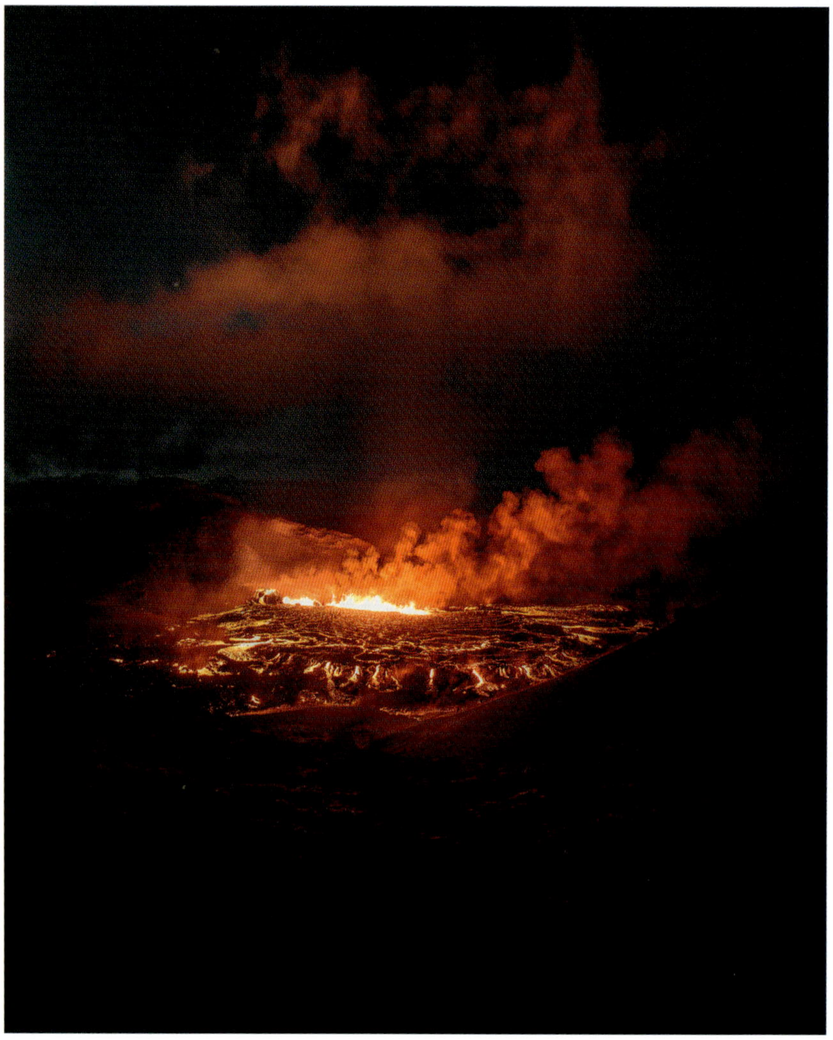

▲ MERADALIR

With colossal power and no concern for its surroundings, newborn Earth emerges from its womb to shape our land as it pleases. It has decided to put a new generation of mountains right here, with no regard for us humans or our insignificant time on this land. All we can do is admire the newly birthed feature and take a step back as the lava creeps closer.

➤ SUNDHNÚKUR

Nature once again leaked a bunch of glowing hot rocks all over the place.

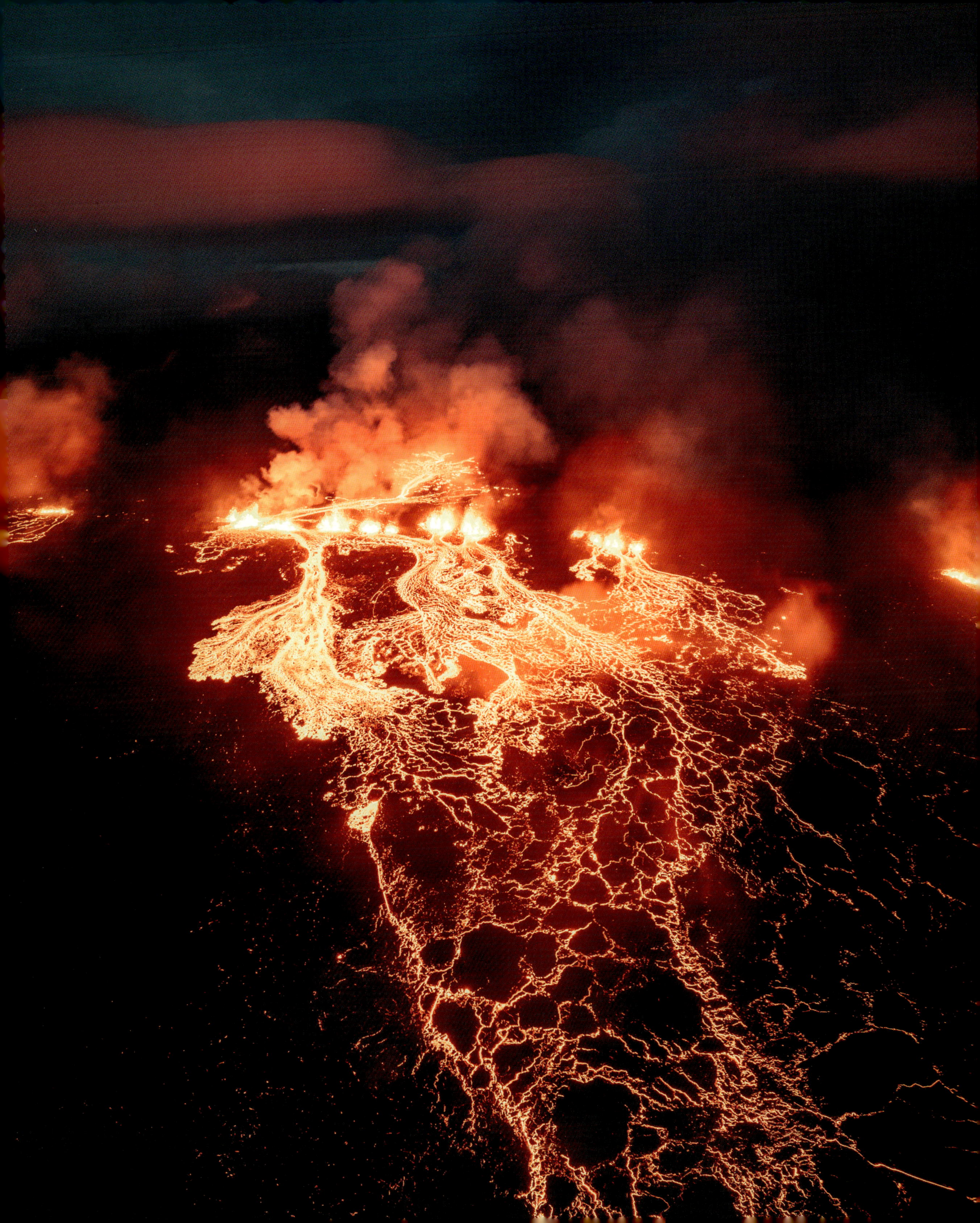

FAGRADALSFJALL VII

From my field notes: "The old volcano from two weeks ago has started filling up its valley, meaning that we can't get close to it anymore like we used to. So, Iceland just went 'lol you guys getting bored? Let me open up some new cracks for you then.' Seeing one volcano being born was a life-changing experience. Seeing two more pop up blew my mind a few times. And then three more craters emerged the next day, just where we had put our tent up last weekend."

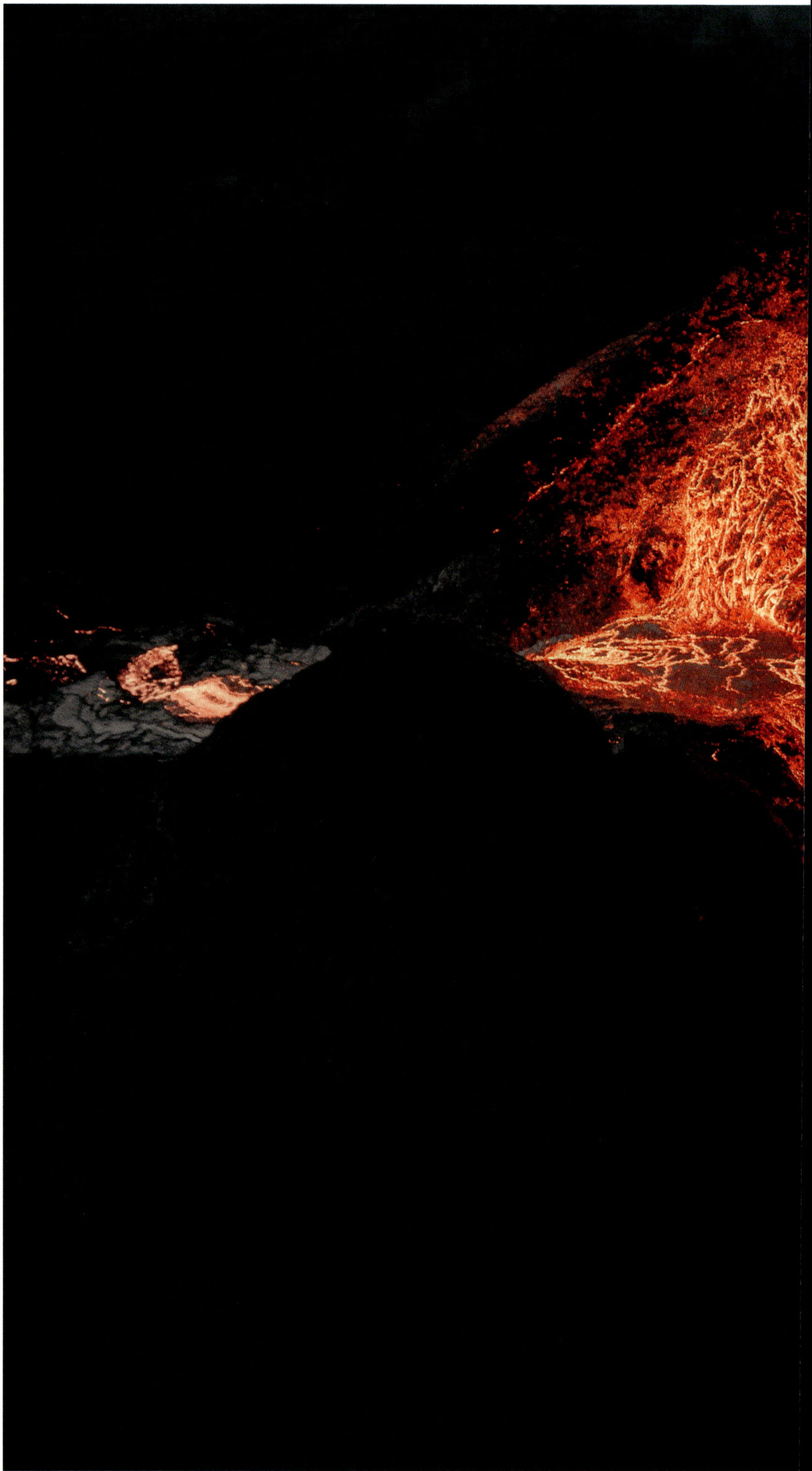

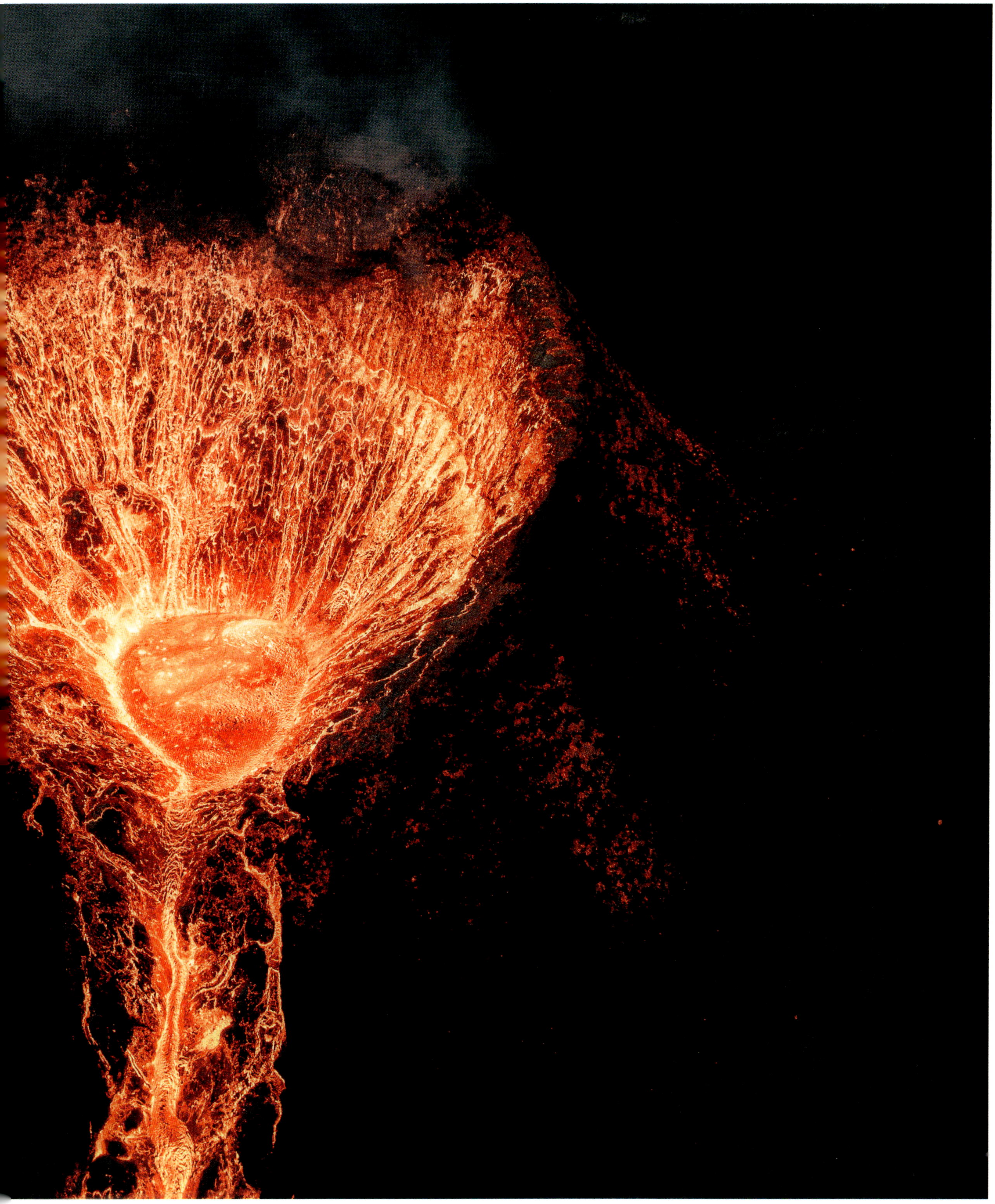

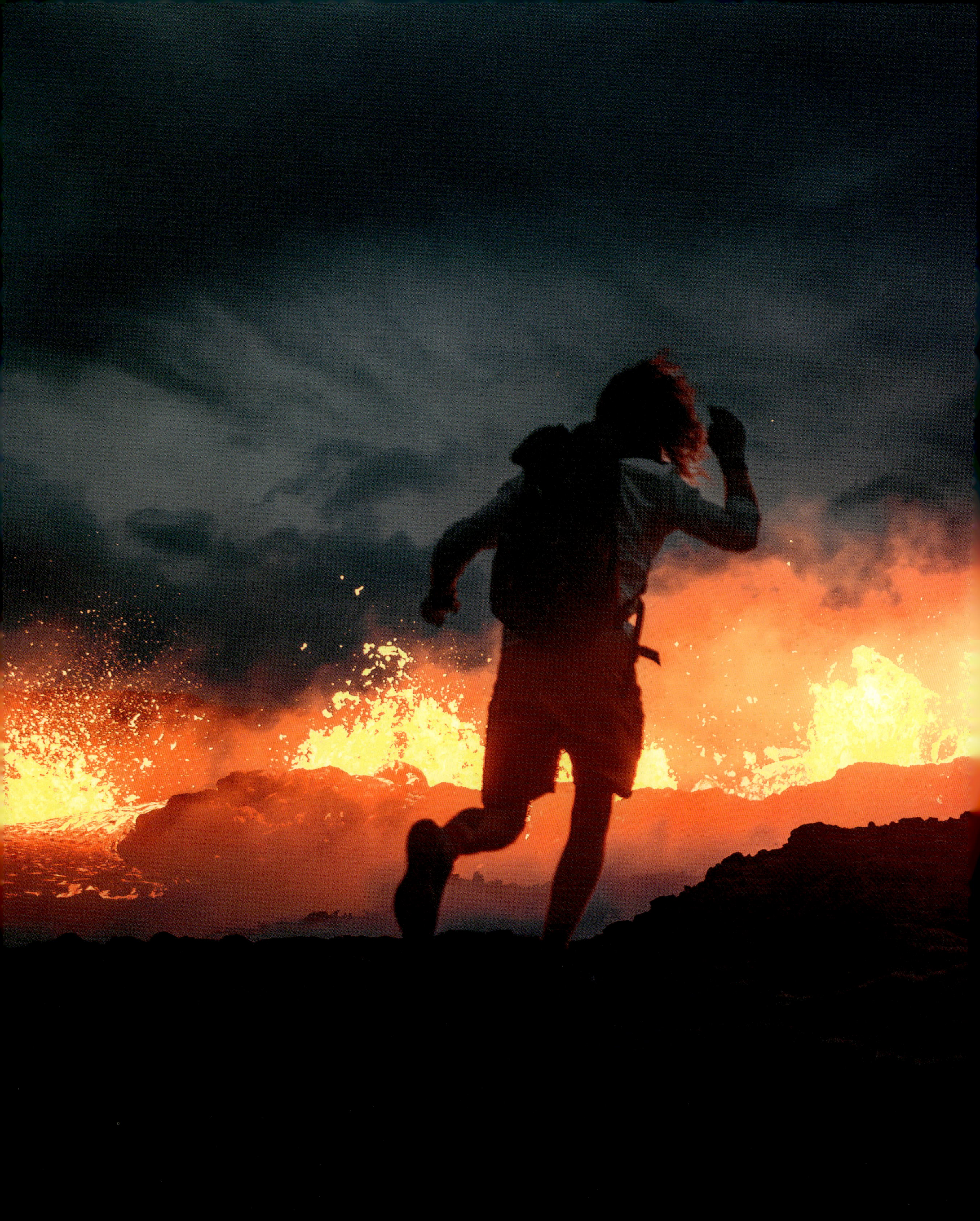

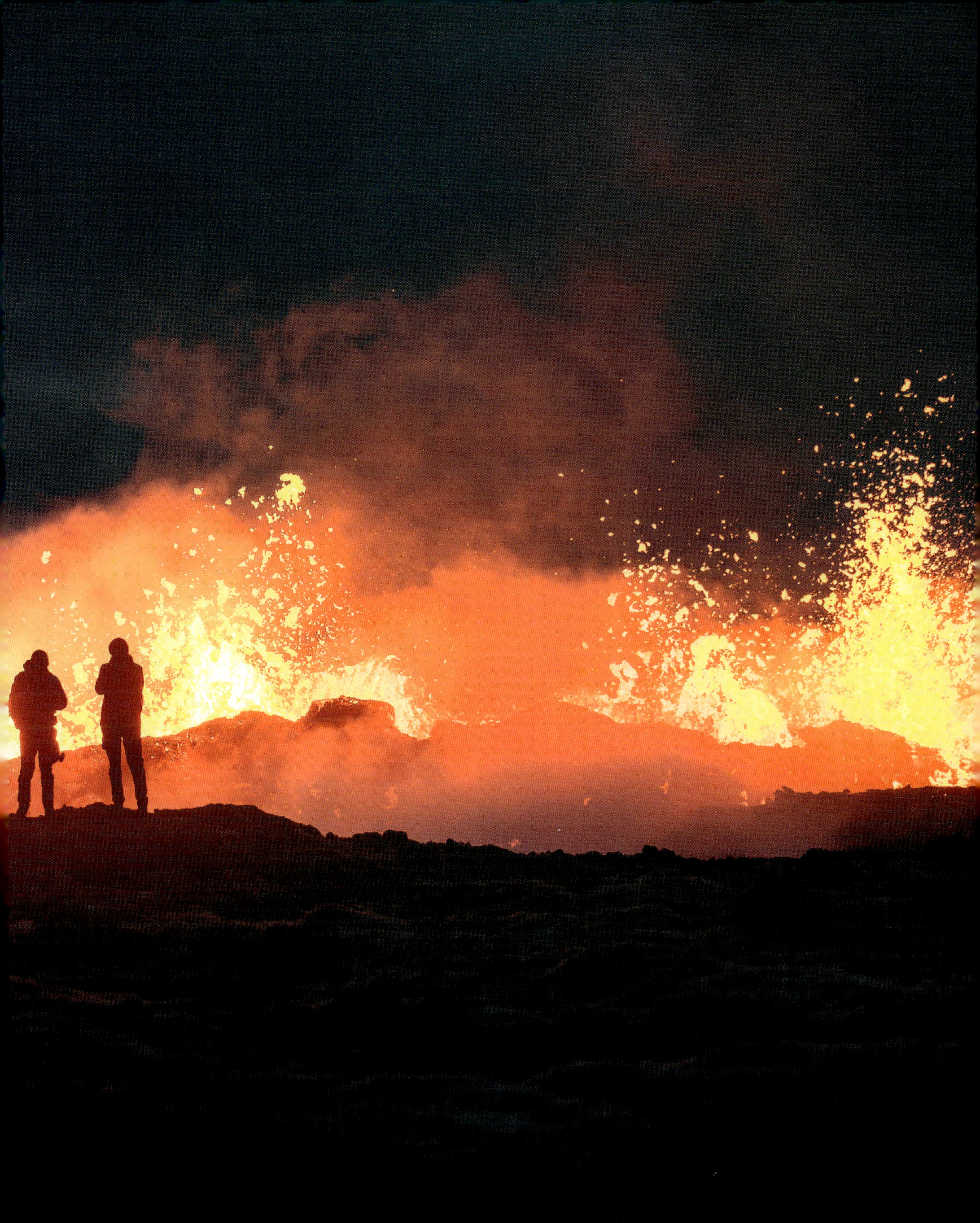

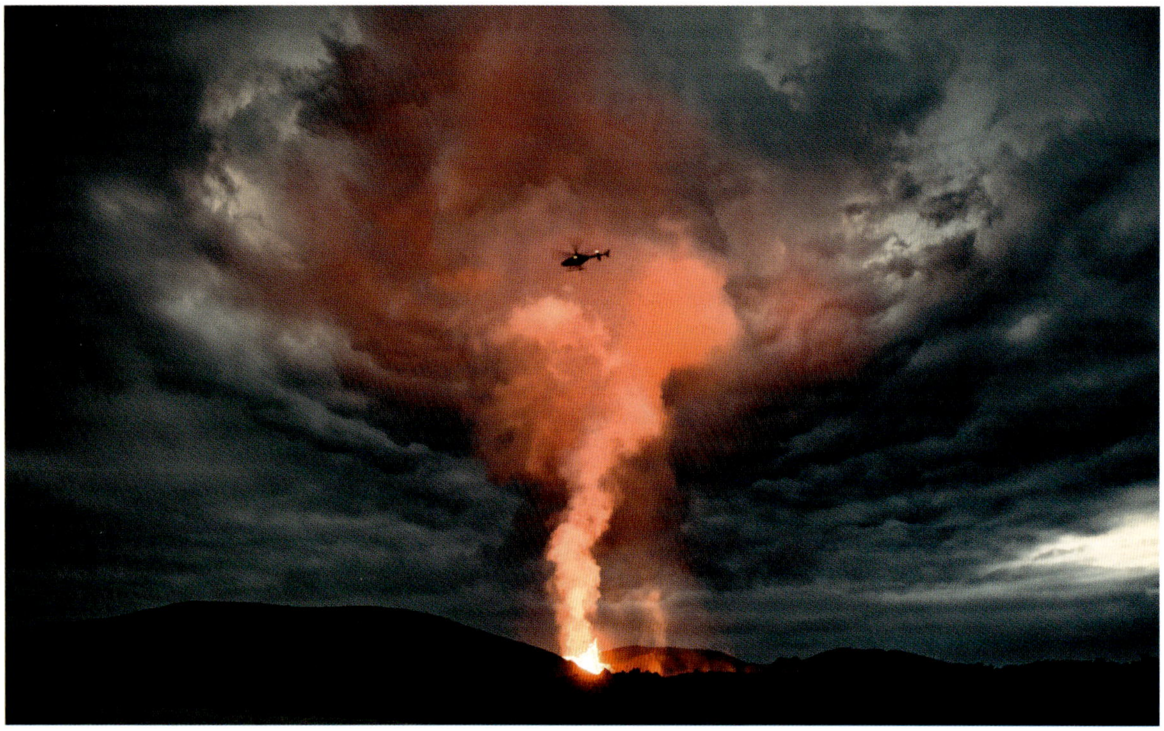

◀◀ MERADALIR II

We really did run there.

This is insanely fresh lava pouring out of an eruption. The eruption is just four hours old.

As the lava moves over the land, looking for purpose but only finding the path of least resistance, it gathers the best kind of people around its spectacle. The crazies, the adventurous explorers, the ones who want to connect with nature. As we flock in our hundreds to the greatest outdoor show on Earth, all watching the same forces, it brings out the most primal feeling in us. We are all once again connected by fire.

Normally, getting close to a volcanic eruption means helicopters, planes, or flying over it with your drone. But in the last few years, something completely new has happened. On the Reykjanes Peninsula, the Earth cracked open just an hour's walk from the nearest road.

For the first time, tens of thousands of people could experience this wild, ancient force, not alone, not through a screen, but together in real time. And somehow, that made it even better.

We like to think that nature is best experienced in solitude. That to really feel it, you have to be alone. But this volcano brings people together. It would be terrifying being there alone, but the chatter of the crowds, the bonfire smell, and the hundreds of headlamps shimmering in the darkness make it feel like an experience meant to be shared. It's beautiful to enjoy this moment together. And after a few visits, I knew that I would always run into most of my friends out there–filming, shooting, or just enjoying the show.

The volcano was the performer. And we were lucky enough to be its audience, shoulder to shoulder in the glow of something far older and wilder than ourselves.

▲ FAGRADALSFJALL VIII

Helis, drones, sightseeing planes, and commercial airlines–all flying in to warm up by the fires.

▶ MERADALIR III

He had camped out for five days prior to witness the birth of the eruption, and when it did, he came down from his hill to finally warm up.

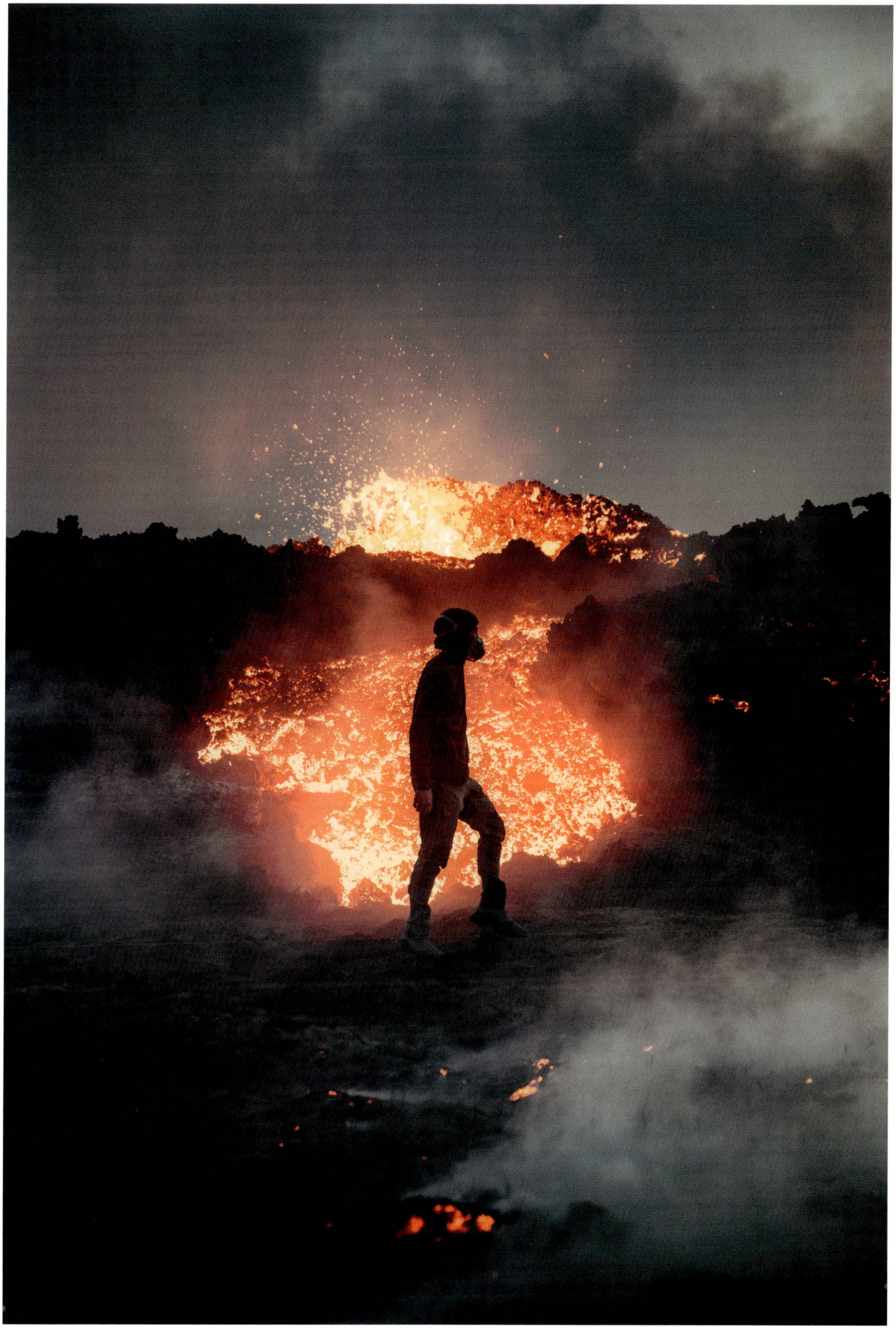

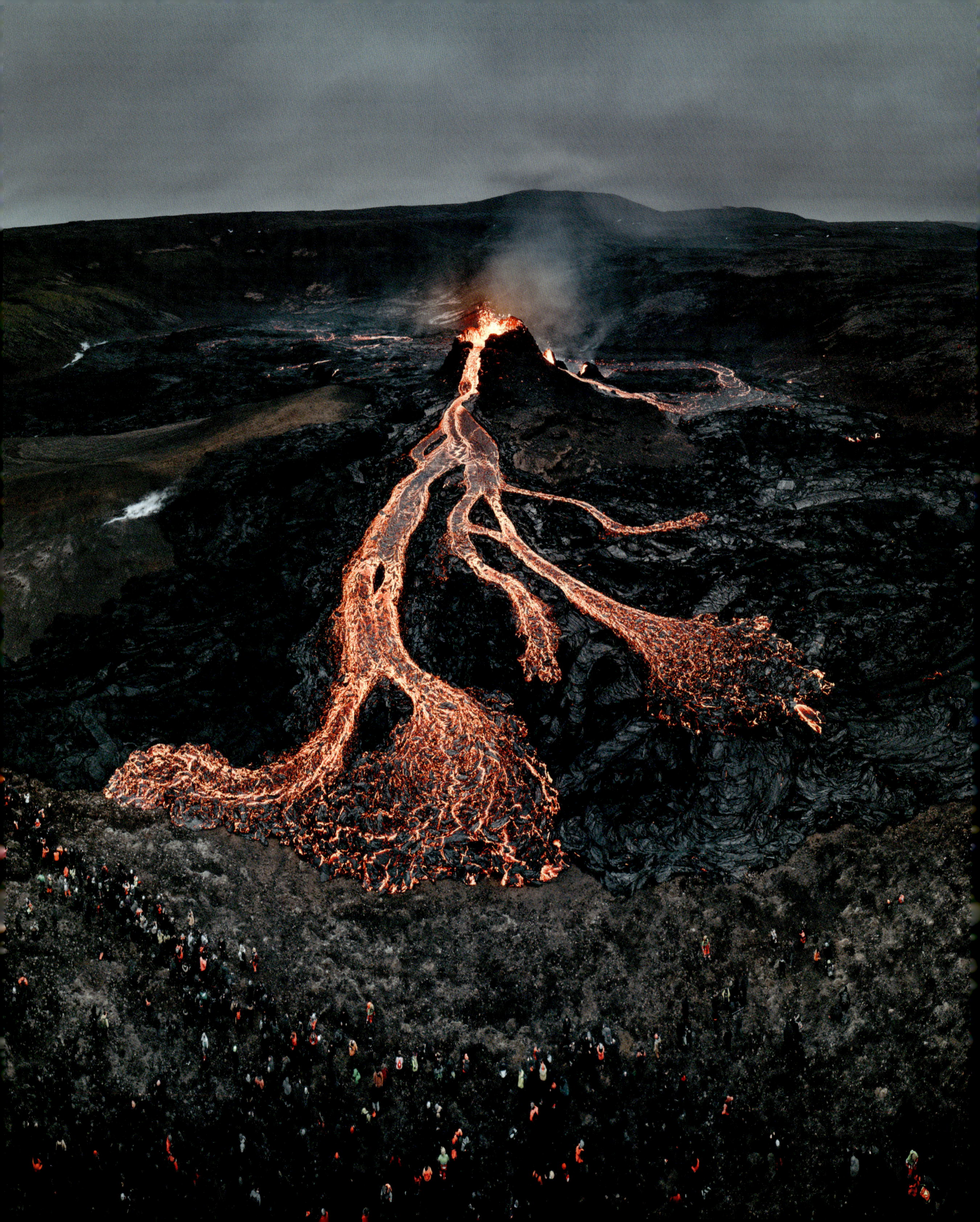

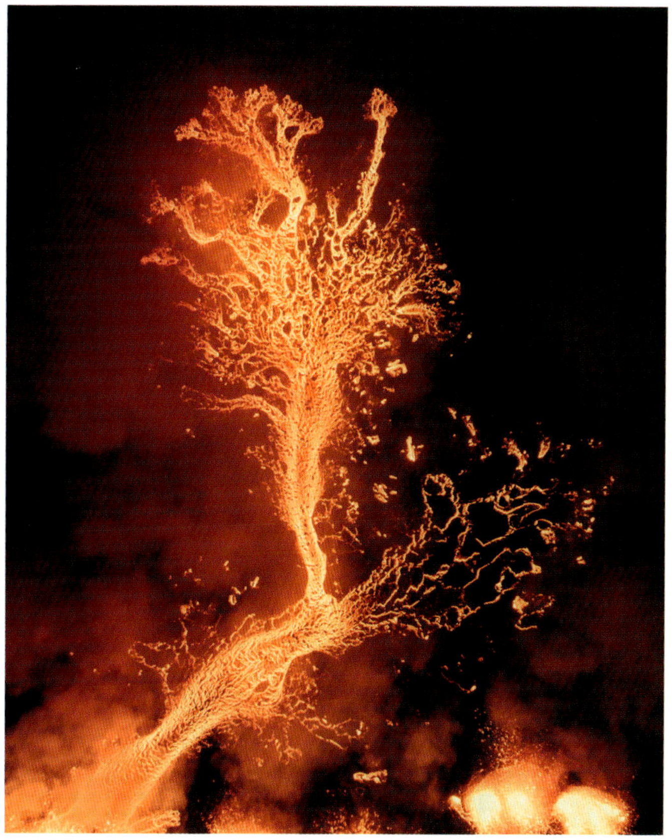

◂ GELDINGADALUR III

Eruption, day two.

We arrived at 7 a.m. There were a few hundred cars pulled over on the road in front of us, so we abandoned our vehicle there with the rest of them. Yesterday, someone walked to the volcano and survived. Everyone else semi-adventurous thought: *If that someone survived, so would we, probably.* So, we all set out to chase the fire.

The volcano had placed itself, perfectly tiny and innocent, in a valley. It became the stage for the greatest, but also most humble, outdoor live show in the world. We followed the heat. Whichever way the lava was spilling, the crowds quickly migrated towards it to stay warm.

We also arrived there to meet everyone we knew, a reunion that, in those pandemic days, was almost more of a draw than the heat of the lava.

It took a volcanic eruption to get people to unconditionally stop what they were doing, get outside, and find each other by the fire. In the end, we stayed not for the volcano show, but for each other's company.

This was a volcano for the people, like a giant bonfire festival. And I think everyone who was there gained a little bit more human connection from it, while also staying warm.

Except for my friend who got hypothermia.

▴ MÝVATN II

Energy making art. Forces in the universe have their own patterns, deeply ingrained and familiar to us on a subconscious level. The science of these patterns and how everything in the universe was created is fairly new. It comes under the umbrella term "Complexity Theory." This is the observance of how simple mathematical relationships cause chaotic systems to become ordered works of art in the presence of energy. And there's no better illustration of this phenomenon than a photograph of lava shot high up from a drone.

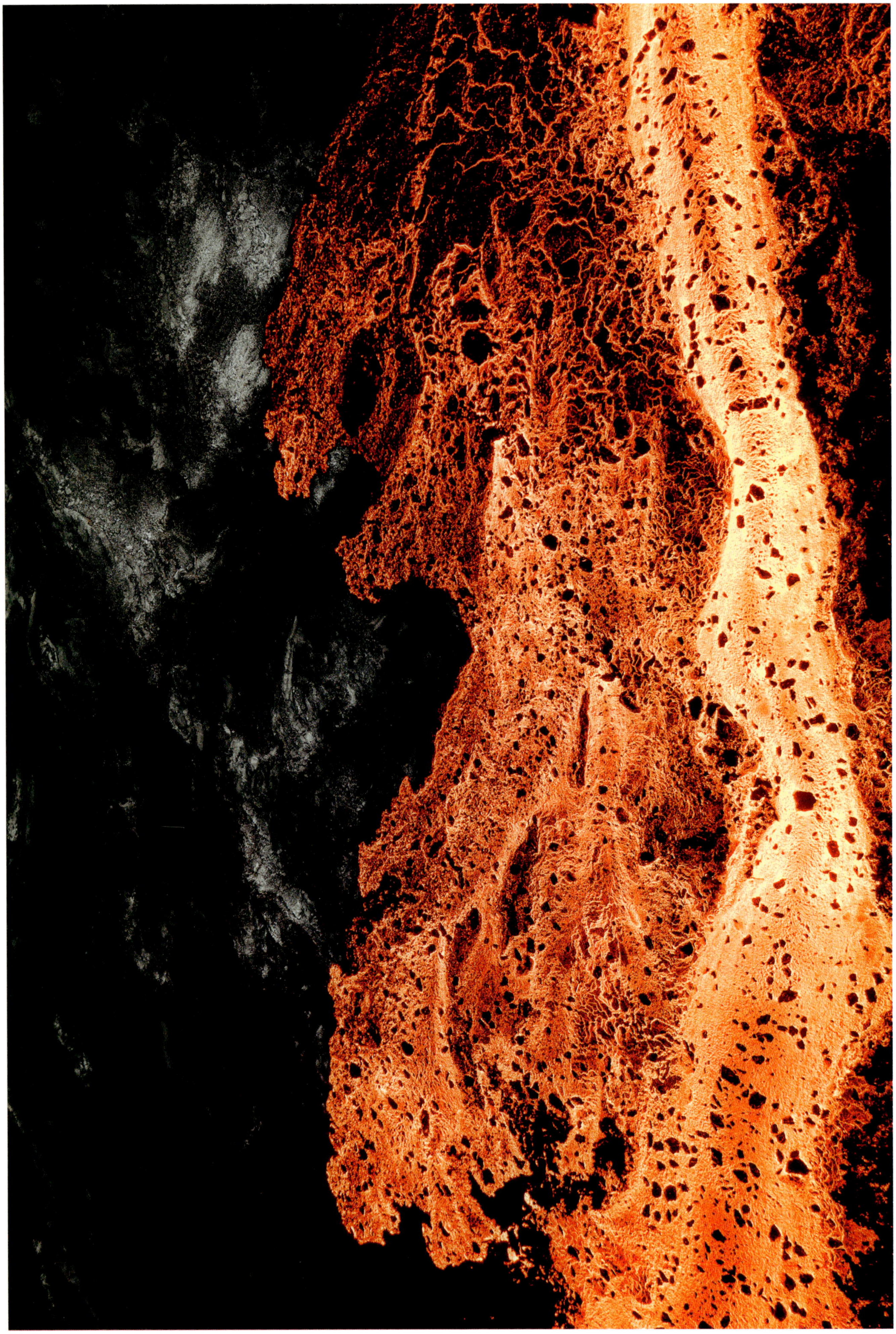

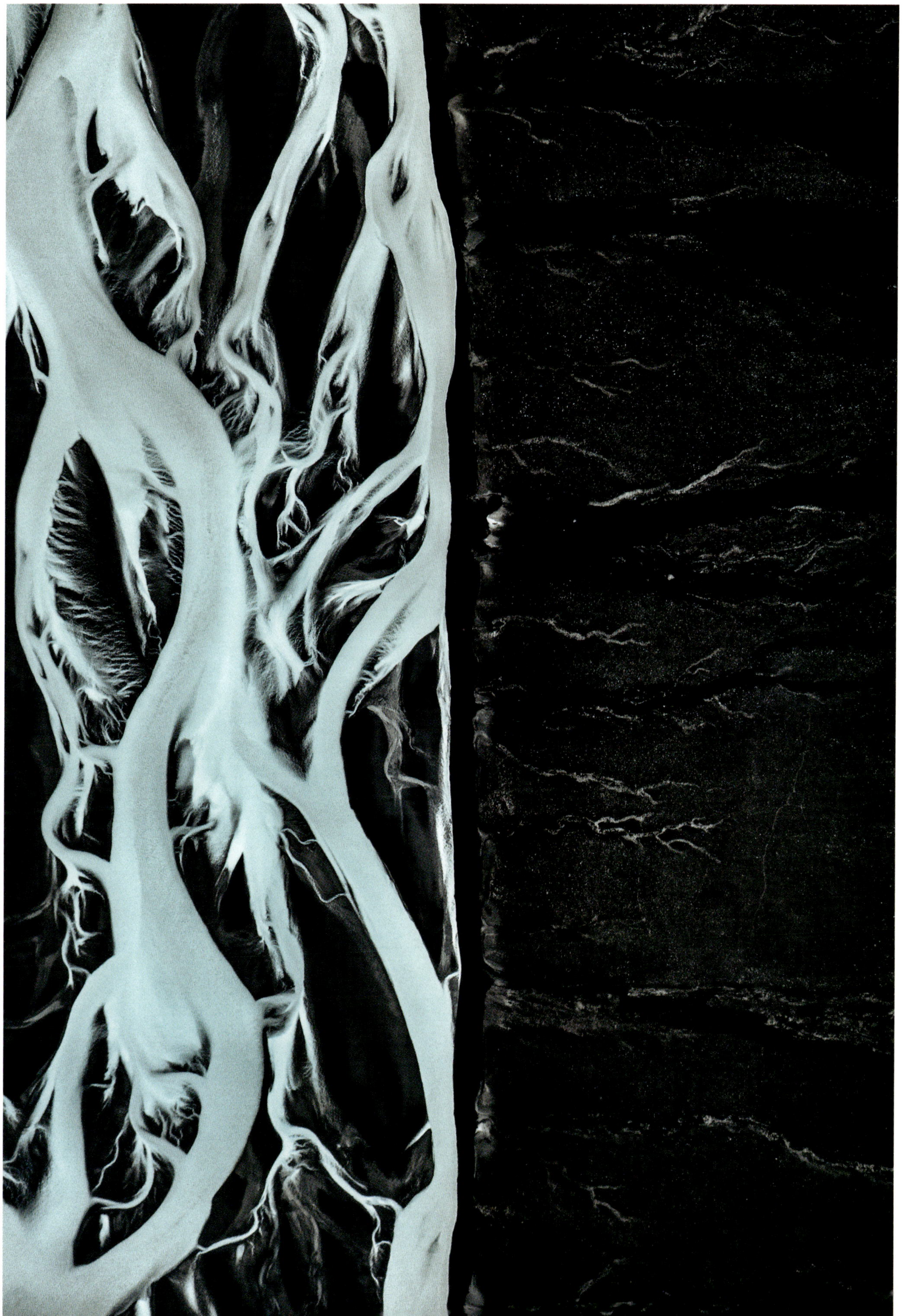

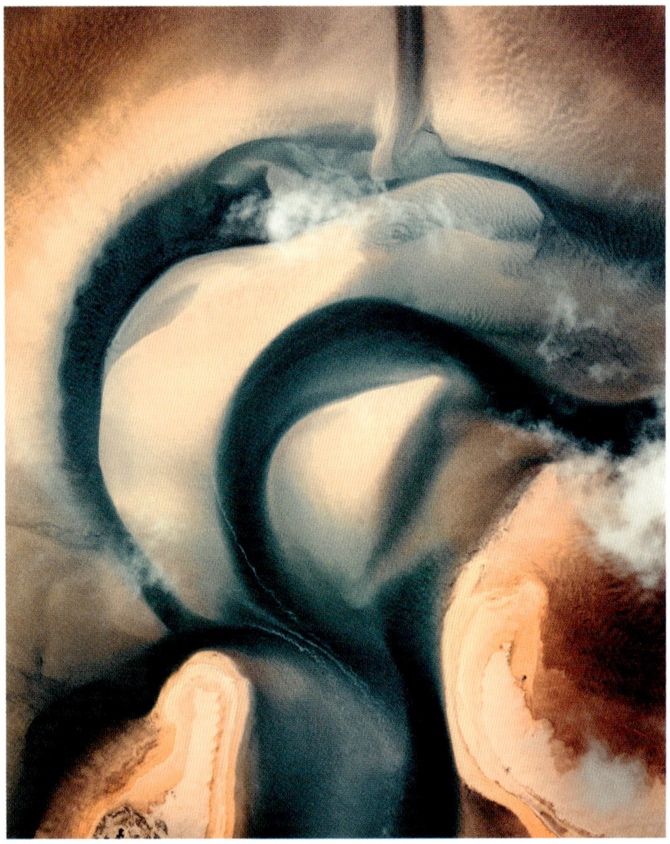

MERADALIR IV (L)

Fresh ground building itself. New lava is now covering up the old lava because the old lava did a bad job at covering up everything else.

THE HIGHLANDS (R)

Fresh off of Vatnajökull—the main ice cap of Iceland and Europe's favorite glacier—this river searches everywhere for lonely oceans in need of company. It spreads and spreads. But the black volcanic sand has been here longer. It takes pride in its loosely put together claim on the land. And at some point, it fights back, making it clear to the rivers that they are not welcome here. It pushes them further downstream.

RAUÐASANDUR

In Iceland, this is called a *red sand beach* because it's not black. And that's so rare that the Vikings didn't even know what yellow looked like when they named it.

KERLINGARFJÖLL

I can't paint. I can put paint on a canvas, but I wouldn't call it painting. But knowing that nature makes its own amazing art, I set out to capture it and sell this art as my own.

In a geothermal area in the middle of Iceland, the shallow underground magma boils the groundwater, which in turn melts the sedimentary rock and spews it up as hot mud in all kinds of crazy colors. I spent hours shooting. The mud took over, covering my consciousness, painting my memory cards, and I couldn't stop. Everything was a painting. But a boiling one that made sounds and smells.

Then the mud and water spoke. All they want is to be understood. This is the earth getting in touch. Trying to touch you, with its hot paint.

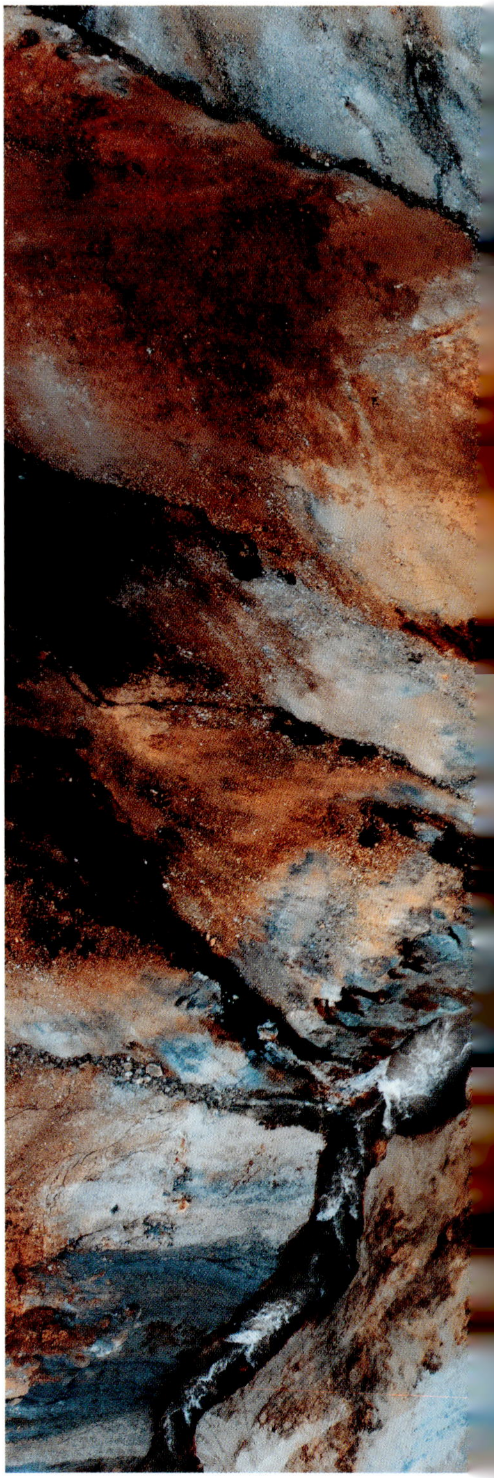

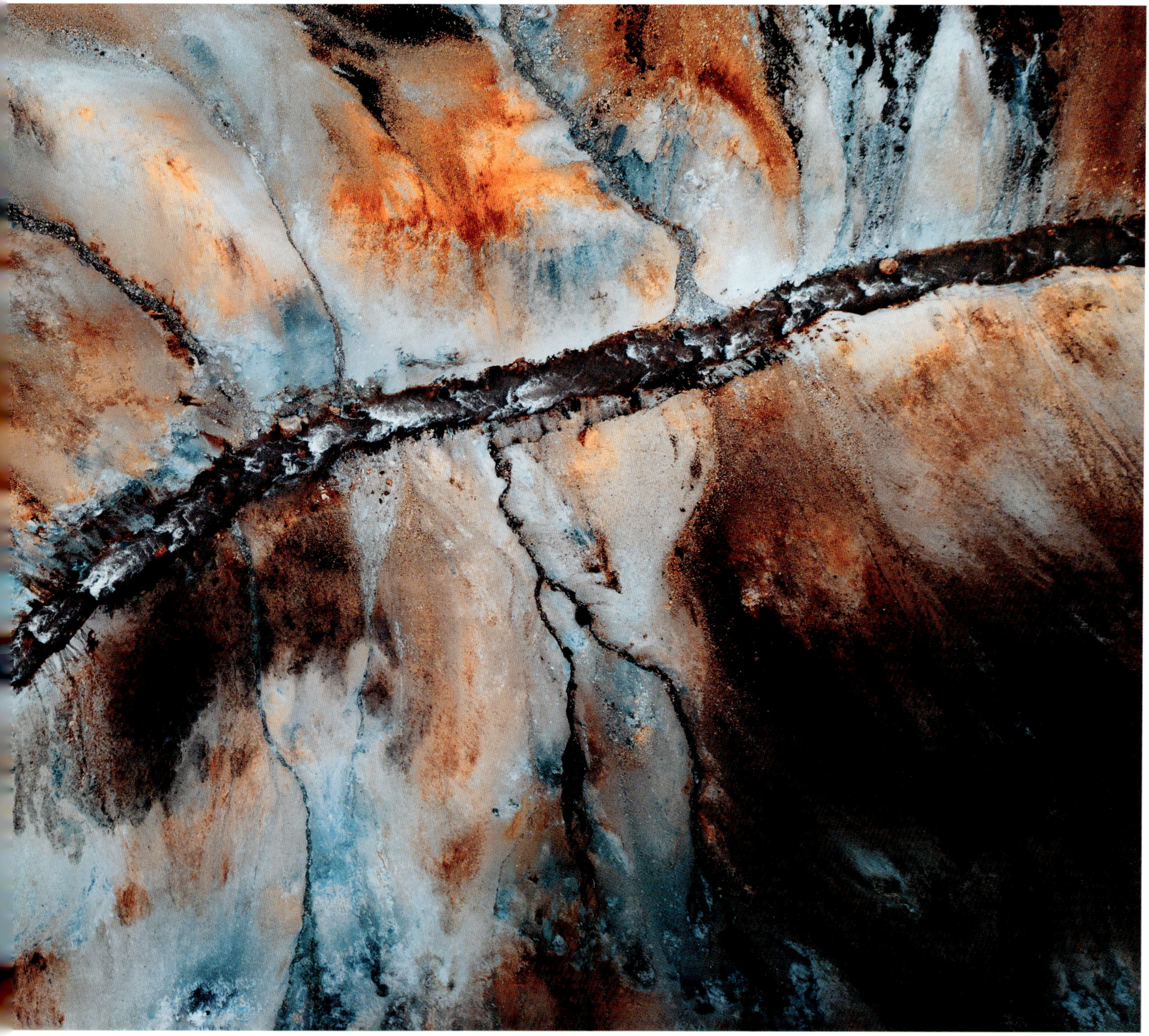

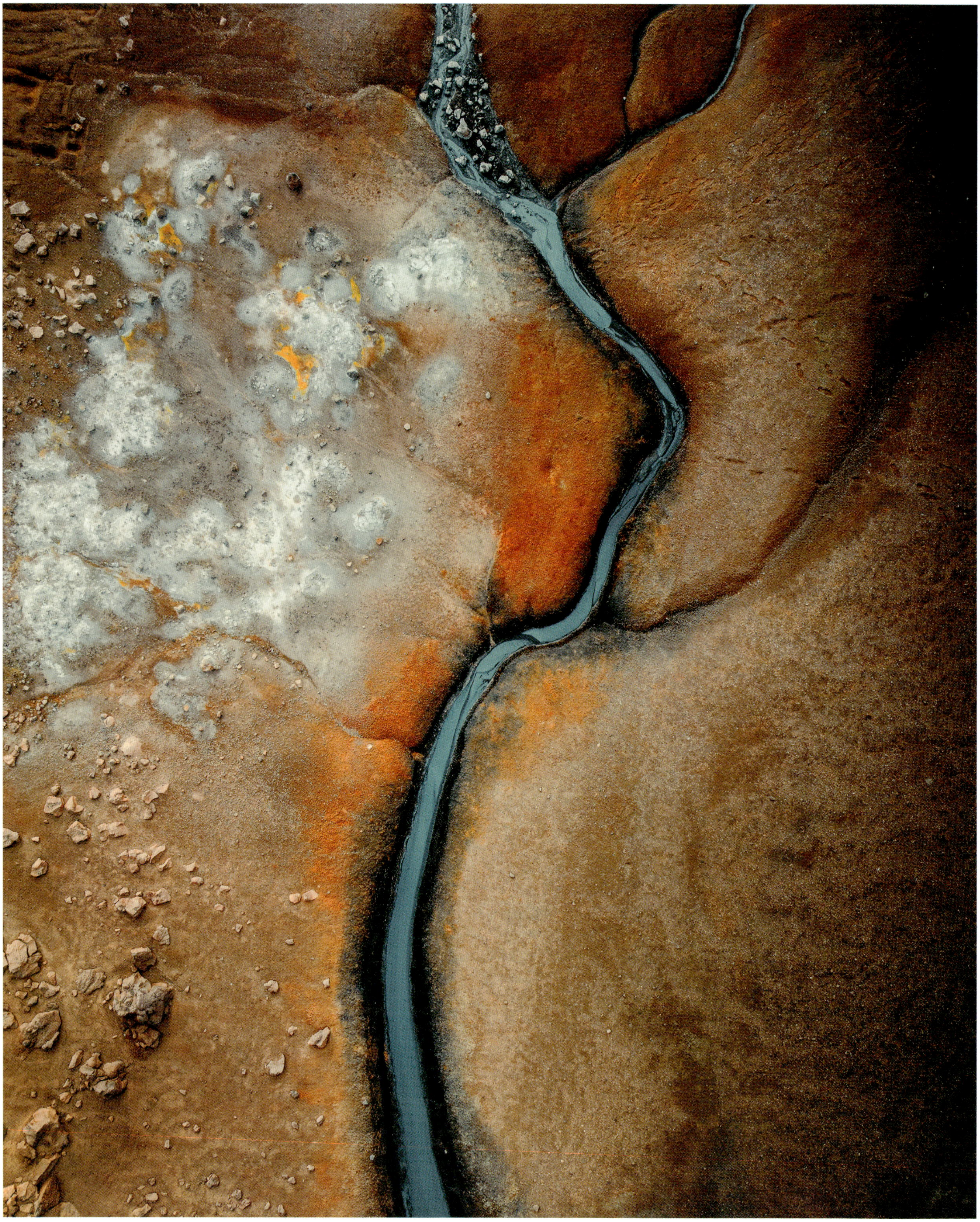

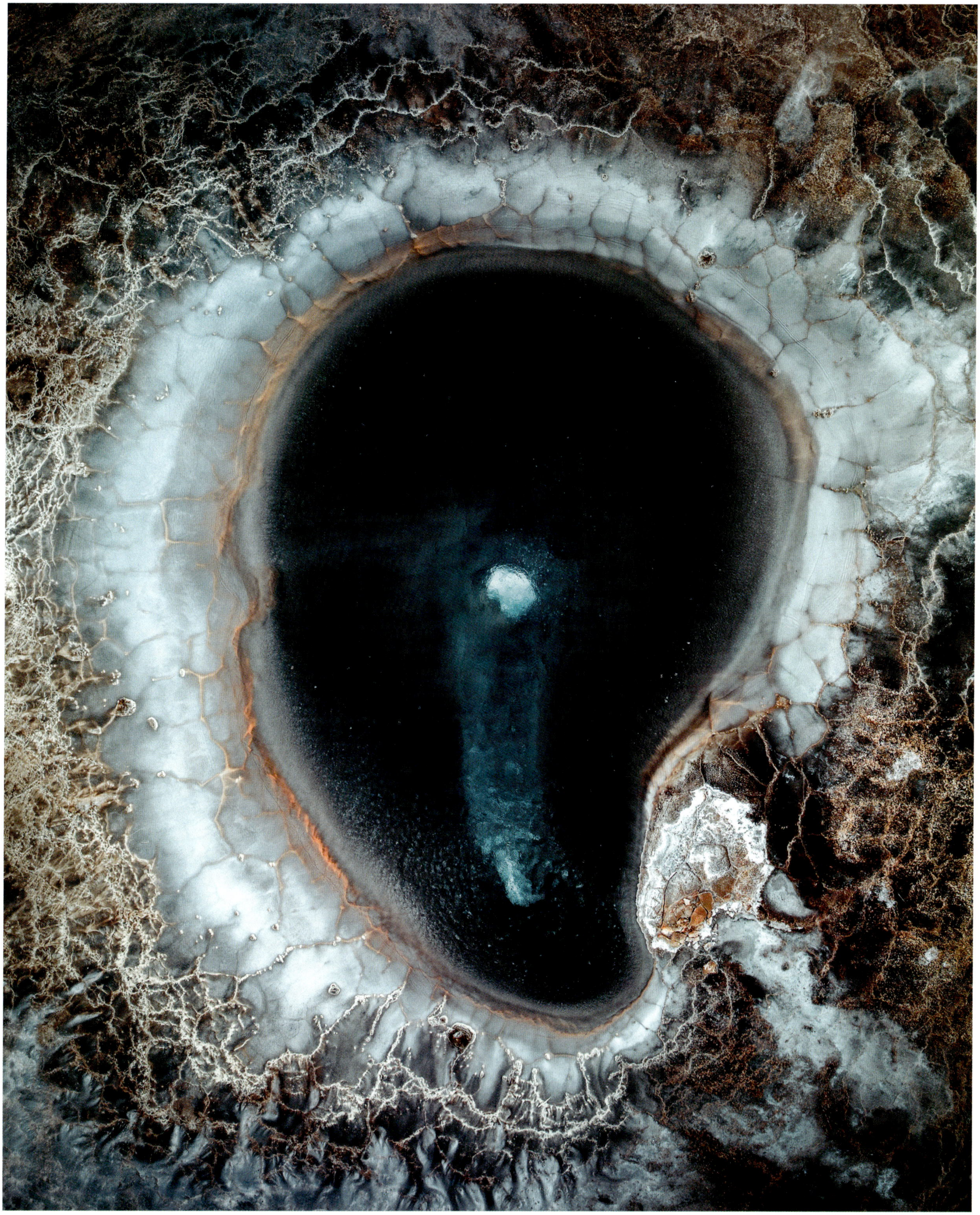

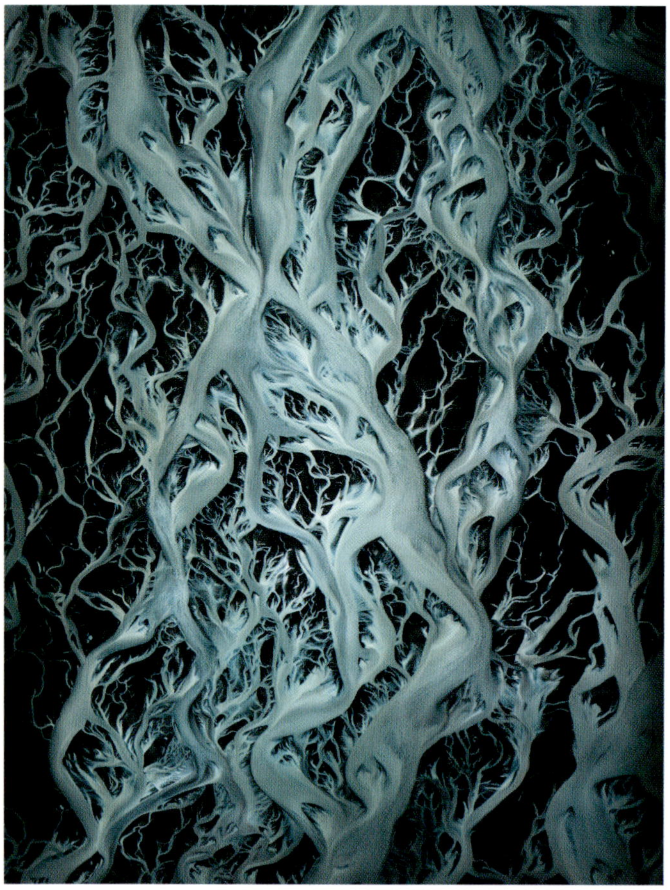

◂◂ MÝVATN III (L)

A small stream hoping to one day grow wise and forge its own river deltas, only to eventually discover that it knew its way all along.

◂◂ HVERAVELLIR (R)

A geothermal embryo, hoping to one day go full volcano. For now it's only making bubbles.

▴ DEEEEP IN THE HIGHLANDS

As the glaciers retreat, their offspring embark on a long migration towards warmer waters. In search of equilibrium, they fight their way across the lands in organized yet chaotic patterns.

I've always wanted to capture the scale of this wet migration and finally came close by digitally gluing together forty-six individual top-down drone photos to create this massive one. And this is still just the tip of the iceberg, as they say.

▸ HVERAVELLIR II

Hot water imitating the universe.

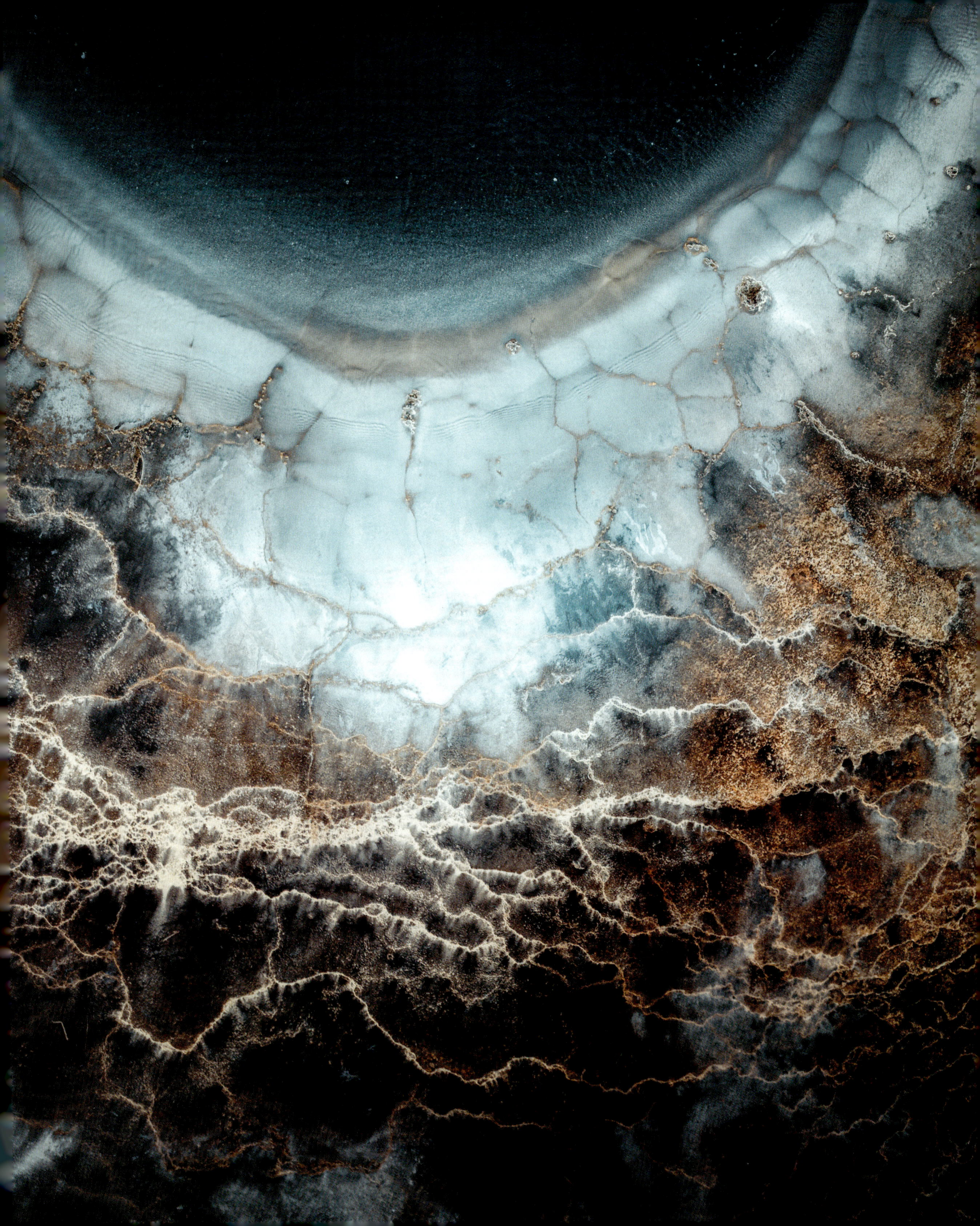

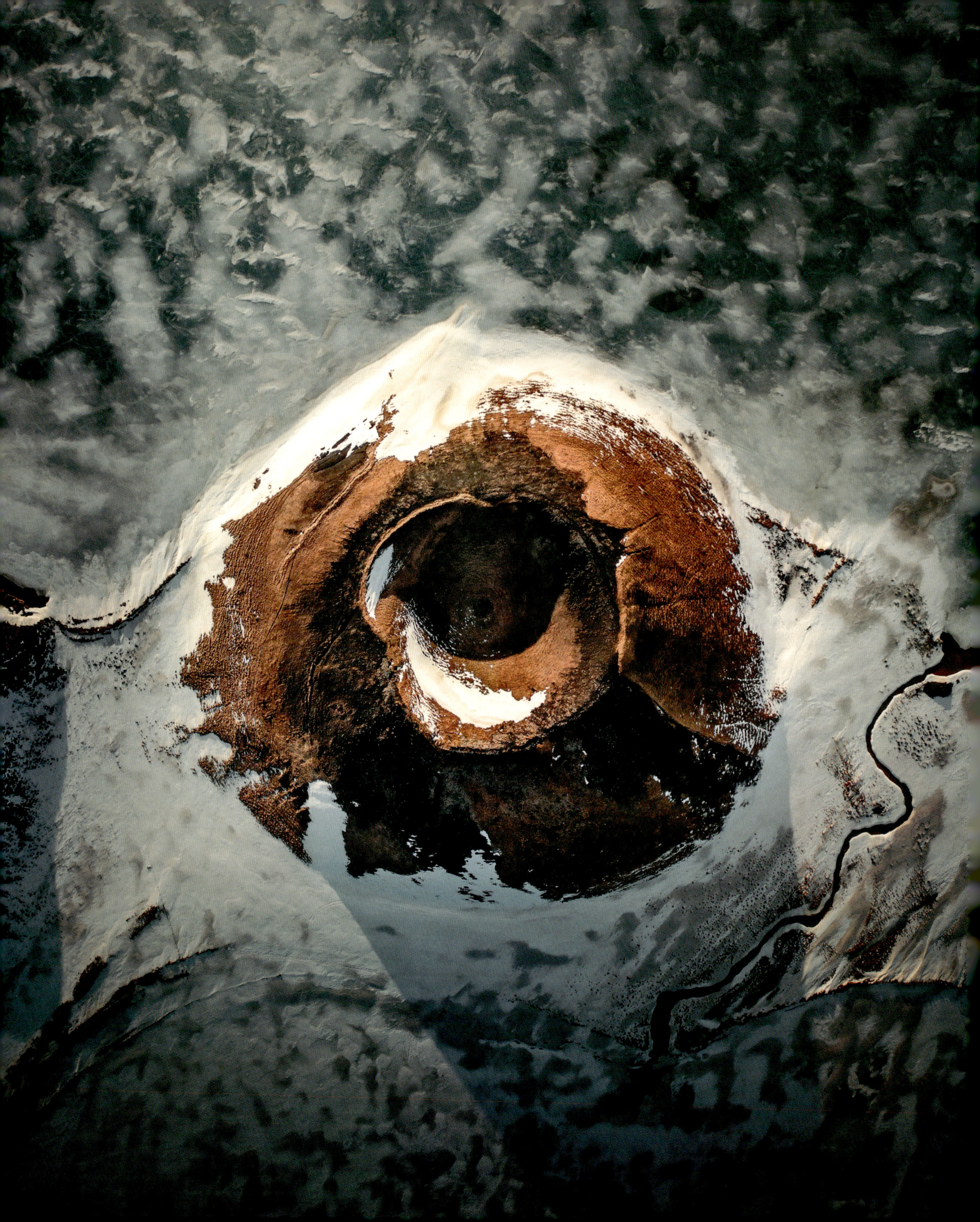

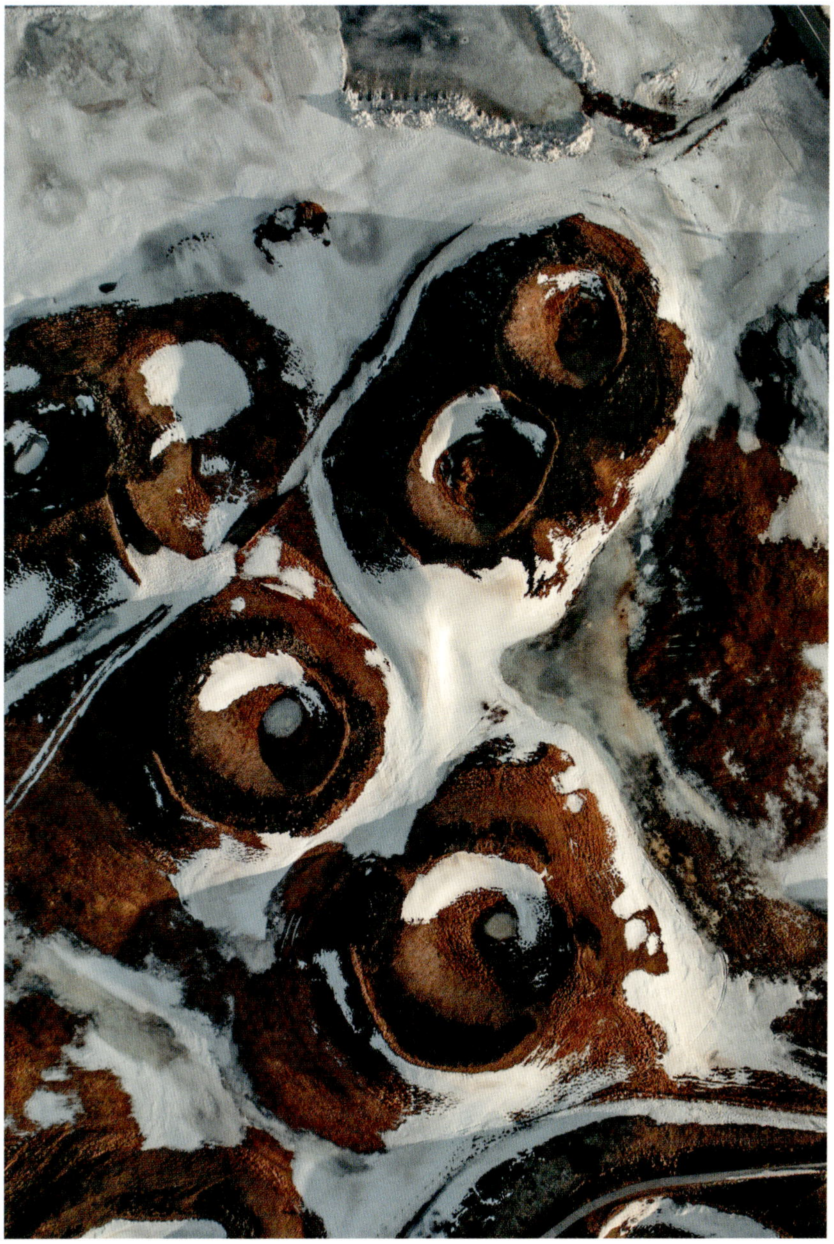

◀ MÝVATN IV

The young Icelandic landscape growing a pimple.

▲ MÝVATN V

And more of them.

▶▶ VATNAJÖKULL VI (L)

The deep mouths of the glaciers, where you'll be chewed up if you don't fight your way out with an ice axe.

▶▶ IN A PLANE FLYING A LITTLE TOO LOW (R)

The glaciers are crying out. Here are their tears.

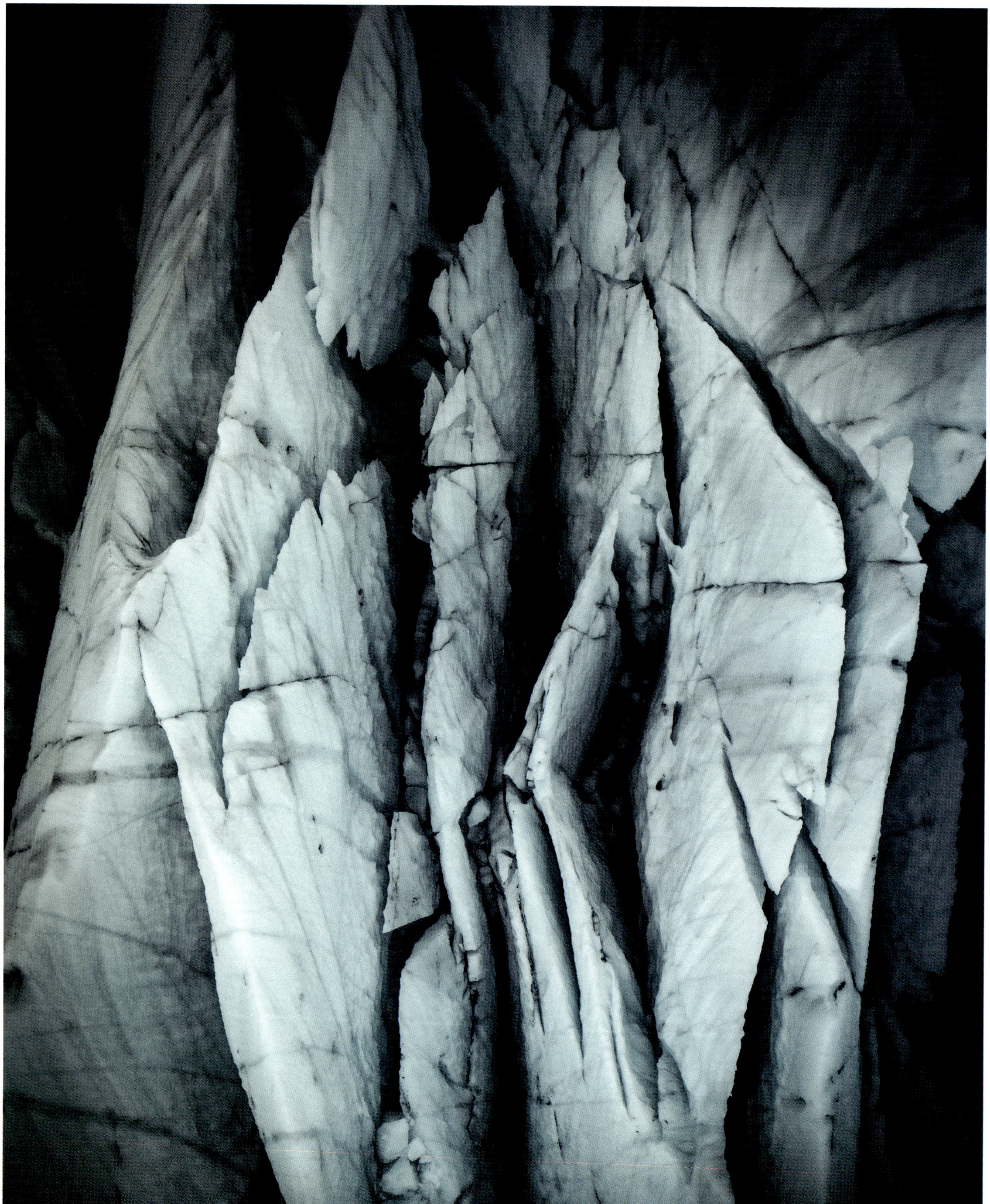

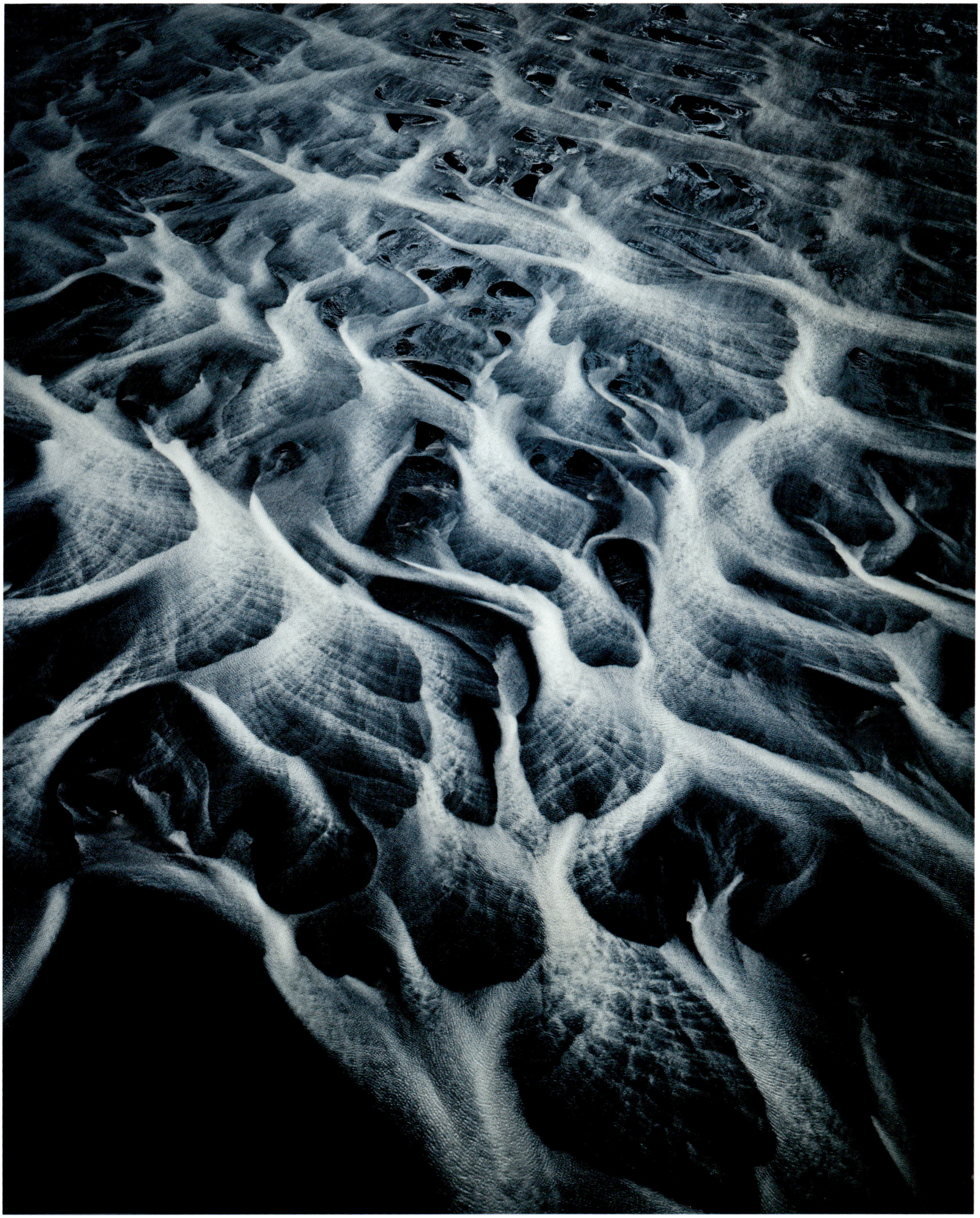

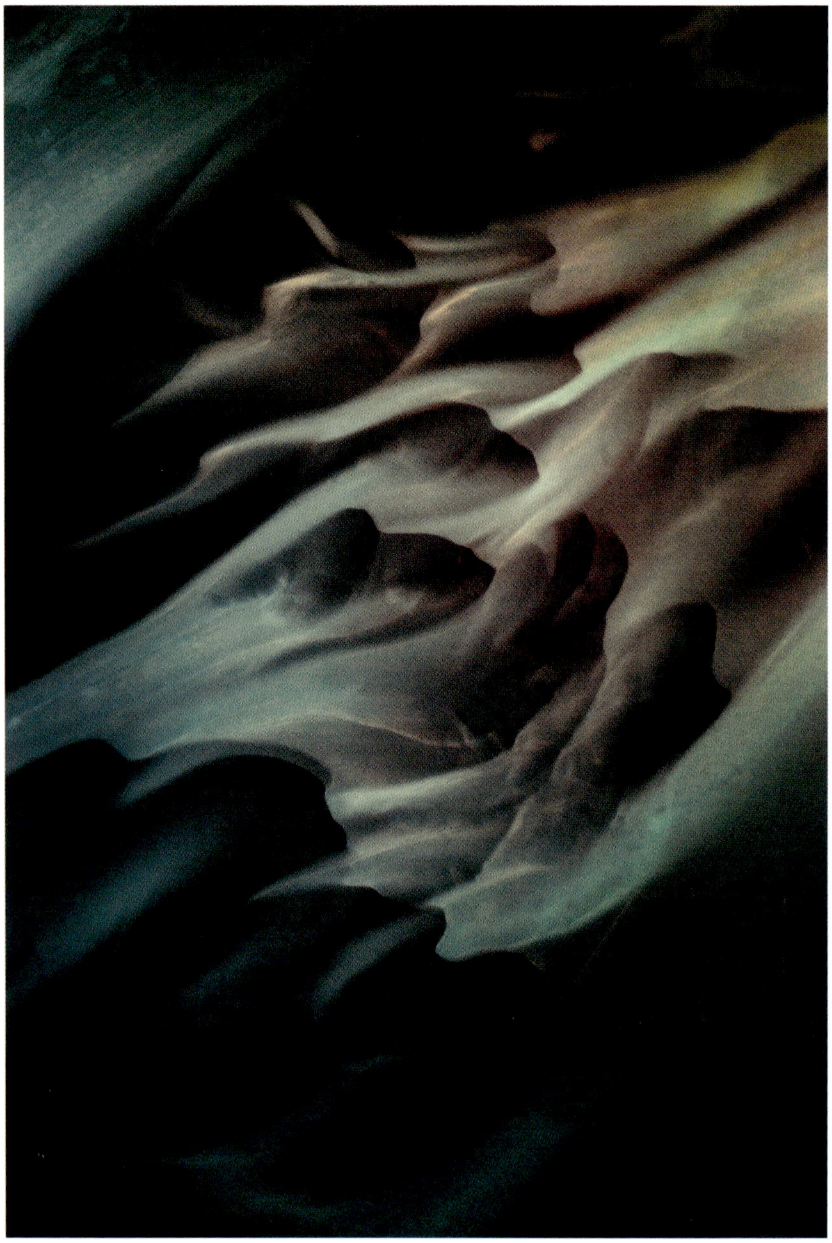

▲ SOUTHEAST ICELAND

Rivers touching each other and having river babies.

▸ VATNAJÖKULL VII

If you look hard enough for meanings and patterns, anything in the world can look like a badly drawn heart.

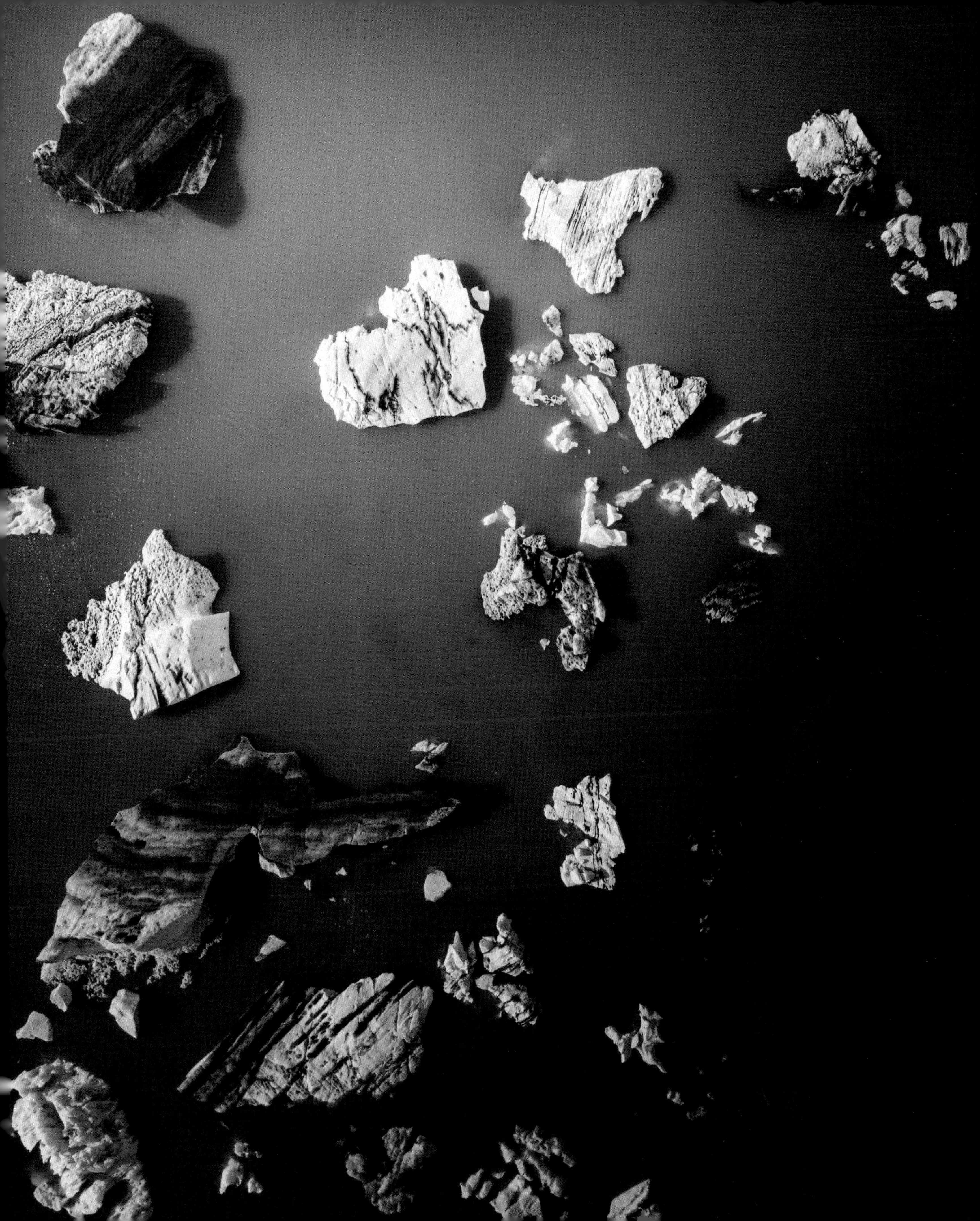

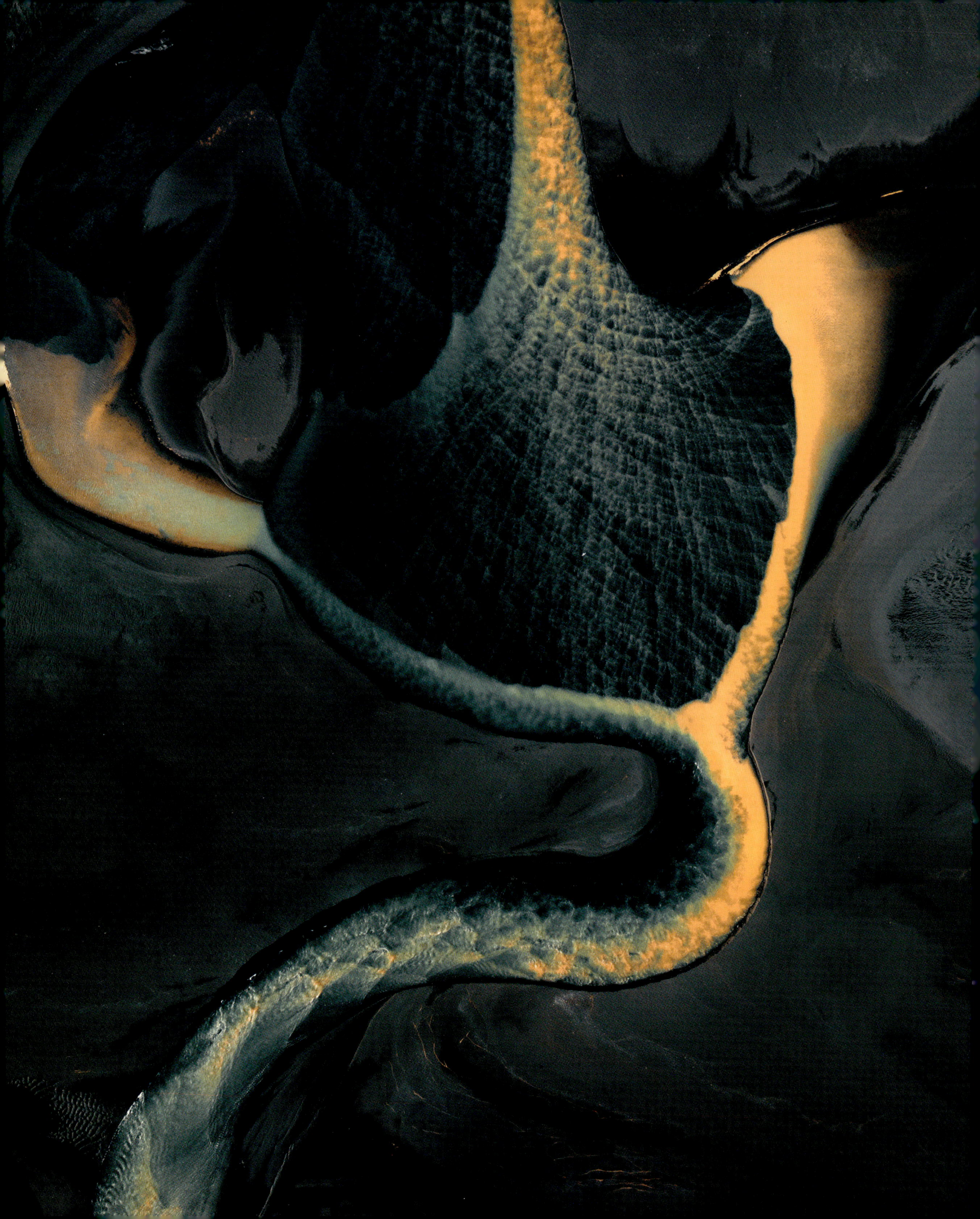

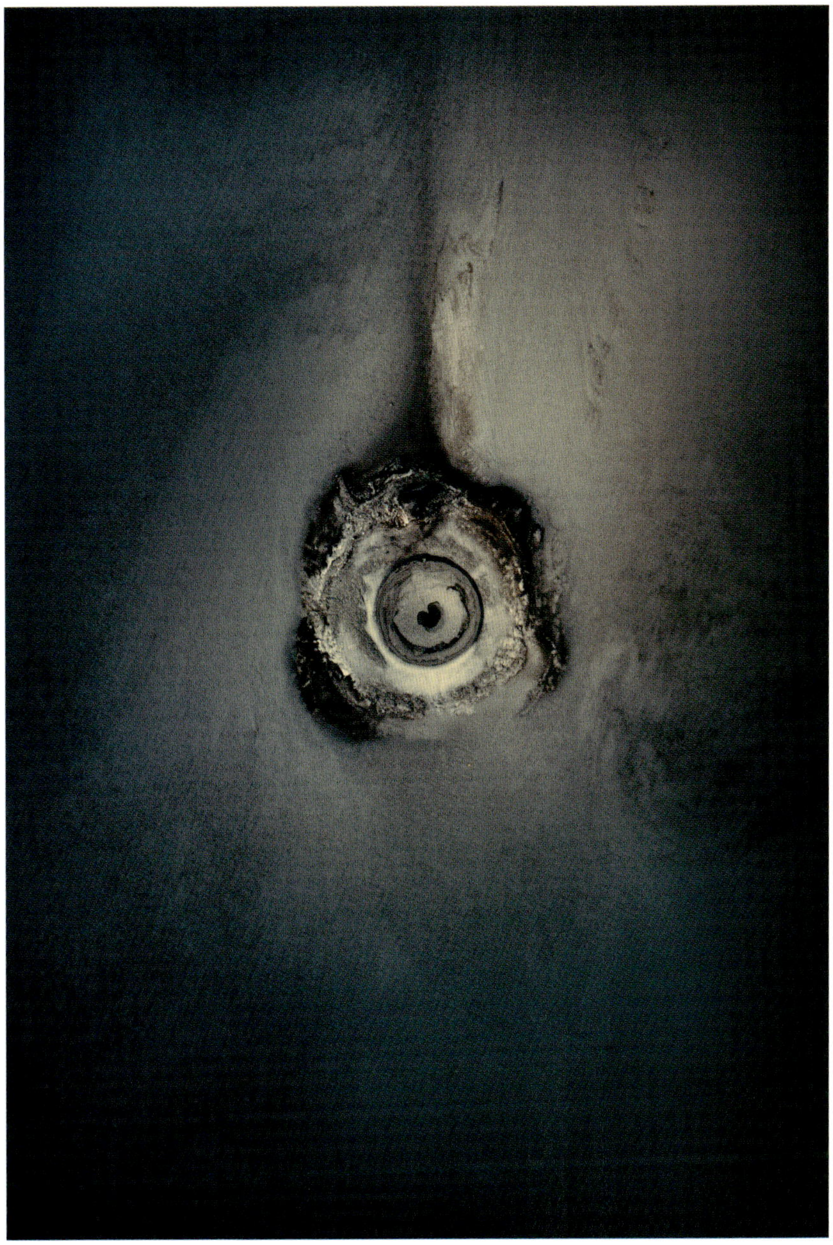

◂ GULLÁ

Rivers used to be blue, but this one wanted to be special so it painted itself with gold.

▴ HVERIR

Take a guess: Is this a close-up or a drone shot?

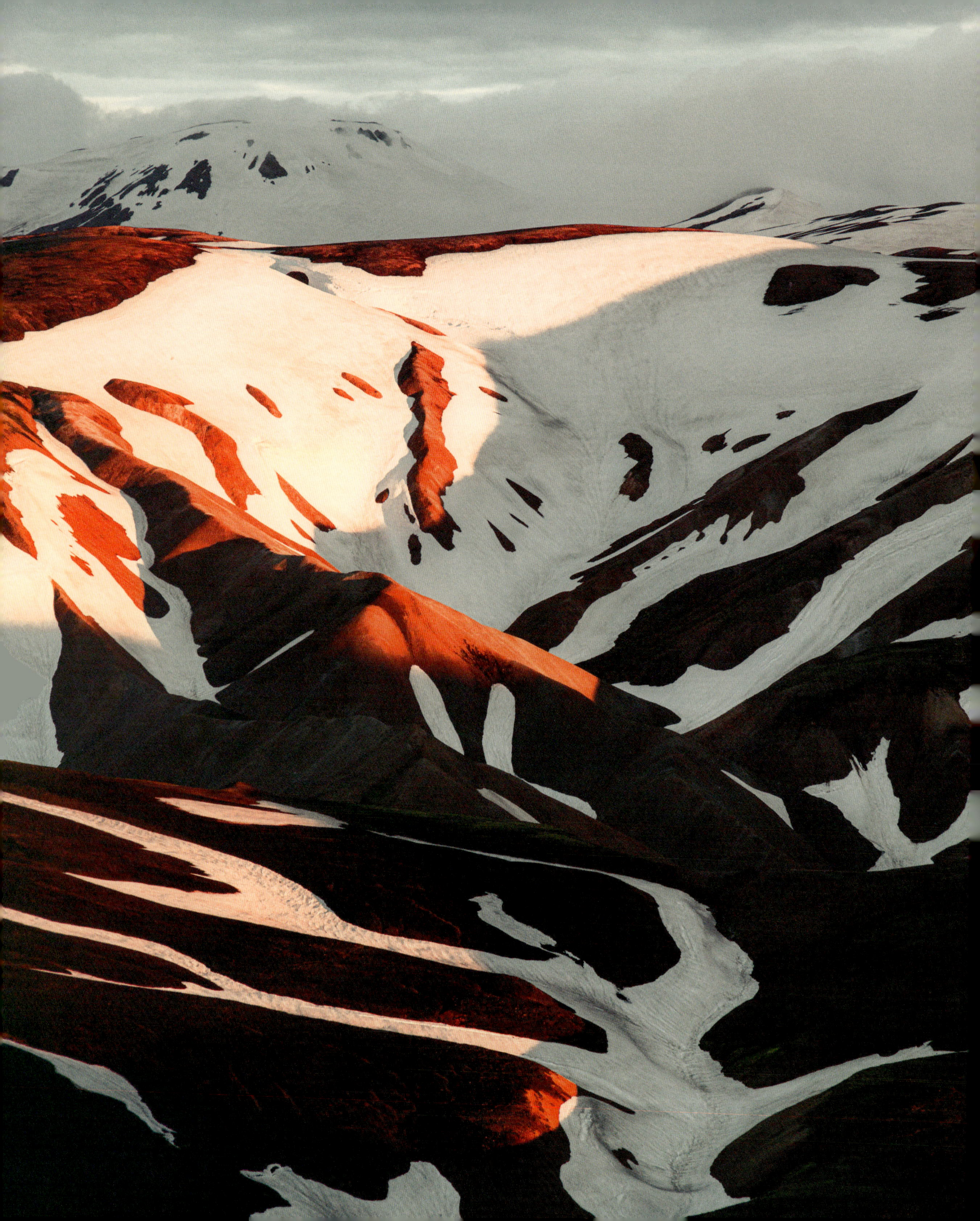

MIDNIGHT SUN PARTY FOREVER

July and August

Everything happens all the time. Existential clarity in excess. No one ever stops, everything is oversaturated, and the sun is trying to light it all up at once. Does chaos leave stains? Yes. Can we just take a break from the outside? No! It's too nice.

The season of the sun is here. And that means drive, desire, striving, wanting more—more reach, more projects, happiness, quality time, friendships, intimate moments, unforgettable experiences. And the sun's passion burns hot until it almost burns you down.

After having spent the dark parts of the year in hibernation—preparing for this season or recovering from it, depending on your perspective—it's easy to become overwhelmed when we can suddenly do all the things all the time. The social pressure is on. We feel bad for every second of sunshine we spend indoors, every mountain we haven't climbed yet, the people we don't meet because we're out meeting other people. It's great to stay out on a peak with friends, sharing views all night, with no idea how it got this late. Or early. Or both. Meanwhile the dishes are piling up and the full memory cards are towering over the uncharged batteries. No time to even think about tidying up.

But all these worries fade into the backdrop of our vast landscapes. The bright nights stretch time in the most abstract ways, diluting any sense of urgency. There is a theory that we are at our happiest when we forget about time—while dancing, playing music, or writing poetry, painting, skiing the perfect line, running at sunset, or vibing at a really good party. It's simply called "flow," when the forgetting of time leads to the dissolving of future worries.

As children, we seek the great outdoors to play. We embrace the magic of discovery and movement. Nature gives us the space to release our energy, find new worlds around every corner. The outdoors becomes a canvas upon which we can unleash our creativity, a classroom in which to learn, and a place to thrive without constraints.

As we grow up, these sensations can become muted.

Instead of exploring, we are stuck resetting passwords, choosing bread at the grocery store, waiting in line for coffee, and sitting at home scrolling through TV shows.

But nature is still out there, stubbornly refusing to grow up with us.

For me, the mountains, the oceans, the trails, the wilderness—they're not just places to conquer or photograph. They're playgrounds. Giant, messy, harsh, beautiful playgrounds. Places to laugh at yourself, to lose track of time, and to find others who refuse to grow up. Out there, it's all about feeding your curious mind again, painting your imagination onto the sometimes stormy and extreme canvas, and having fun.

Nature is our playground. Come out and play.

◄◄ LANDMANNALAUGAR

Iceland grew its mountains to be more photogenic than the rest of the world. Then it laid some patches of snow down to make them fun, too.

► THE HIGHLANDS II

It's amazing how good piles of dirt, moss, and water can look in the right light.

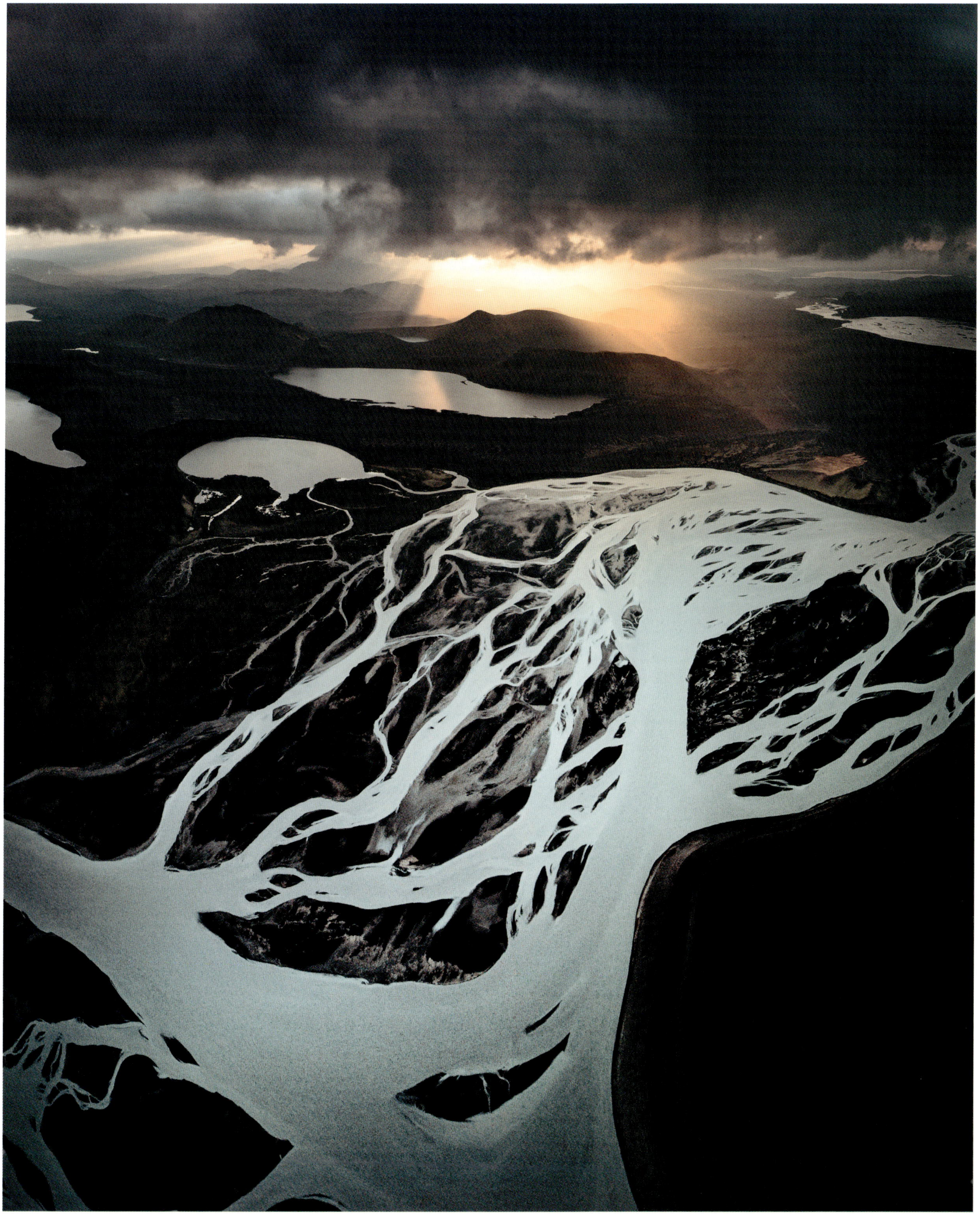

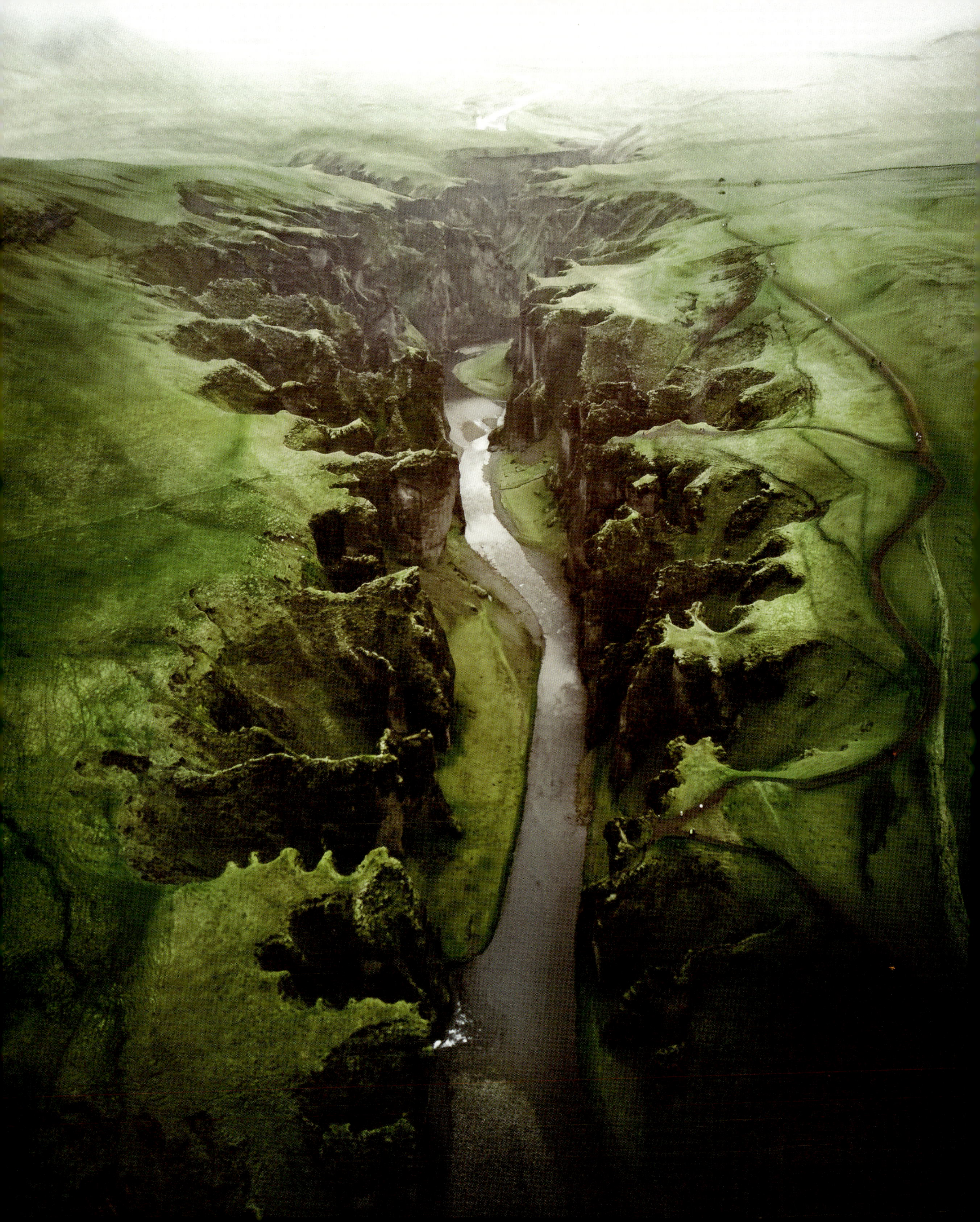

◂ FJAÐRÁRGLJÚFUR

Earth giving way to let a small stream pass on by.

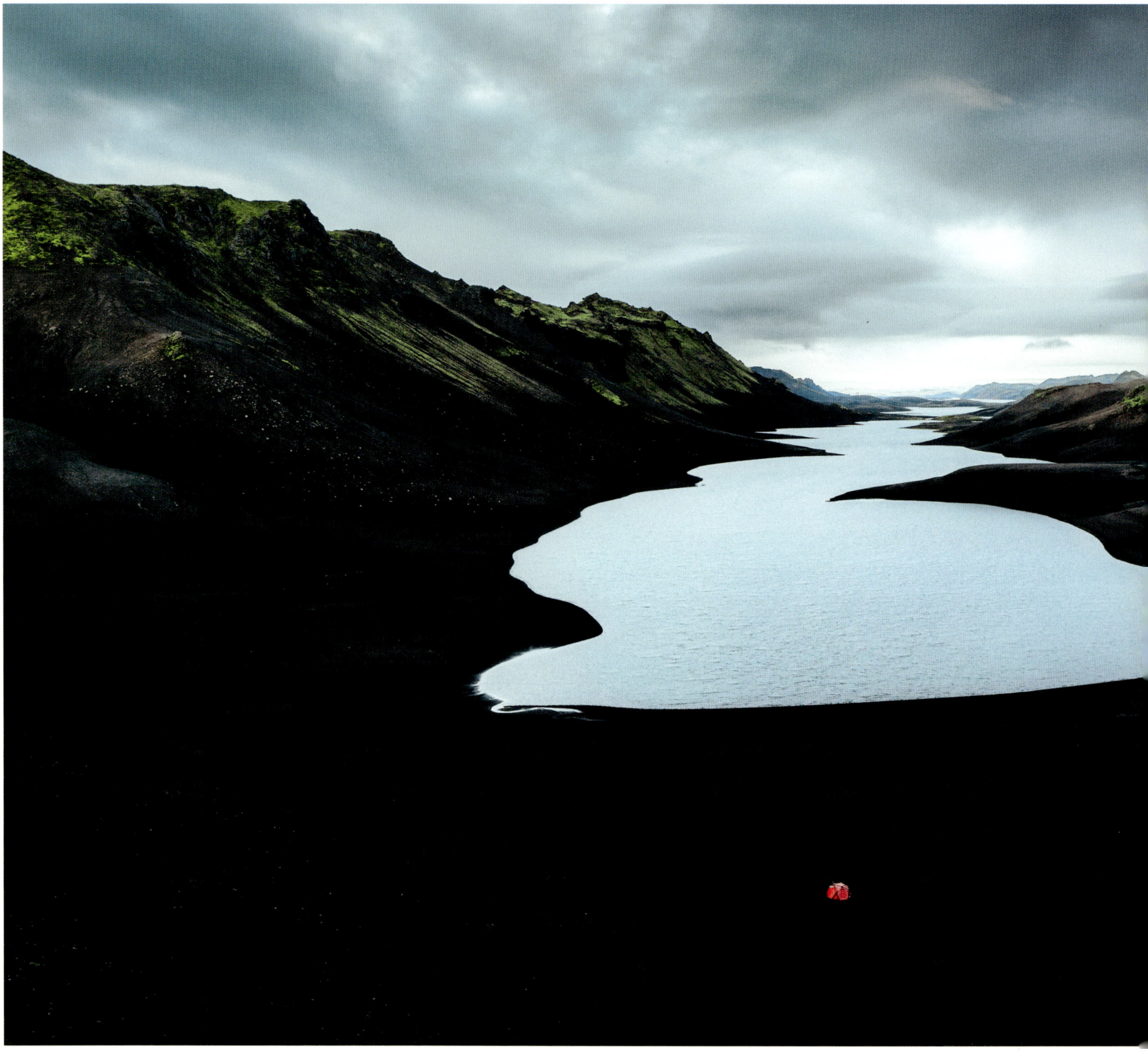

◂ LANGISJÓR

A great place to live if you love landscapes or don't like people.

▾ EAST ICELAND

A "horse" that grew horns so it could point at what it wants.

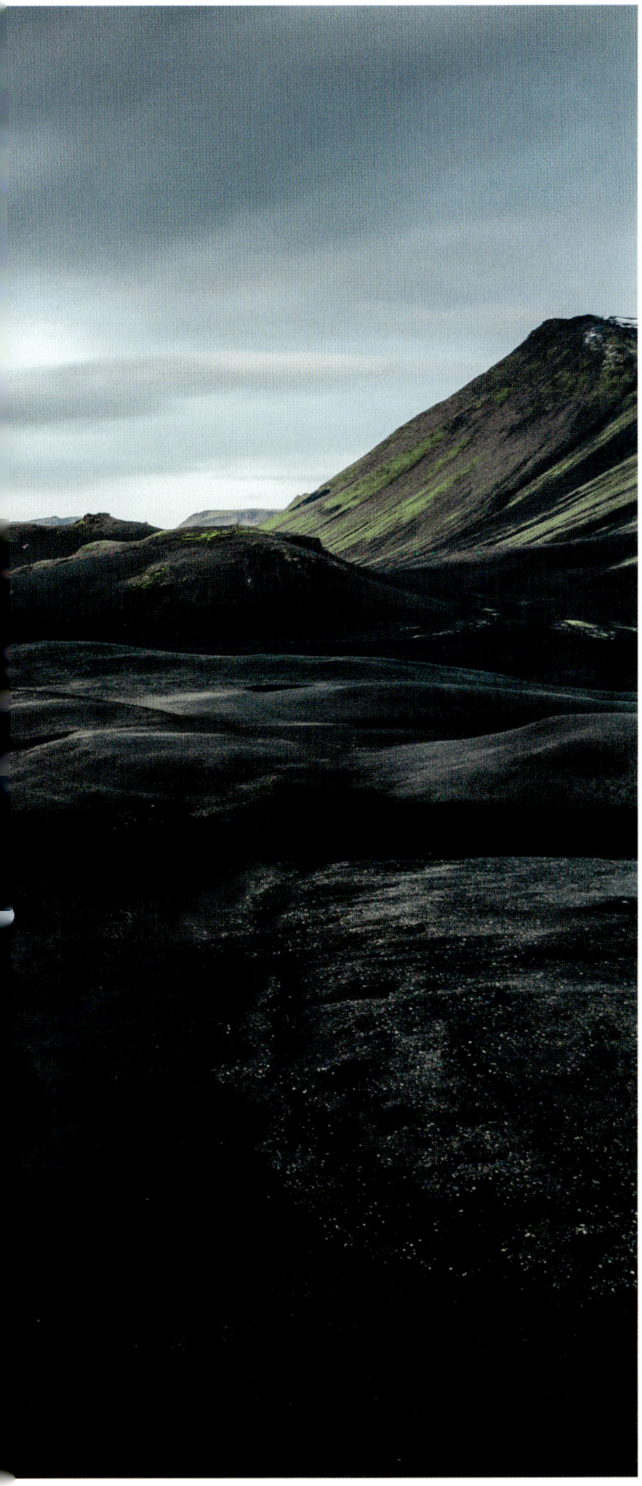

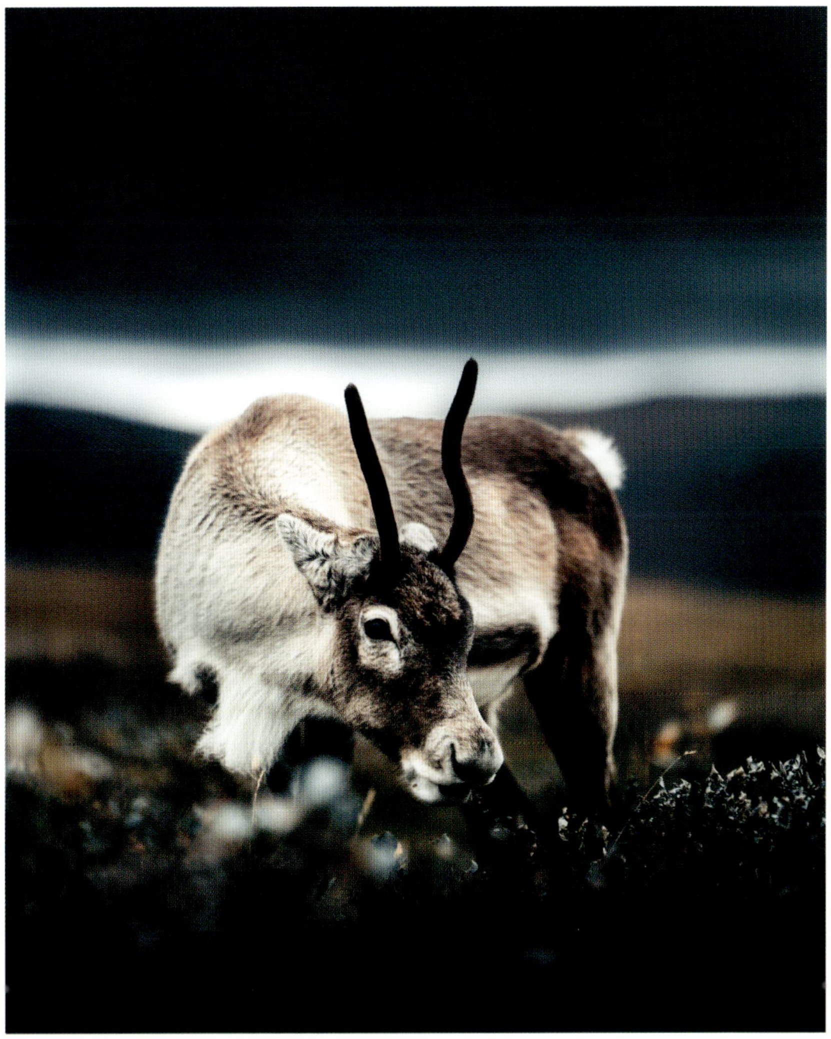

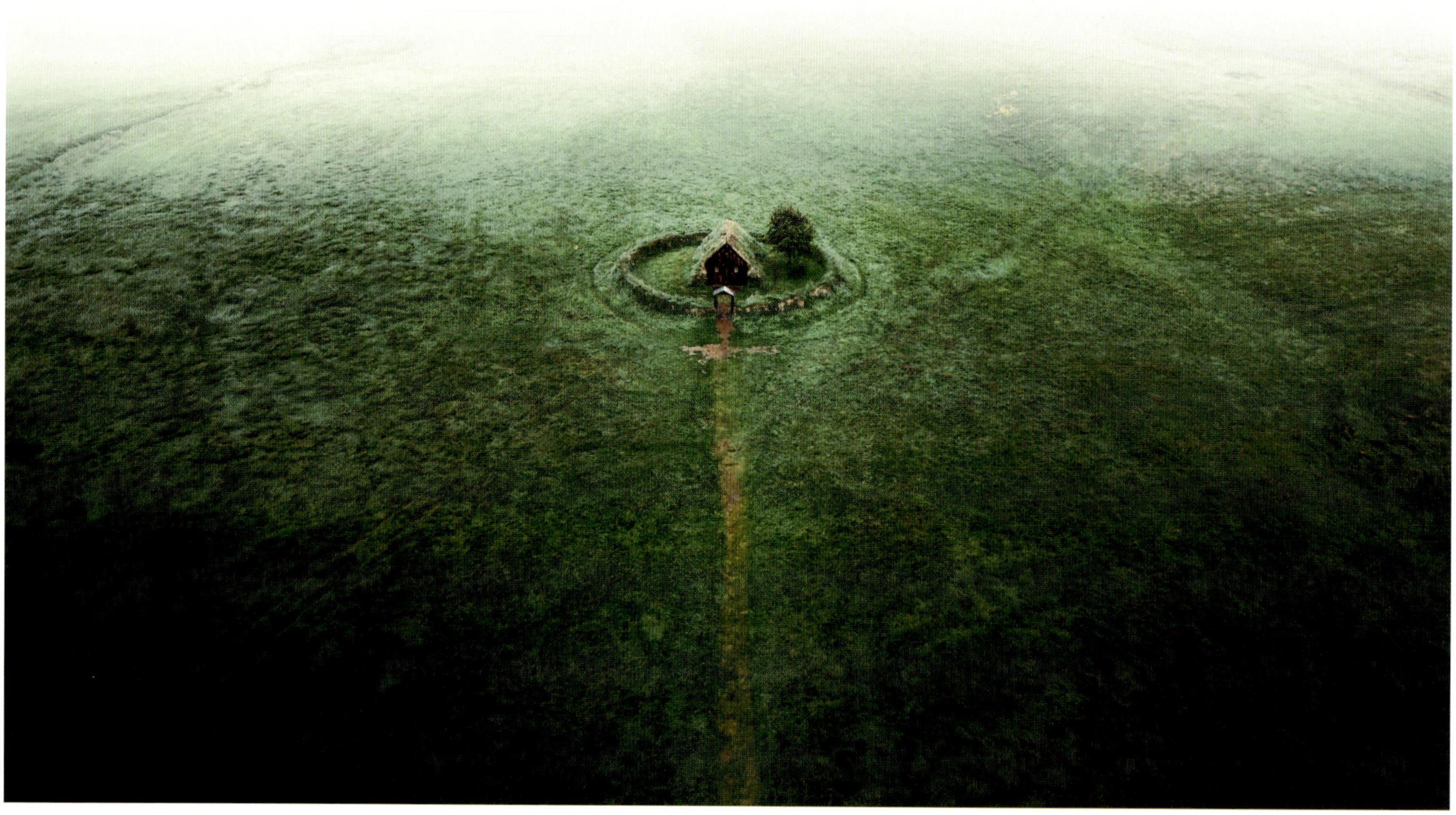

▲ GRAFARKIRKJA II

When the Vikings first came to Iceland, they quickly used up all the trees to build houses and keep themselves warm. Once they ran out, all they had left to build with was turf.

This is one of the country's oldest churches, showing how little the early Icelanders had to work with–and that they left one last tree for decoration.

▶ ALL OVER EVERYWHERE

These are some of the original explorers of Iceland. The true eyes and hooves of the landscapes. Many of the island's hidden gems that now have easy, five-step instructions for how to get there, or trails of dropped Google pins, were originally discovered by these sheep–and later by the farmers who had to traipse out to get them back.

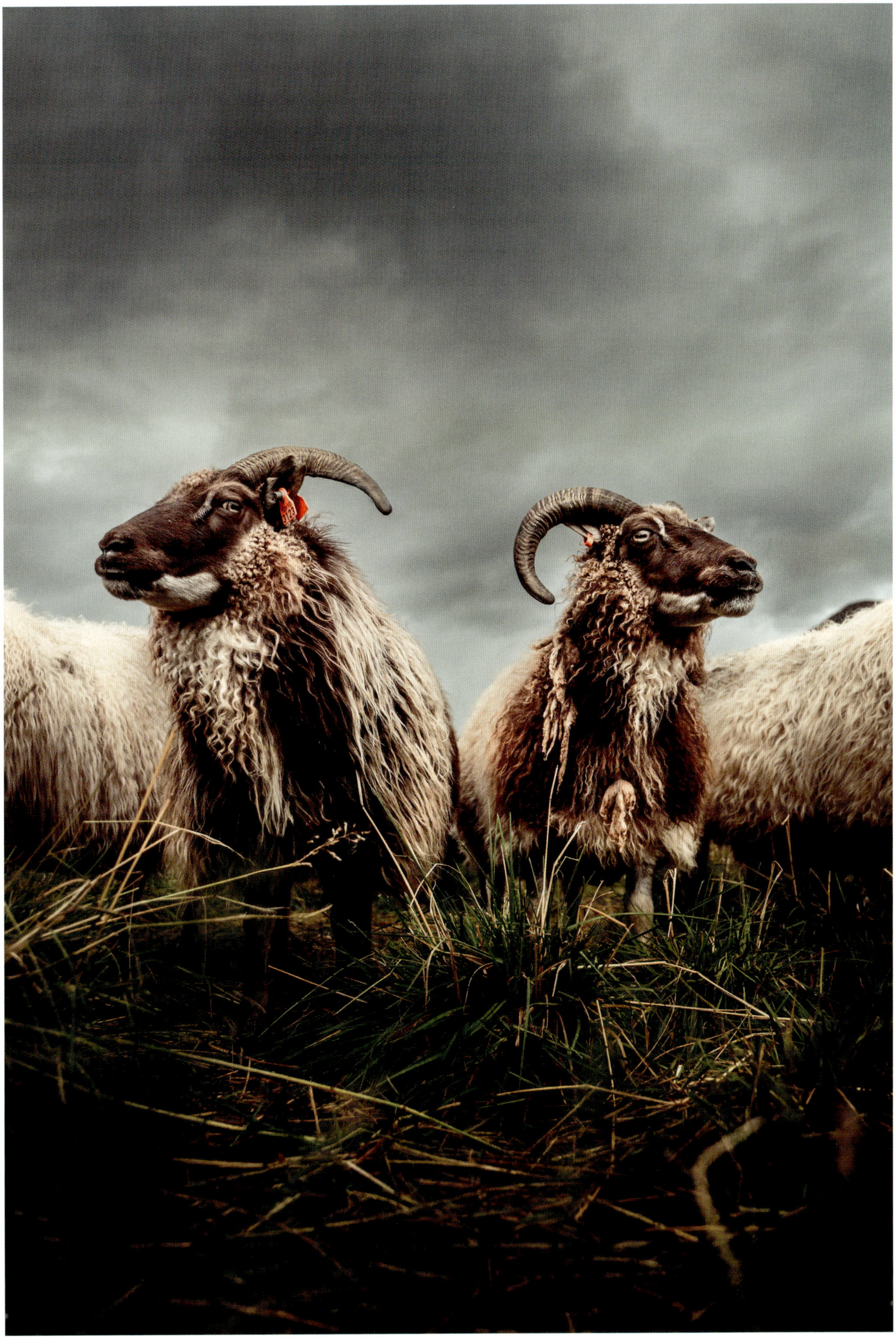

➤ EAST ICELAND II

The locals appreciate the good views.

➤➤ THE HIGHLANDS III

A classic shot that has been captured many times before. Nonetheless, photographing Iceland is a little bit like collecting Pokémon. Gotta catch all those epic pics even if everyone else already has them.

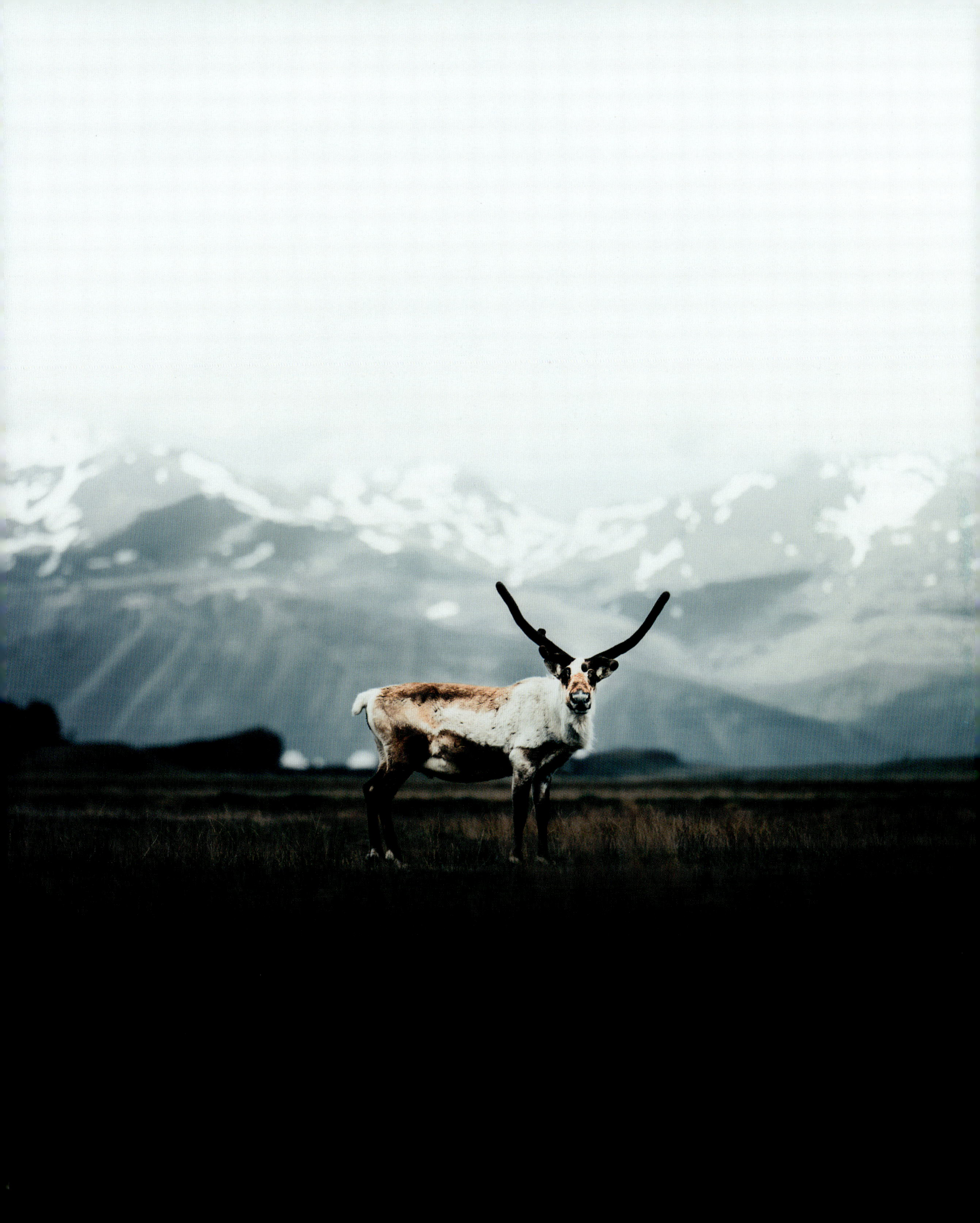

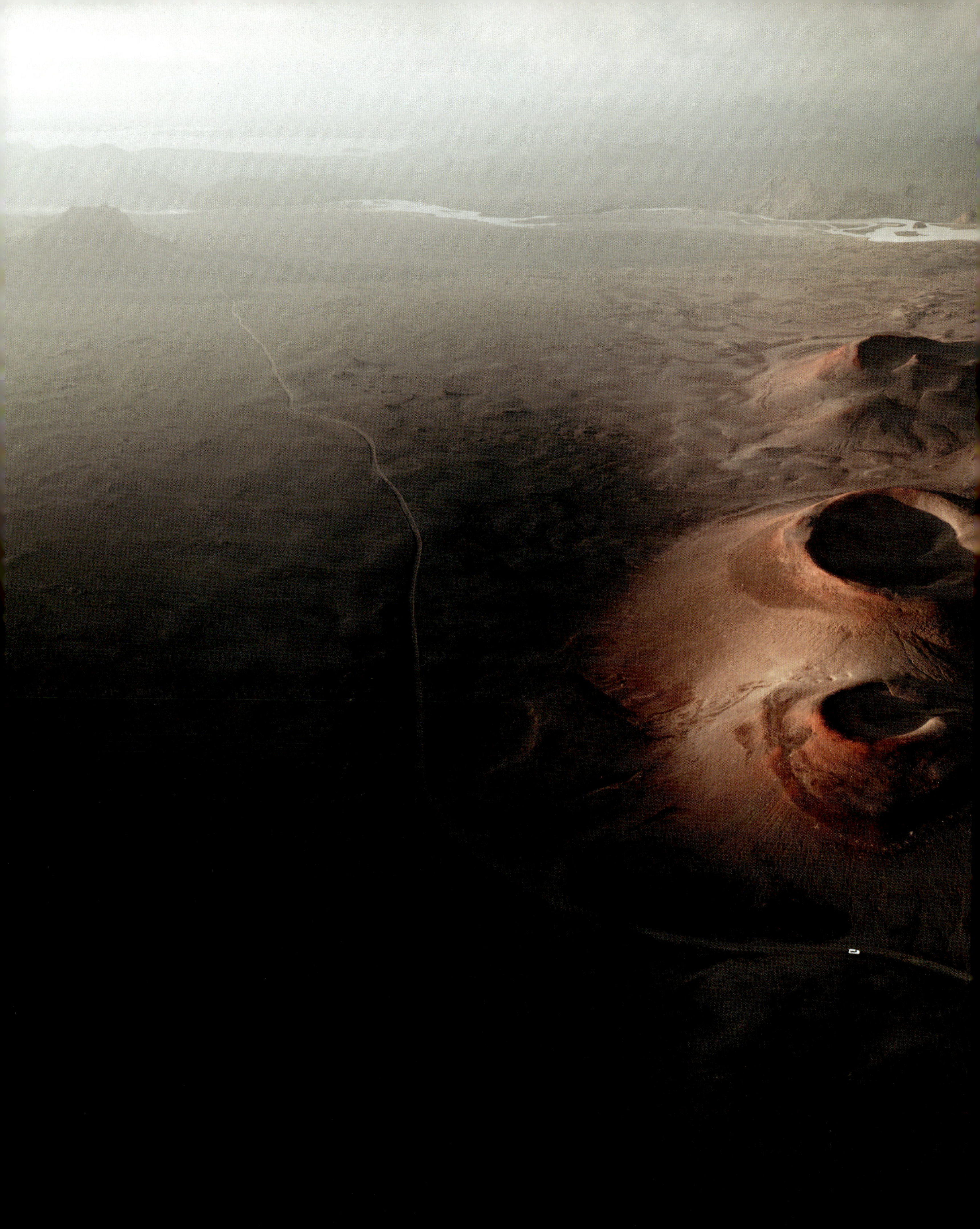

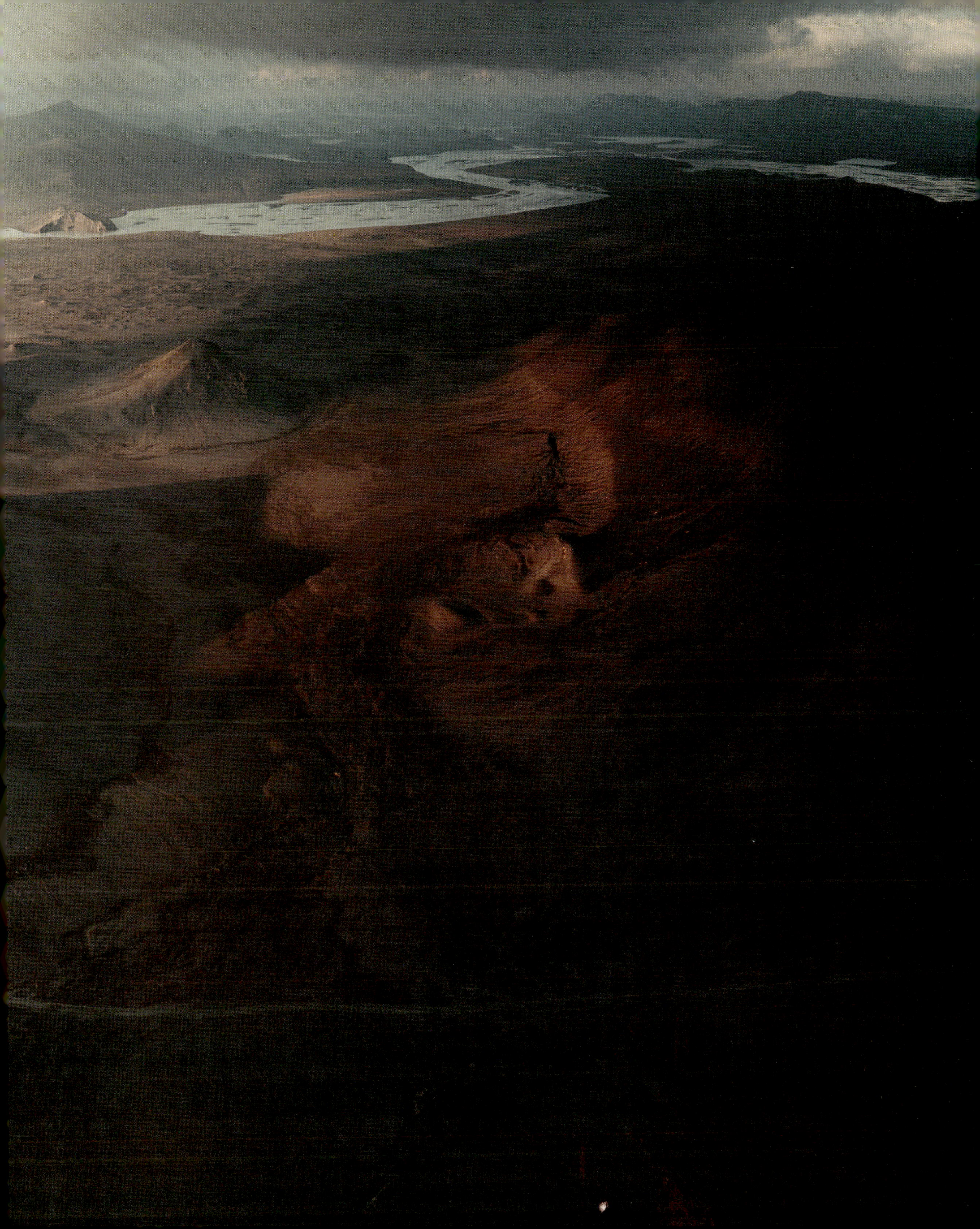

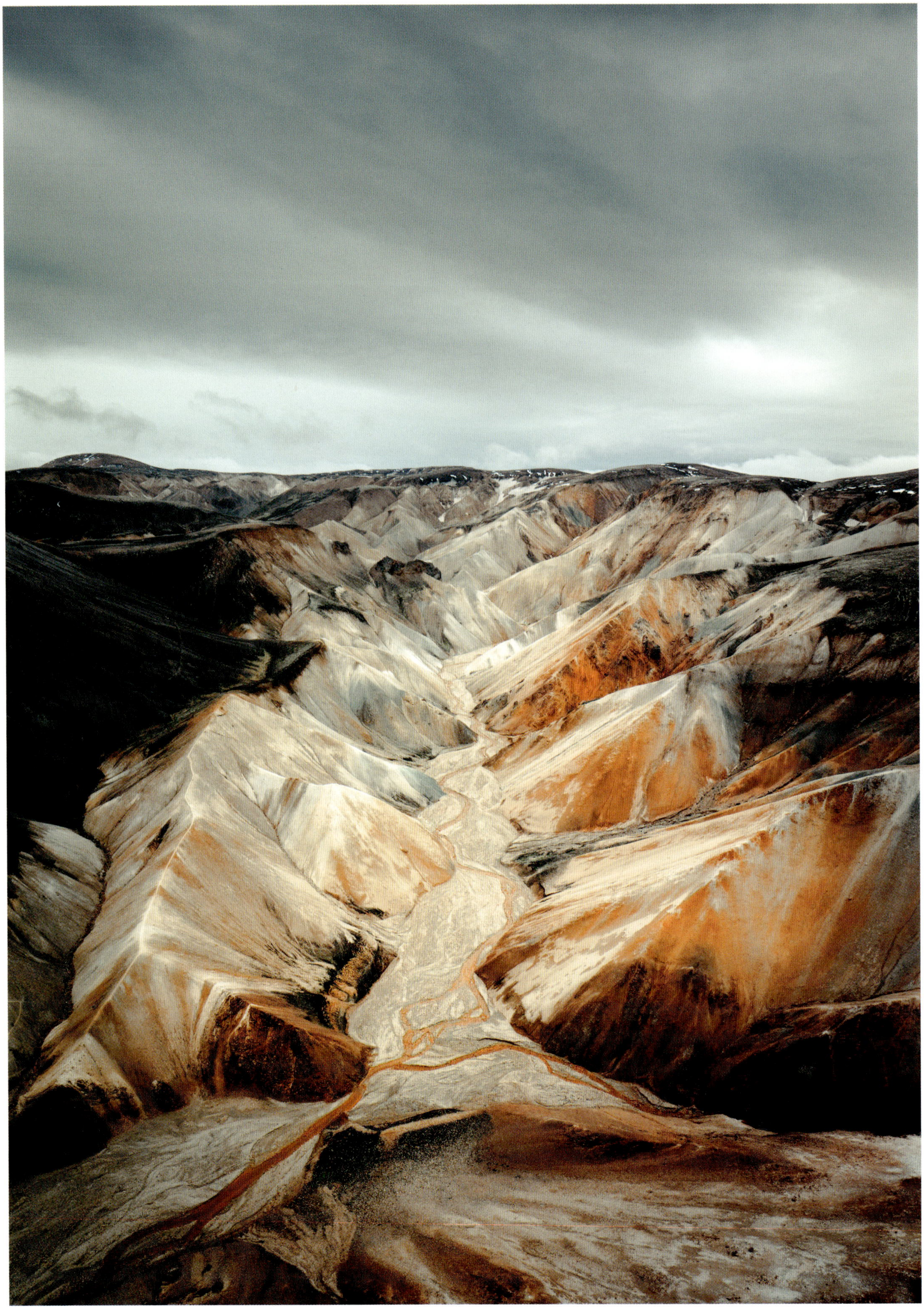

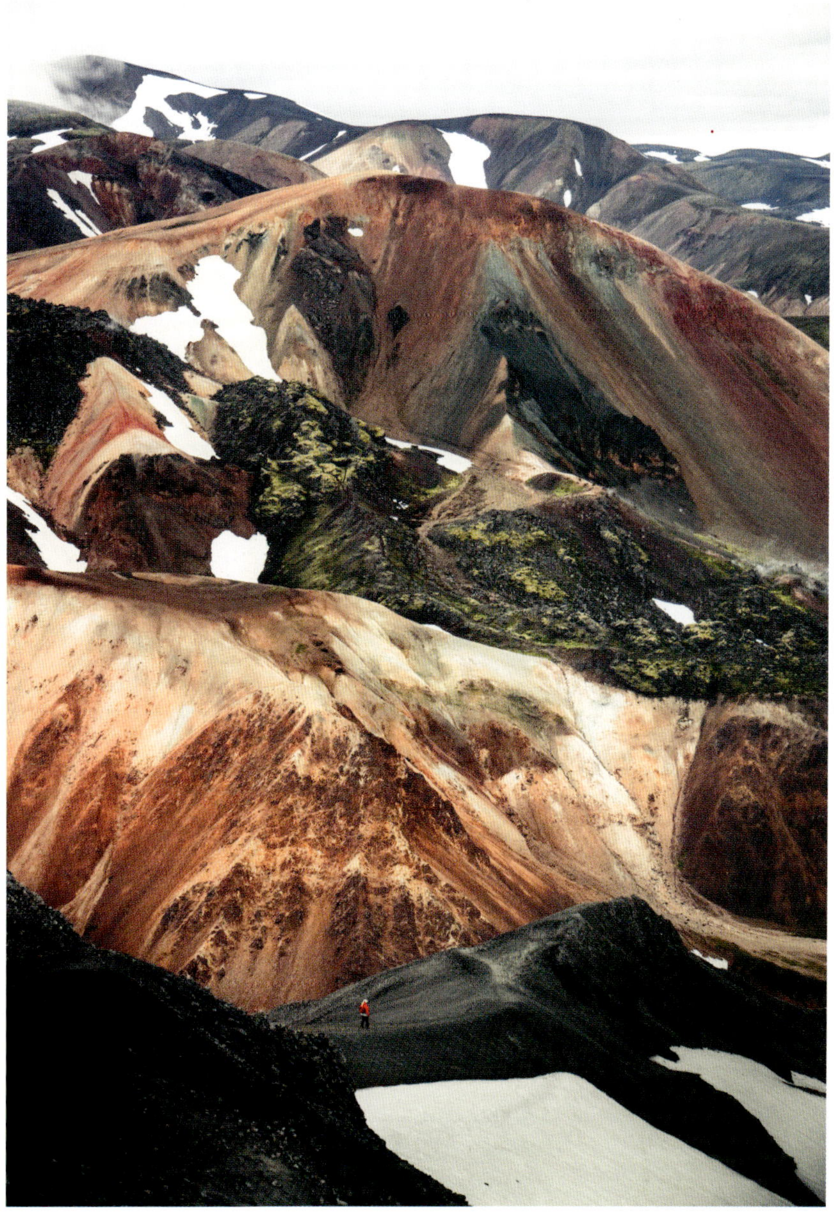

◀ LANDMANNALAUGAR II

This view made itself so beautiful that it had to hide deep in the unconquerable Icelandic highlands so people wouldn't quit their jobs and just sit and stare at it for the rest of their lives.

▲ LANDMANNALAUGAR III

After Odin was done painting the world, he dumped all the leftover color here.

▶▶ LANDMANNALAUGAR IV

A place that deserves to be seen by most but is best experienced when empty.

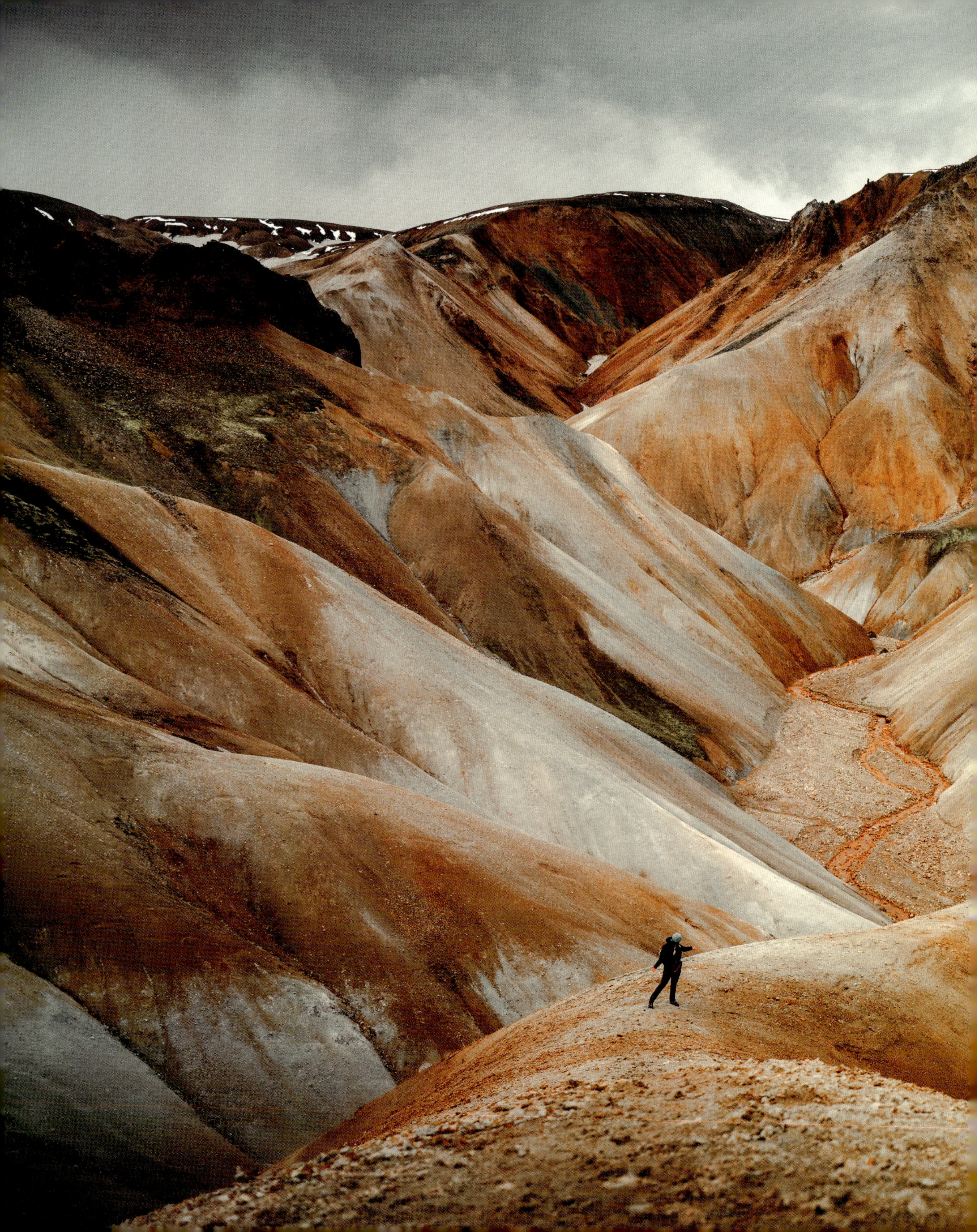

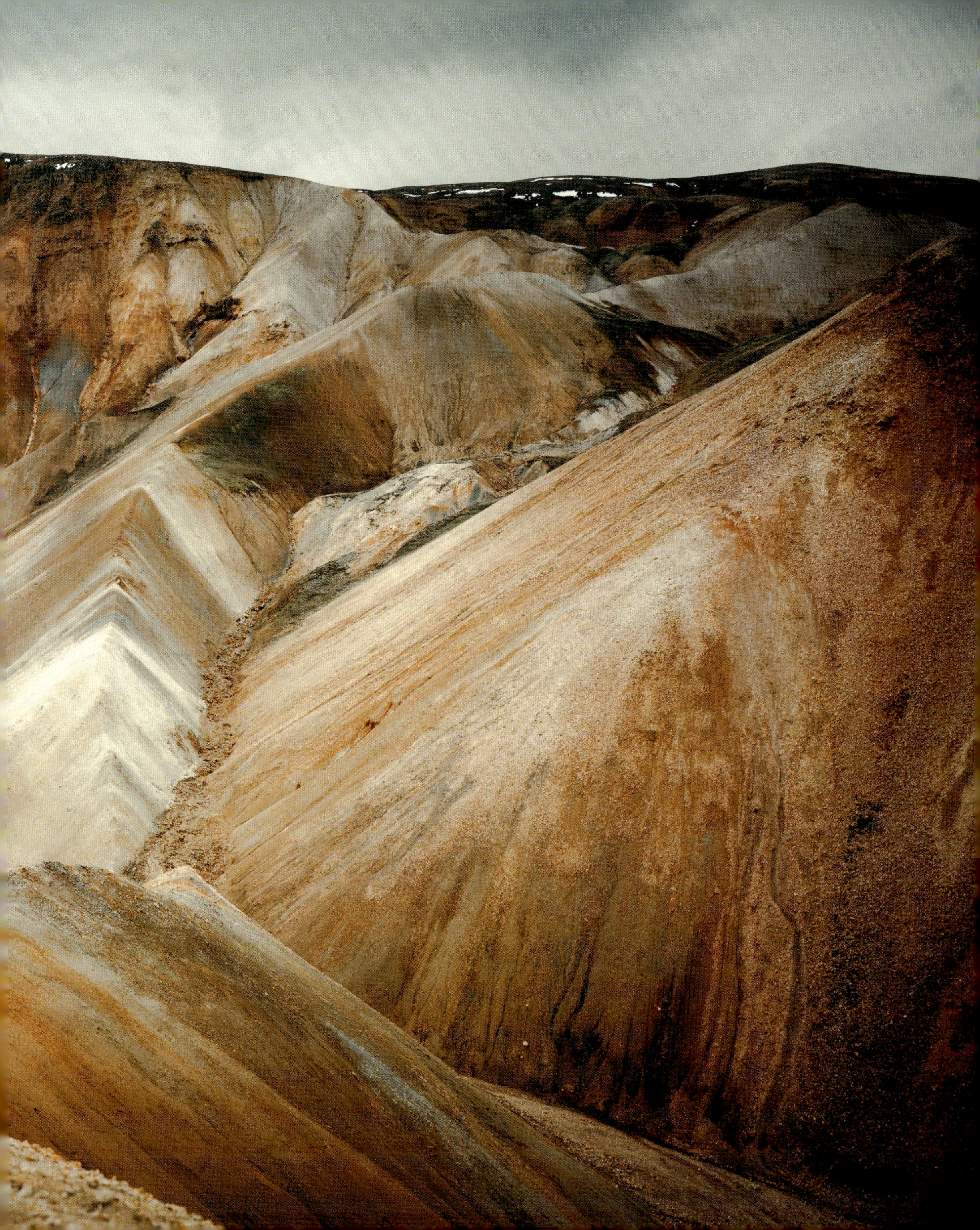

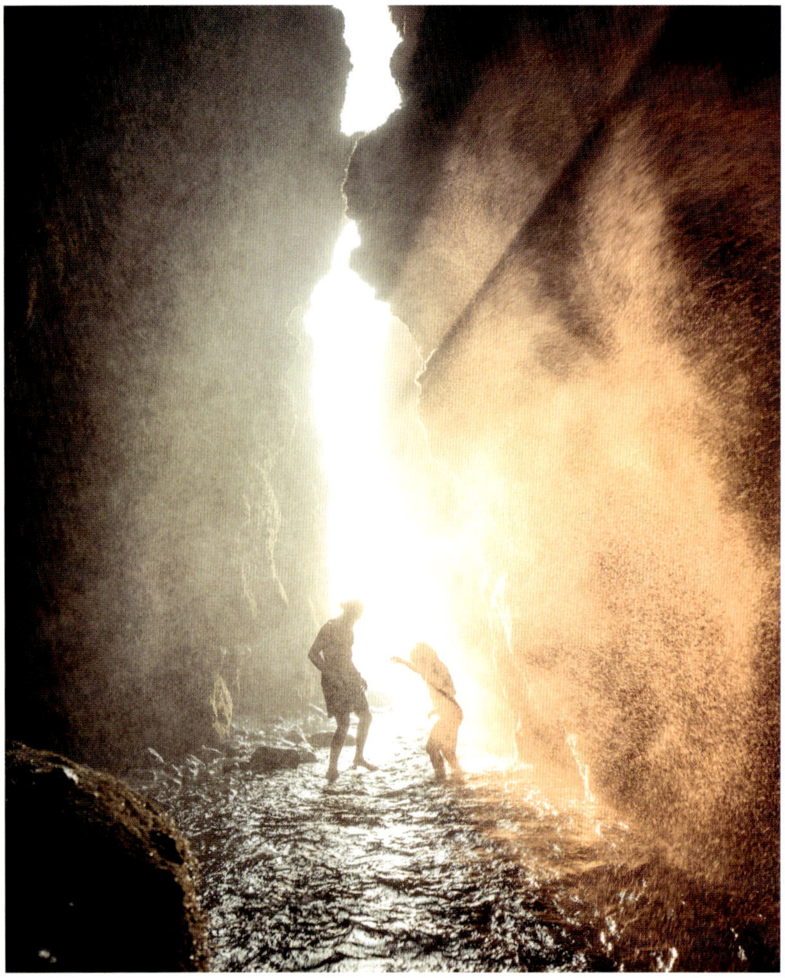

▲ GLJÚFRABÚI

The sun never really set, so we woke up too early and showered in a tiny canyon that always brings its own storm.

▶ SIGLUFJÖRÐUR III

As a lighthouse is made seasonally obsolete by the surrounding brightness, its body parts gradually leave their home seeking new purpose on the seabed.

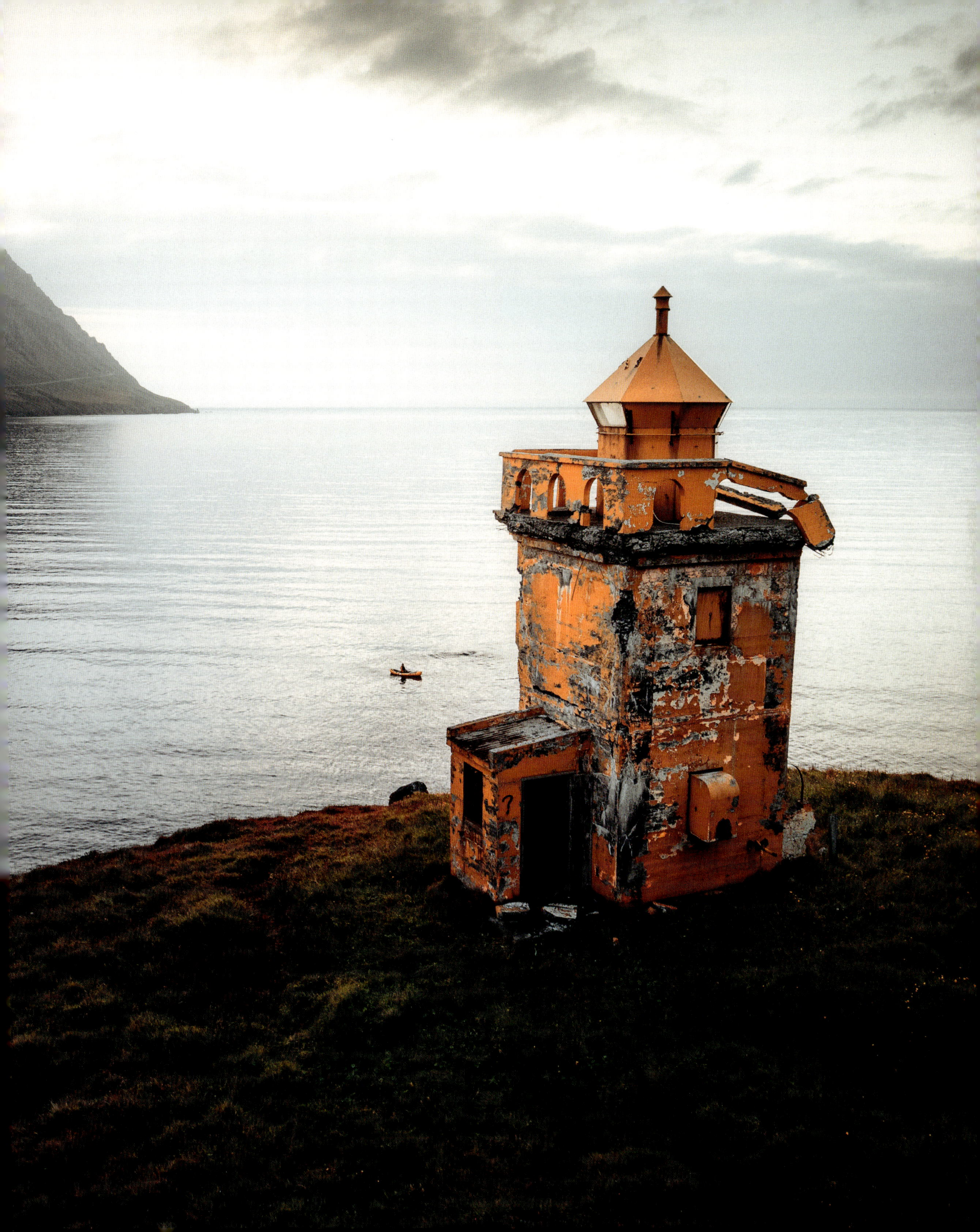

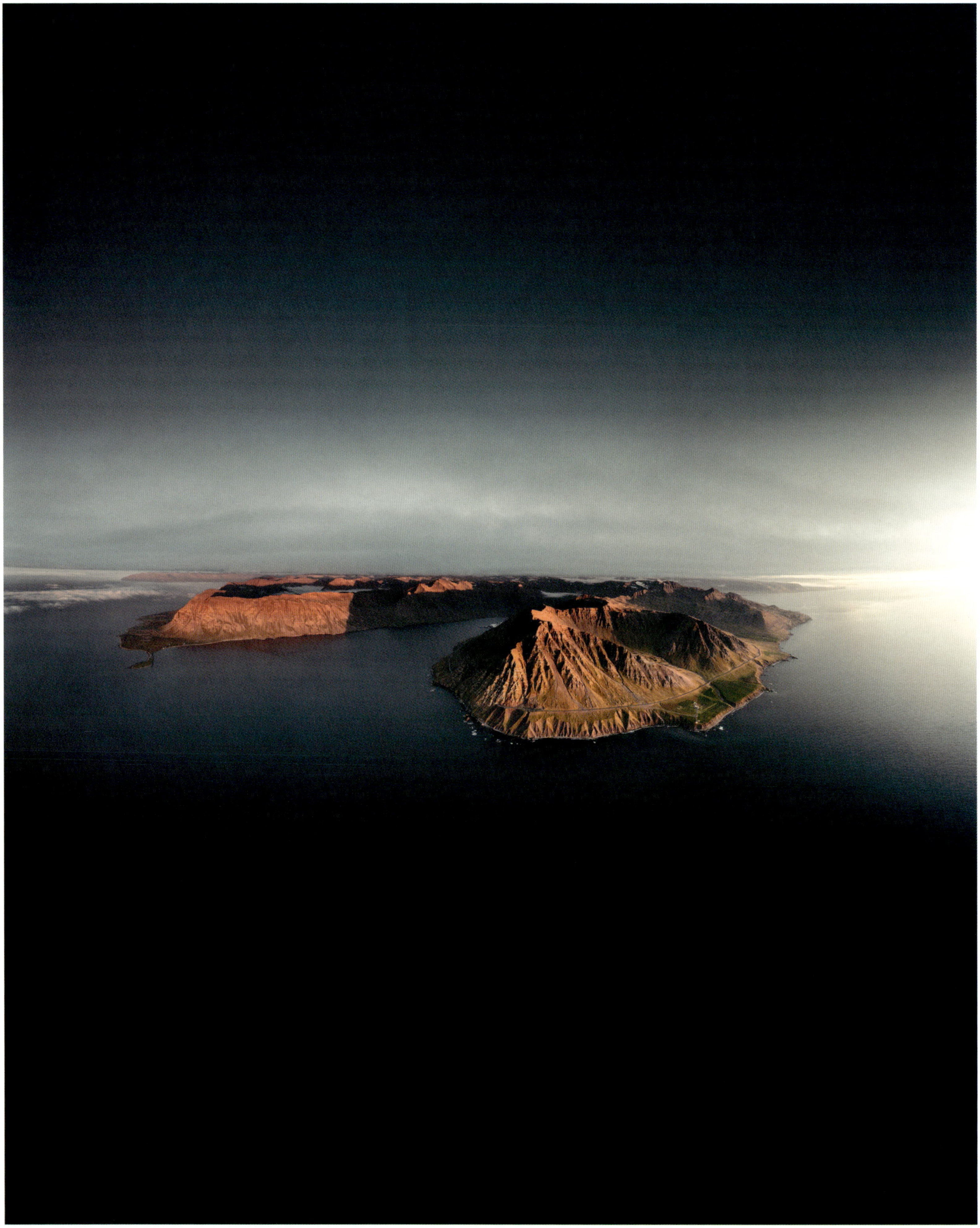

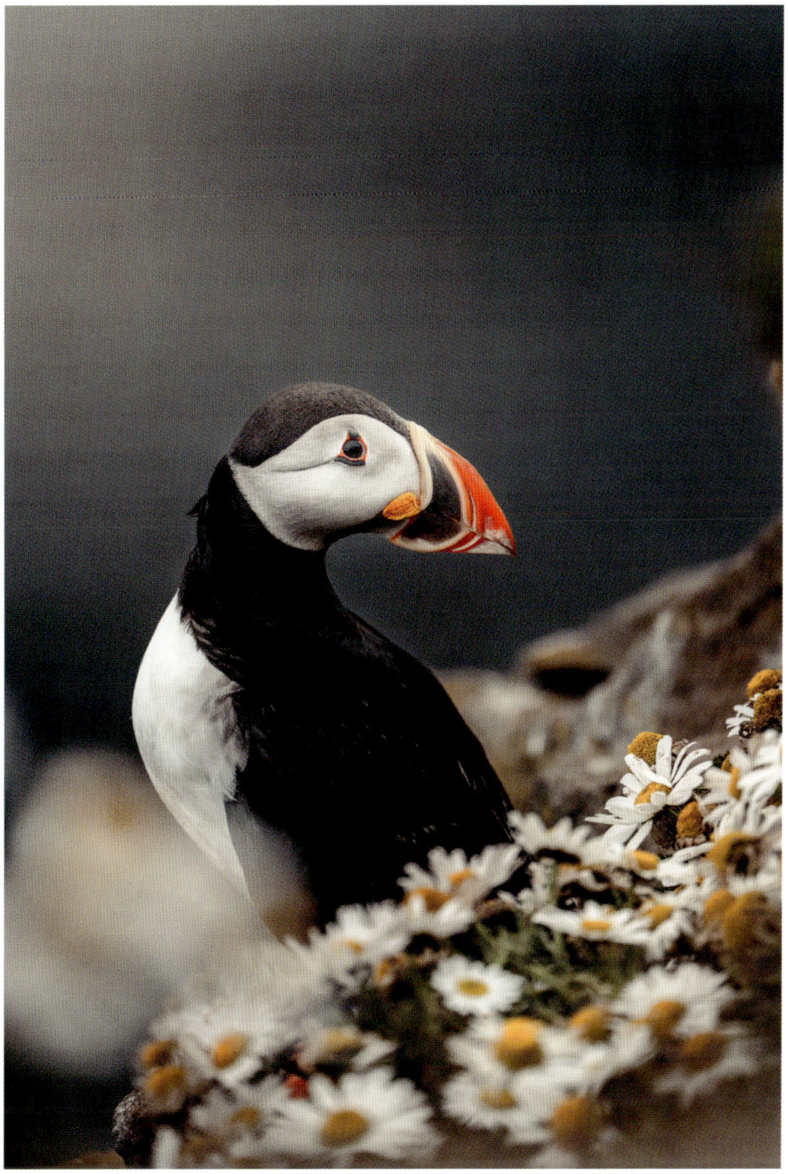

▲ WESTFJORDS

Puffins often nest around flowers so they will look prettier in pictures.

◂ THE EDGE

Having moved to the edge of the world, I discovered that the top of that edge is only a three-hour hike from my house. And from there, I can throw rocks to the bottom of the edge. Or fly my drone and take panoramic selfies where I am really, really, really small. You probably can't see me in there, even if you buy the largest version of this print. I dare you to try. they will look prettier in pictures.

▸▸ SIGÖLDUGLJÚFUR

A 3 a.m. sunrise. It was romantic. Hands were almost held. Tears were almost shed. The night was almost remembered. But at least there's this photo to remind us that it happened.

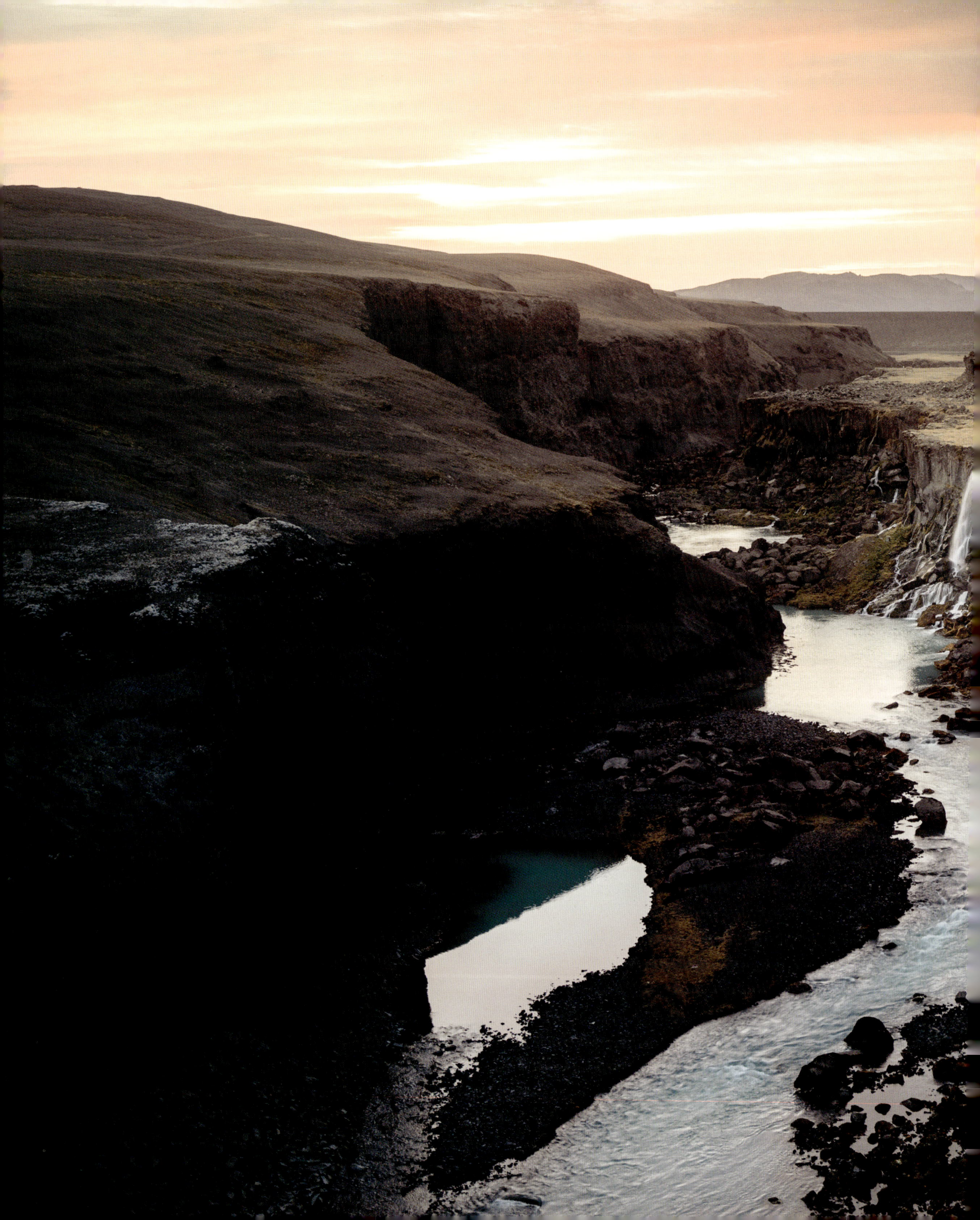

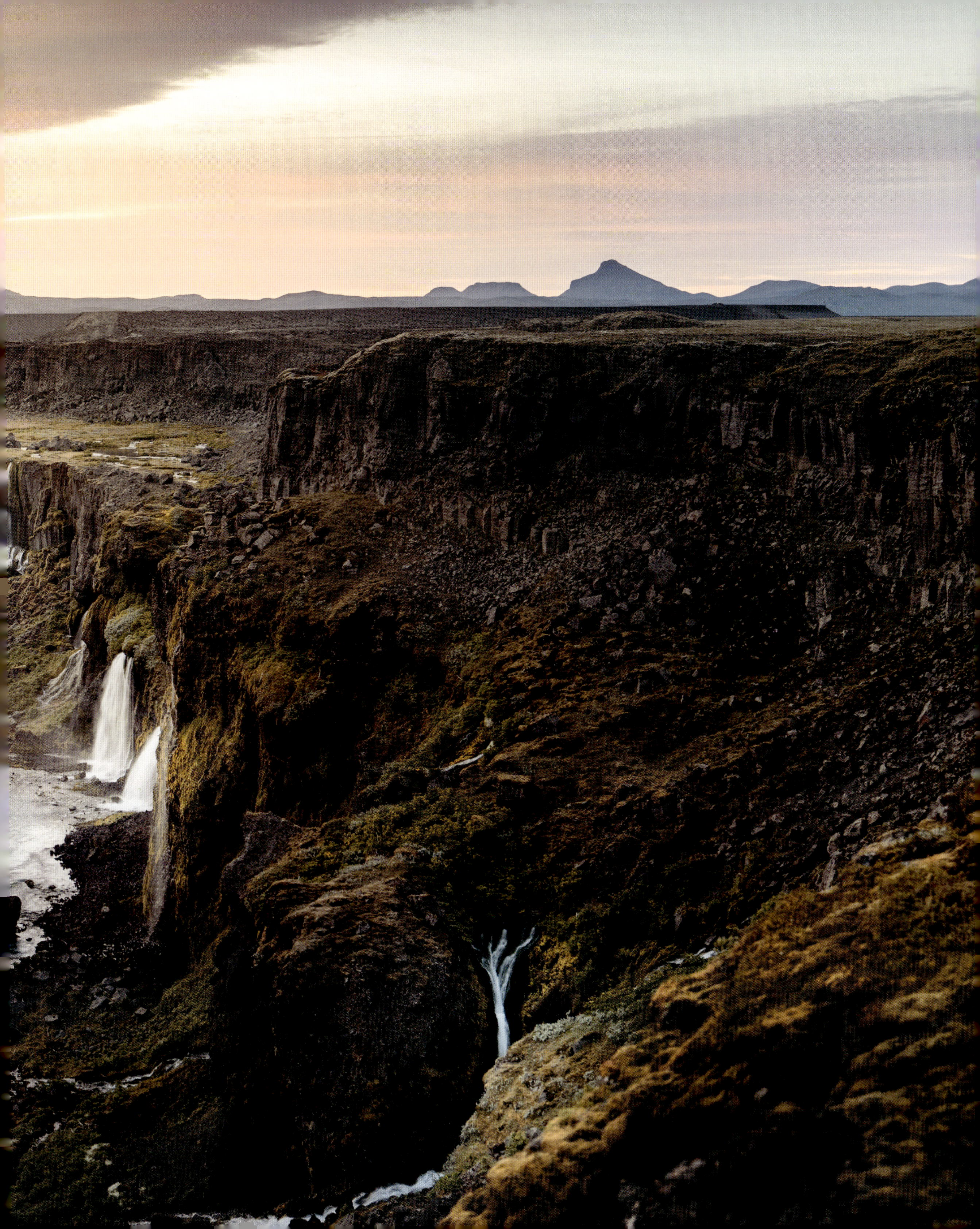

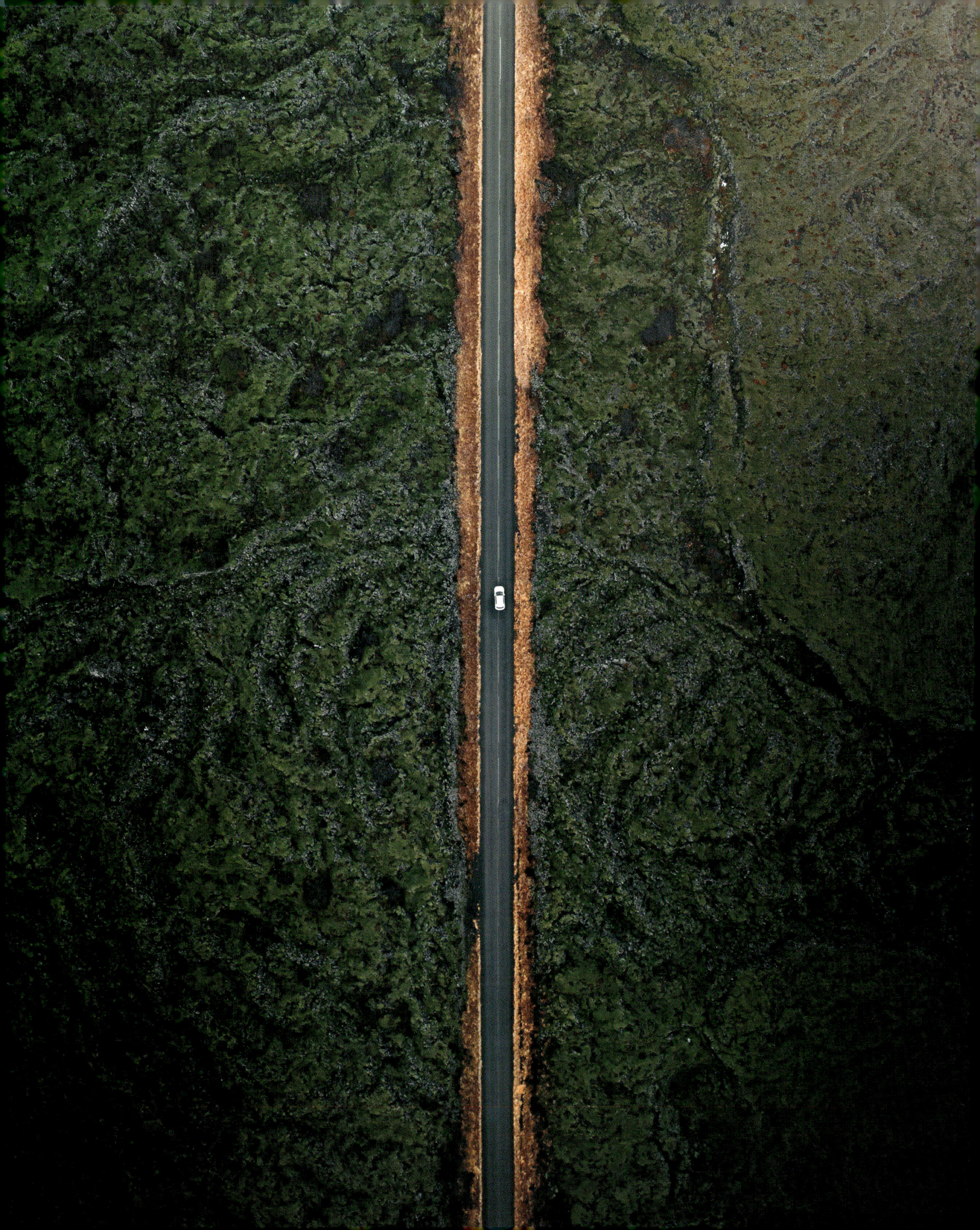

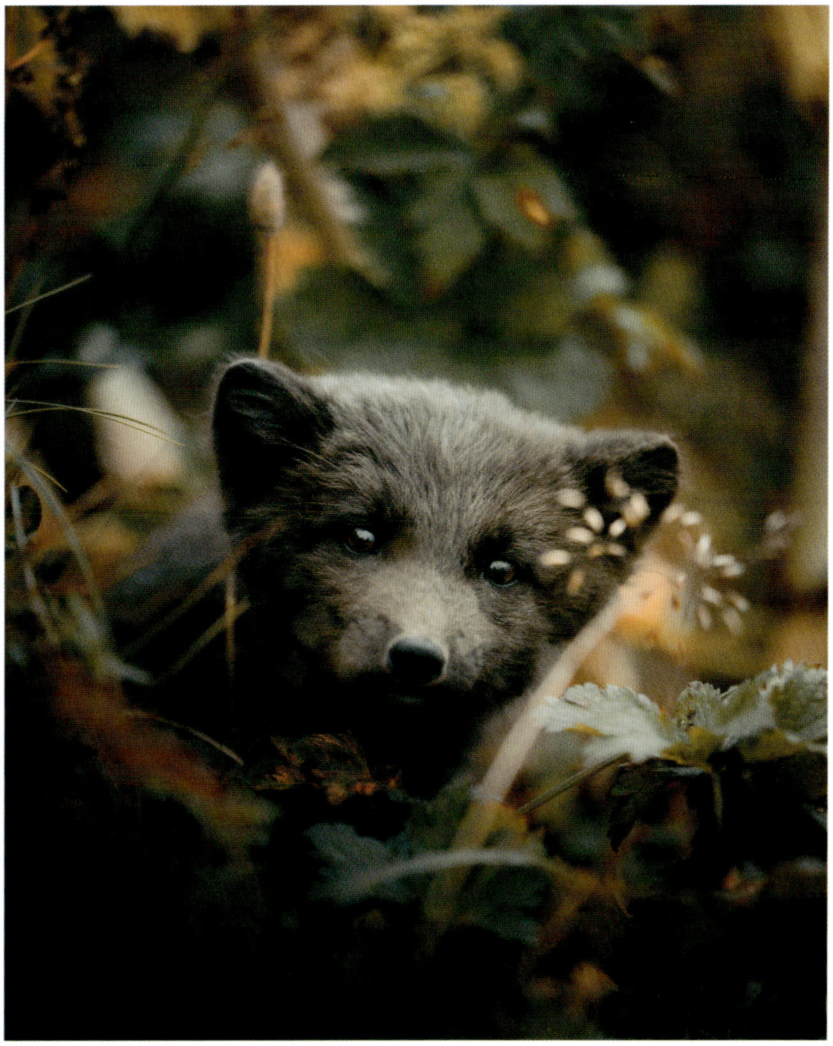

◀ REYKJANES

Sometimes you just have to take a few steps back, or up, to see what nature is trying to show you.

▲ HORNSTRANDIR

I asked this arctic fox cub to stare into my lens and bare its soul, but in the end all I found in its gaze was my own reflection.

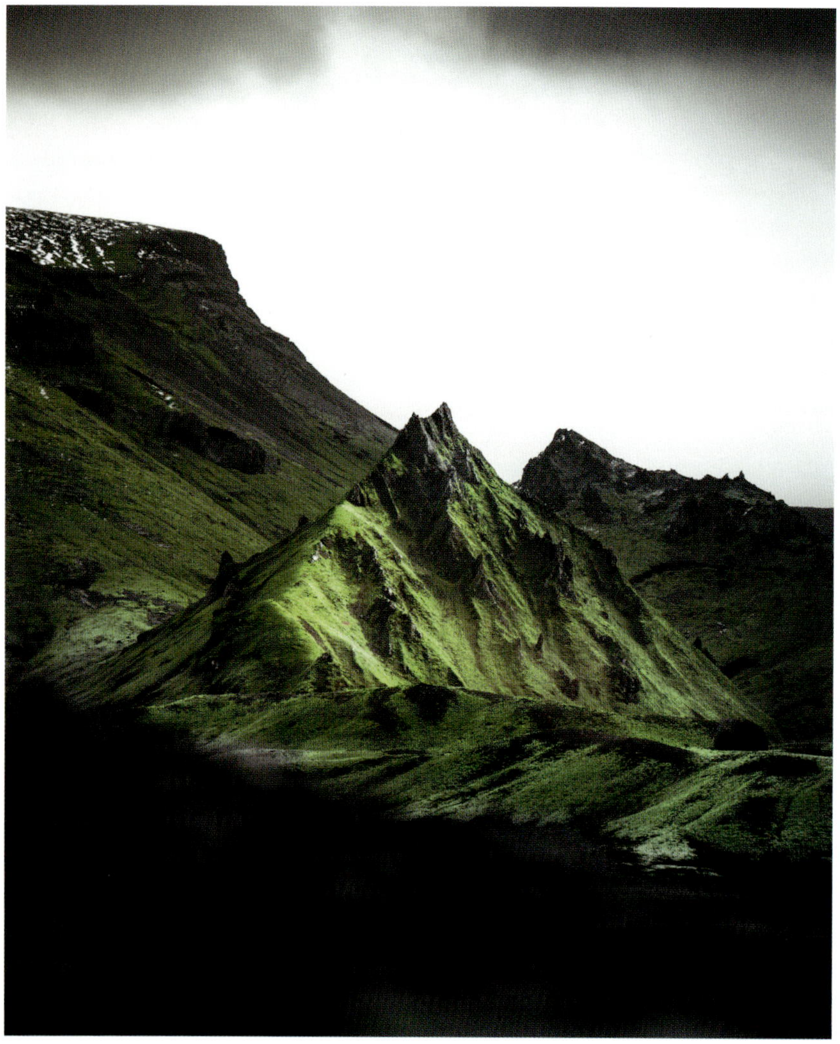

▲ KURL

Over time, the Vikings got better at building mountains. Here, they started building from top to bottom, making the peaks sharper than their old tabletop mountains.

▶ FJAÐRÁRGLJÚFUR II

Nature's own zipper. Broken and unfixable just like the rest of them.

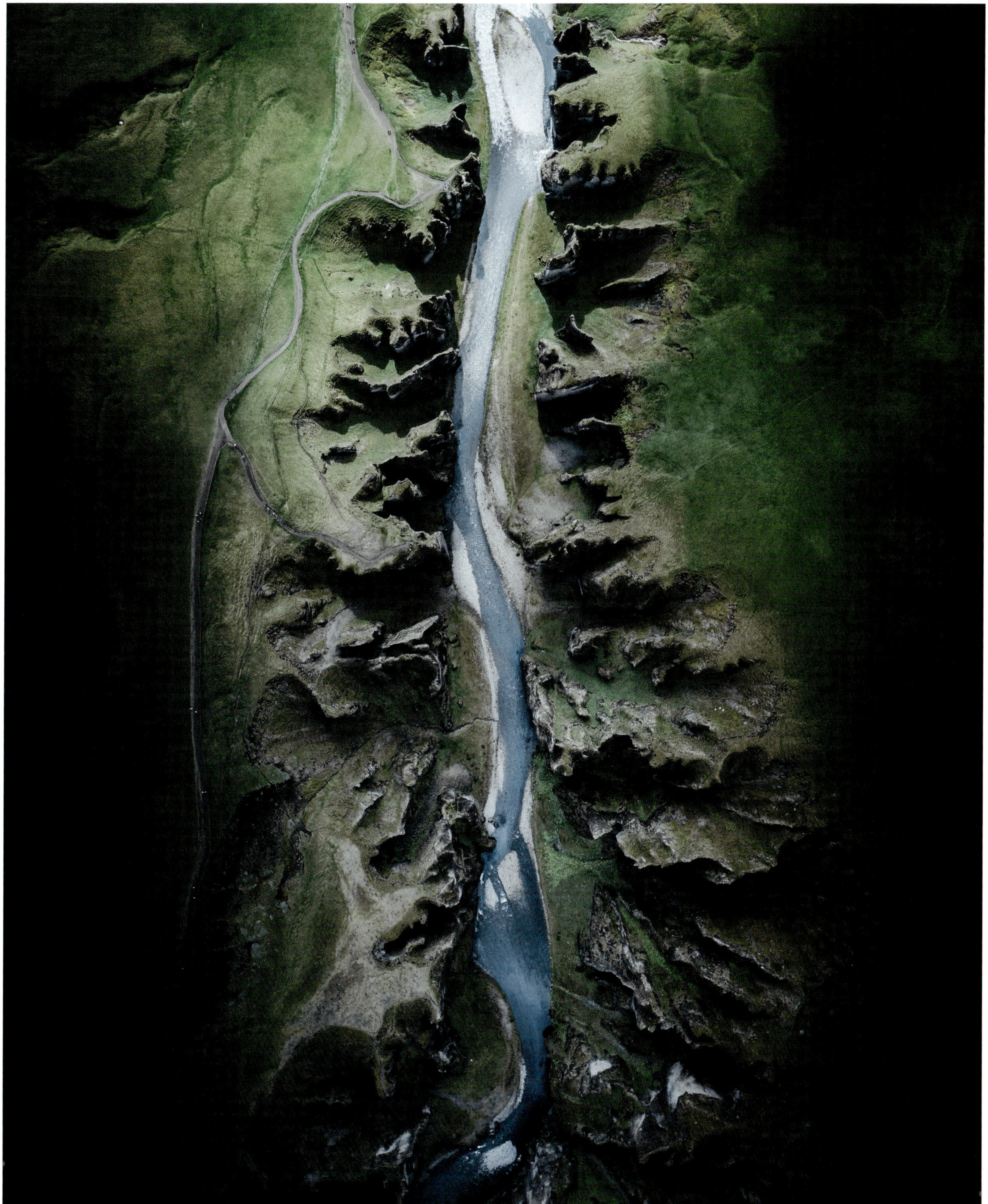

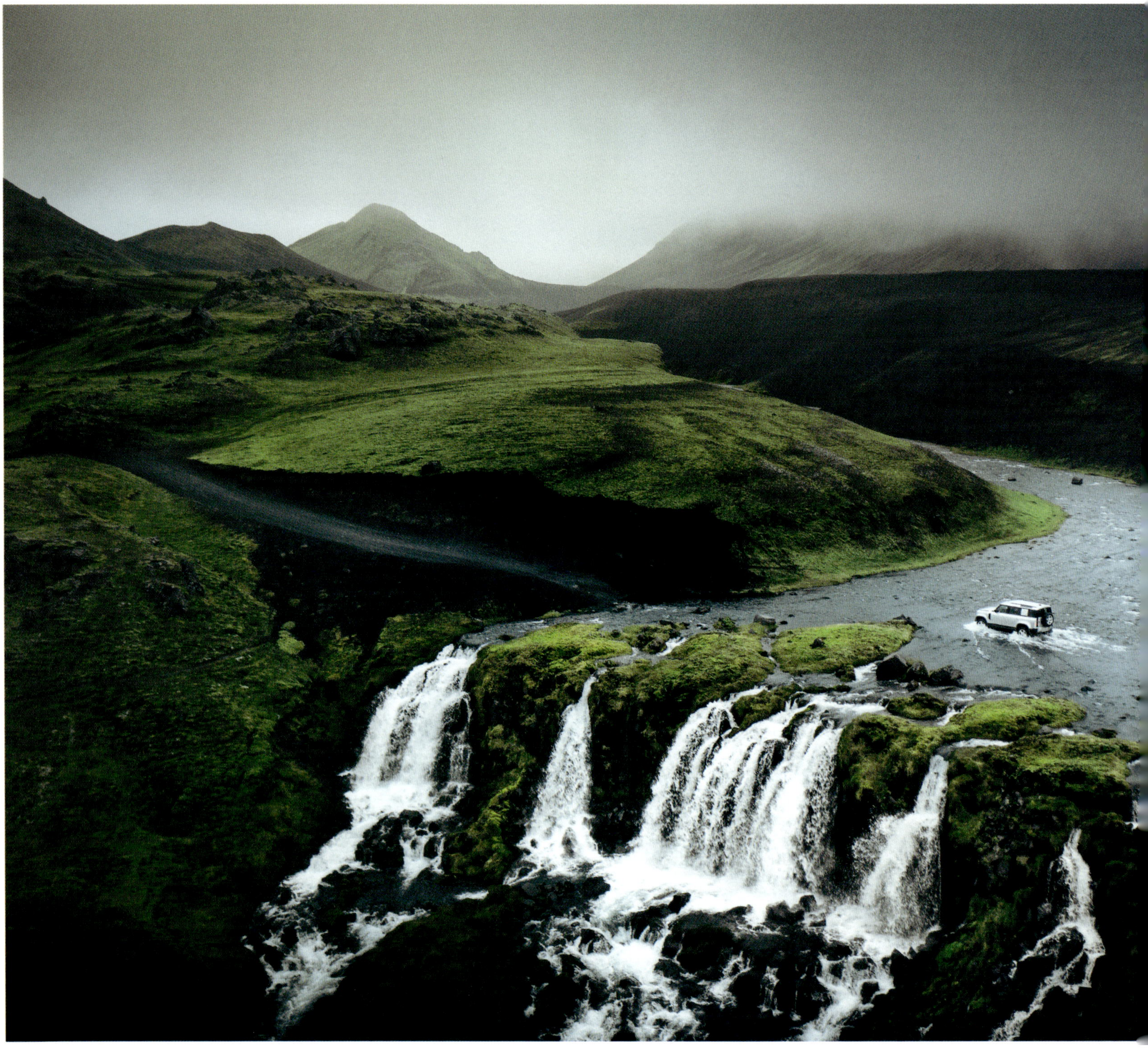

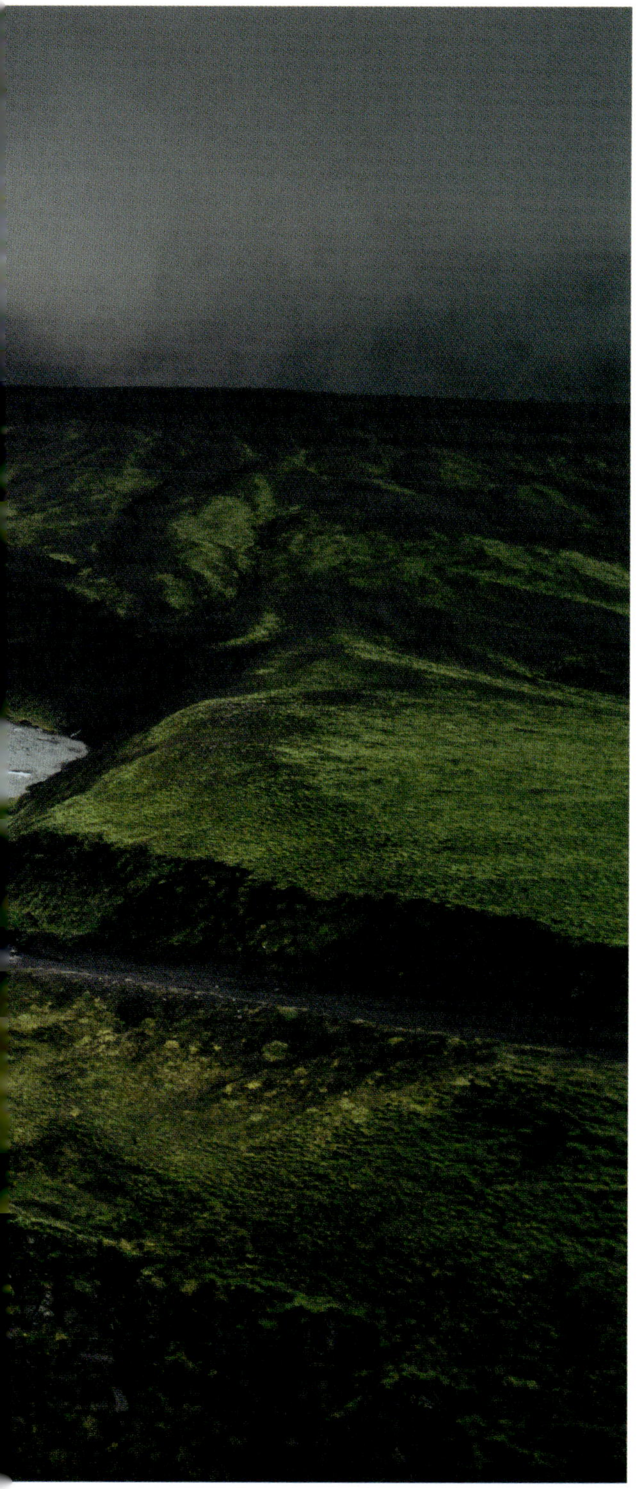

◀ THE HIGHLANDS IV

Driving off road in Iceland is highly illegal because you might run over the elves. But this is an official road, car wash included.

▼ STRÁKAR

Once, as the great protector of the fjord, this mountain would only let across the people who truly meant to make it here. Those who didn't want to risk their life for it could just sail around it instead. These days there's a tunnel, though.

▶▶ ÁLFTAVATN

It might seem like the wrong planet to look for a bar, but actually there is one by the lake on the right. Just so you know, in case you ever find a way to get there.

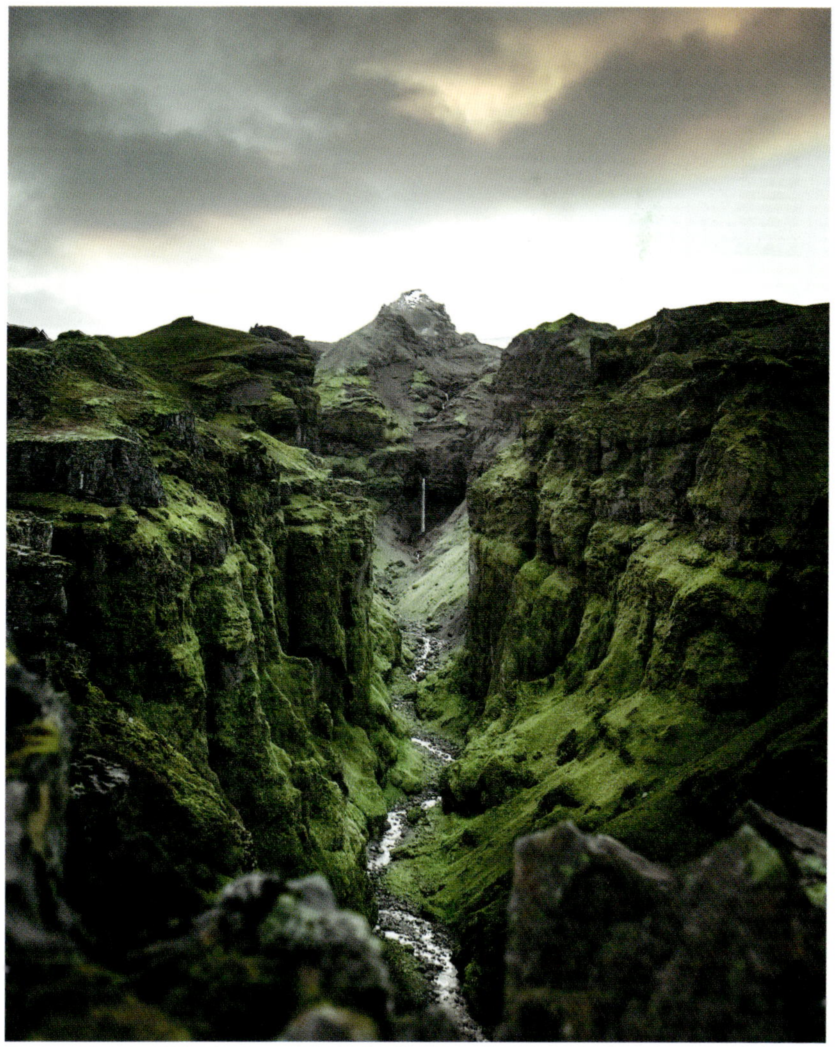

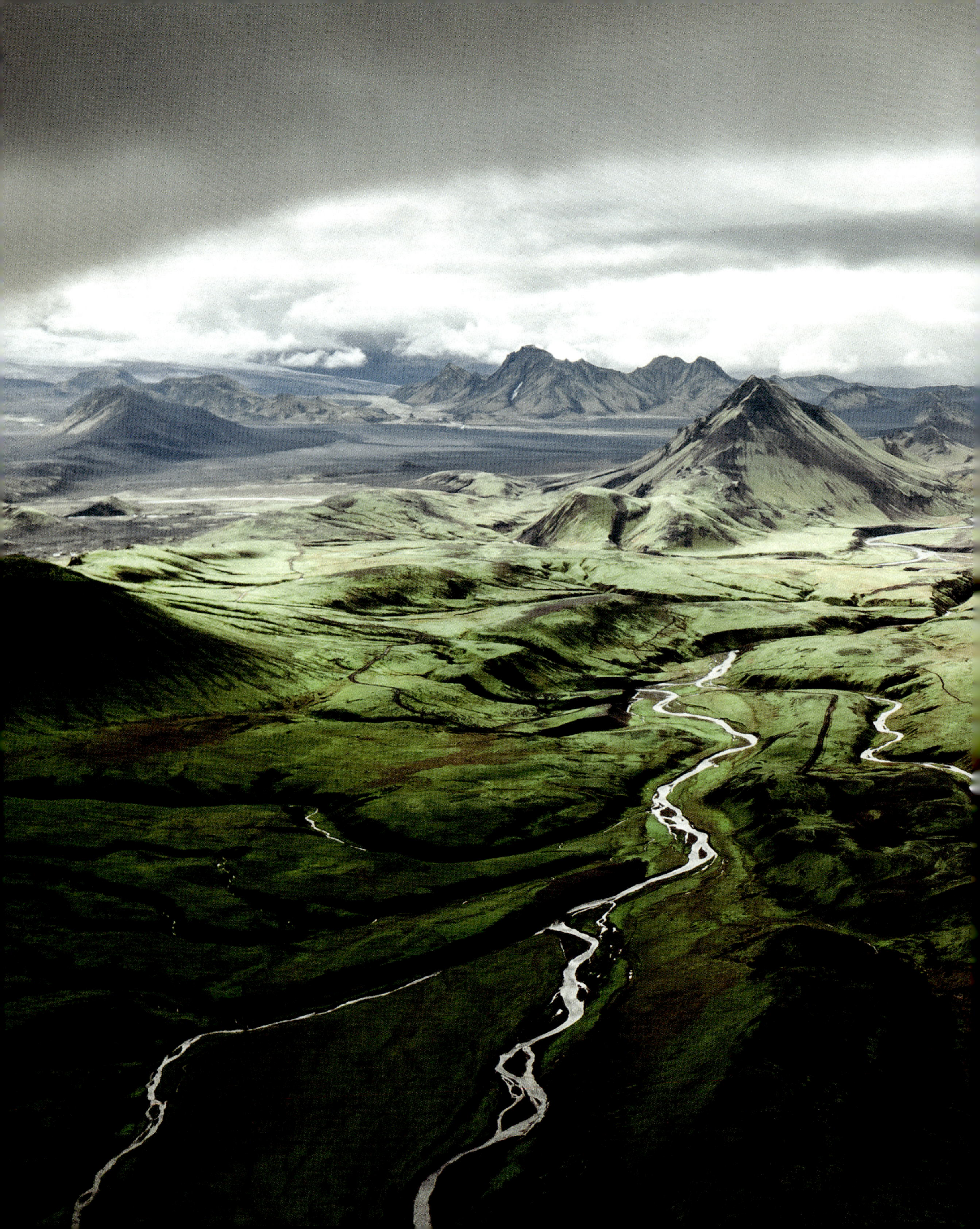

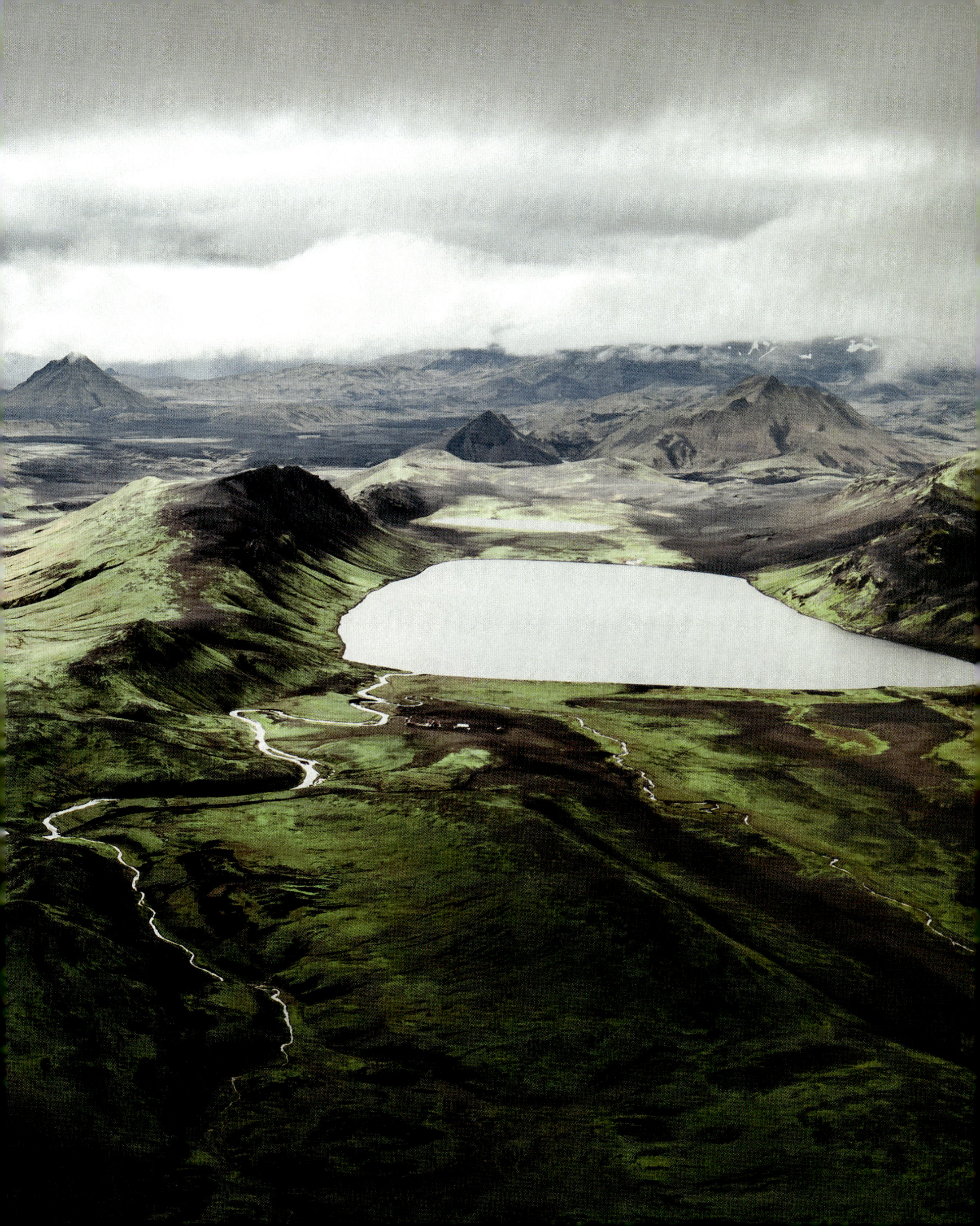

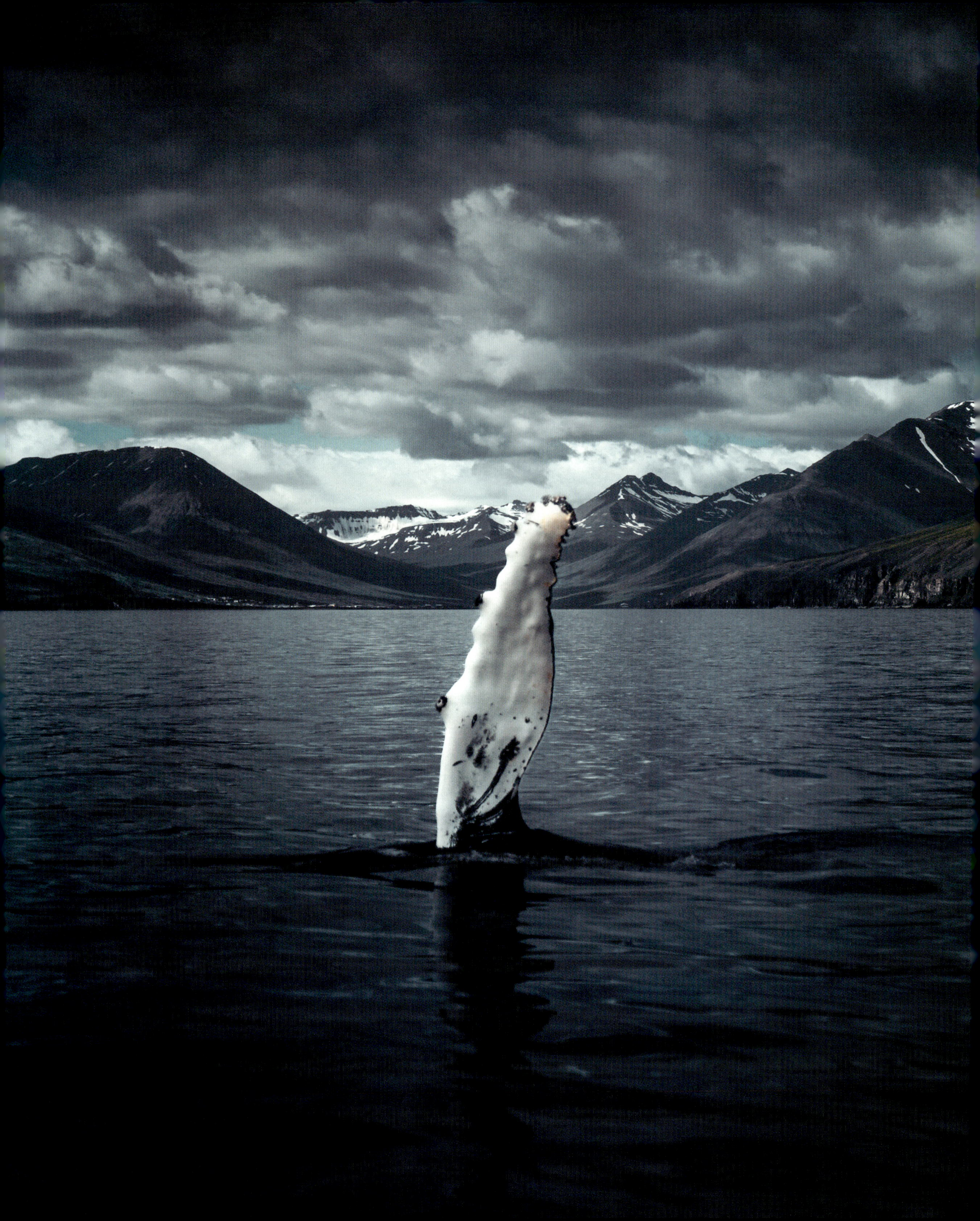

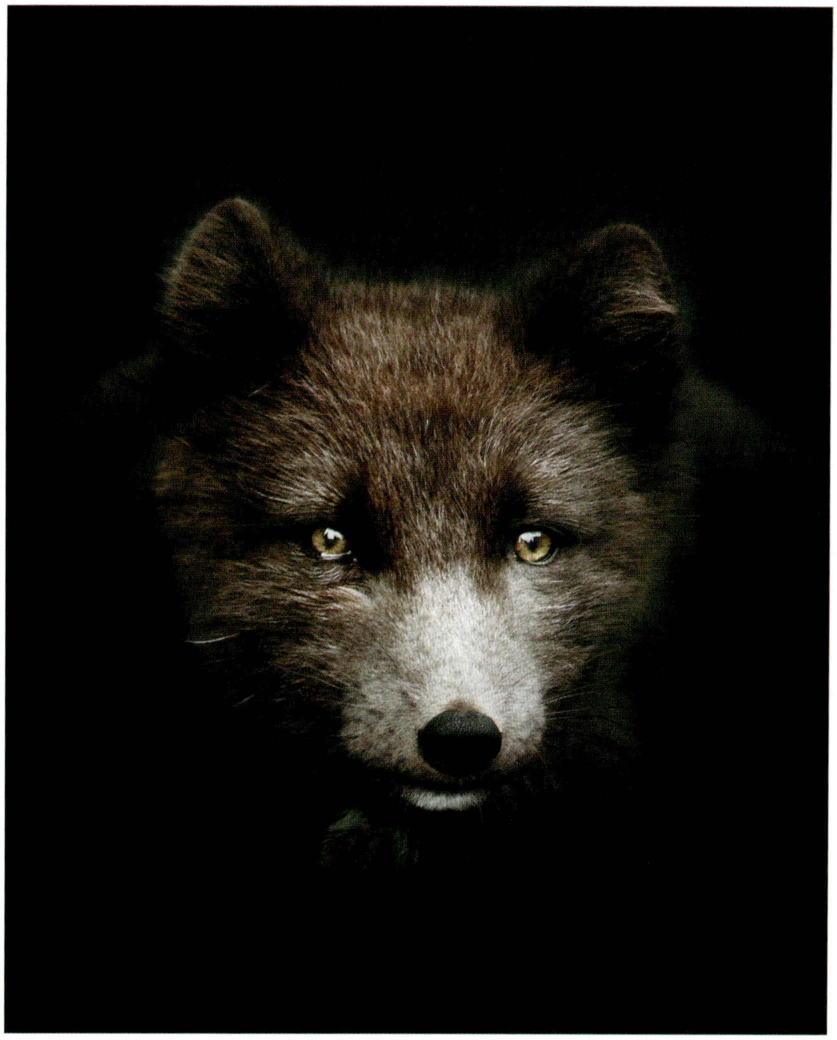

◄ EYJAFJÖRÐUR II

Just stopped by to wave hello!

▲ HORNSTRANDIR II

An arctic fox trying to figure out how much fur to grow until winter and which color to turn.

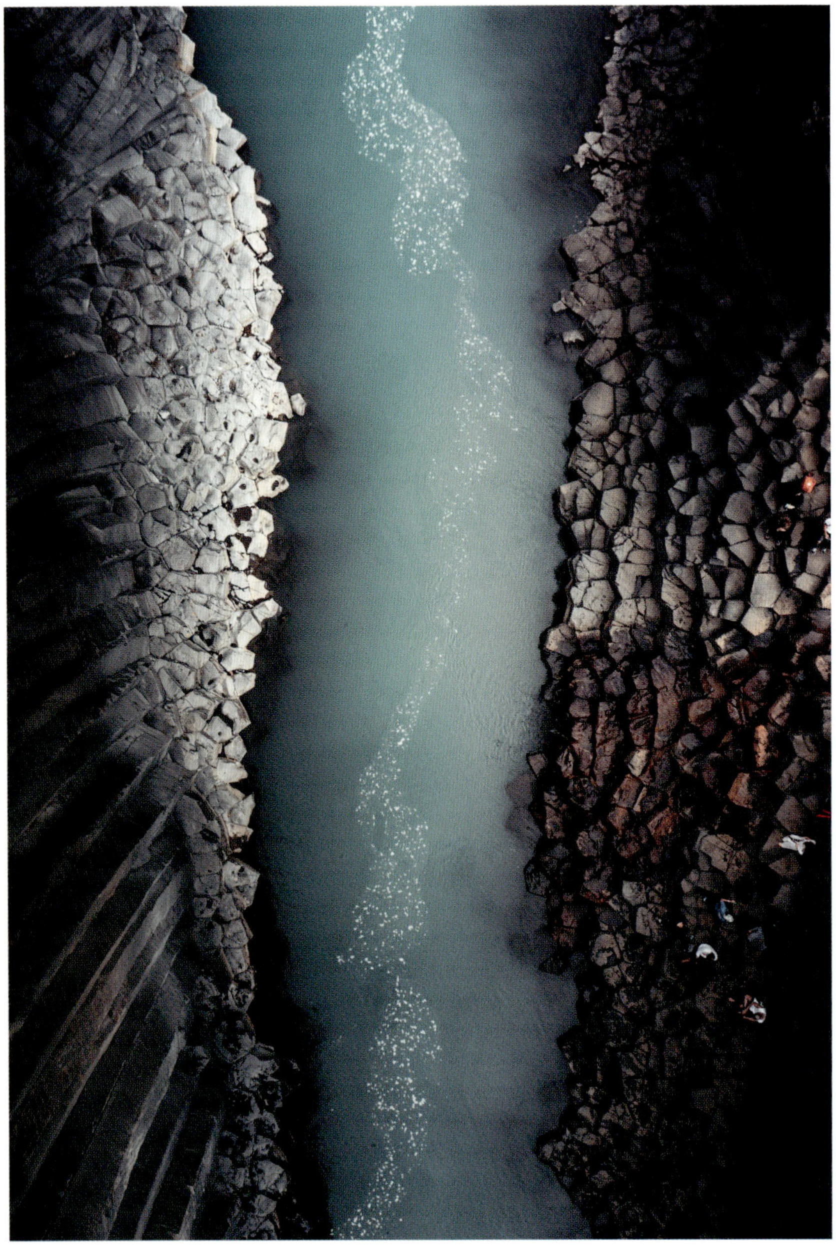

▲ STUÐLAGIL

Everything is slowly floating downstream.

➤ MÆLIFELL

Mountains are just big triangles.

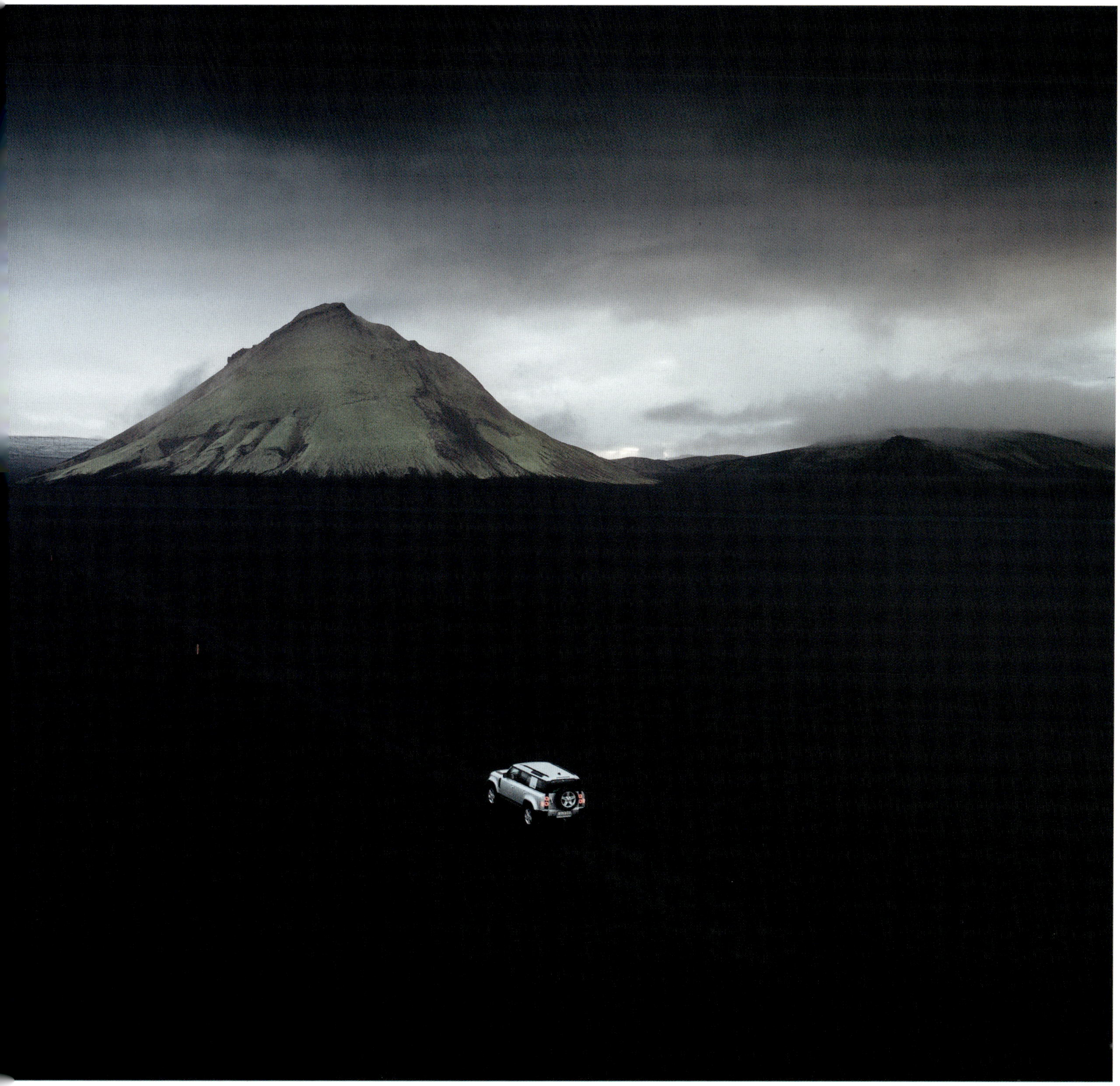

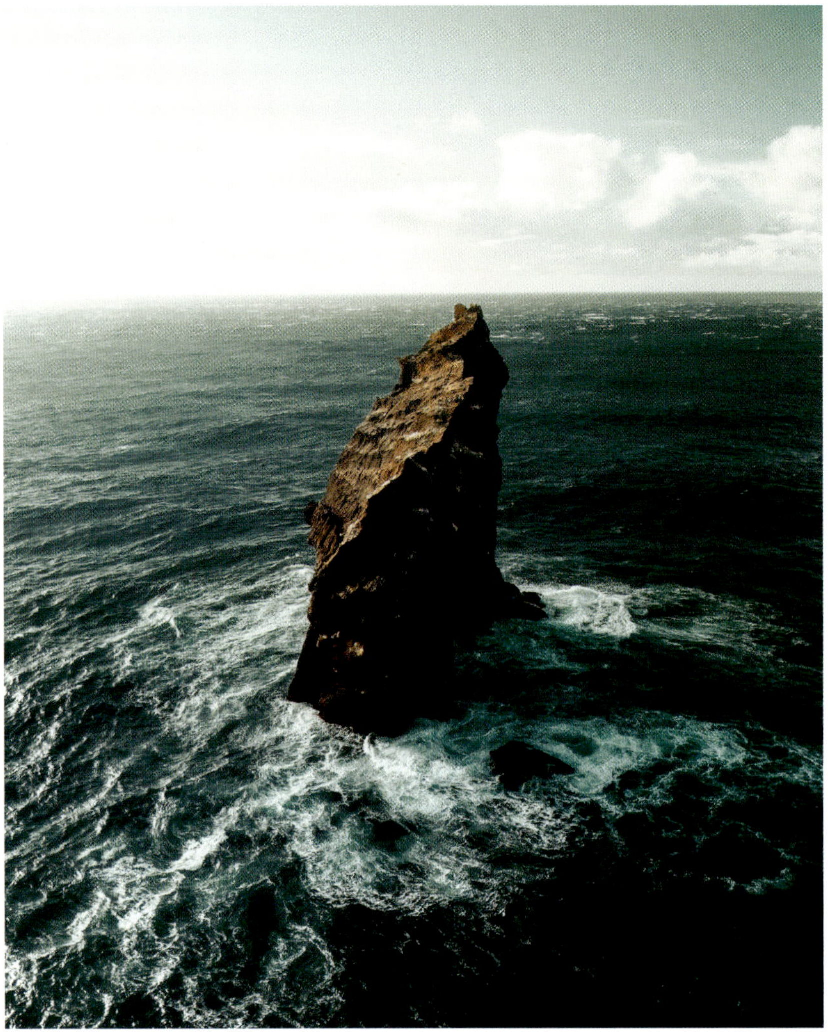

➤ REYKJANESVITI III

Nature can make us feel pretty small. But luckily it also gives us nice views so we can forget about all that existential stuff and be happy instead.

▲ REYKJANESVITI IV

The Atlantic Ocean likes Iceland. It has given us a big hug and doesn't seem to ever want to let go.

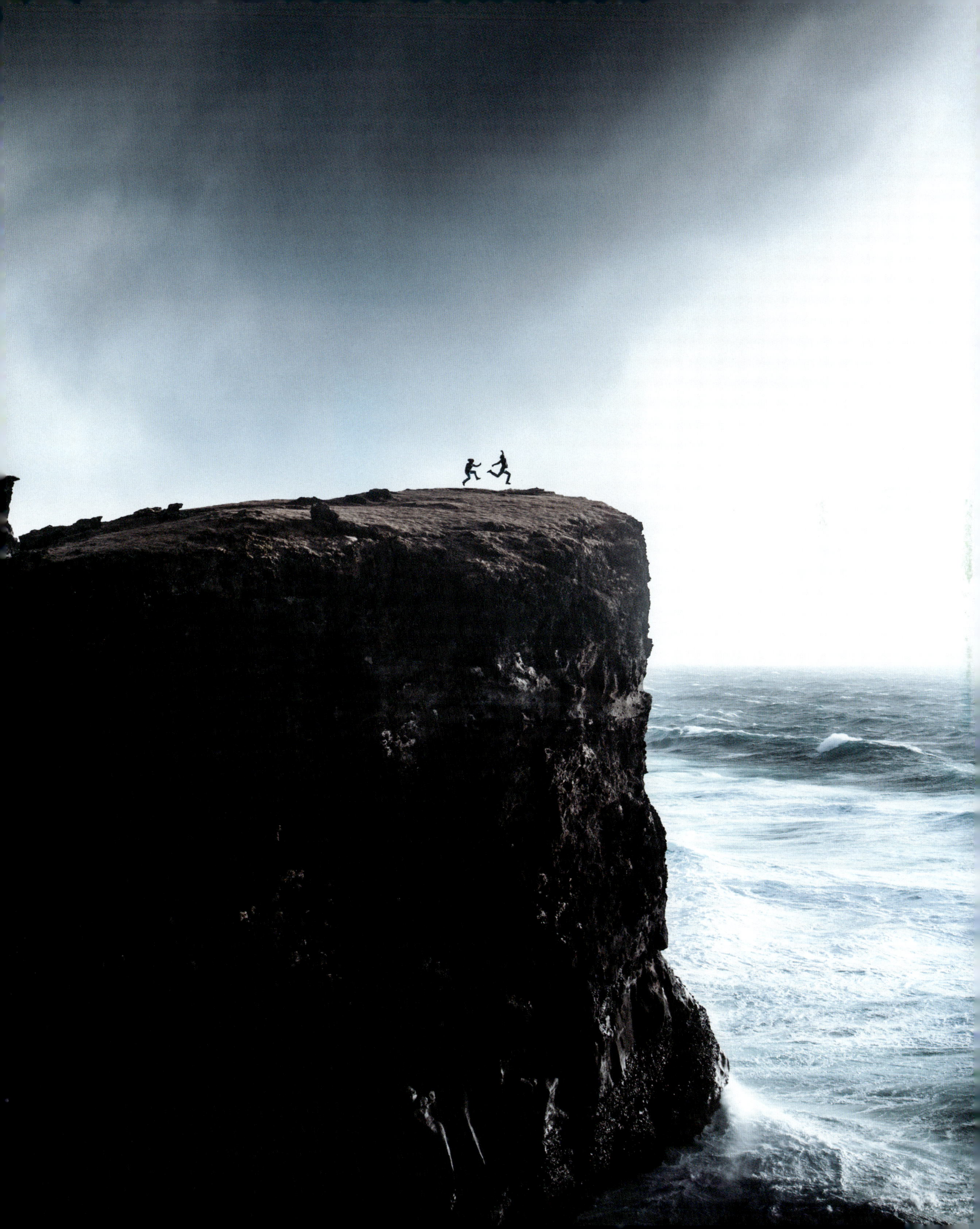

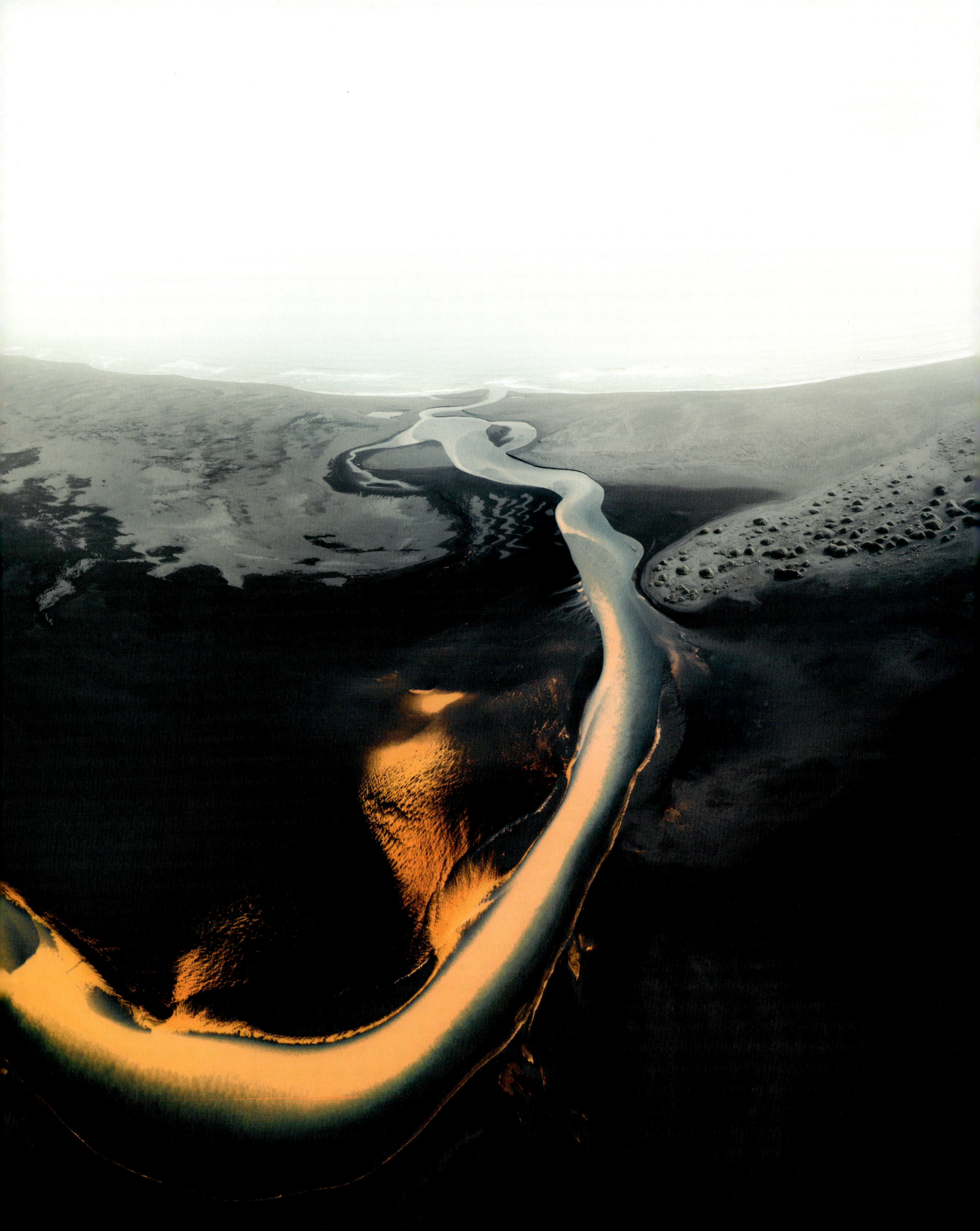

◂ ONE OF THE BLACK SAND BEACHES

A river trying to color the ocean gold but only managing to make itself look special.

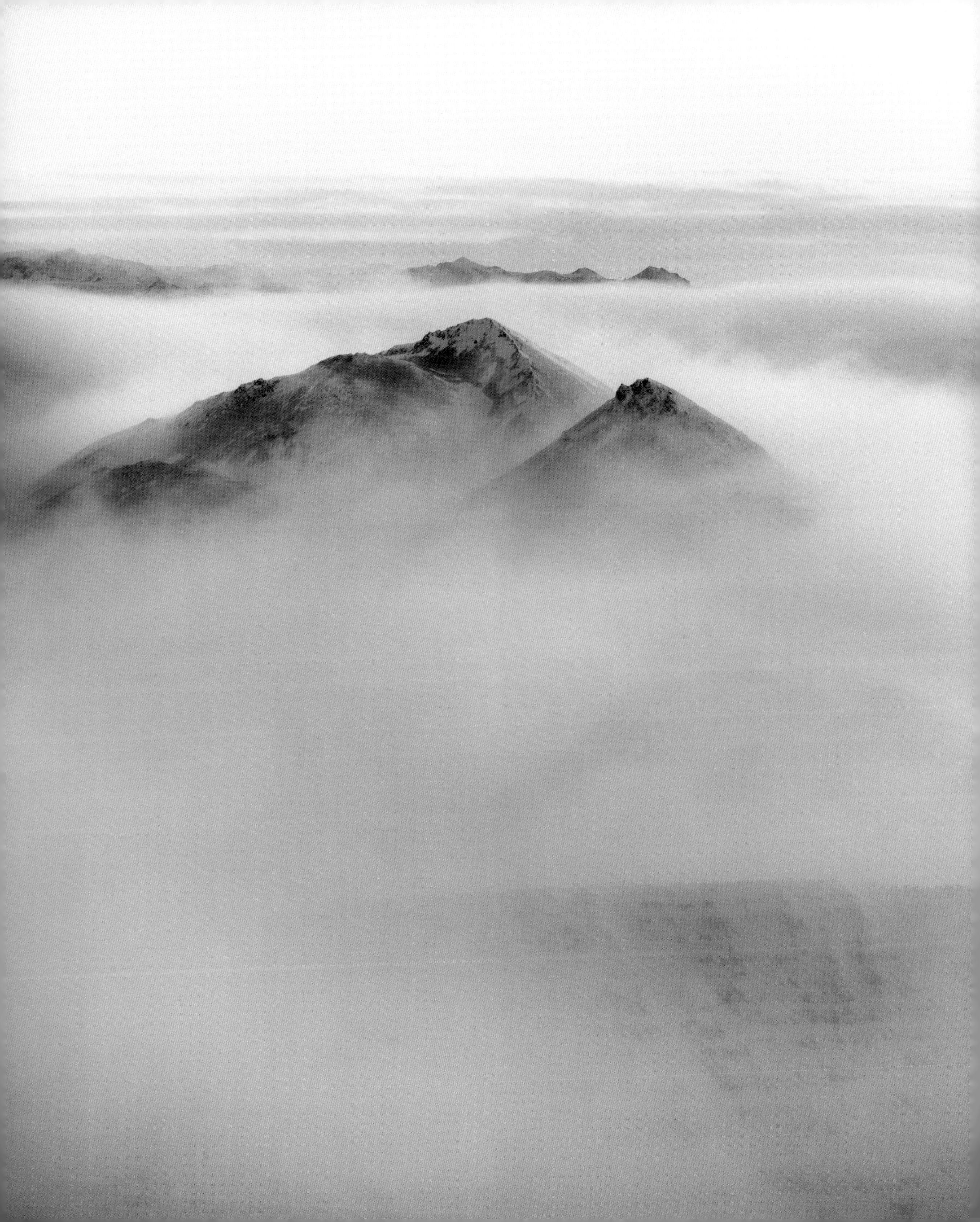

THE SOFT DRAMA OF RETREAT

September and October

Fog has finally reached its destination. Moss puts on its emotional glow. Light slants in with cinematic confidence—this is the angle it was looking for all summer. The weather is bipolar again, even more than before. Everything is mildly heartbreaking, and that's just how we like it.

Retreat isn't collapse. It's the exhale before the quiet. And somewhere in these waning months, for a brief second, Iceland achieves something that most would call balance.

Winter may feel too slow and summer too fast, but it takes exactly this long to reach our short-lived equilibrium, every time.

It was at this time of year that I first came to Iceland. I didn't yet understand the collective hangover from the long summer, or the weight behind the question of whether to stay through the winter. After all, I thought I had only come for a few months.

Photos taken this time of year come out too good without any effort. The landscapes wear their emotions on the outside and tell us all their stories. The weather comes wrapped in packages, with the sky delivering each new gift openly so you can prepare your layers. (Or wait five minutes for the next delivery.)

This is the season when it all lines up. It's still warm enough to stay out for hours at a time, the modest rain has chased the peak crowds away, and the highlands haven't been snowed in yet but only the locals still dare to go see them. There's time to be out, but the occasional storm provides an excuse to stay in and clean up the messes of personal life.

In this season of balance, we can grow a full appreciation for everything and everyone around us. We've journeyed together through extremes and arrived at this state of just-right, of true well-being.

But we know it won't last. We're already nostalgic for this exact moment.

◂◂ ESJA

Can you call it sightseeing if you can't see anything?

▸ HVALNESTANGI

This mountain grew too good looking, then found that it didn't like all the attention. So, it hid its face in the clouds.

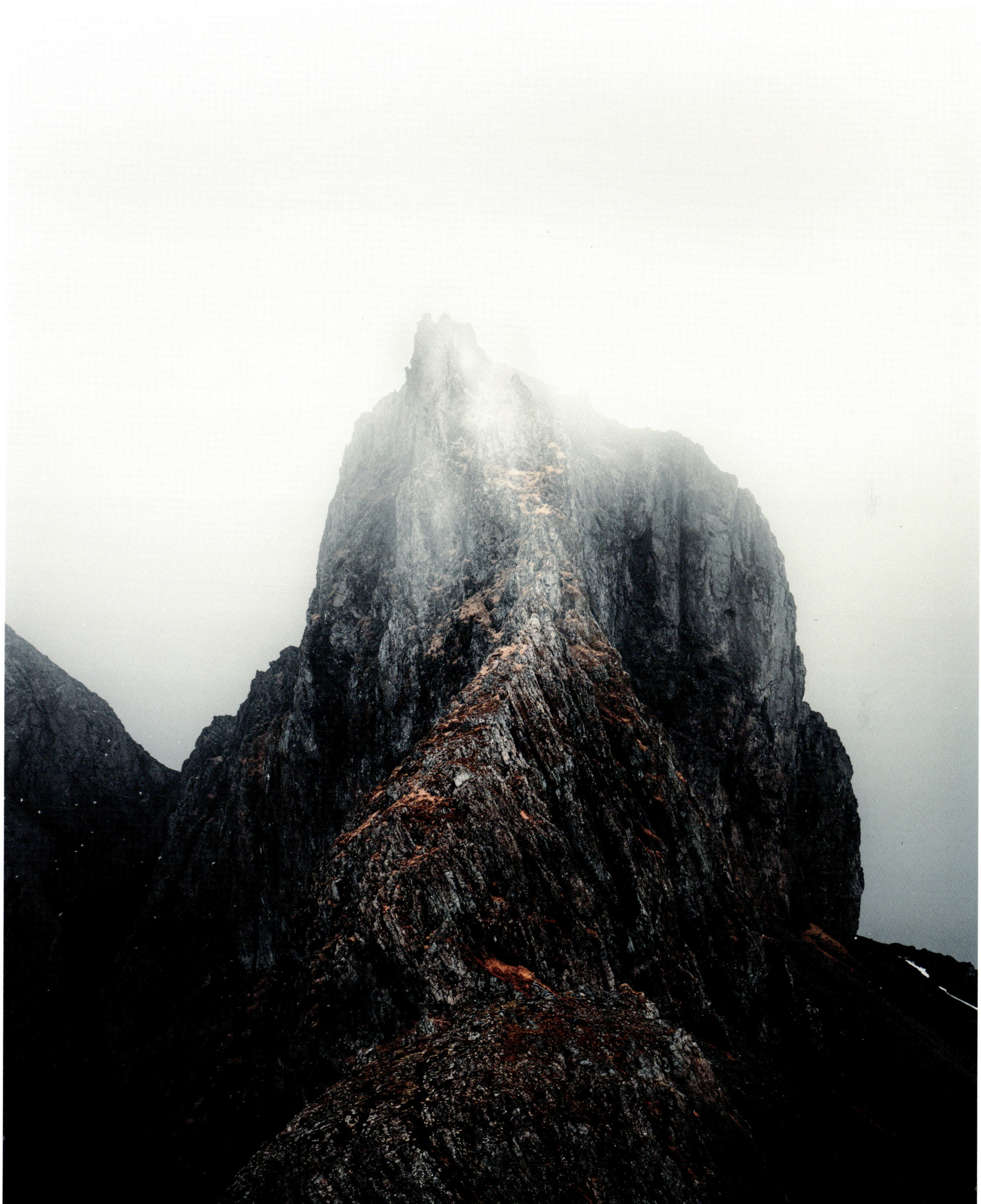

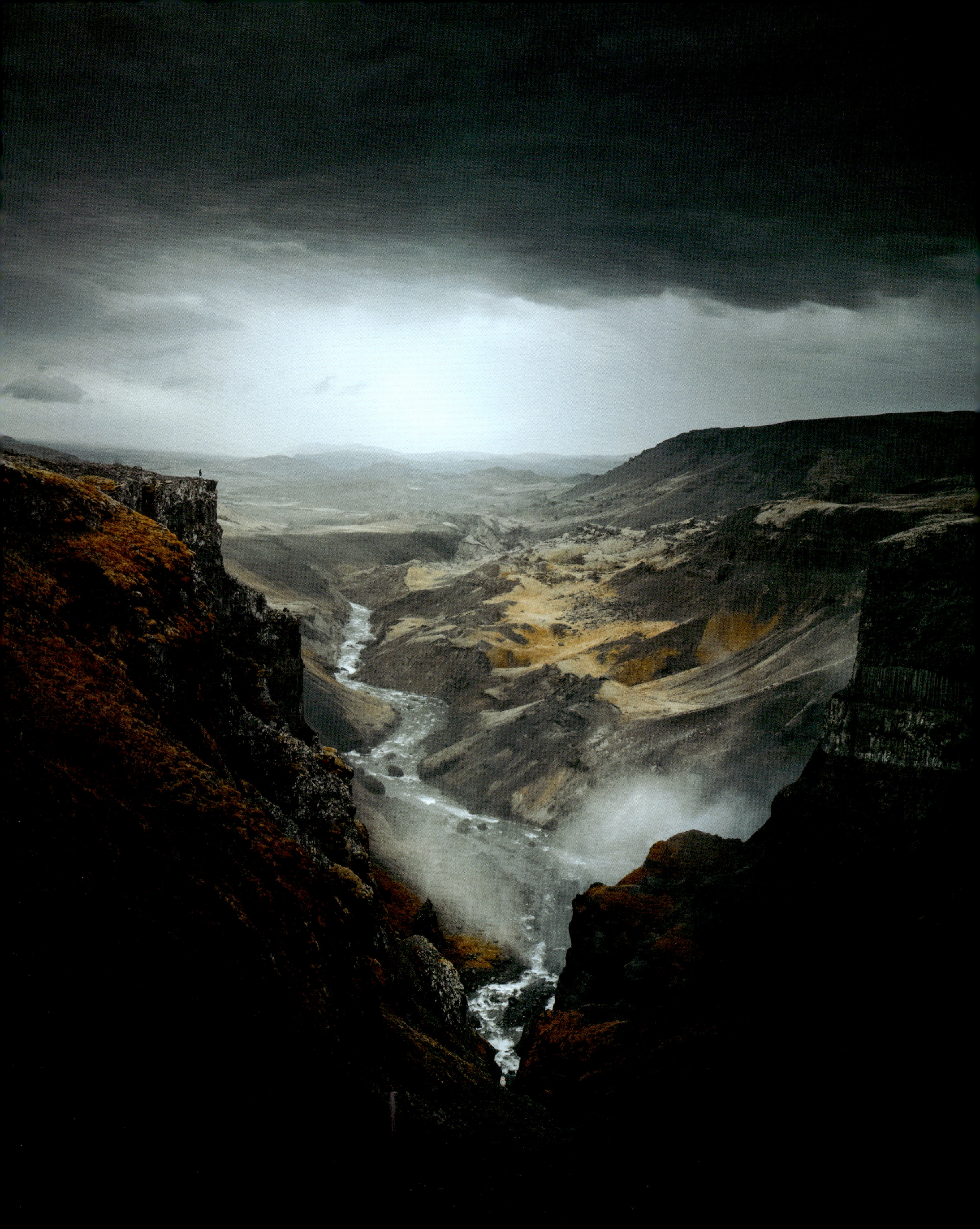

◄ HÁIFOSS II

Sometimes you just have to take a step back and let the moment in. It's also a great way to stay a healthy distance from the edge of this canyon.

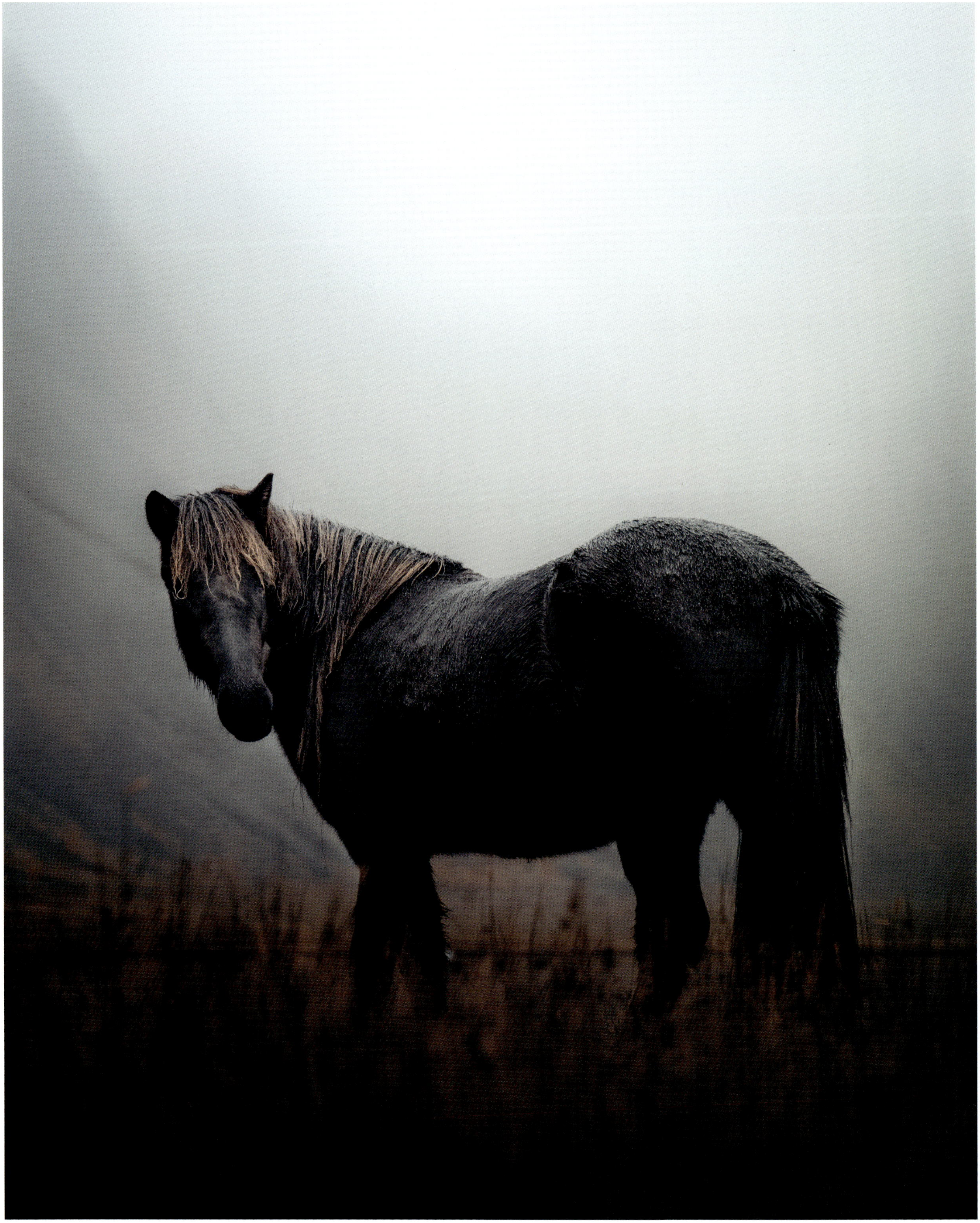

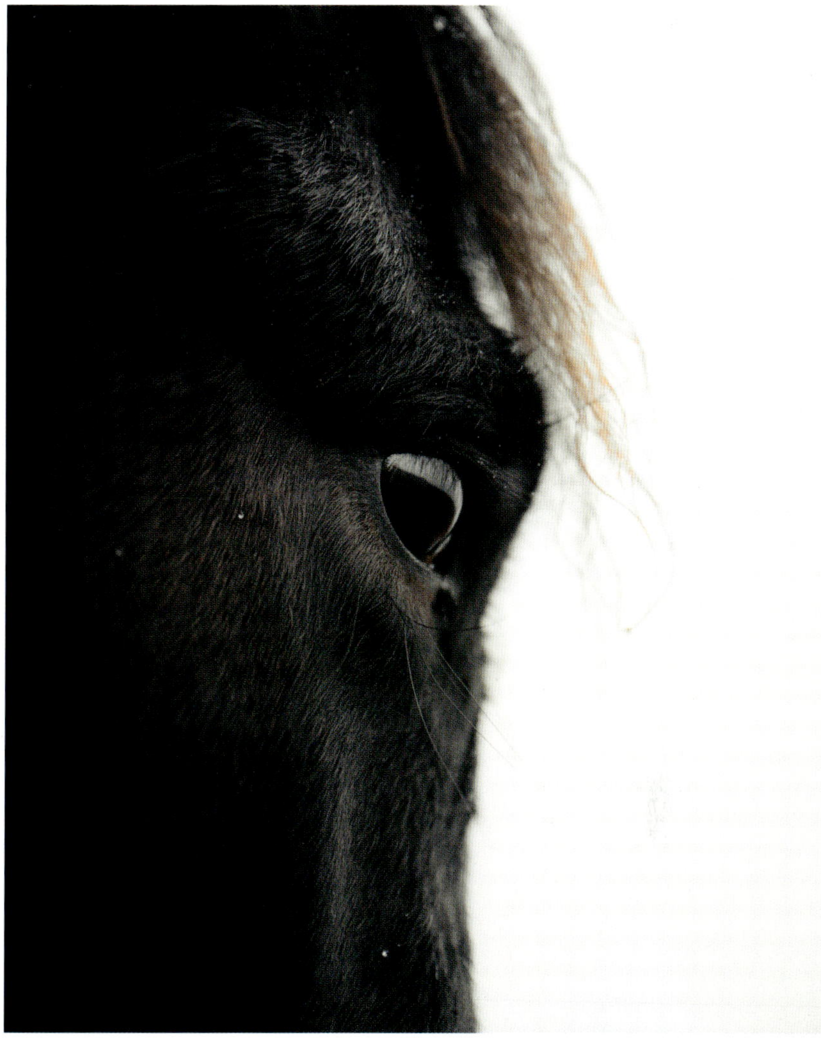

SOMEWHERE COLD

Icelandic horses prefer the cold because they like it when their hairs freeze and go all sparkly.

ANOTHER COLD PLACE

An eye that has seen more storms than any human would survive, thanks to the best shelter: thick fur and a big butt to block out the wind.

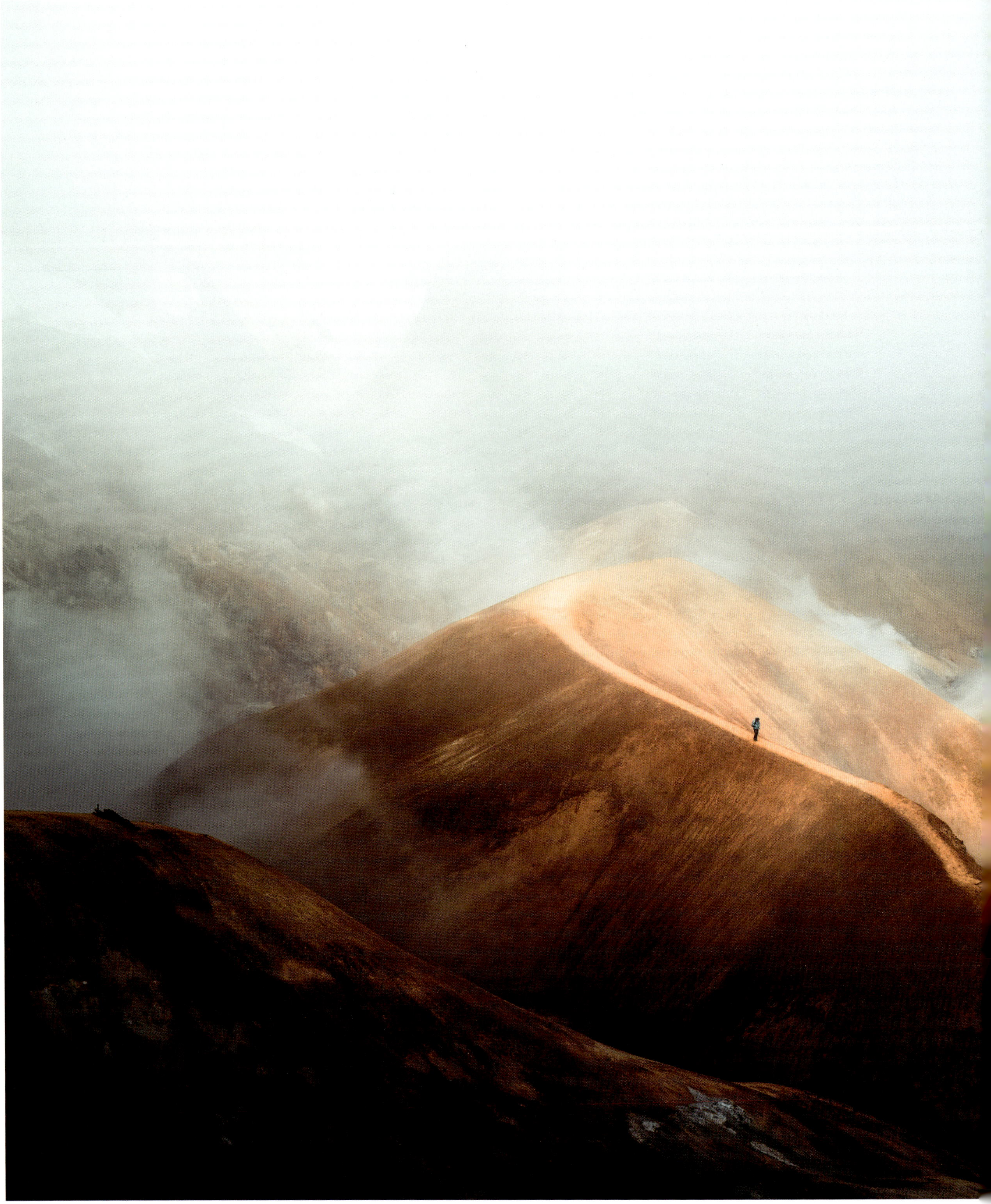

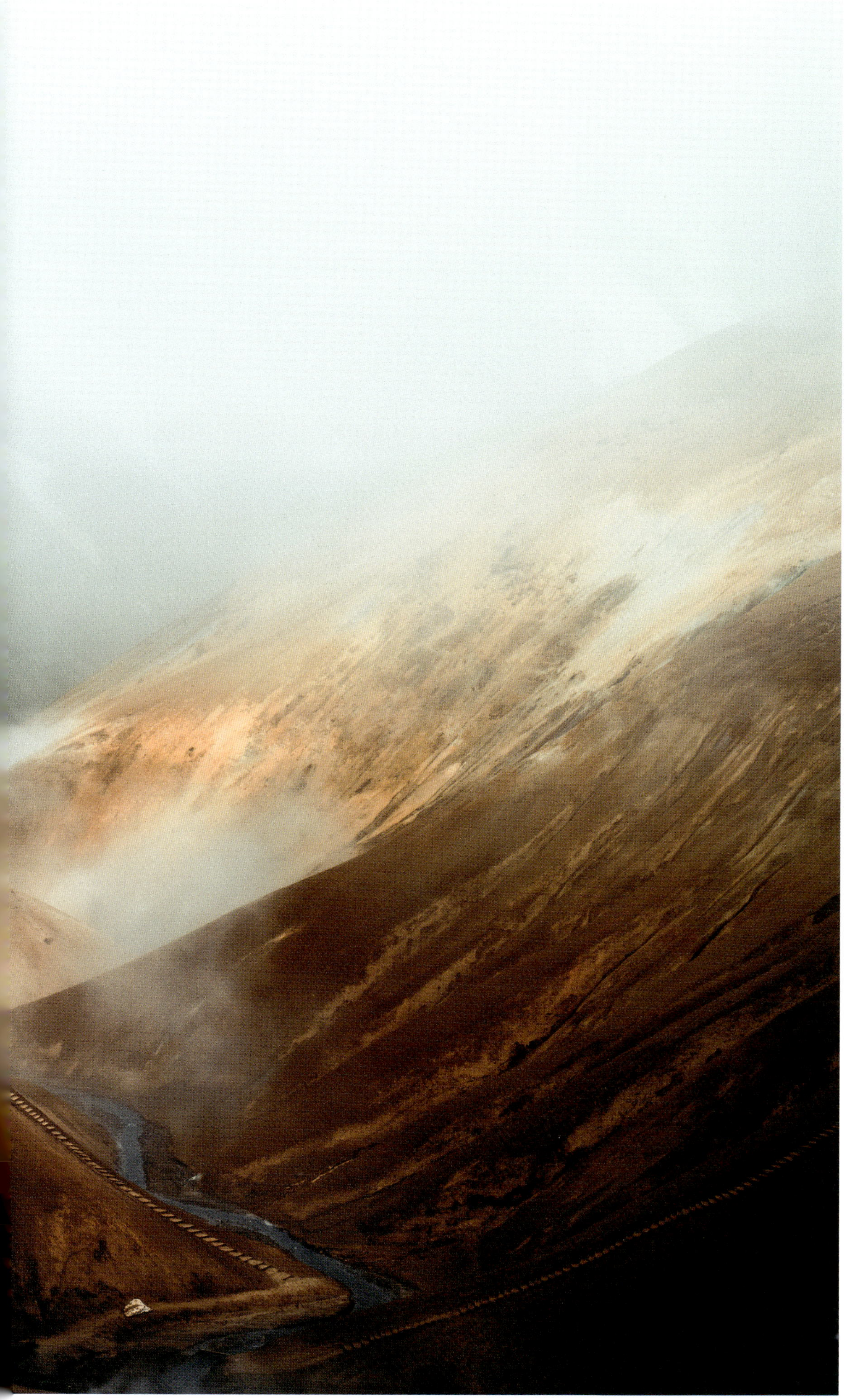

KERLINGARFJÖLL II

Fog-ography is always changing. You just have to accept it and work with it out here.

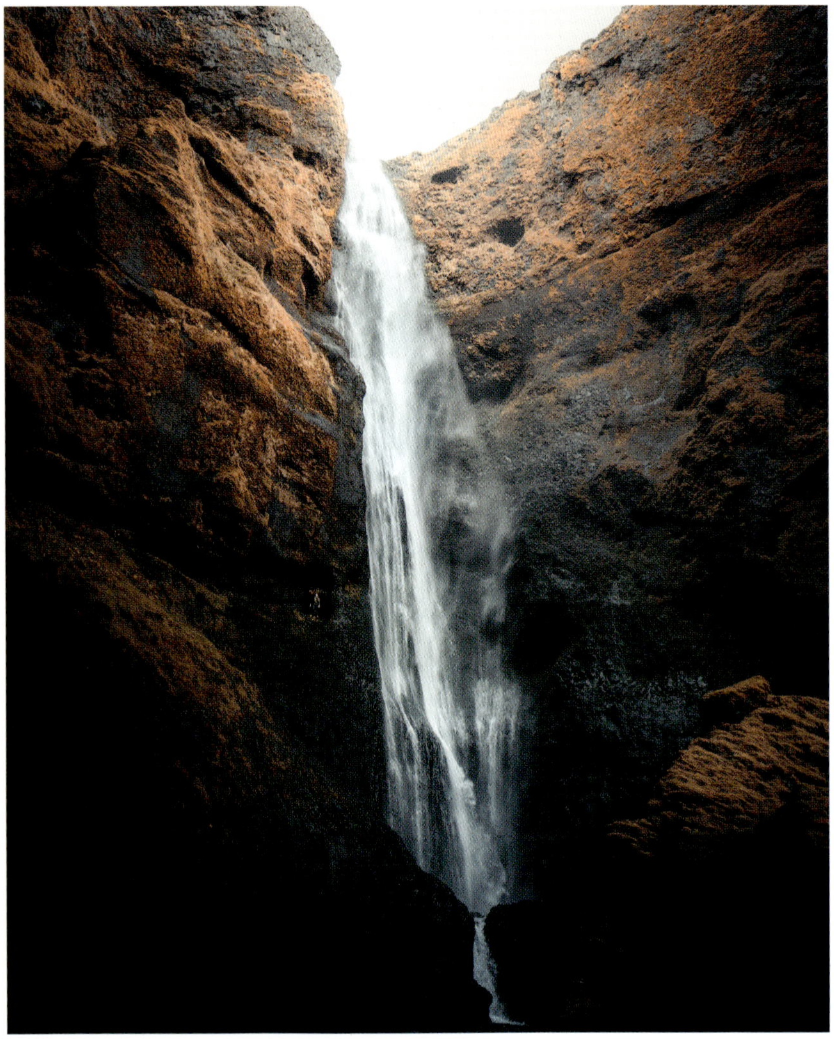

▲ ÞÓRSMÖRK

The waterfalls here fall many Icelandic meters every day just to look good for us. Support their cause by taking a moment to be amazed.

➤ THE FOREST

It's taken me hundreds of years to finally nail this shot of an Icelandic forest. First, I had to gather all the trees in Iceland, get them to stay upright through all the storms, and then paint every leaf I could reach with my own hands. I can only hope it's appreciated and that I haven't caused anyone too much trouble by blocking their views.

➤➤ ÞÓRSMÖRK II

This land was struck by the hammer of Thor, opening up all these crying canyons.

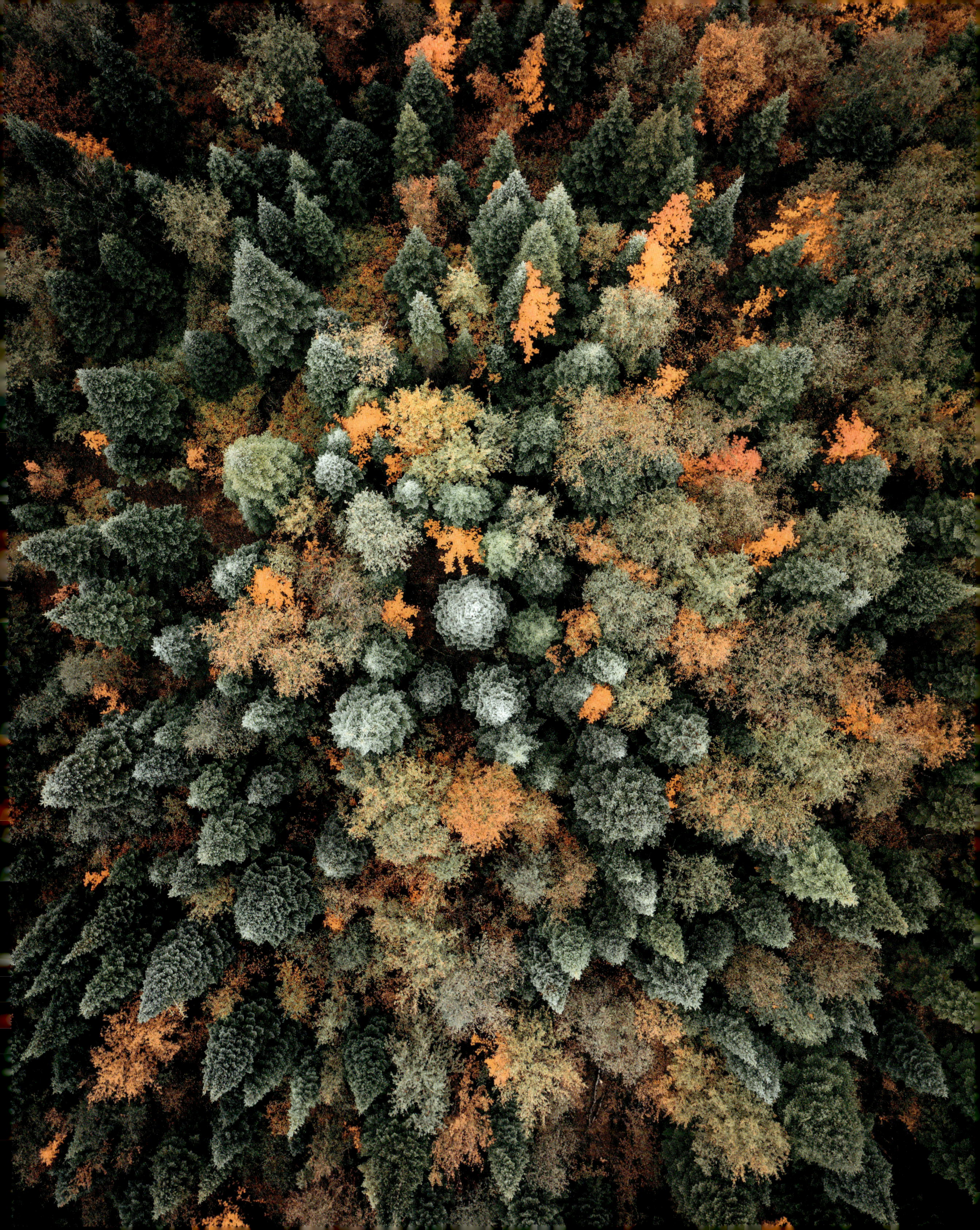

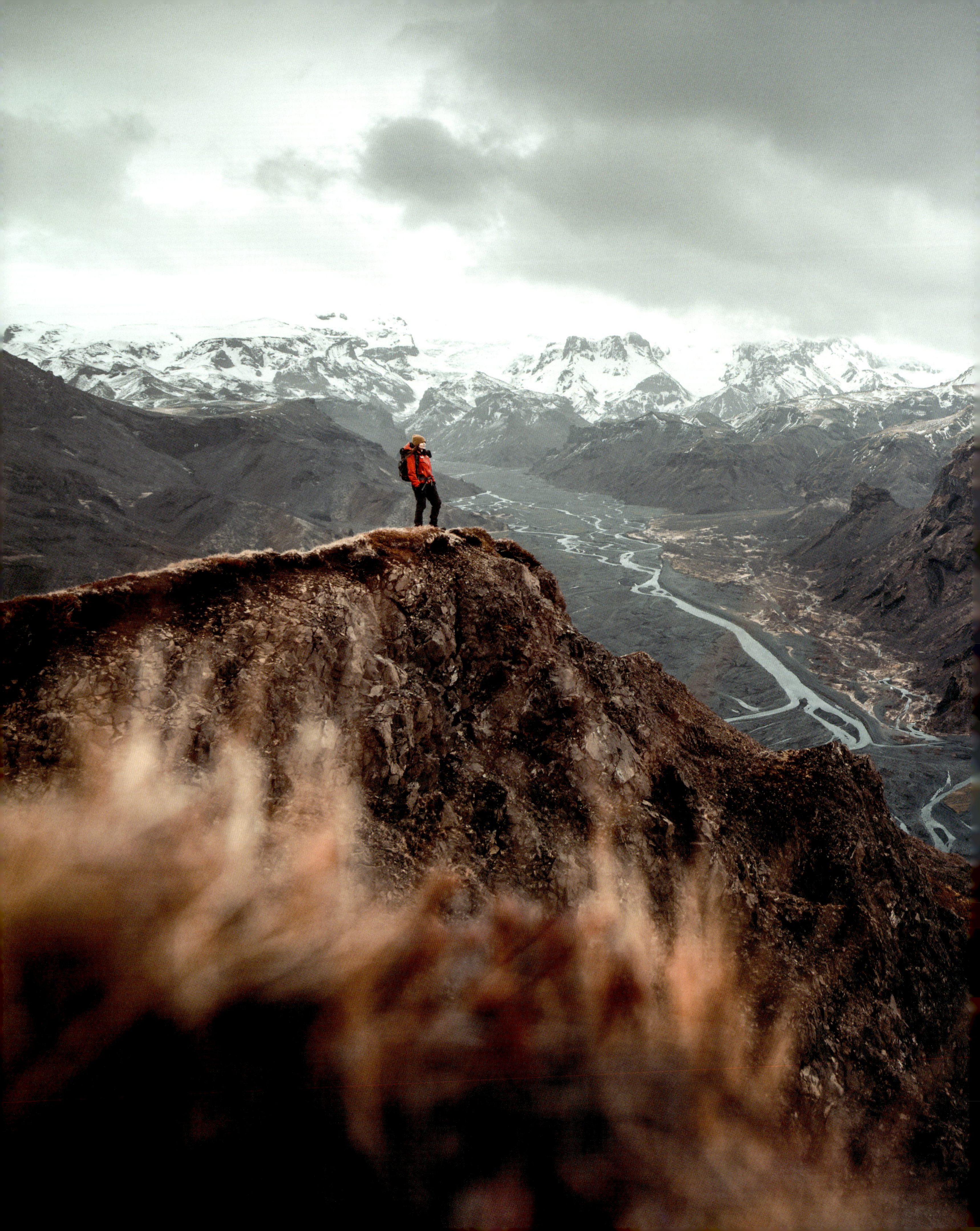

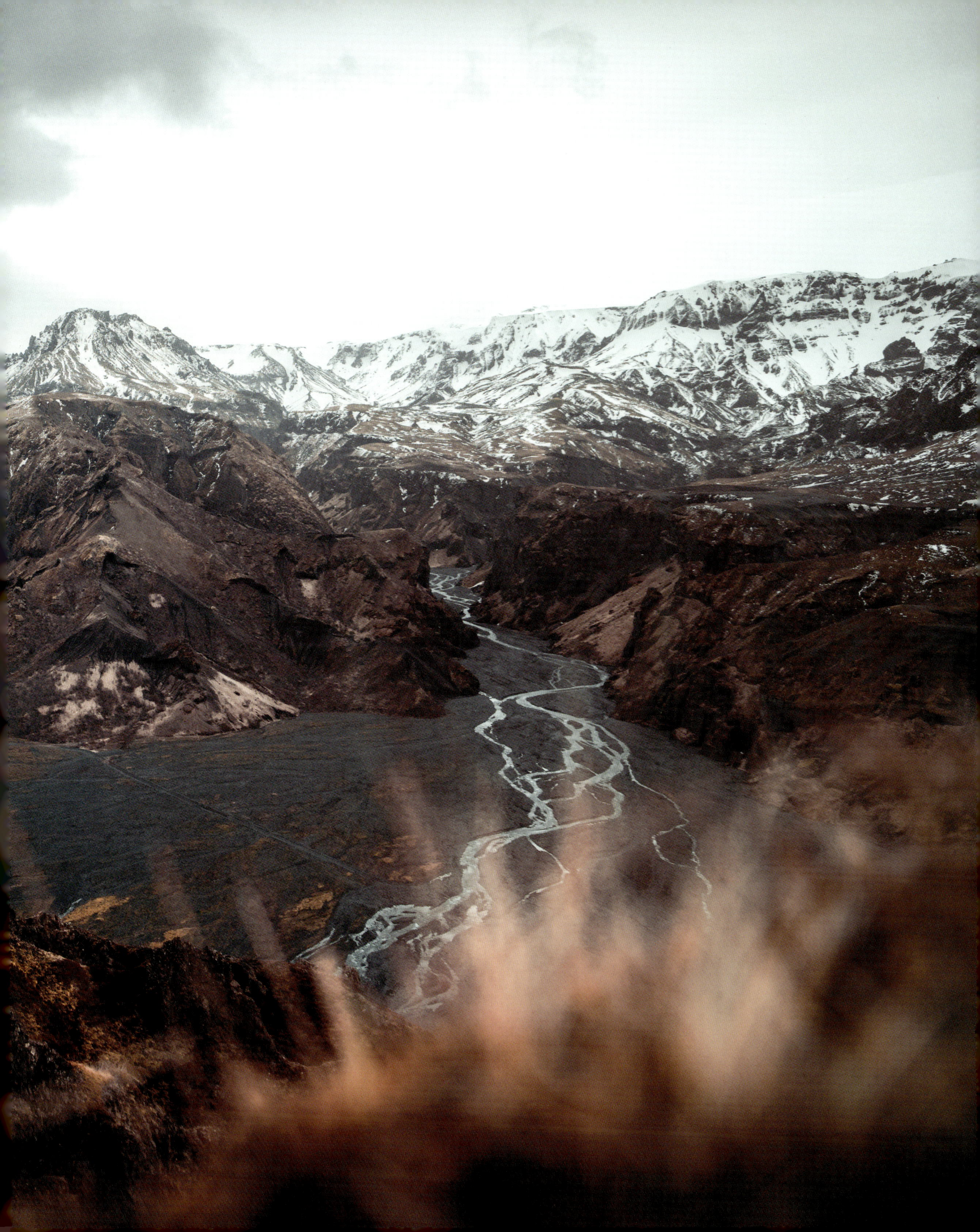

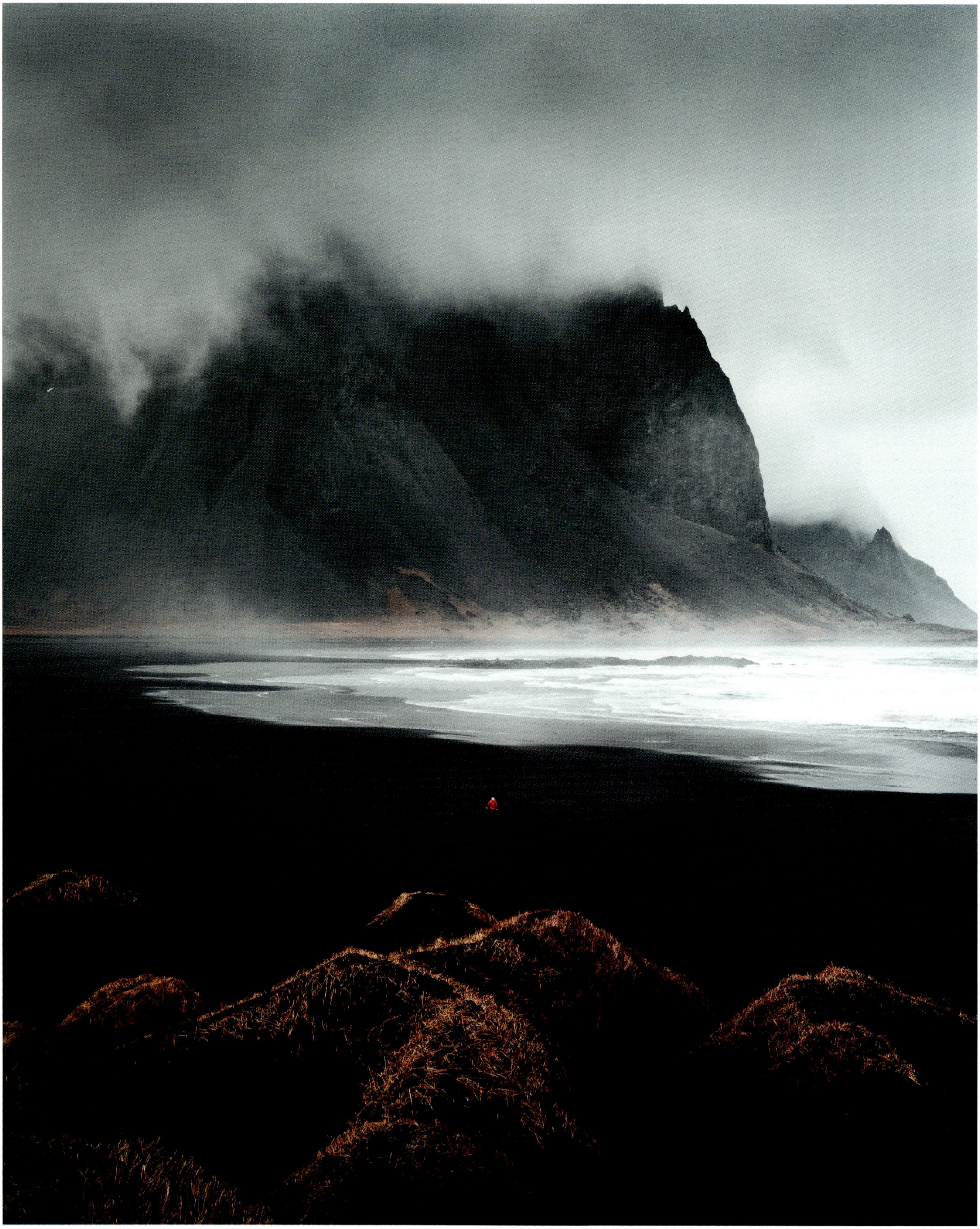

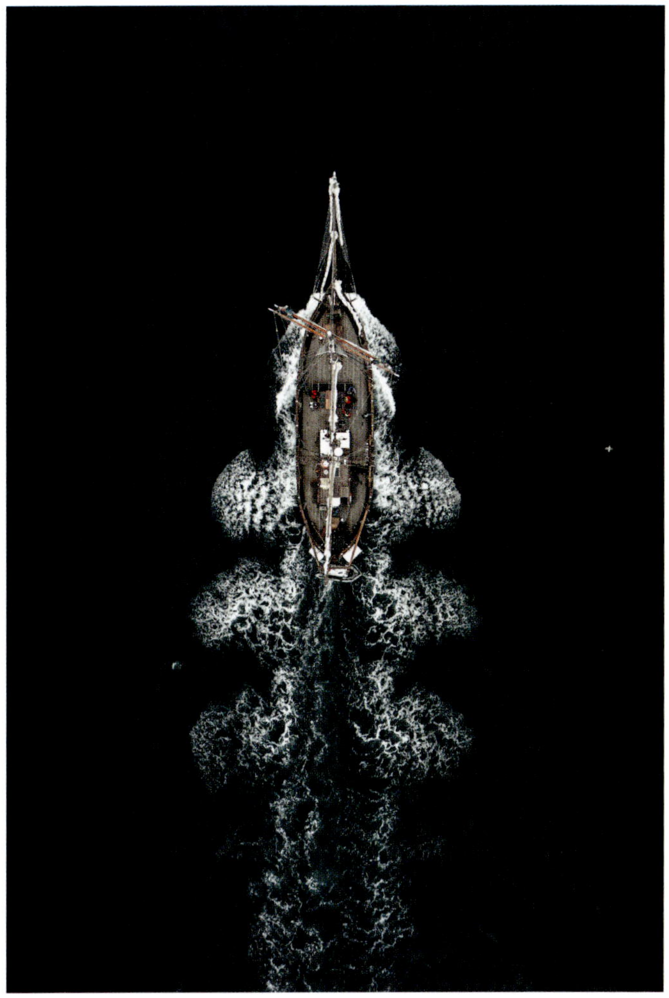

▲ OPAL

Using our sailboat as a temporary paintbrush to paint the seas with a dance.

◄ VESTRAHORN VIII

Every now and then a photo needs a person to stand in a red jacket and act like there is nothing more important in the world than staring at the scenery.

►► SVÖRTULOFT (L)

The ocean tried to climb a cliff but the lighthouse stood its ground to defend it.

►► THE HIGHLANDS V (R)

Icelandic waterfalls grew tall back in the wet ages so they could drown the little Vikings when Ragnarök finally came around. They never figured out how to move, though, so now you can get pretty close to them without them hurting you.

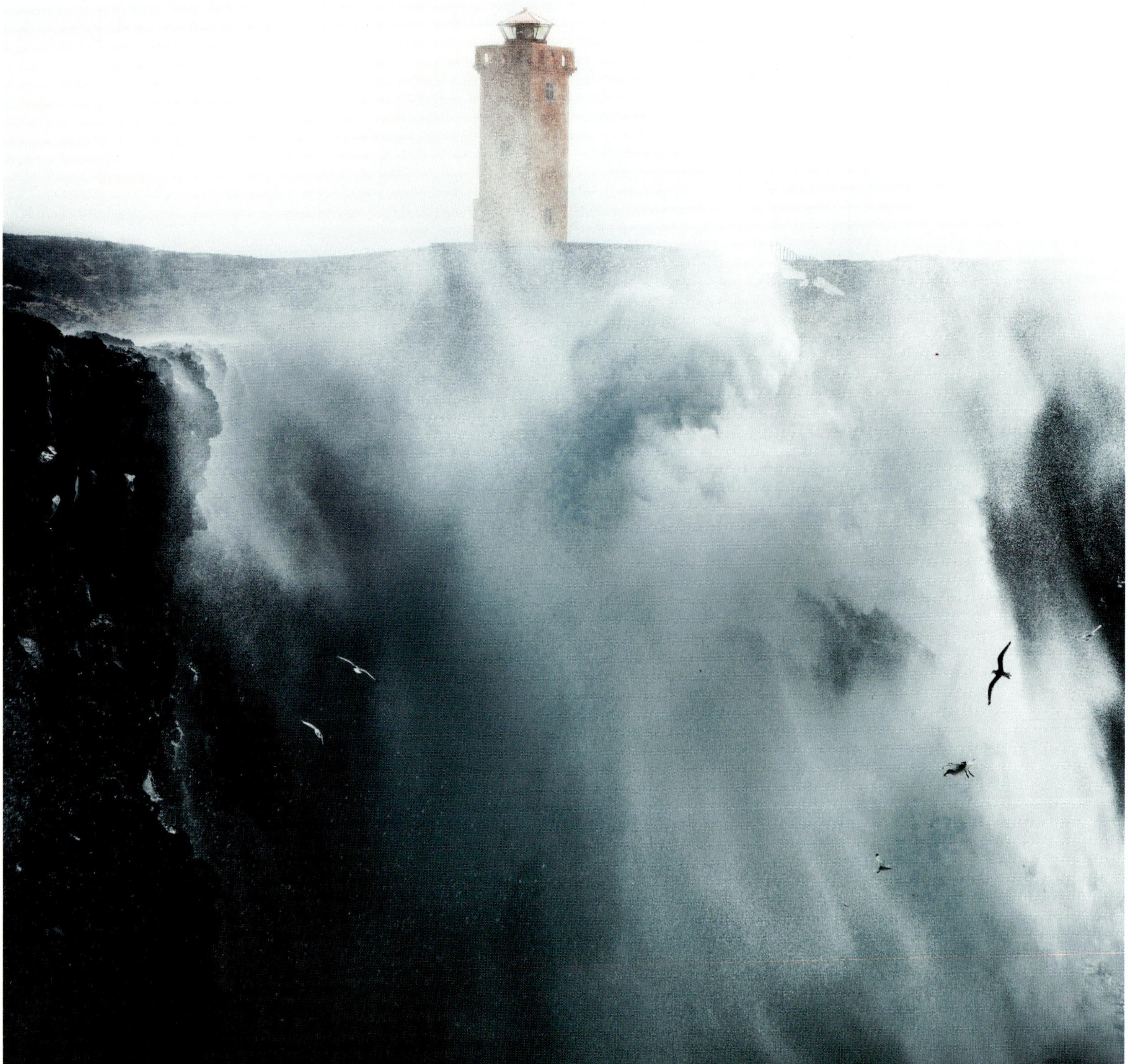

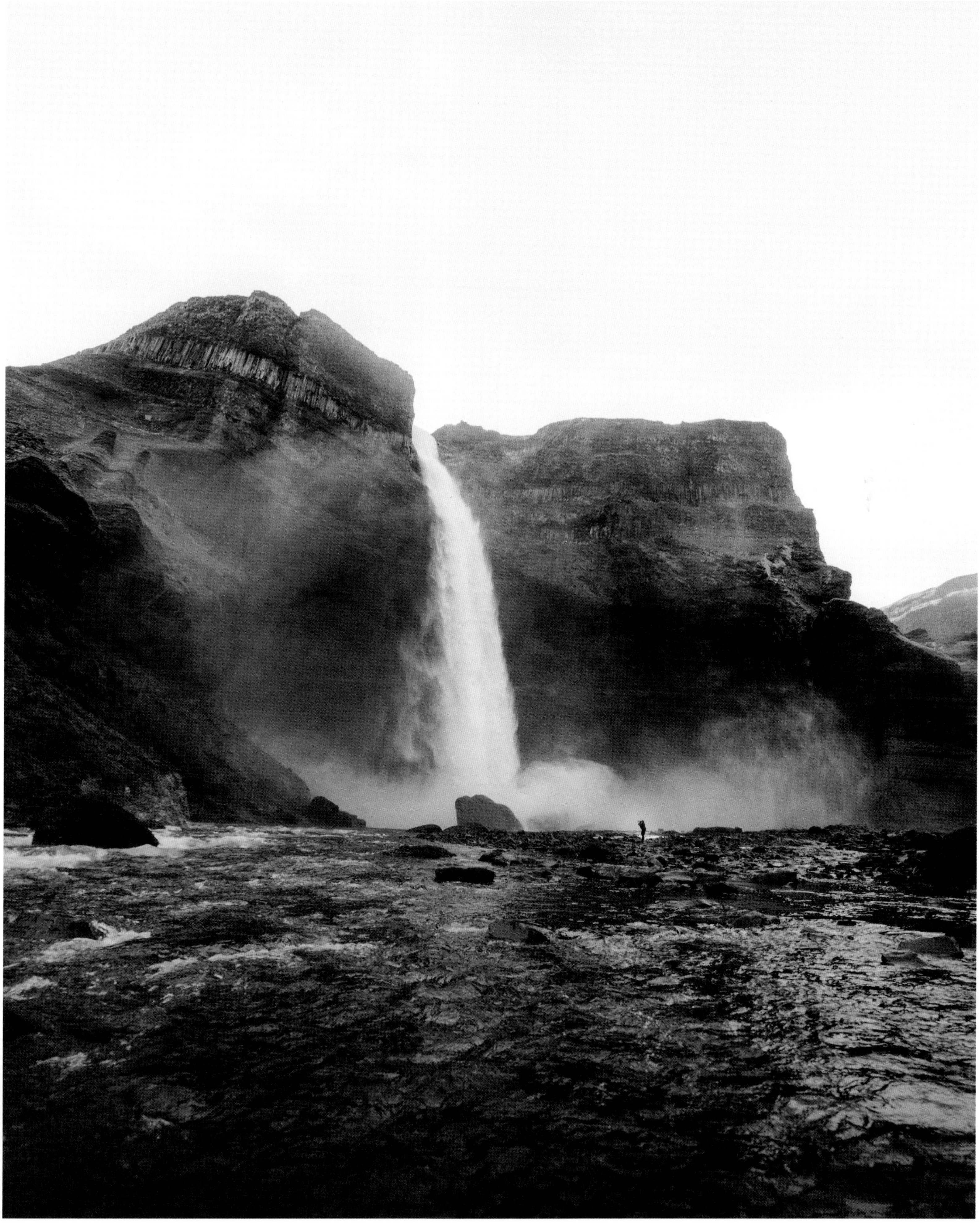

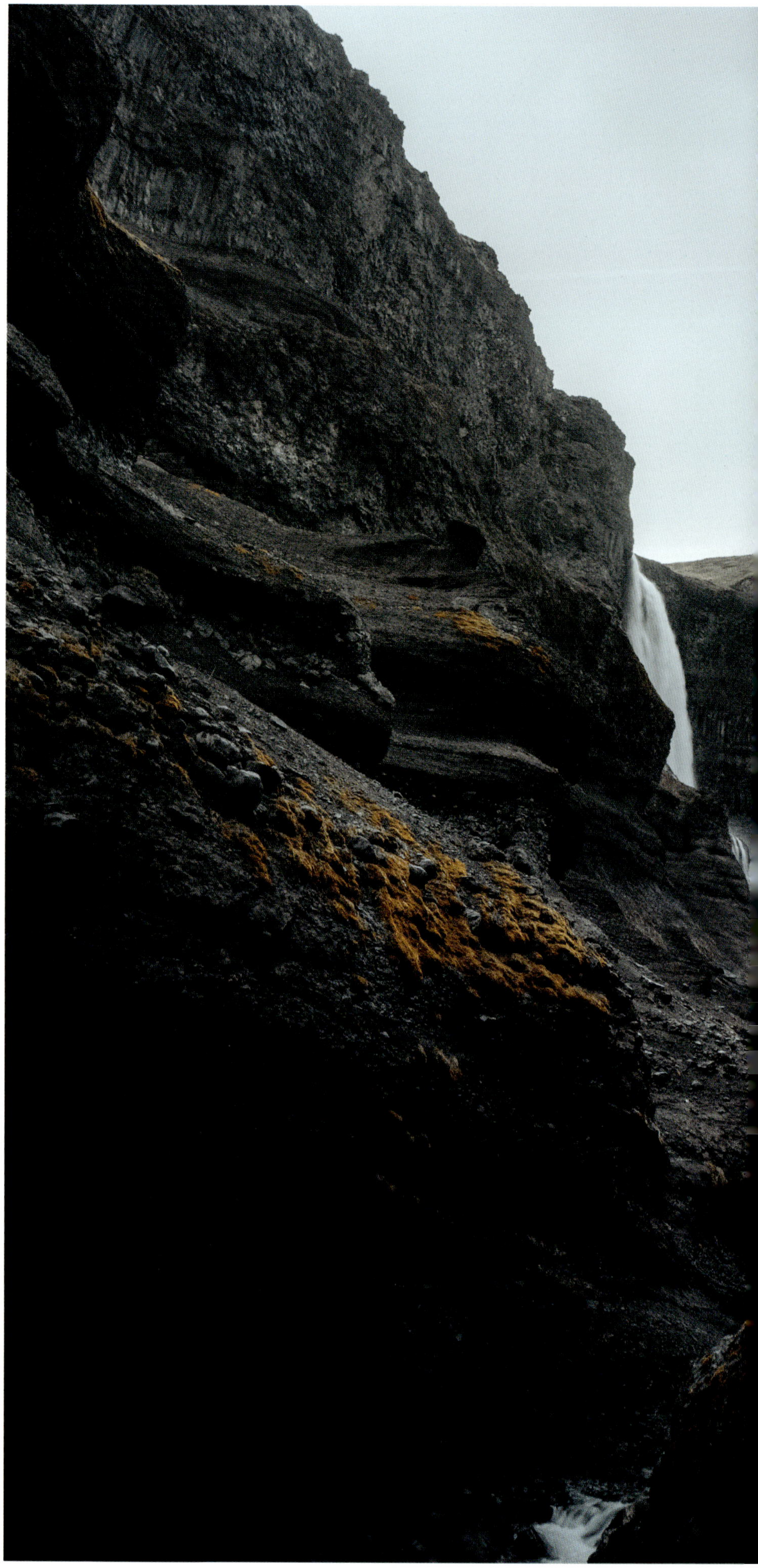

➤ THE HIGHLANDS VI

This is where lakes go to dump all their excess water.

➤➤ LÓNDRANGAR

Elves sometimes build their churches along the coast to revel in nothingness and solitude.

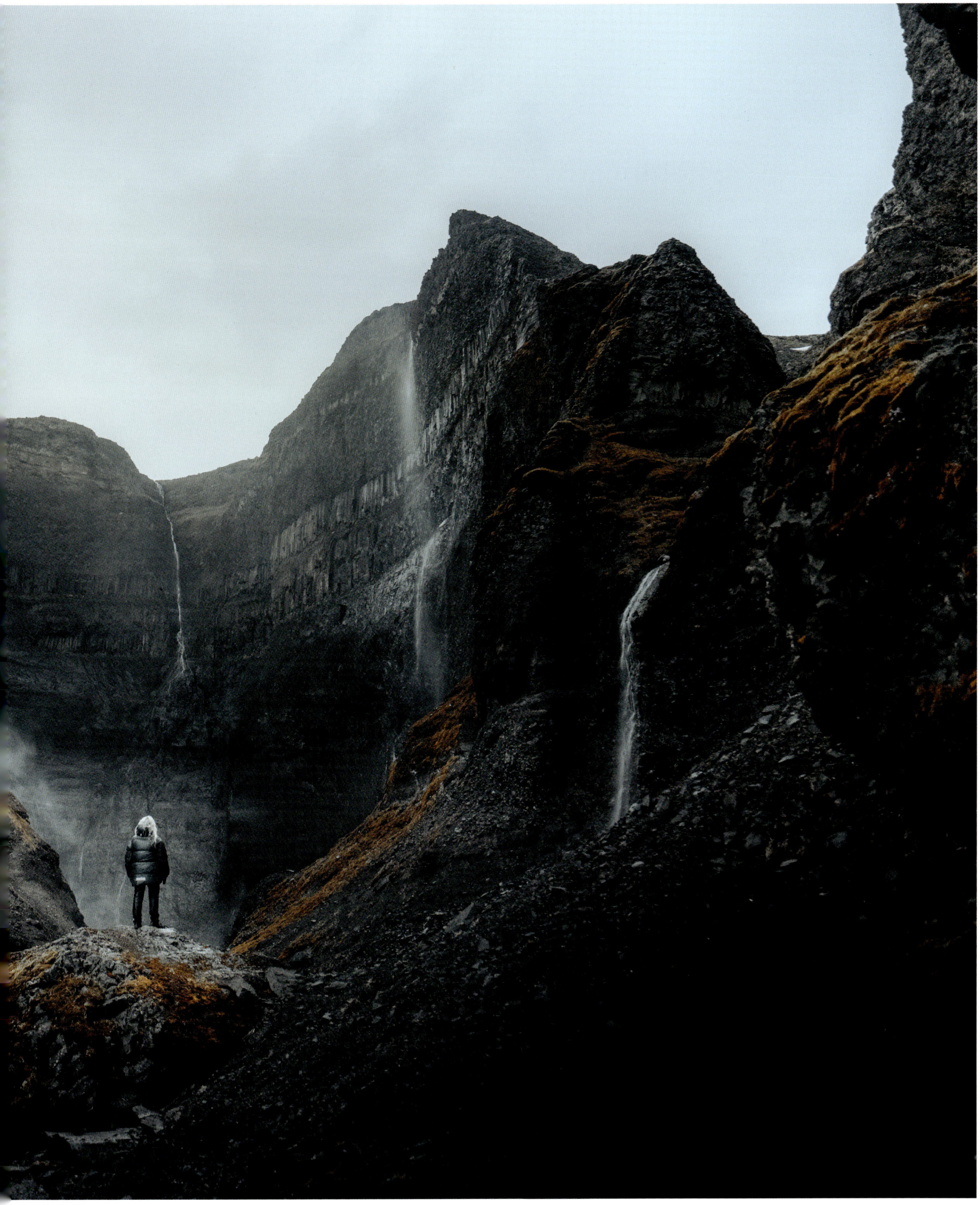

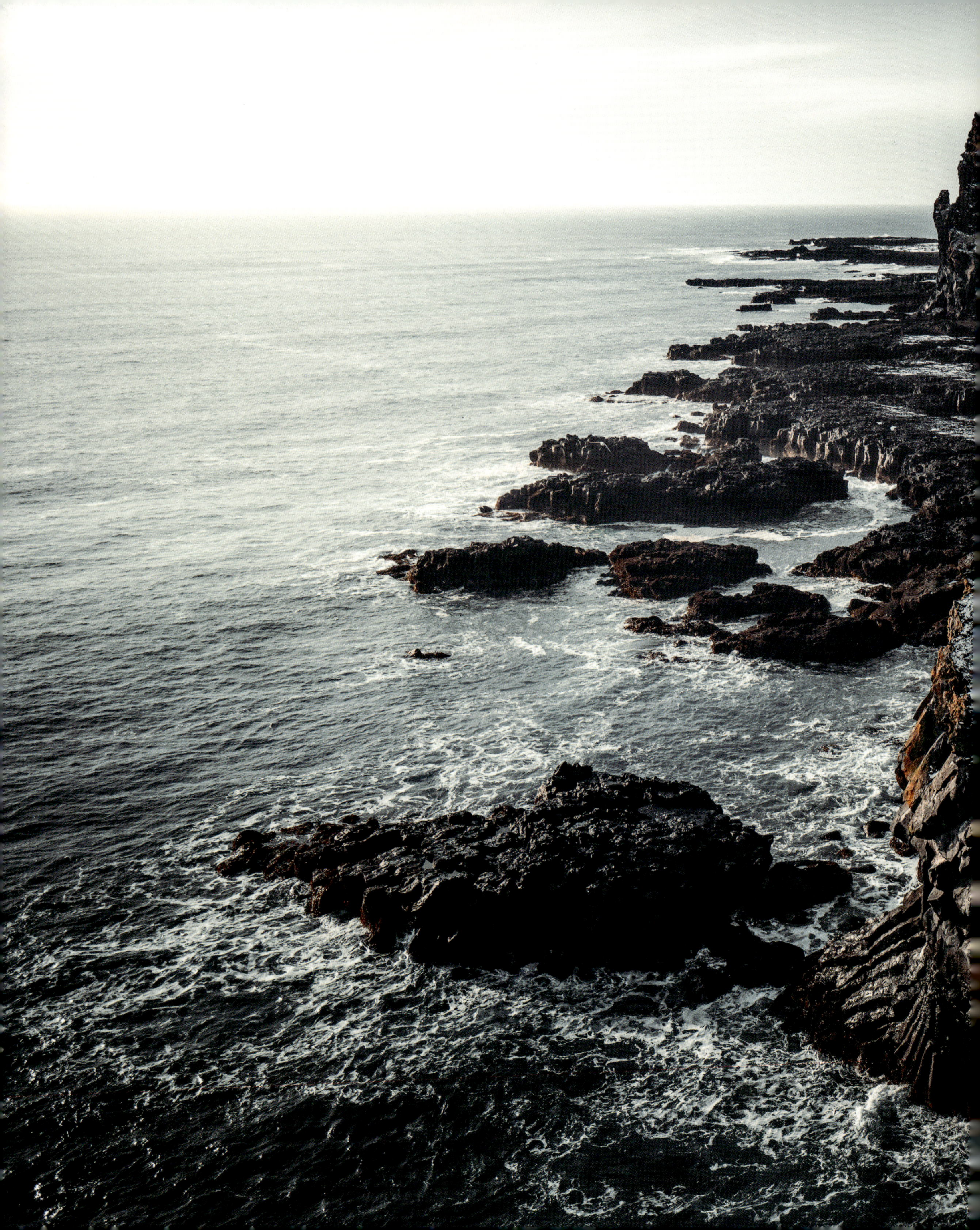

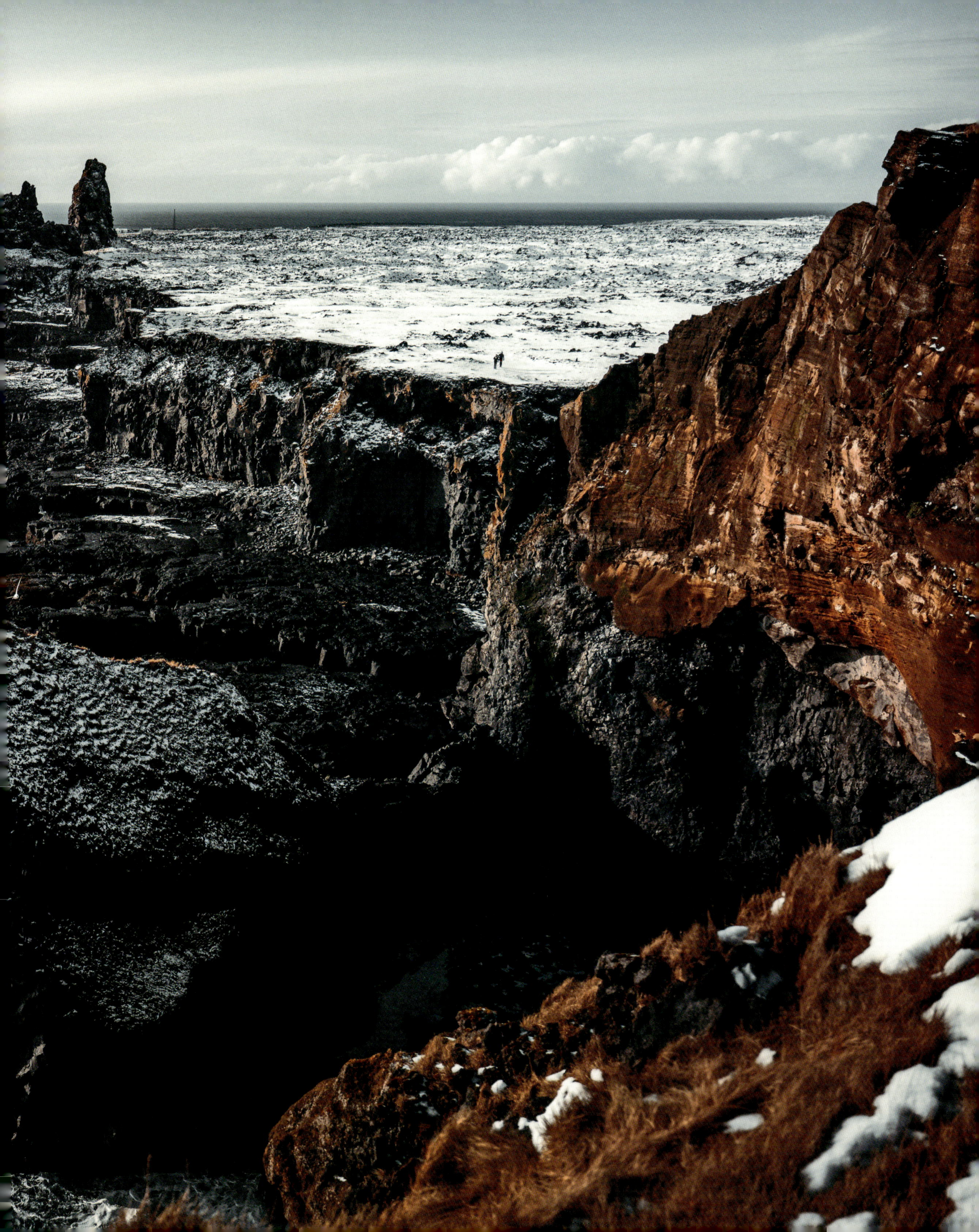

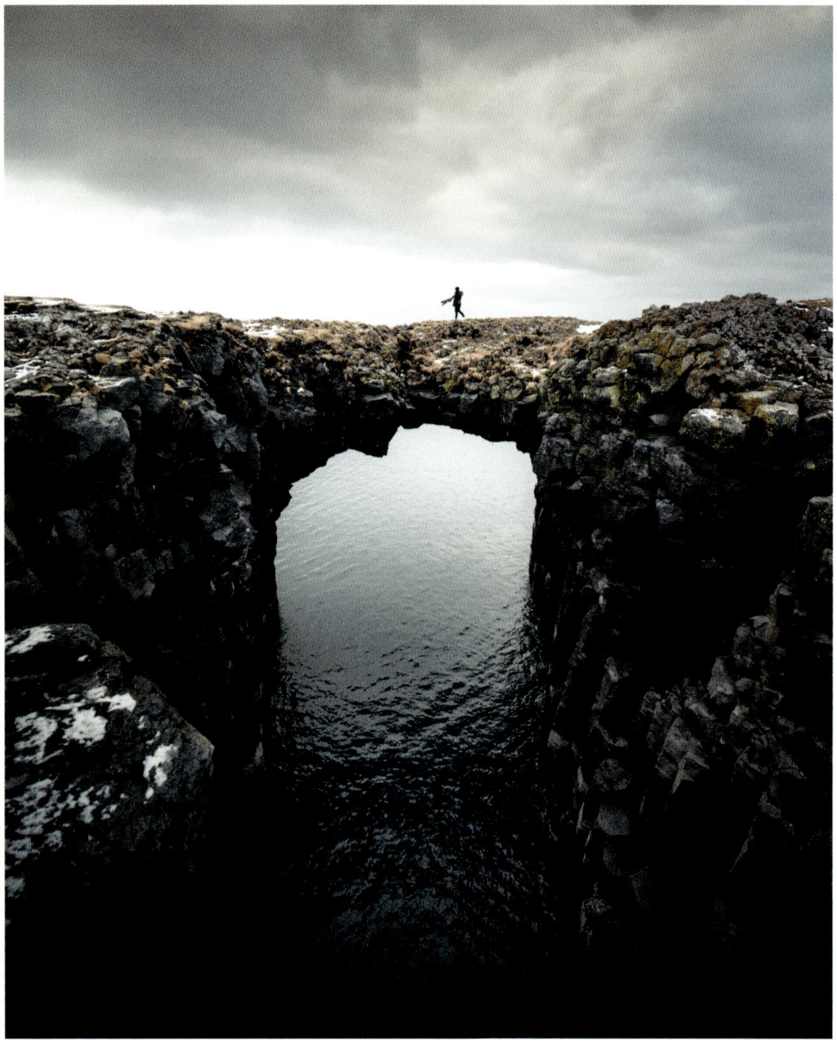

▲ ARNARSTAPI

Two trolls got petrified while fist bumping and now they're a bridge across the ocean.

➤ ARNARSTAPI II

These trolls once gathered to have a drink from a puddle, but then the sun rose and surprised them so they all turned into rocks.

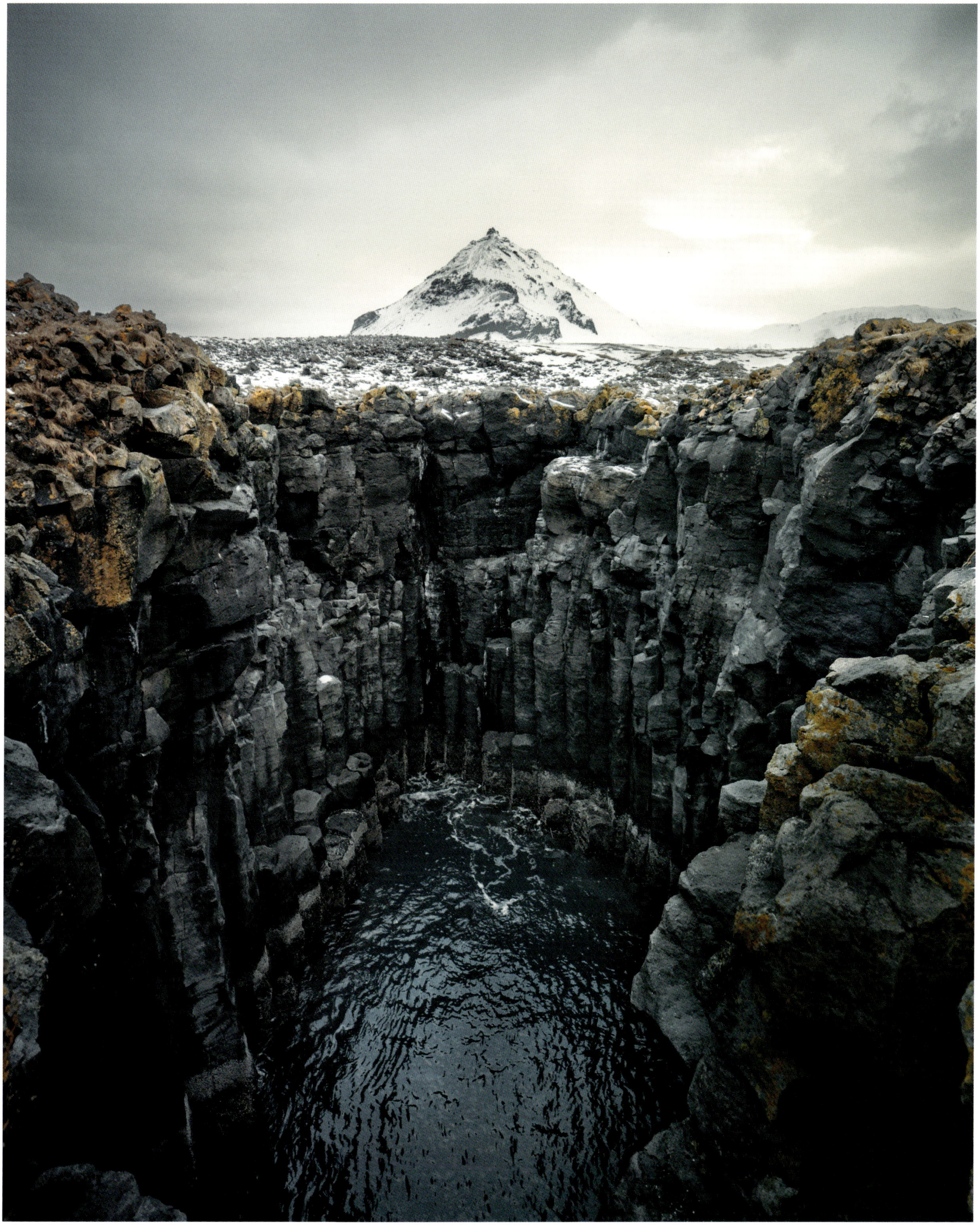

▼ KIRKJUFELL

View from the sea through a boat hole.

▶ NORTH OF ICELAND

A boat eating water—because boats like eating water—as we make our way around the coast, being chased by storms.

▶▶ SIGLUFJÖRÐUR IV

If I were a sailboat, this is exactly where I would be: fighting the Icelandic coast on a journey of self-discovery.

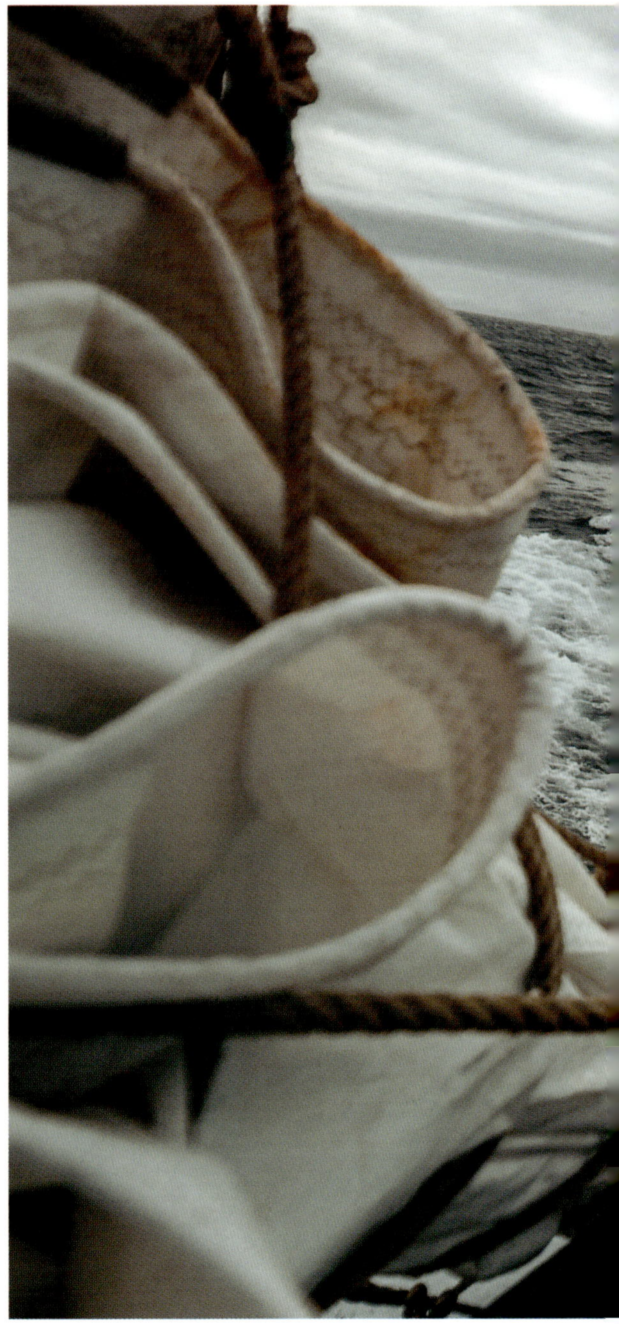

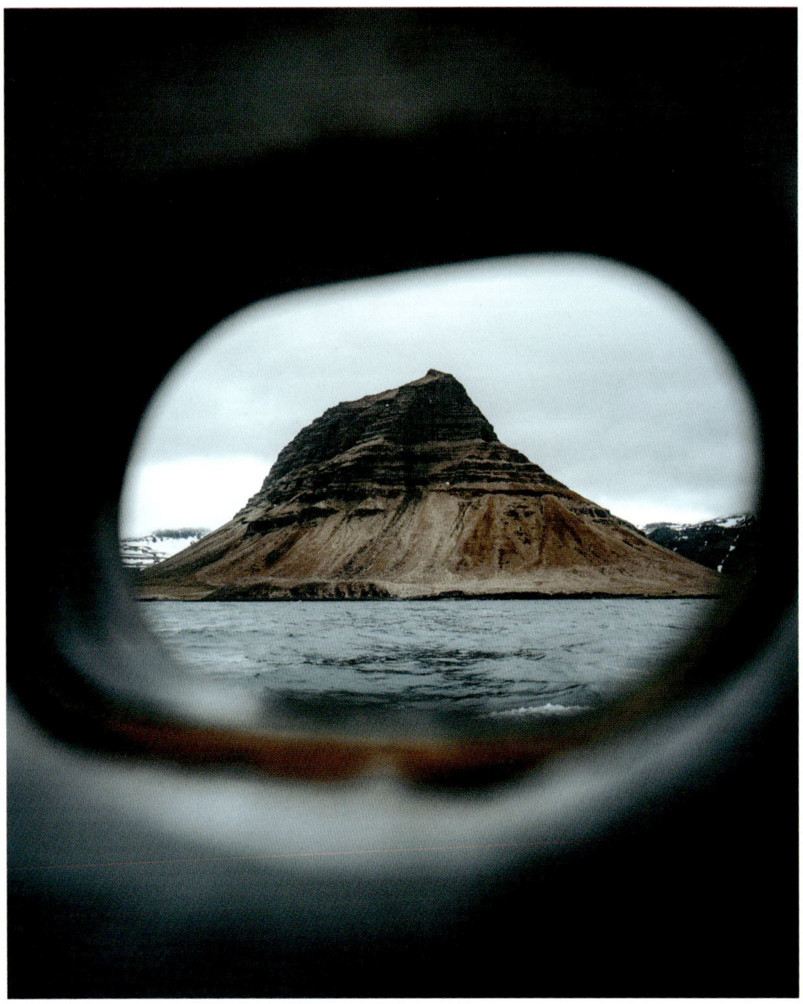

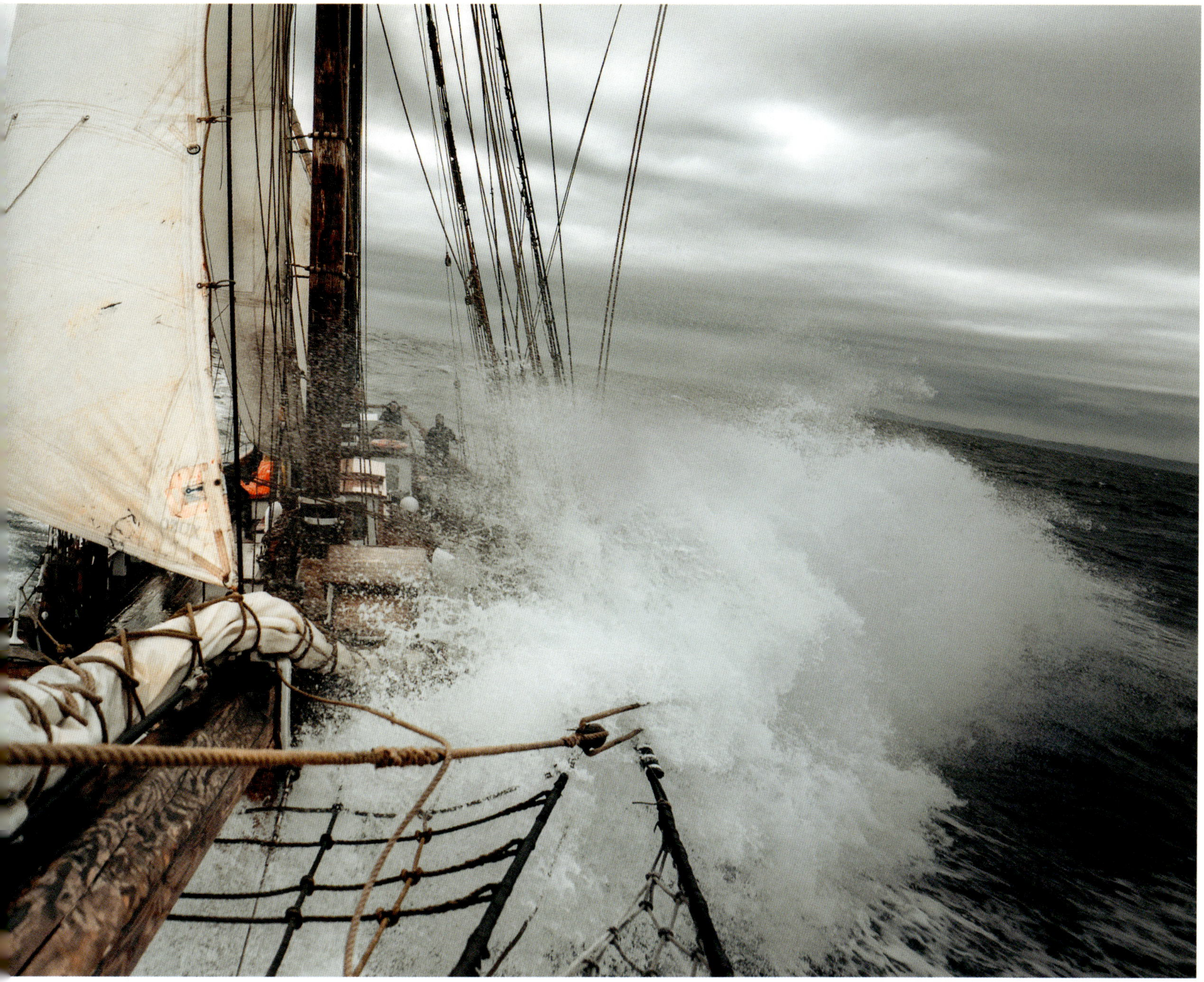

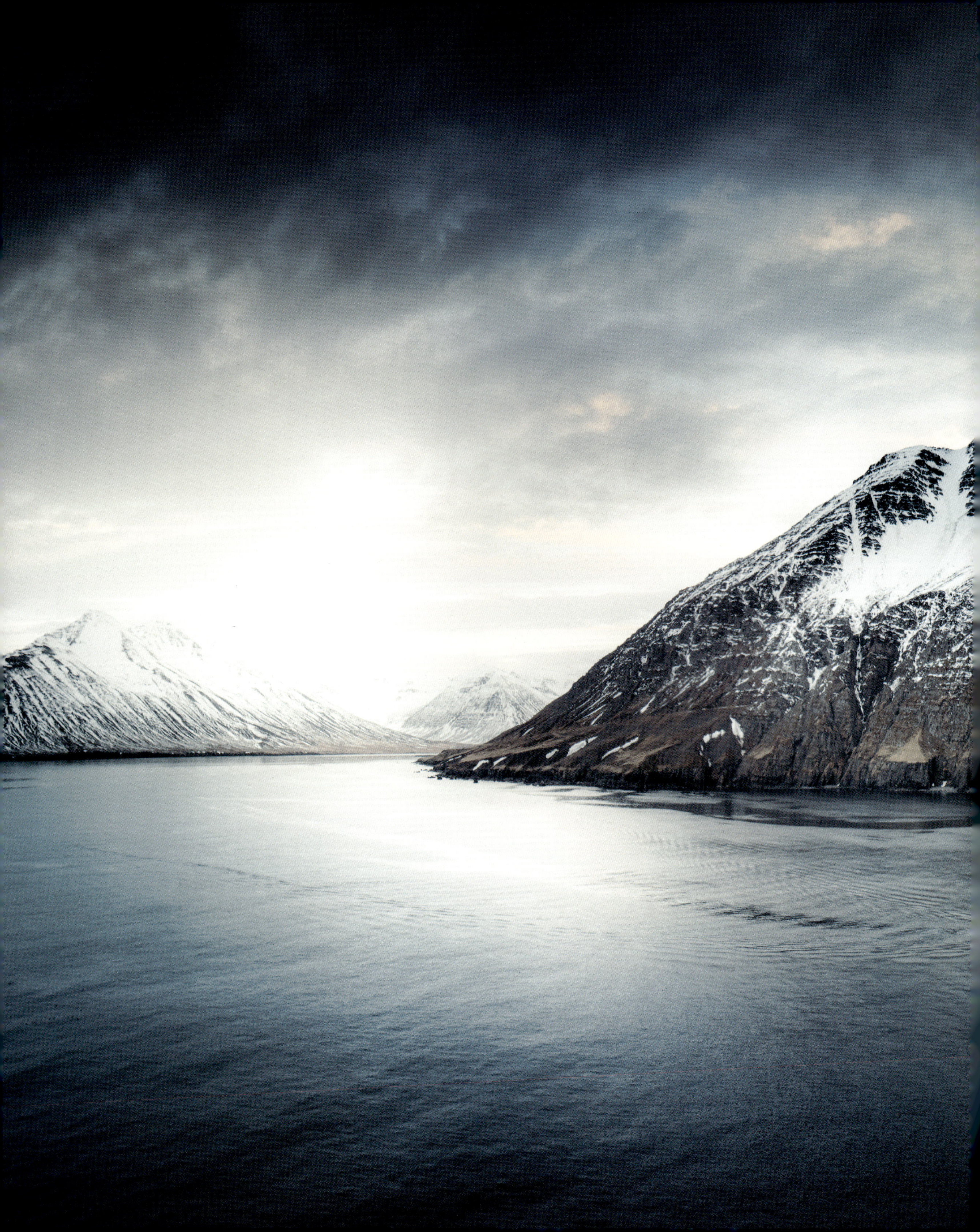

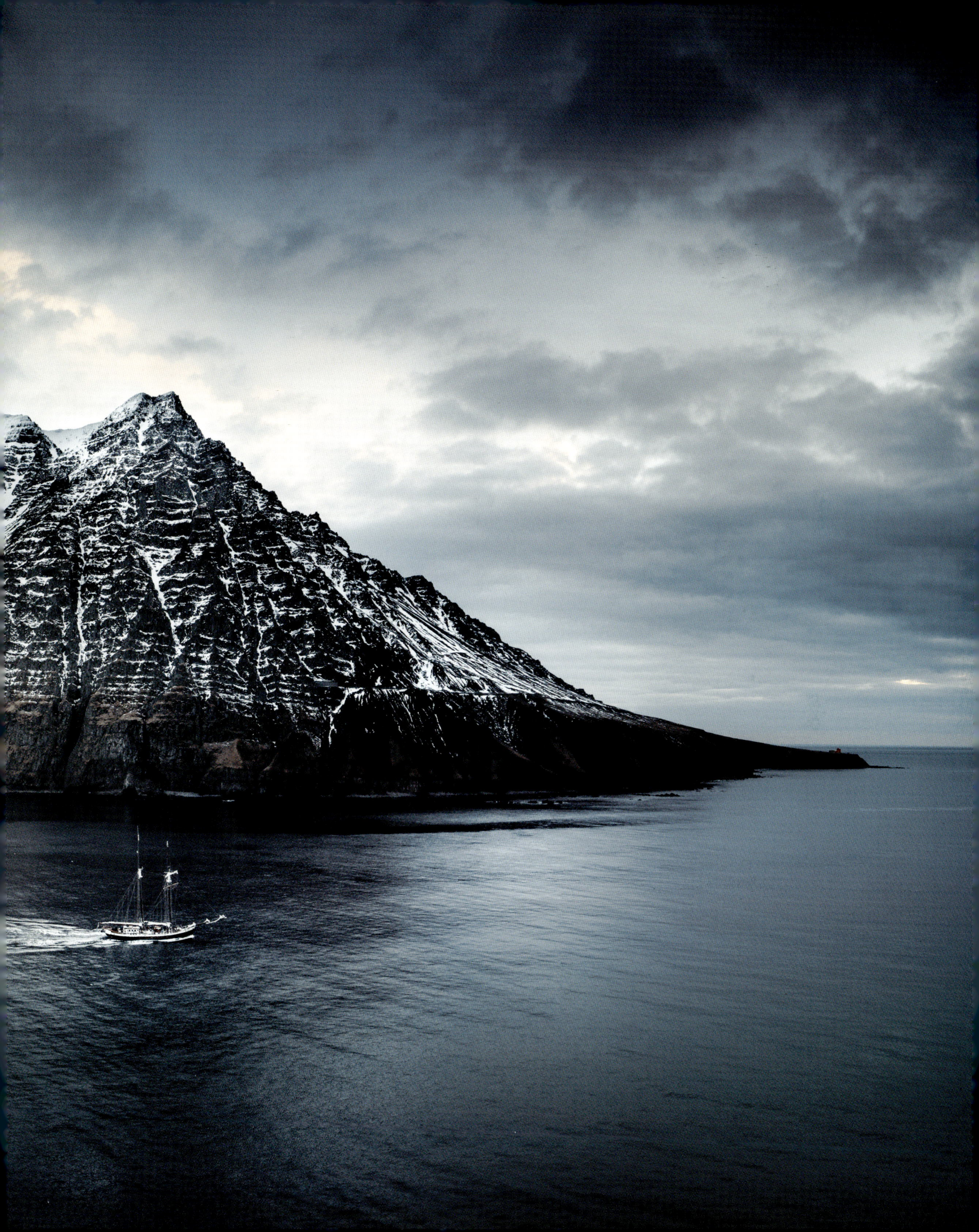

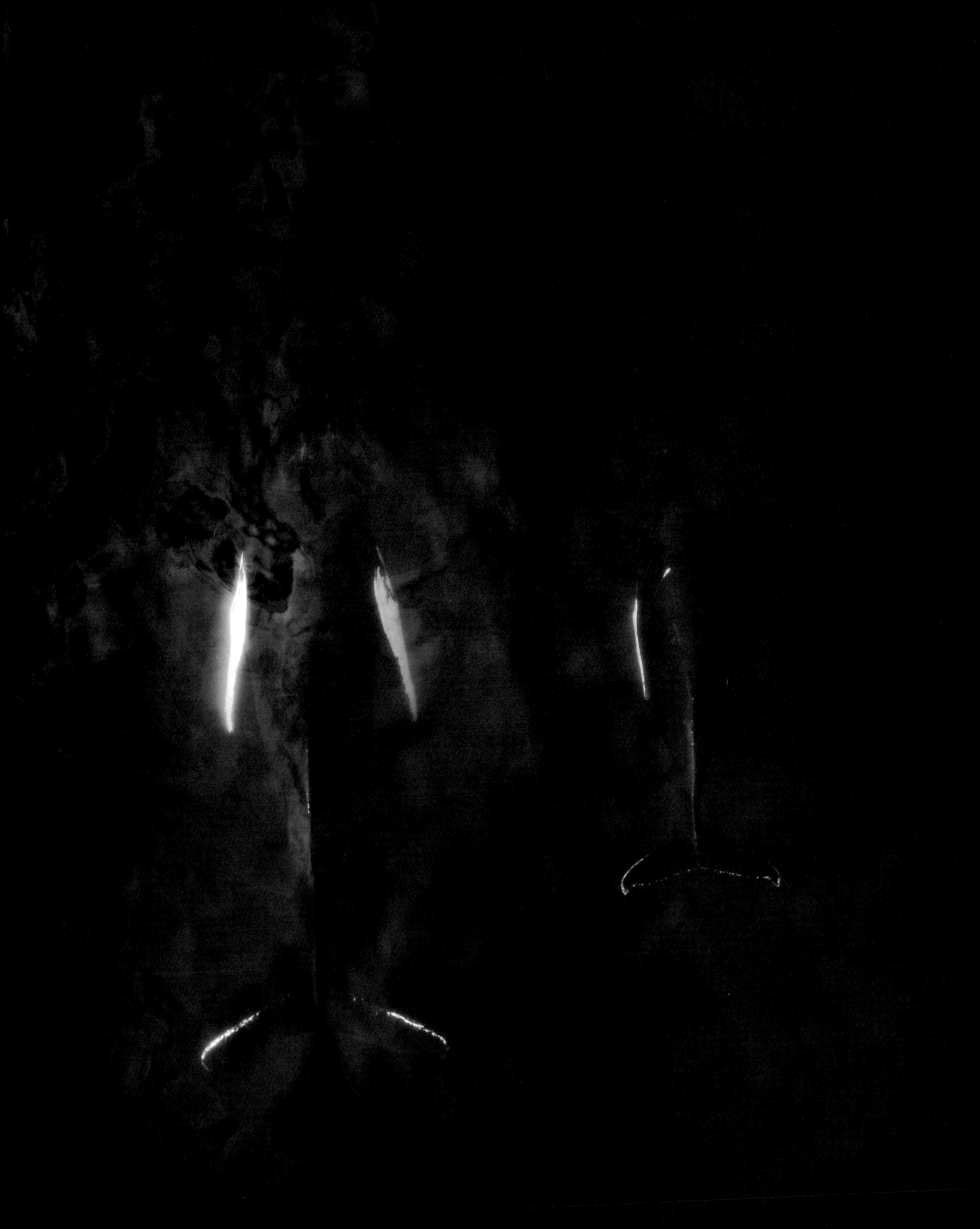

◂ DEEPER AND DARKER

One large organic submarine shows its smaller version around the vast ocean.

▸▸ VESTRAHORN IX

I want to believe I was the first to take this shot in the early days of drone photography, but since it has become such a classic angle I don't even know what's true anymore. The Vikings probably built this road millions of years ago with the intention of one day having it droned all over the interwebs. They just didn't know it would take so long to invent these flying cameras.

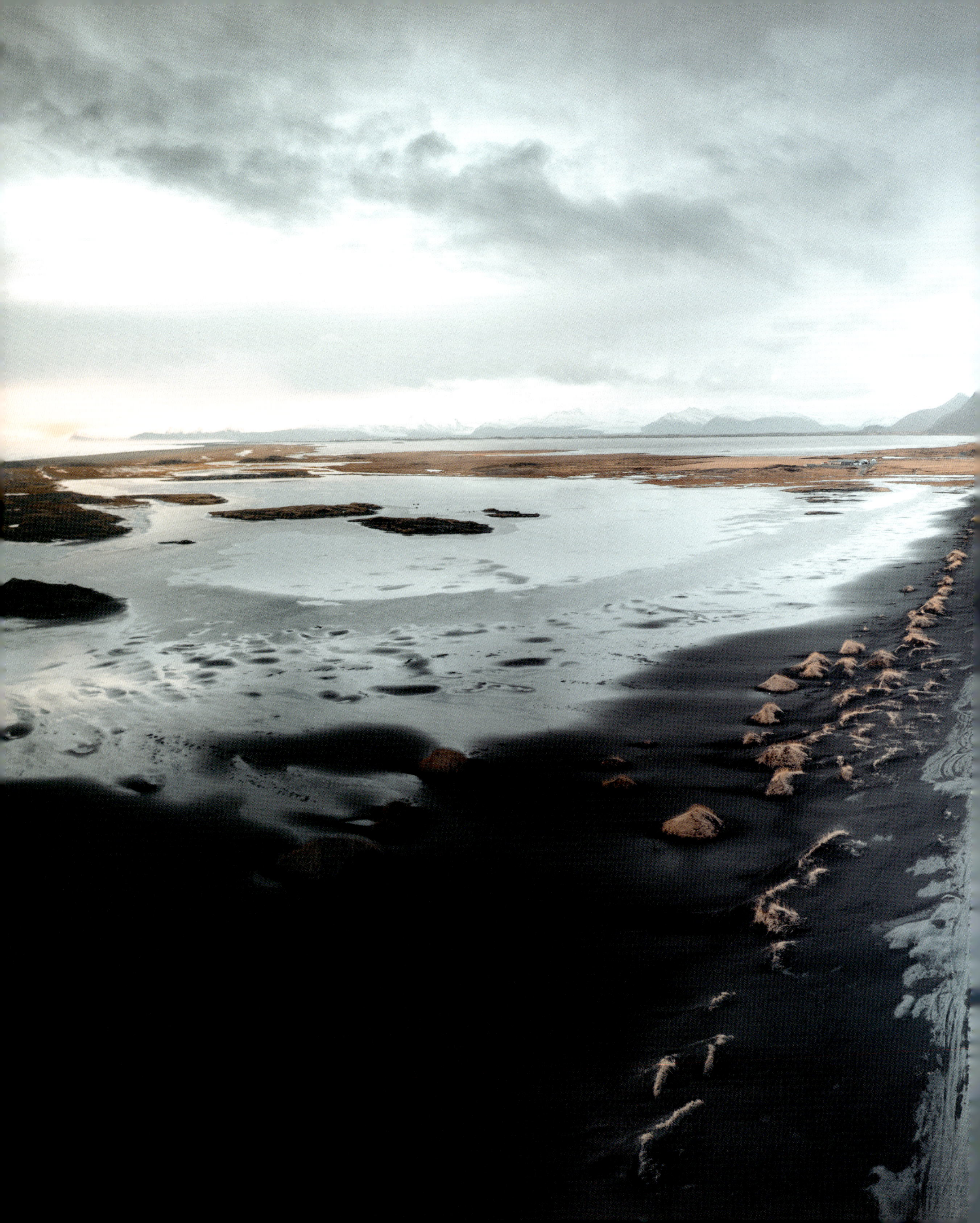

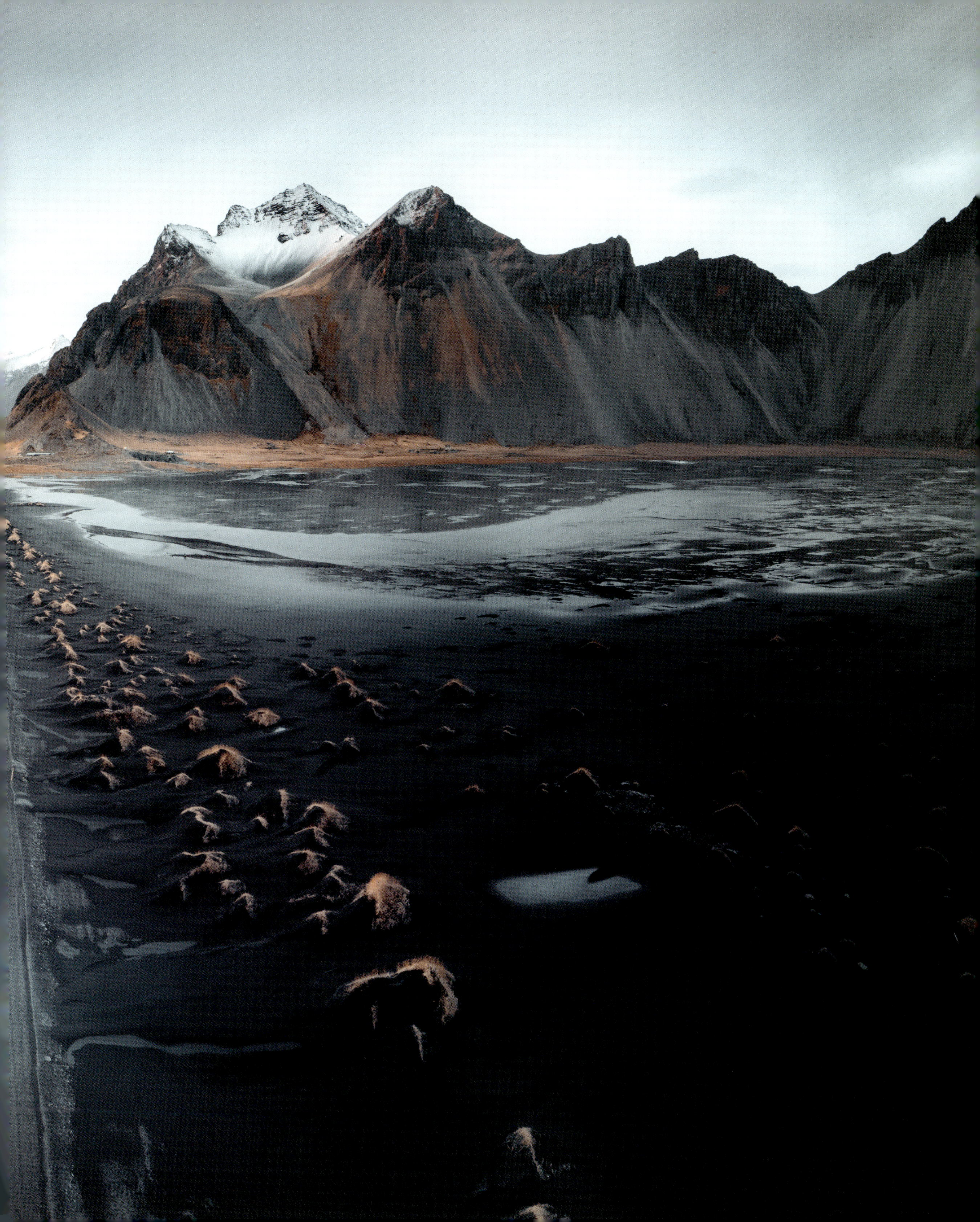

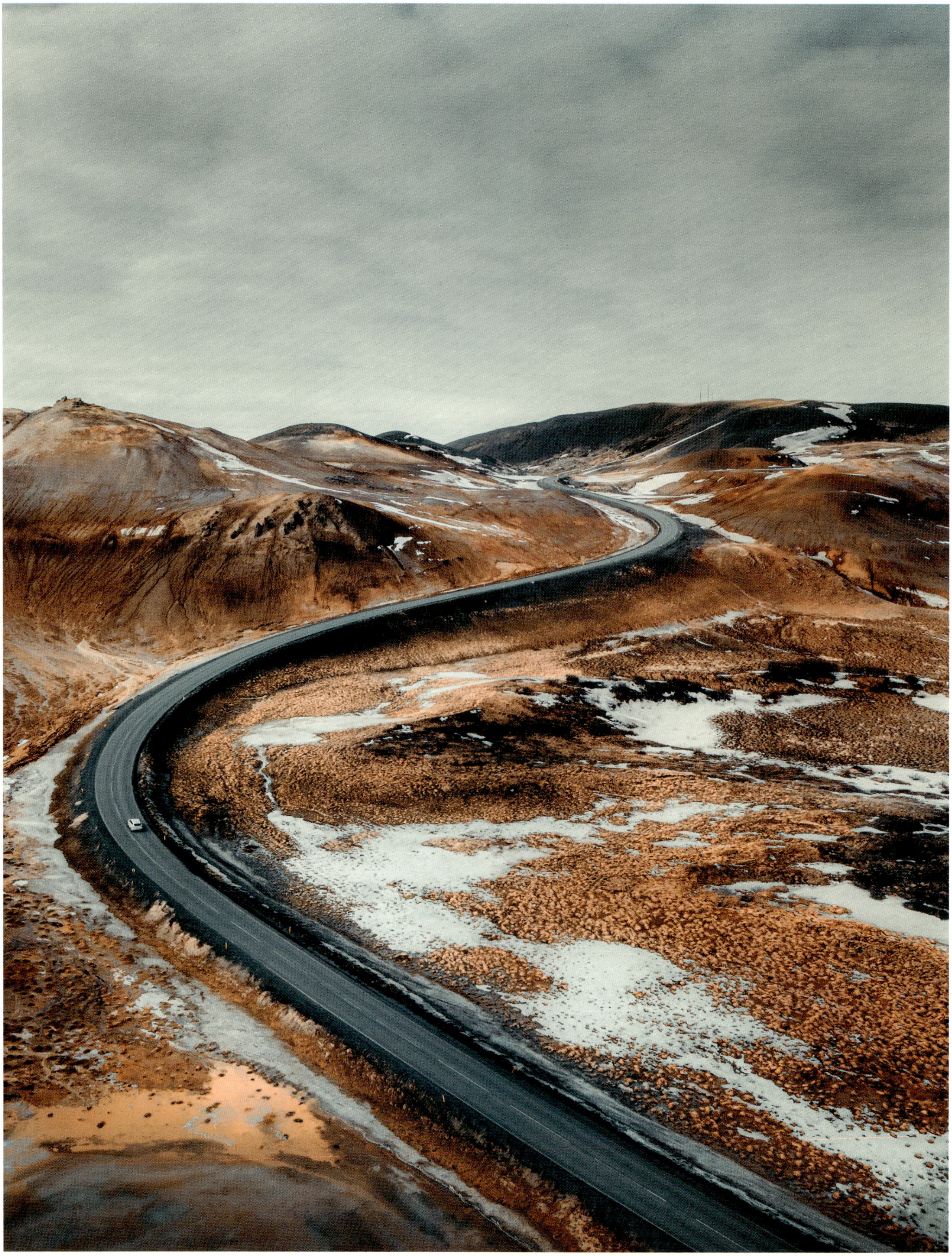

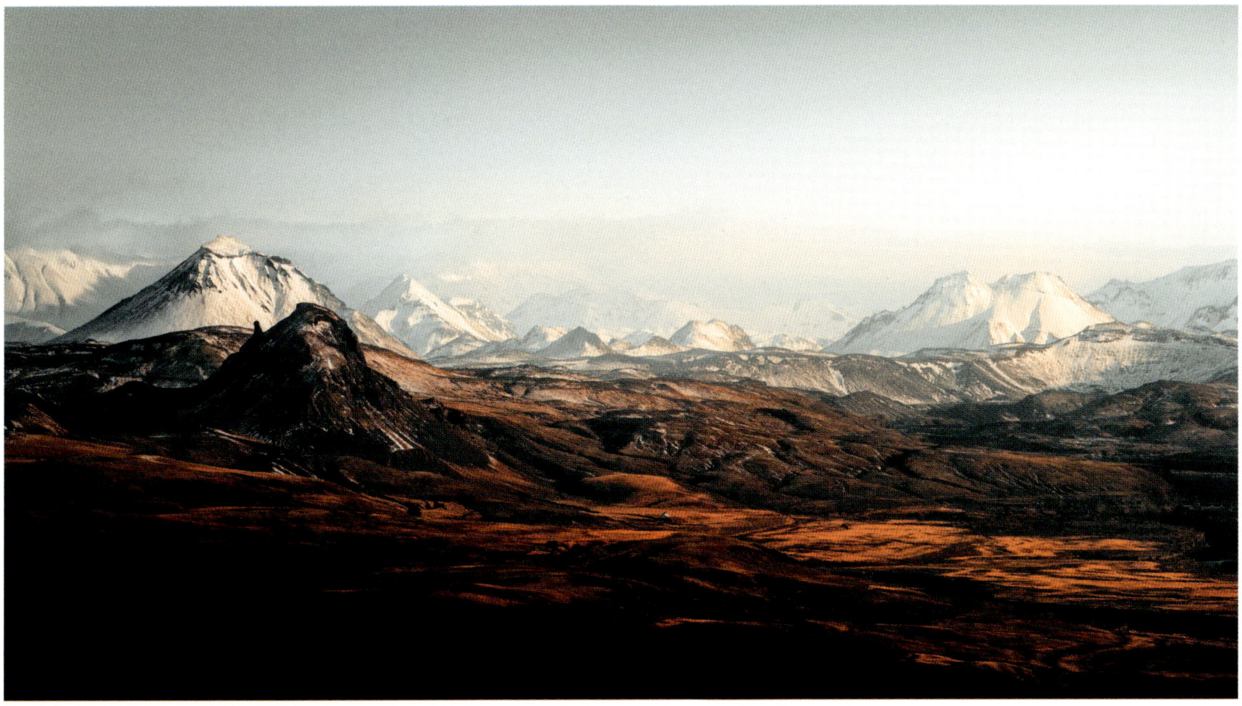

◂ MÝVATN V

Mars stole its signature look from Iceland. They aren't on speaking terms anymore.

▴ FROM EYJAFJALLAJÖKULL

While heading up a steep wall of rock towards the top of that volcano that erupted in 2010, I looked back and saw all these other mountains looking up at me, nervously watching my ascent to see if I would make it. I took a photo of them. And then I made it up and back down again.

▸▸ KERLINGARFJÖLL III

This ridge couldn't agree which color to wear, so it compromised and did a half-and-half look.

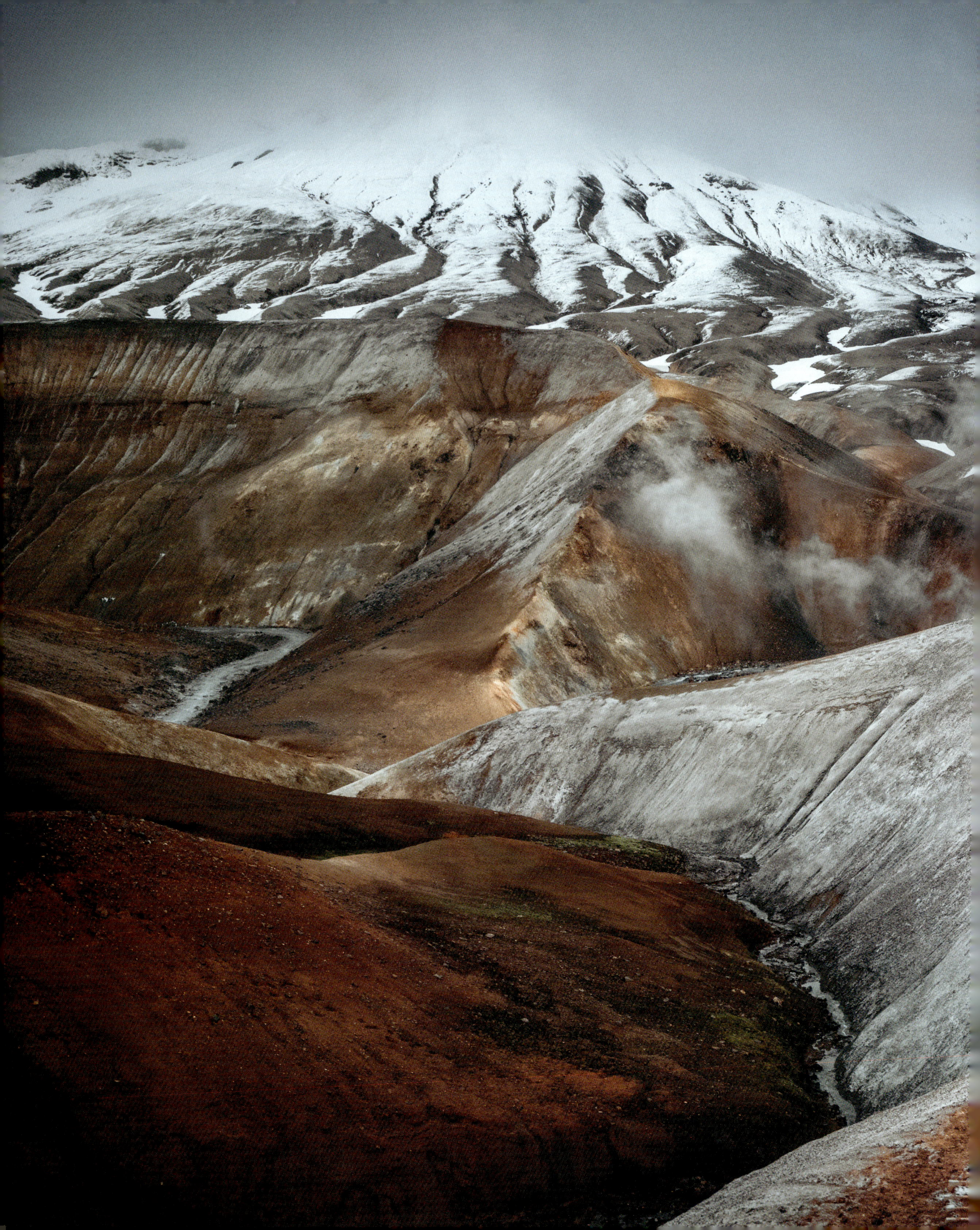

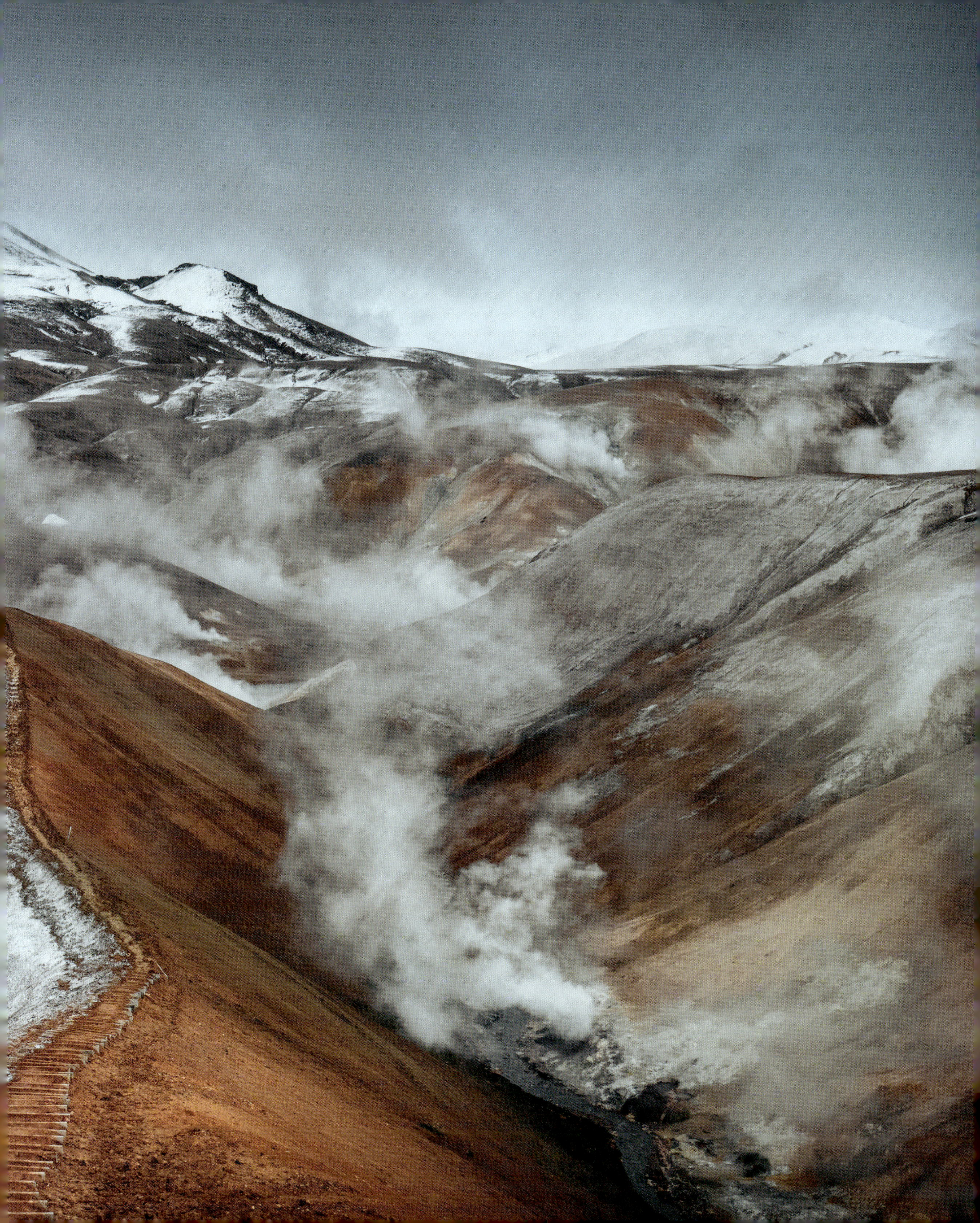

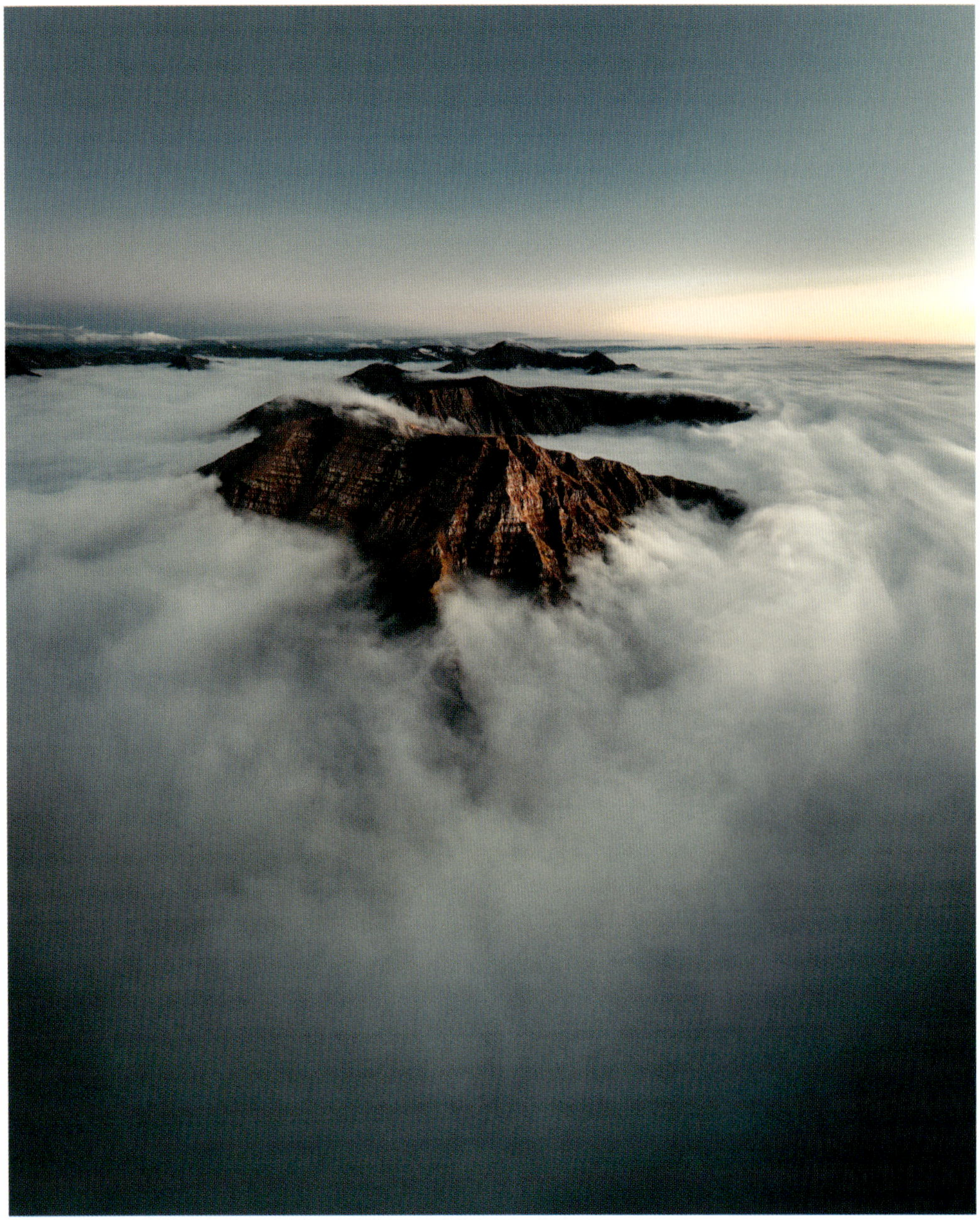

▲ STRÁKAR II

A swarm of clouds attack a lonely mountain that was left behind when the rest of its herd went off chasing warmer climates.

▶ ÞÓRSMÖRK III

That place where Thor hangs out, volcanoes erupt, glaciers form, canyons flood, mountains move, cars drown in rivers, and drones fly away into the beauty.

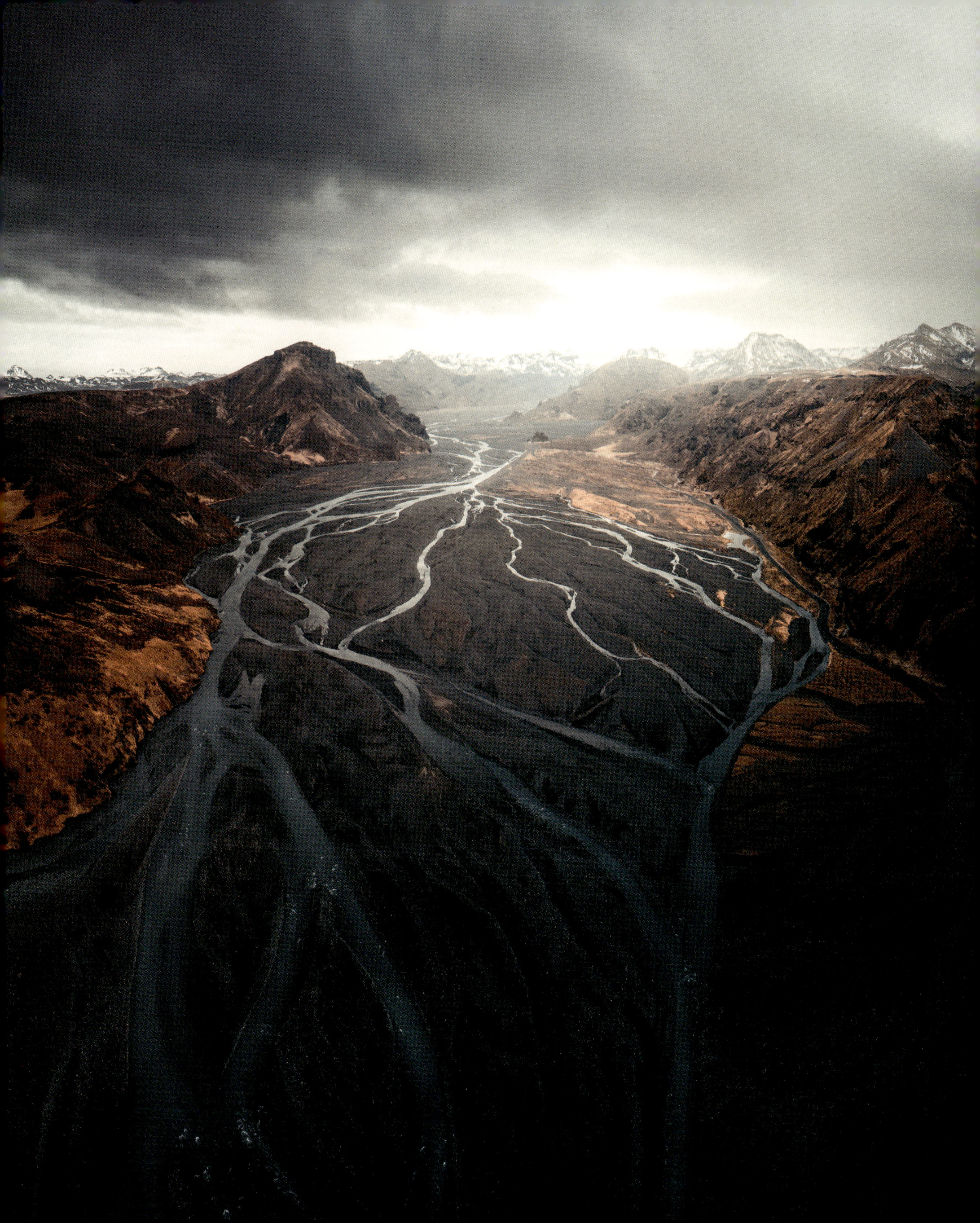

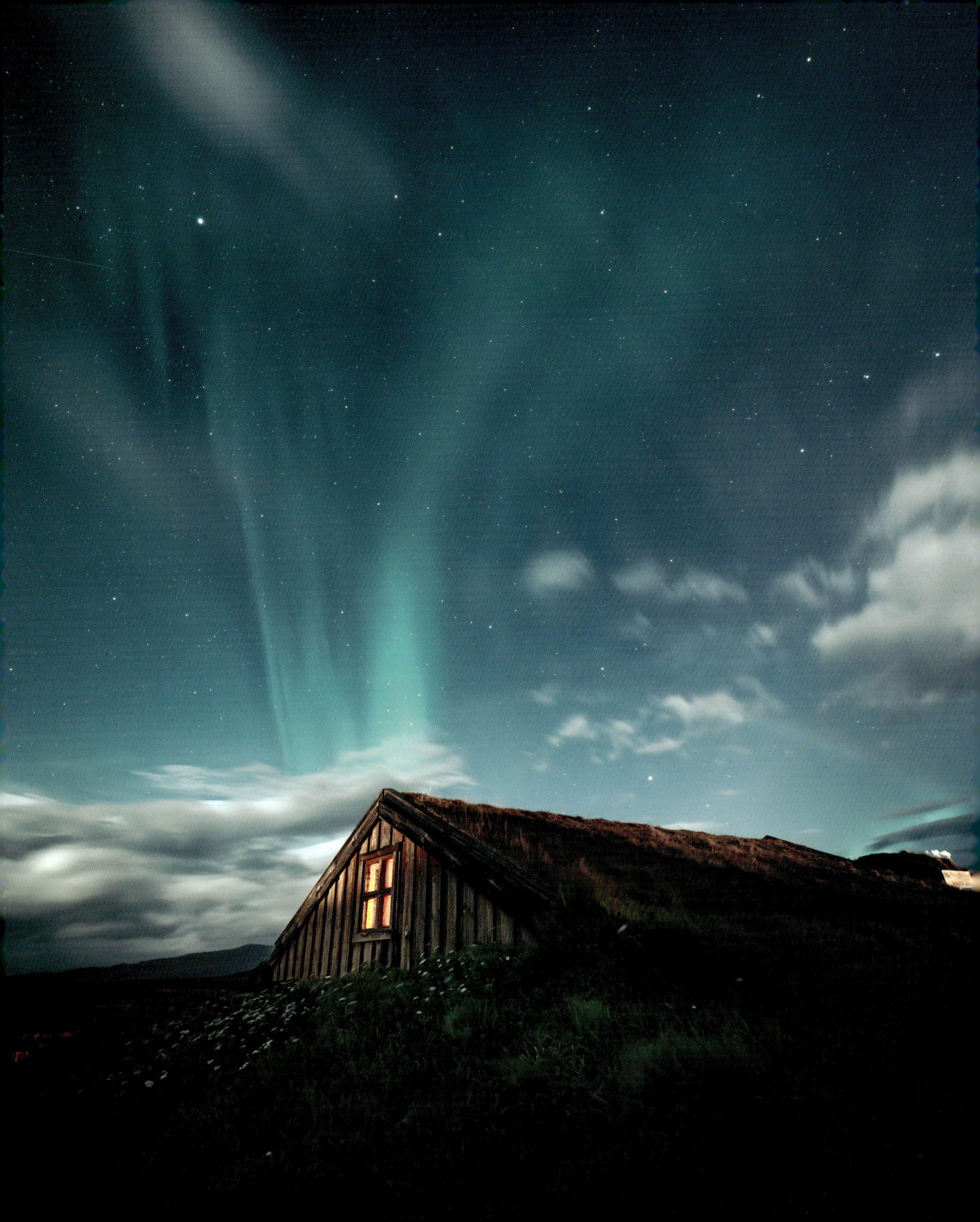

◂ MÖDRUDALUR

When a hut has ideas, it may struggle to get them out in human sentences. So, it projects them up into the sky, hoping that someone will understand.

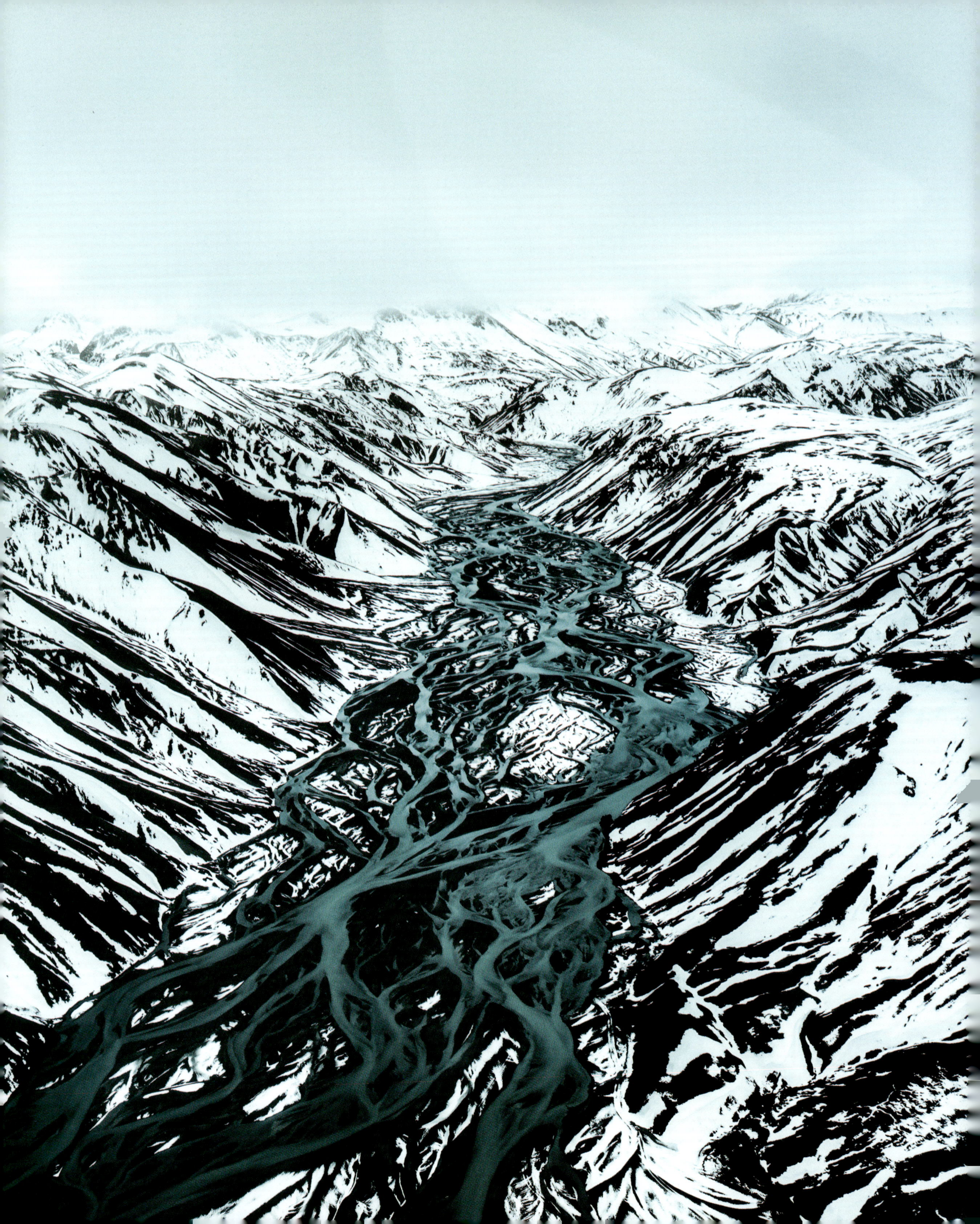

THE QUIET COLLAPSE INWARDS

November and December

The sea eats the sky. Darkness blows in sideways through the fjord. Use common sense with extreme caution. Cold is a state of mind but don't breathe in too fast—it will hurt. Waterfalls freeze mid-sentence, but the auroras return to bring comfort and color in the long night.

Iceland once again becomes a place that doesn't seem to exist—no longer, or not yet. Some days no one is out, and when no one is out and it's so quiet, it's as if no one has ever even been out before.

Imagine locking yourself into a cold, dark cave for a few months. When you come out, anything and everything will feel great. But surviving until then takes some preparation.

This is one of the most important times of year. It's a time to fall back, slow down, go inside, and digest everything. And it can be challenging. As someone who was born into this dark, it's a warming, familiar time for me—but I still learned the hard way how to deal with it.

It's important not to be alone heading into these long, dark months. Because if you are, you're probably going to have a bad time and then you'll never try it again. So, if you don't have a partner or a roommate you get along with, find someone. Even if just for this winter.

Find some hobbies, too. Having the drive to harness the winter is priceless. Outdoor hobbies that involve snow will make you greet the cold, white days with excitement. And when the days get too extreme, it's just as crucial to have something to stay inside for—on your own or with others.

Check the weather forecast before going to the grocery store or bar. People who fail at this may not be seen again.

Don't turn your emotions off. It's easy to numb yourself into indifference during this season, but that's missing the point. You'll need your full emotional self for the next step.

A slow depression may creep up on you. Fighting it will only make it loud, so learn to recognize and accept it. Let it walk by your side and spend some time with you. Get to know it, make friends with it, and you will find a version of yourself in it. Once you know each other, you can channel it, harness it, and ultimately express it.

There is a reason why so much great culture and art comes from these kinds of places; there is a lot of time for learning, growing, and creating in the dark.

Winter can be dangerous, especially spent alone. But instead of trying to fight it, you can embrace its melancholic rhythm. Do something good with it. And remember, we're all in this together, so let the warm hearts of the remote North brighten up your dark days.

This is a season of transformation, and going through it each year will set you up for a deep and meaningful journey through the brighter and more expansive months.

Good luck. It's time to take another breath.

◂◂ LANDMANNALAUGAR V

Before the age of drones, we had to sit in flying sausages and actually look at the landscapes we shot from above, while fighting the reflection of a dirty plastic window. I still do that sometimes because it makes the experience a lot more real and magical, but then I have to eat instant noodles for the rest of that month.

▸ JÖKULSÁRLÓN

A piece of ice so nice it cloned itself, so you can see it twice.

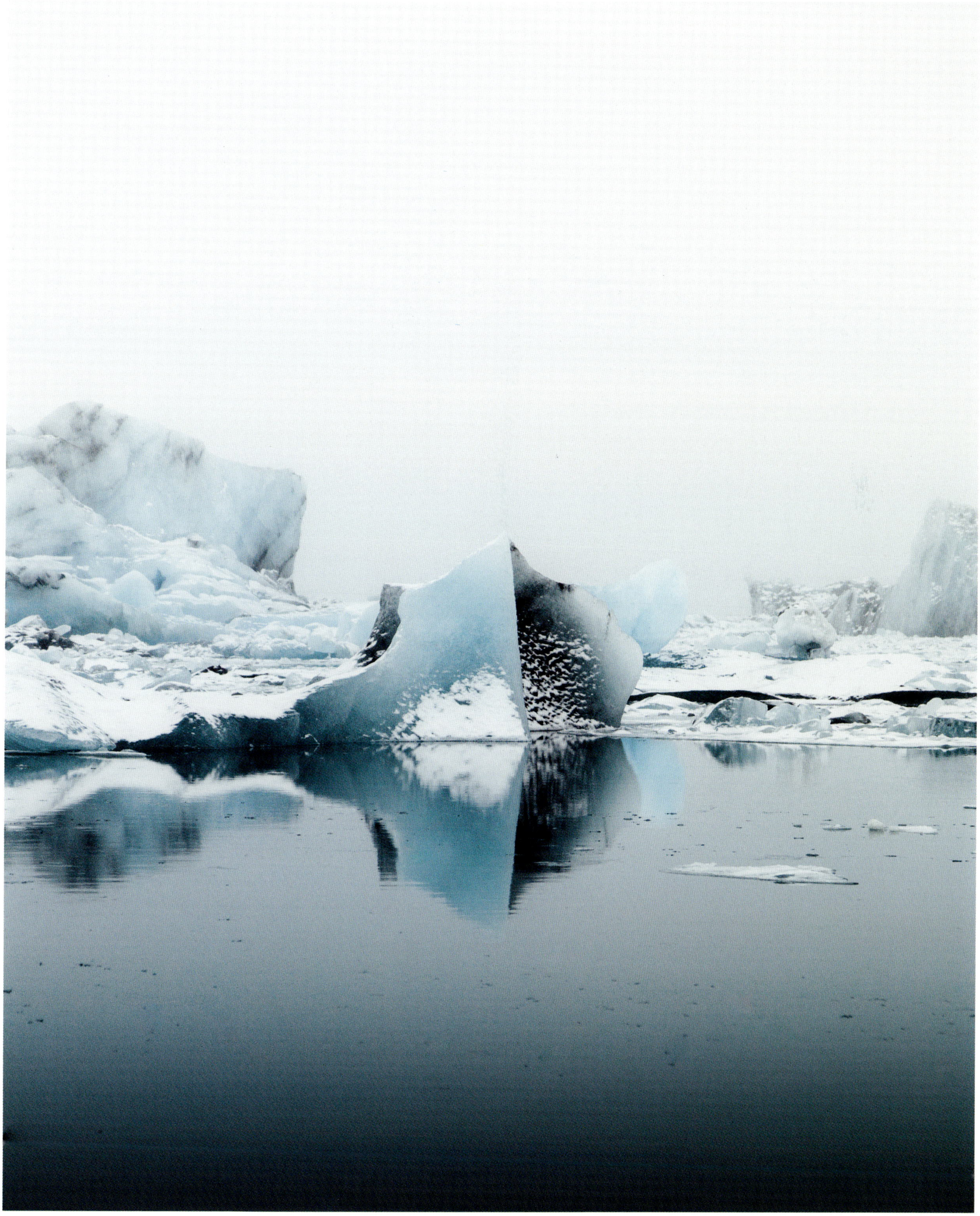

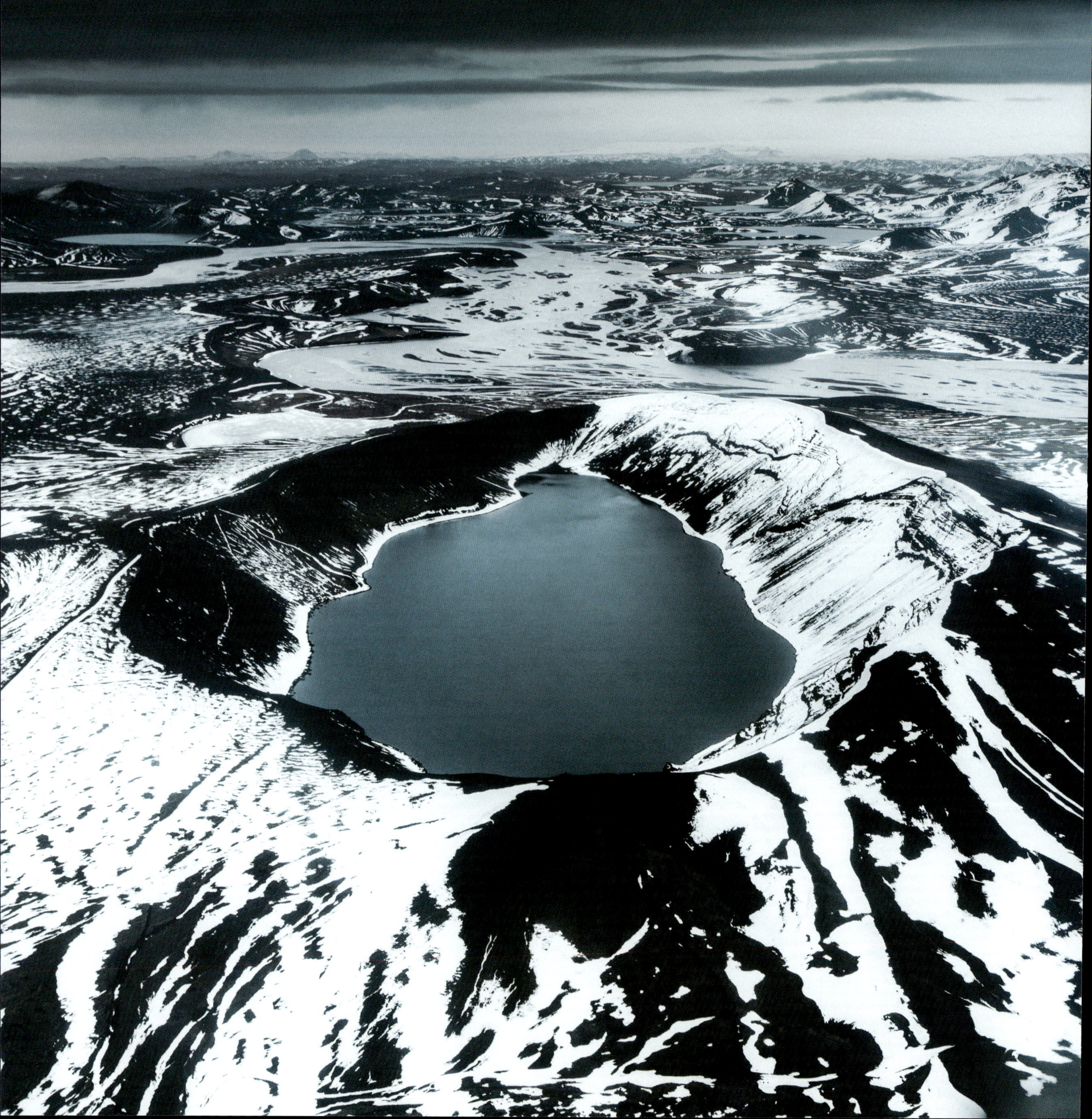

◂ OVER THE HIGHLANDS

A crater dressed up as a lake.

▼ KATLA

I remember the excitement of setting out to find this one. There was a rumor that someone had found an ice cave on Kötlujökull. I Super-Jeeped out of Reykjavik in the fading darkness of 10 a.m. on a Tuesday in December. I forced the Jeep down a black-sand dune, following something that resembled car tracks indicating that it was an actual road, probably ancient. And after many questions about whether this was the right life decision, I eventually stood face to face with a massive wall of ice.

Ten years later, there's a conveyor belt of tourists brought here every day. They even put a door with a lock on the glacier.

▶ BREIÐAMERKURJÖKULL

This seems to be where the best weather is found this time of year.

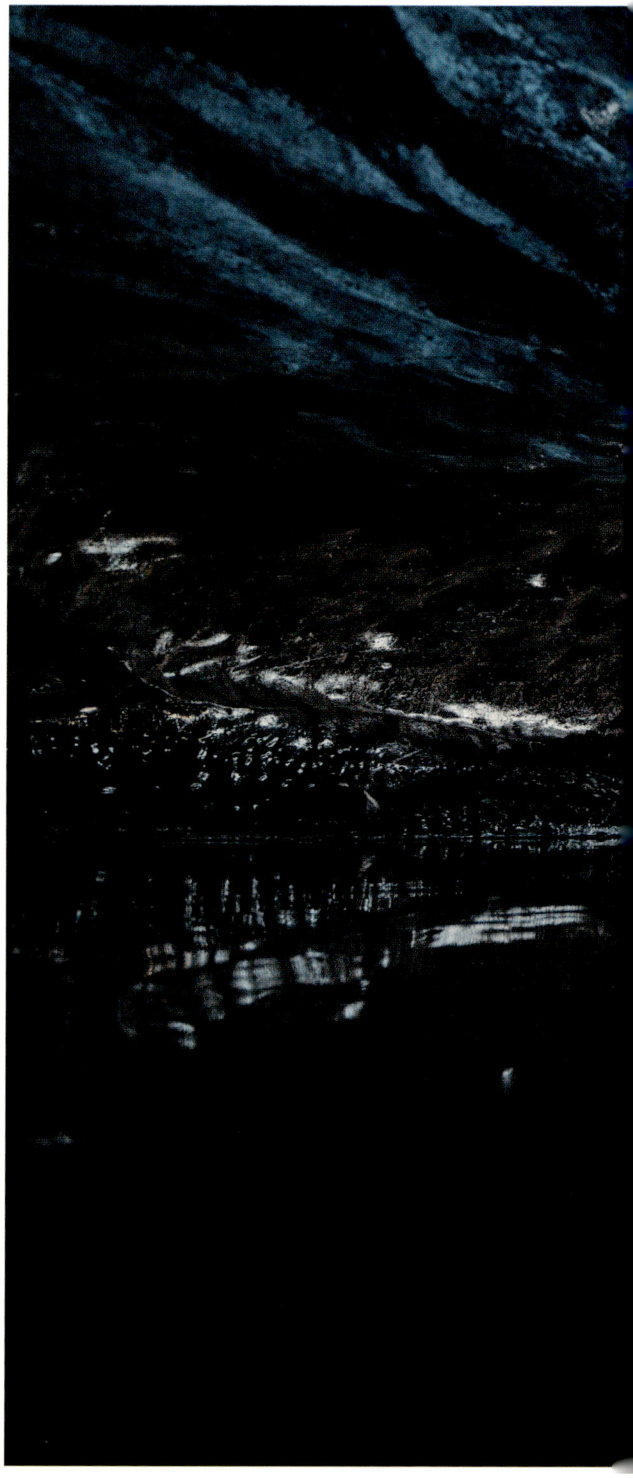

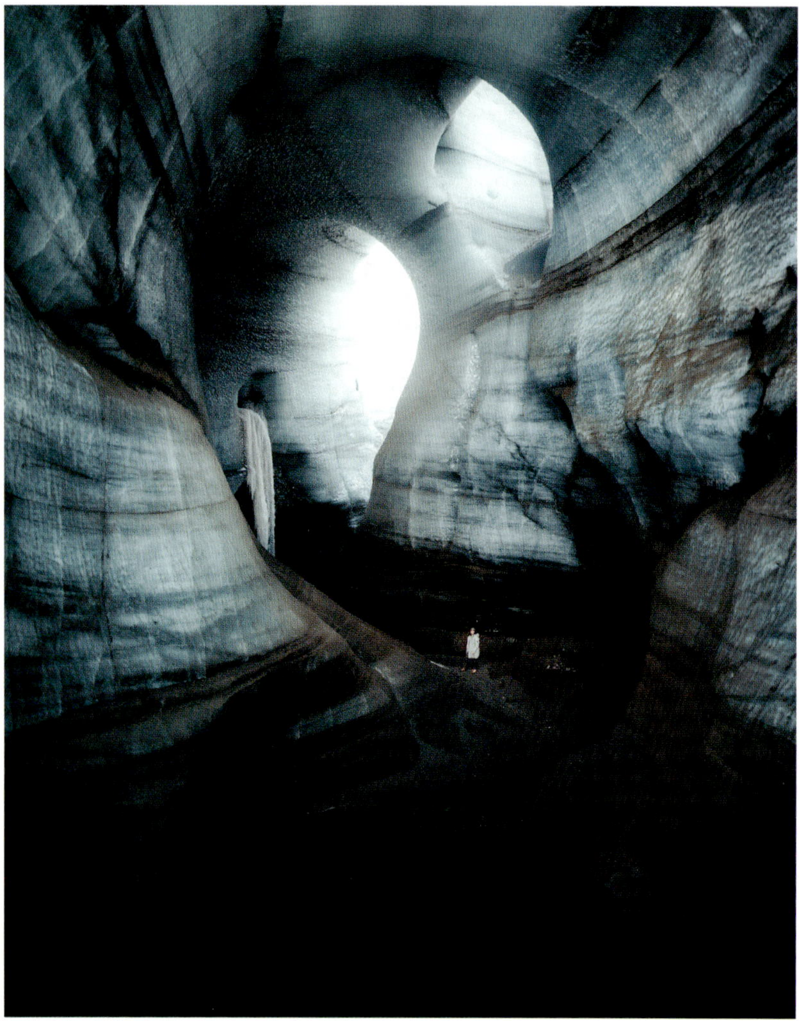

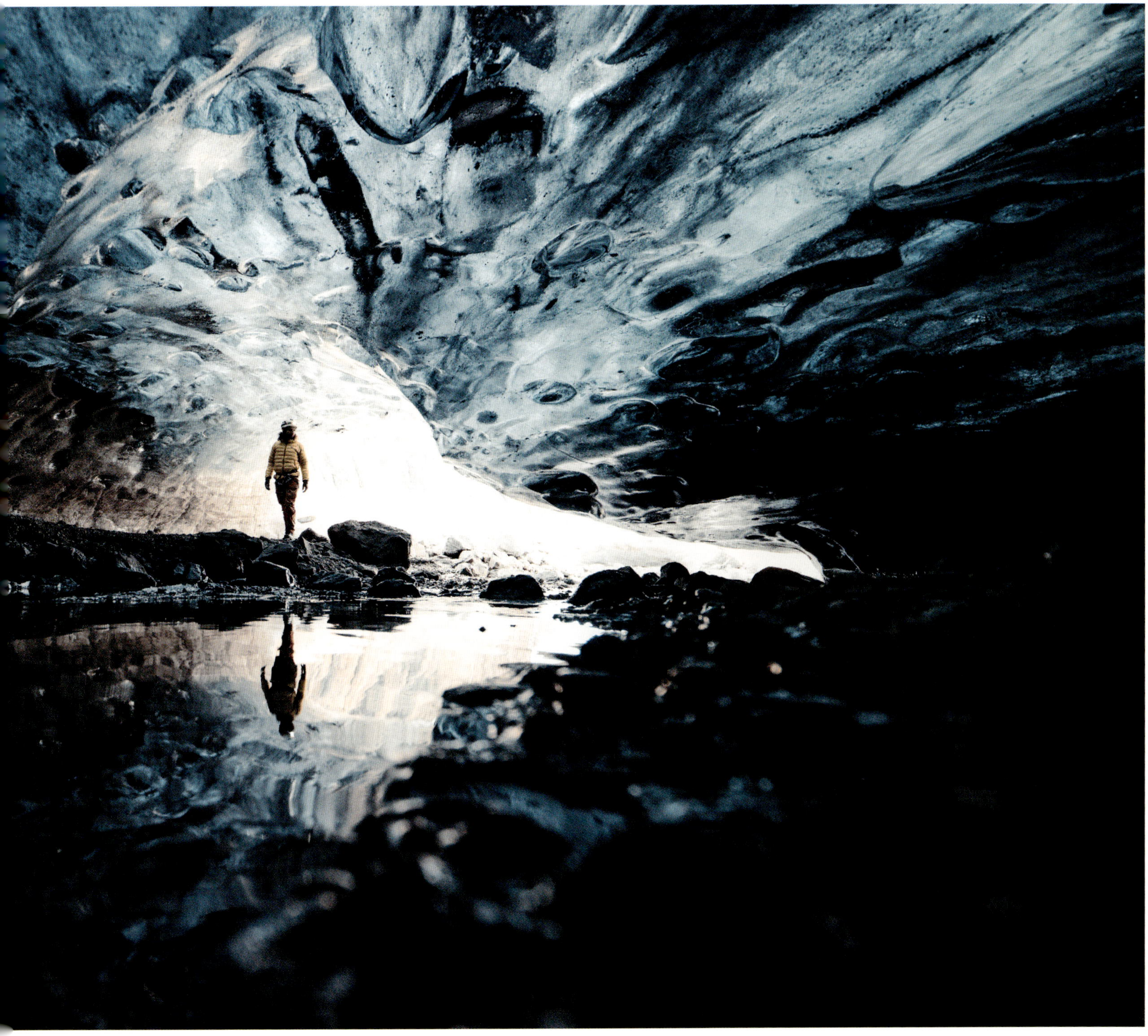

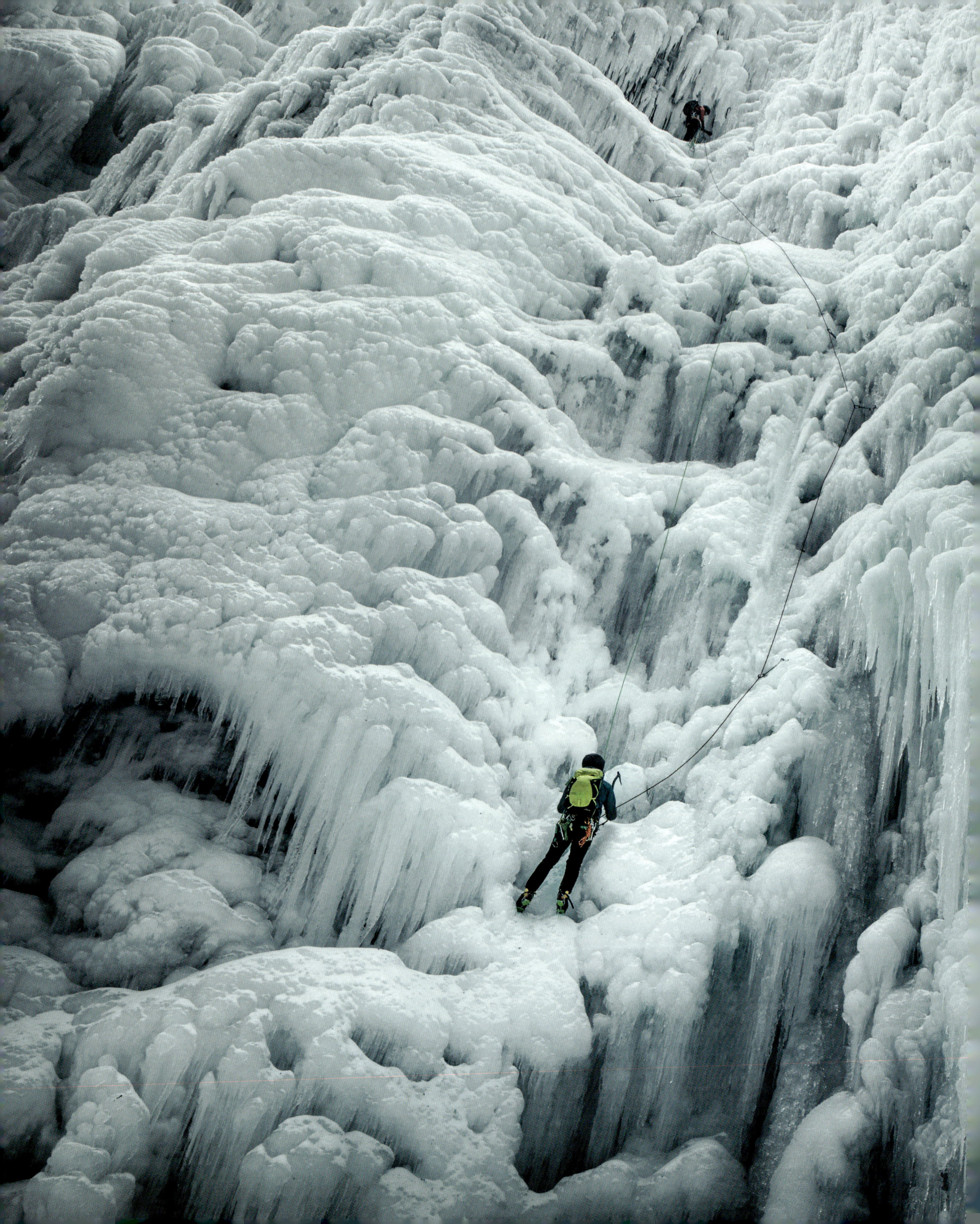

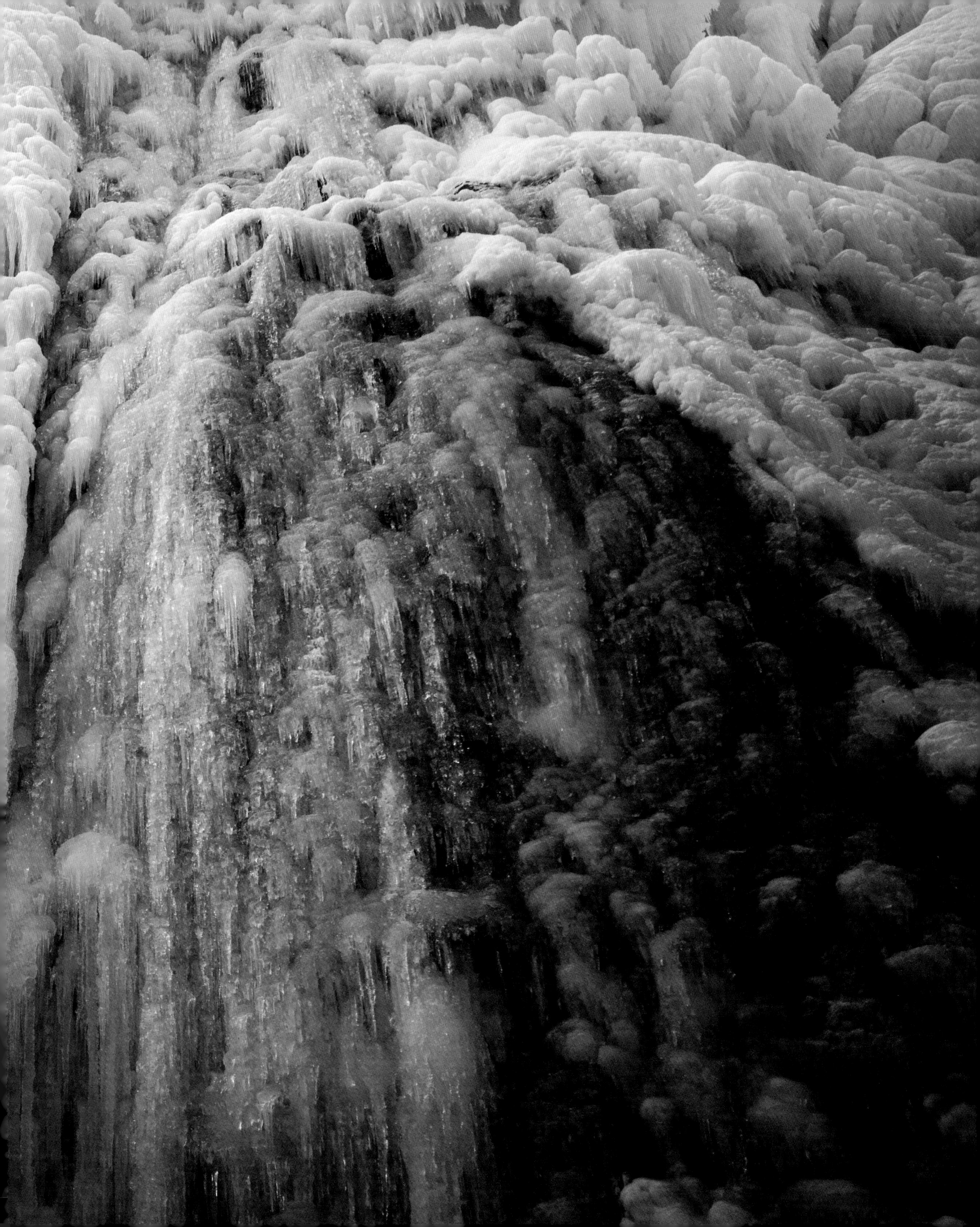

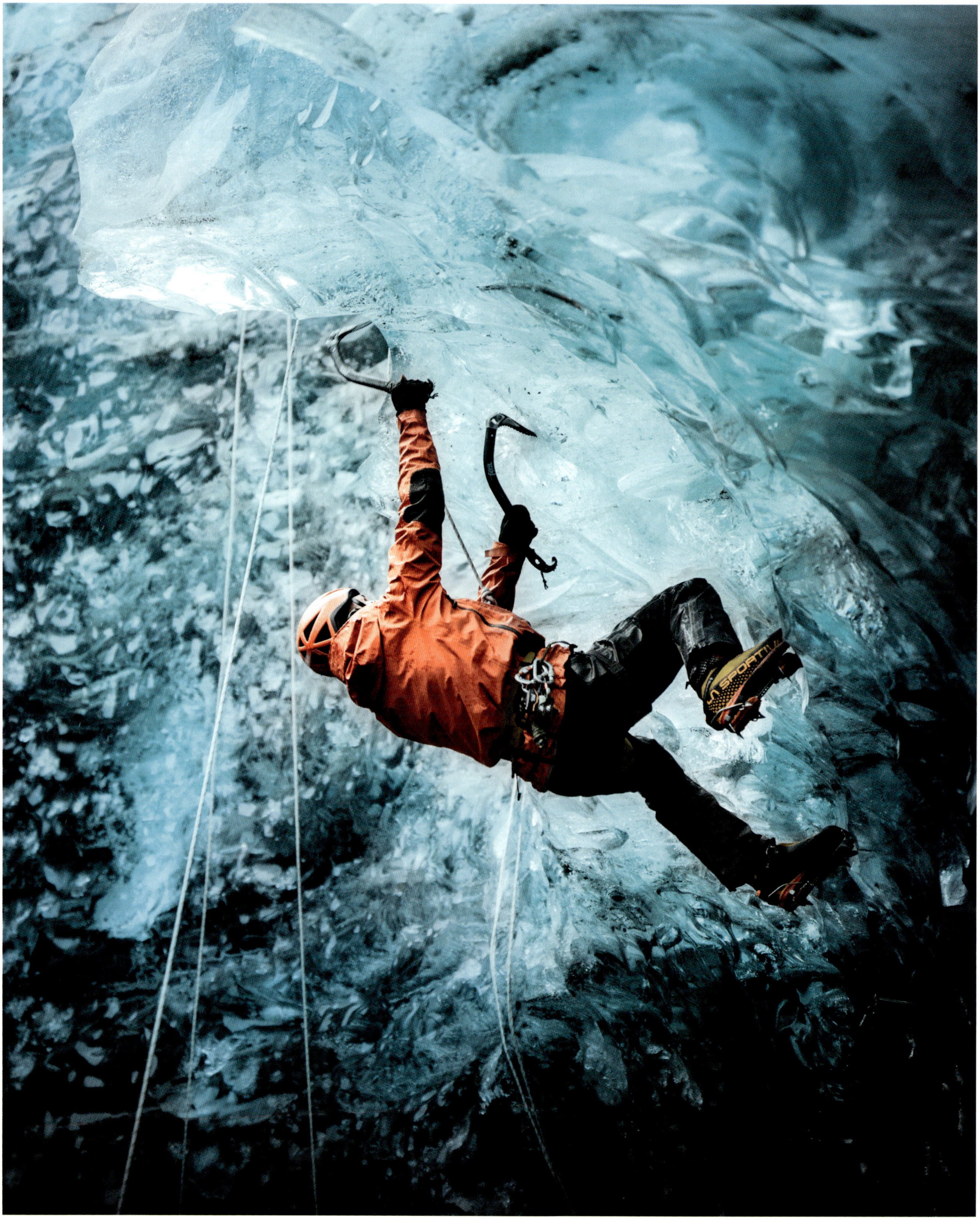

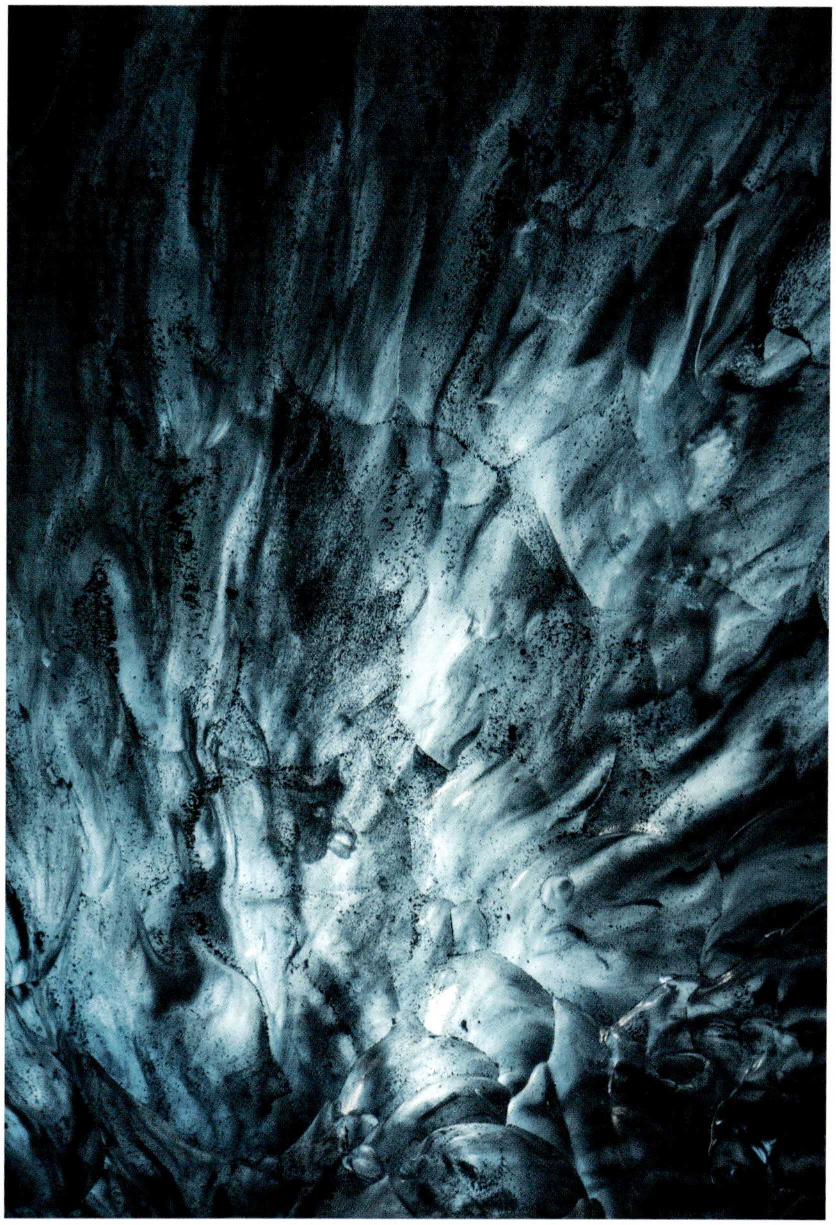

◀◀ GLYMUR

Winter is always coming in Iceland, but you can get to it before it arrives if you know where it likes to hide.

◀ BREIÐAMERKURJÖKULL II

Never growing up makes nature our playground. That's what the Vikings believed when they built the first glaciers of Iceland. Then they grew up and fought each other in family feuds instead. But cold is cold and winter is bad unless you find the fun in it.

▲ VARNAJÖKULL

A glacier expressing its emotions.

➤ FALLJÖKULL III

Not the place to drop your car keys.

➤➤ BREIÐAMERKURJÖKULL III

Looking for lost sheep, possibly frozen in the ice.

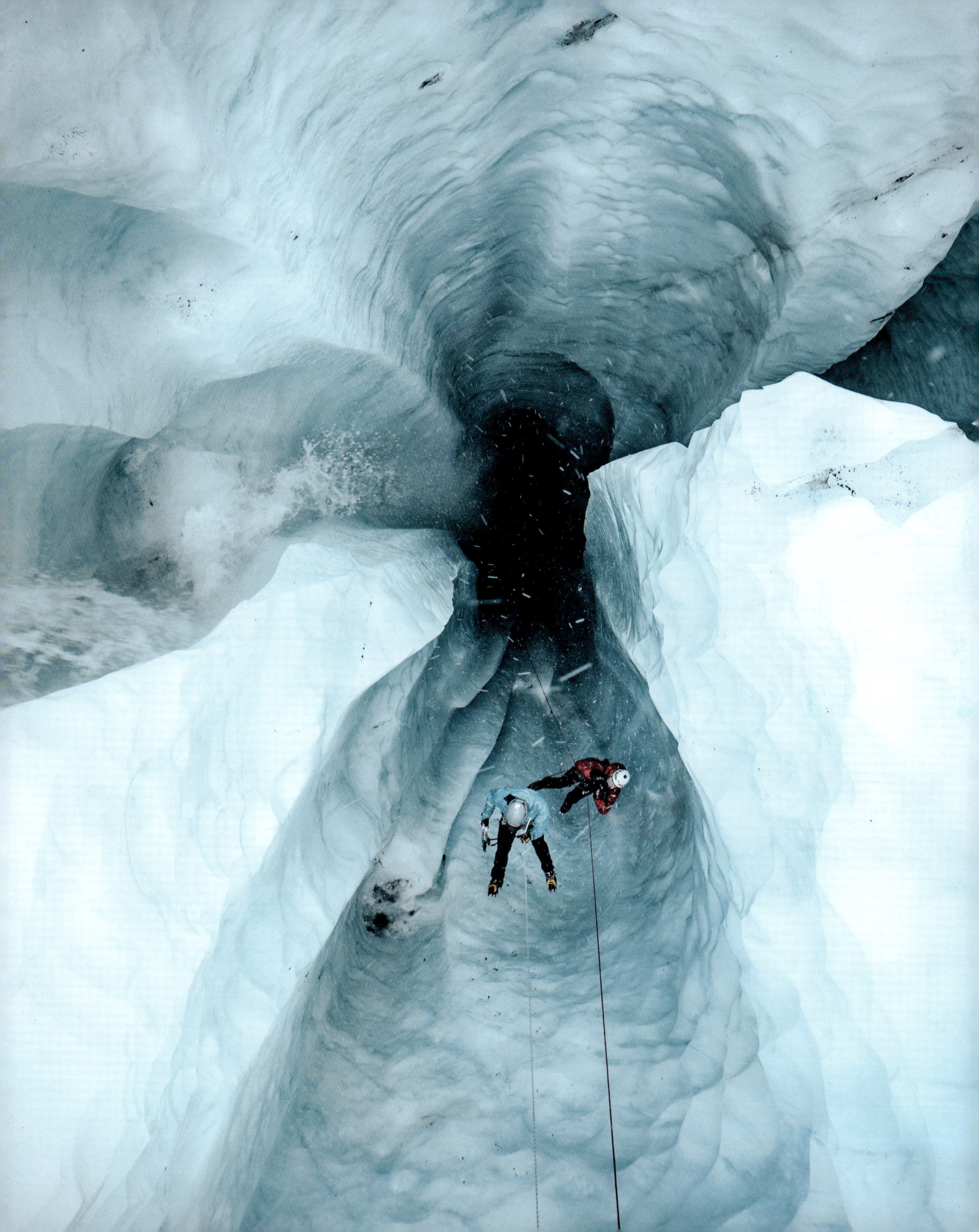

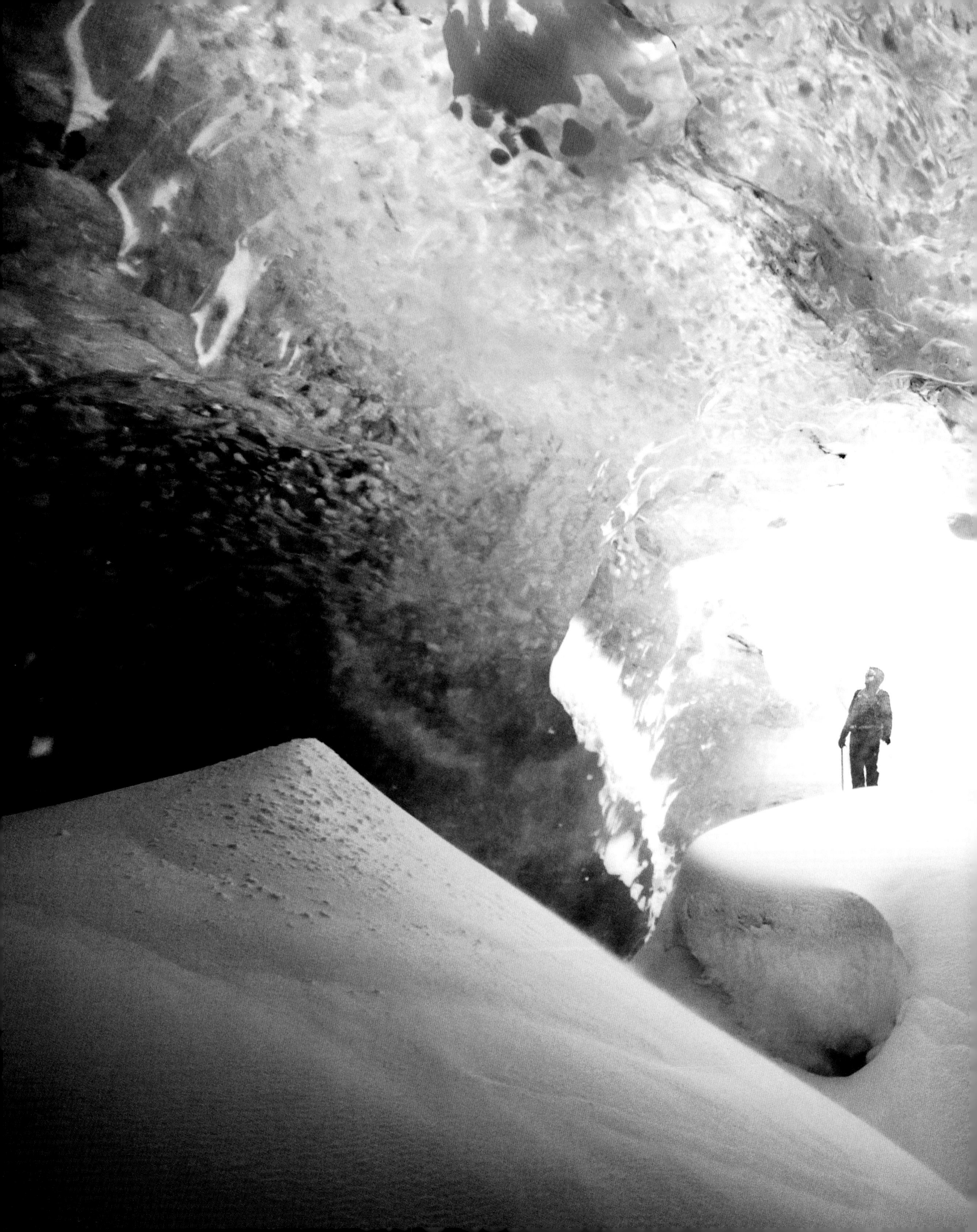

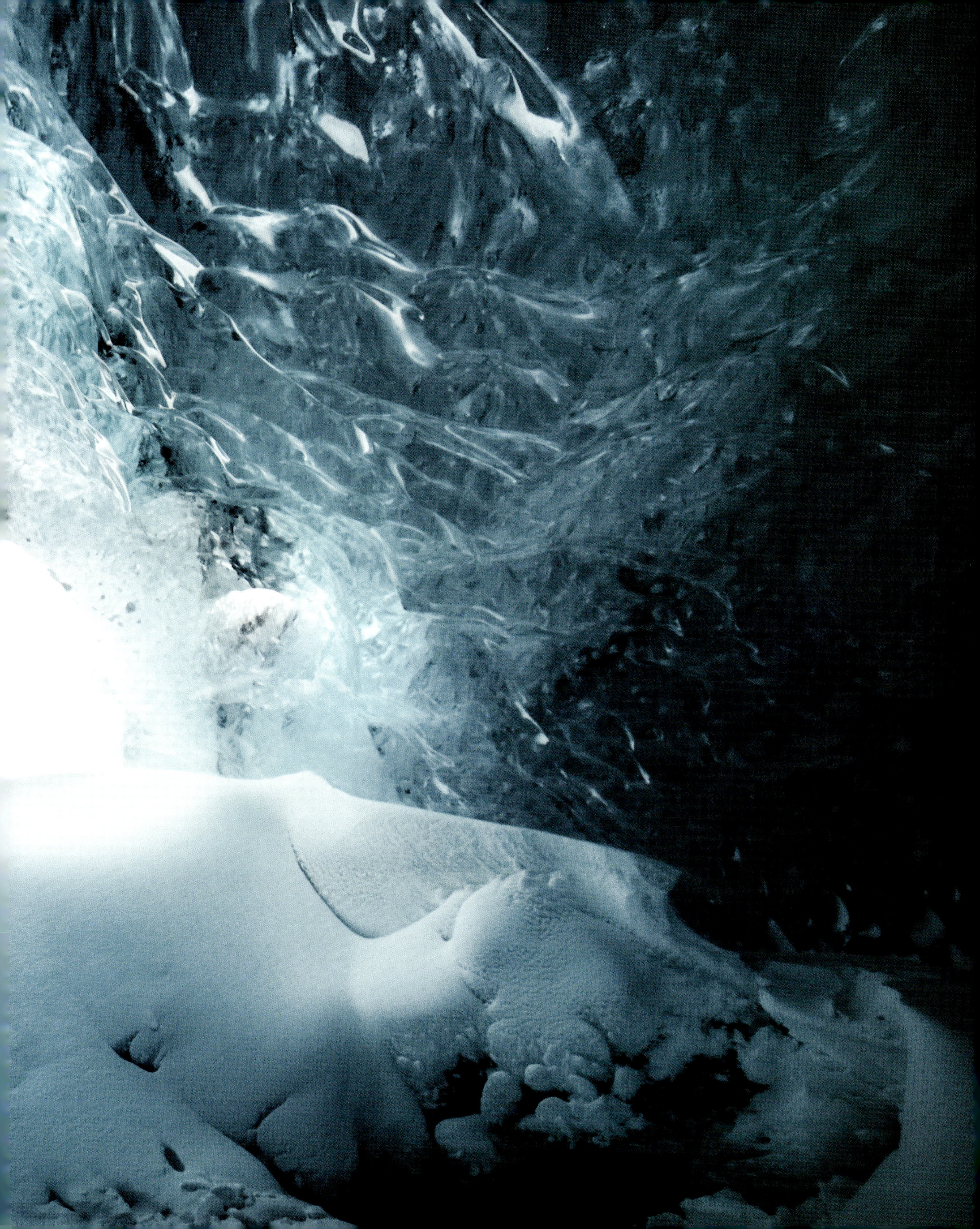

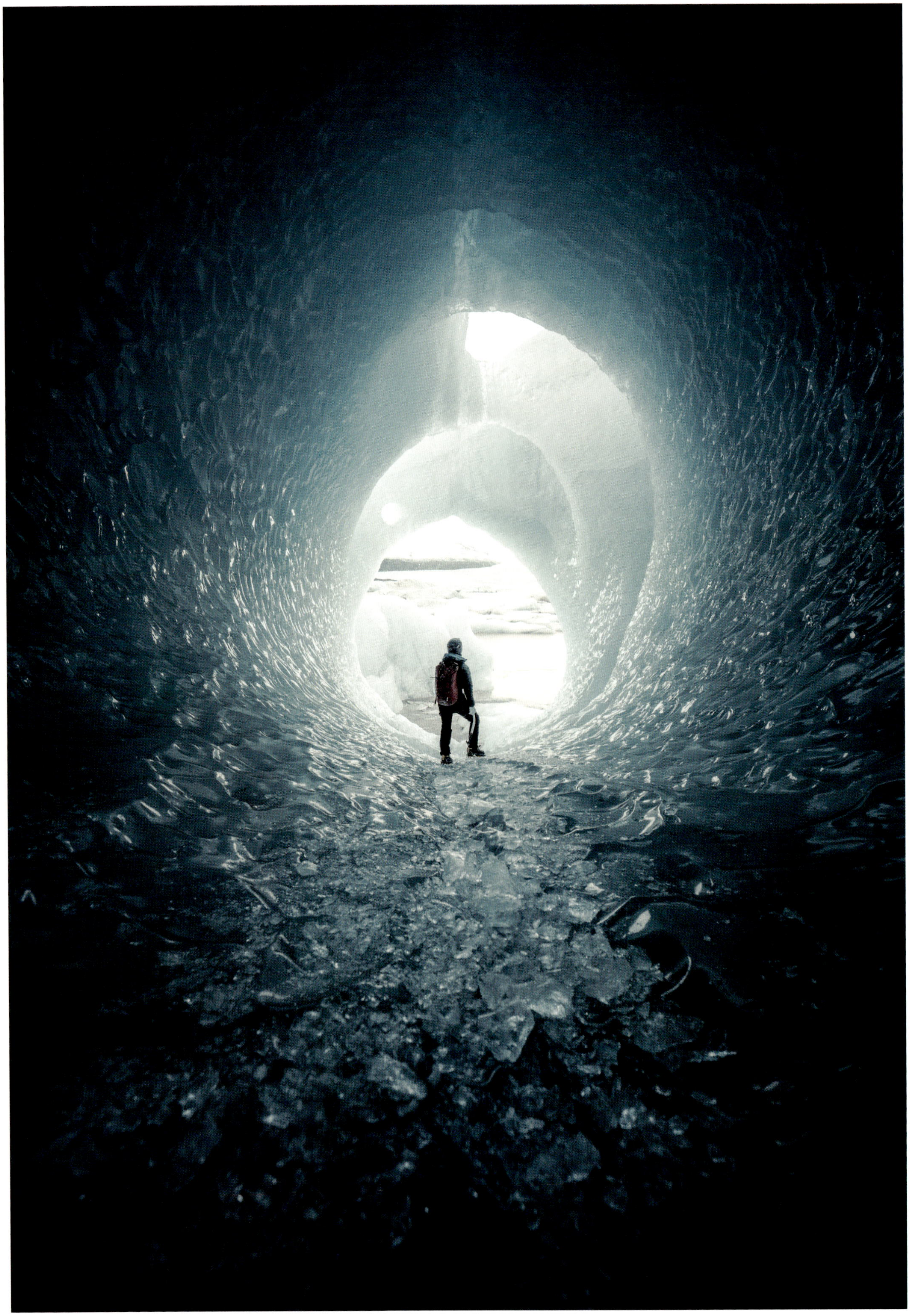

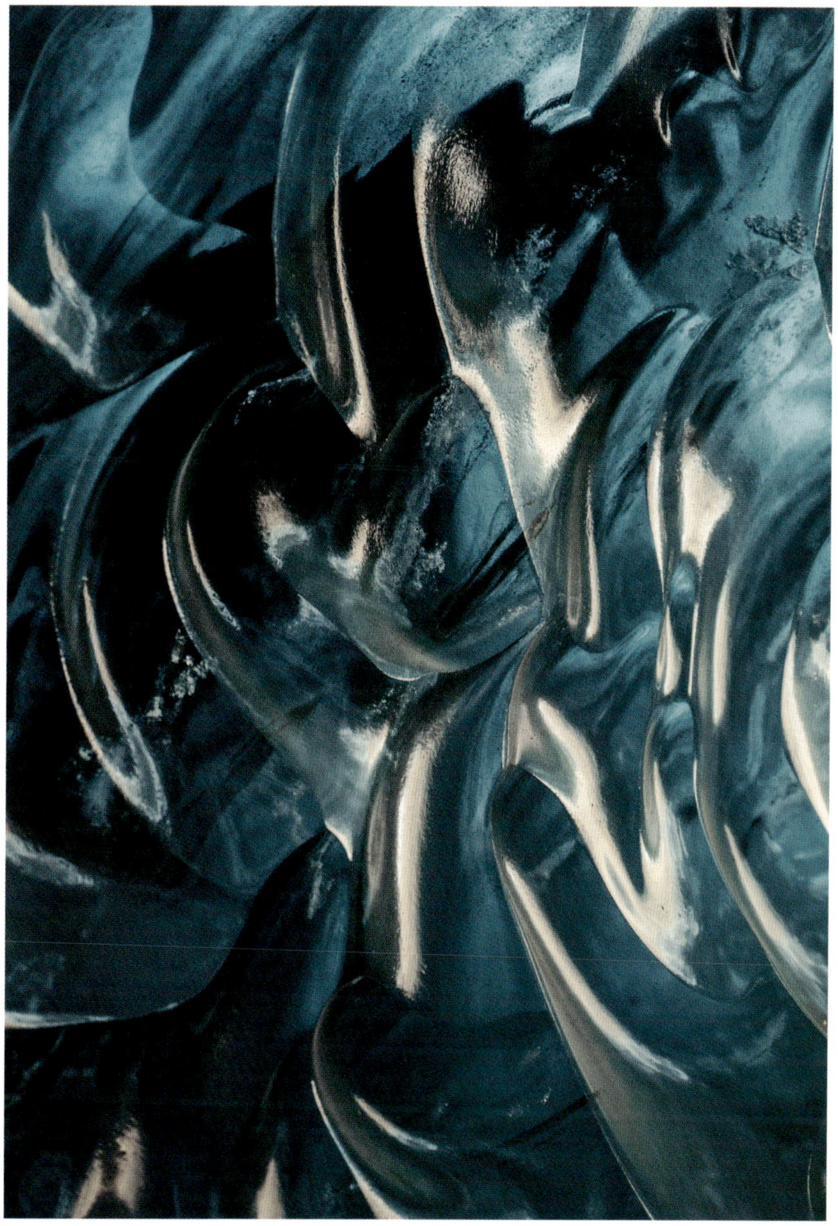

◂ VATNAJÖKULL VIII

The birth canal of a frost giant.

▴ VATNAJÖKULL IX

Walls of ice caves shaped like ripples do on the surface of an ocean. Except here they move in the slowest of motion.

▸▸ GRÍMSVÖTN (L)

When ice gets old, it gets wrinkles, just like us. And this ice is older than anyone here.

▸▸ GRÍMSVÖTN II (R)

Waves frozen in time.

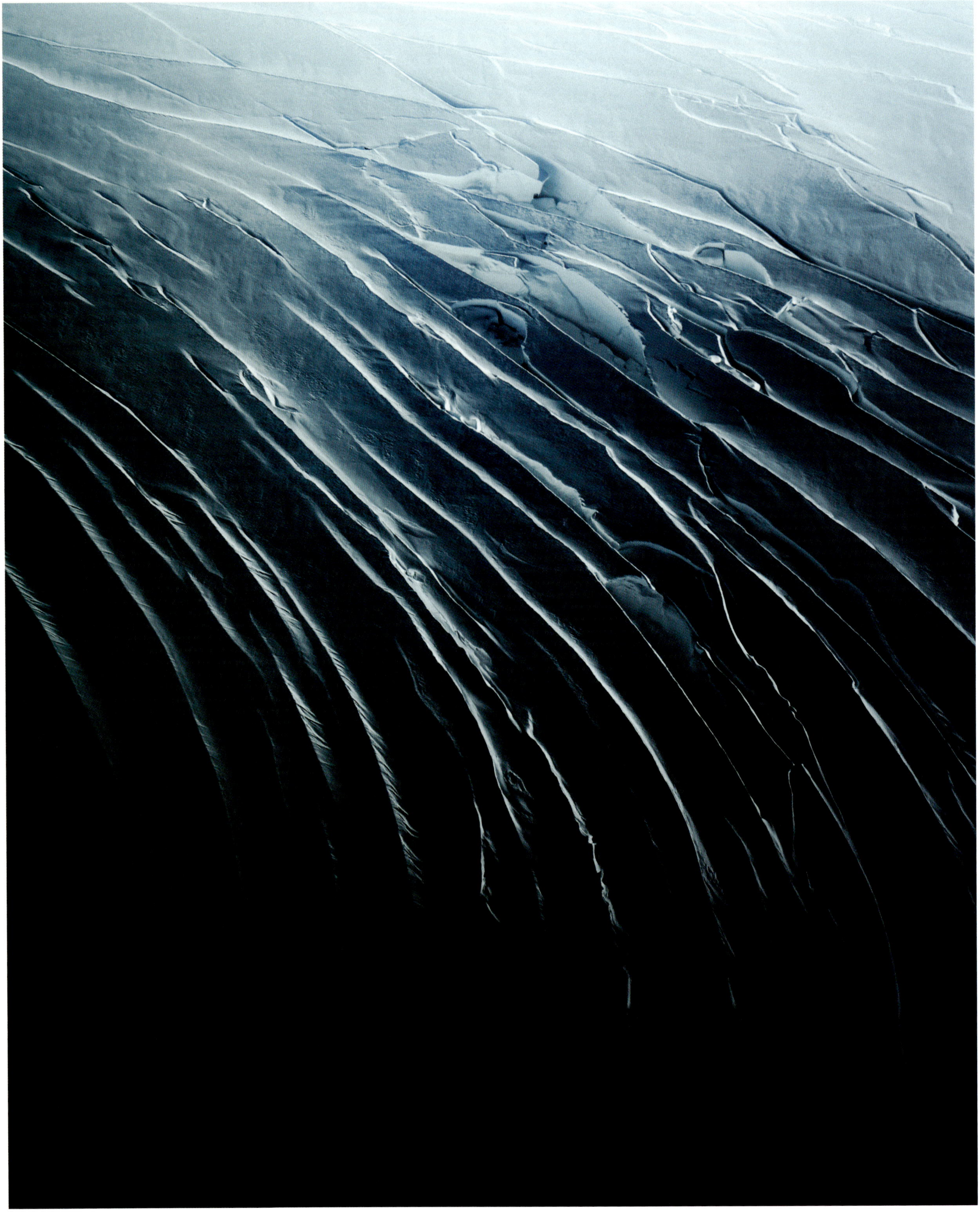

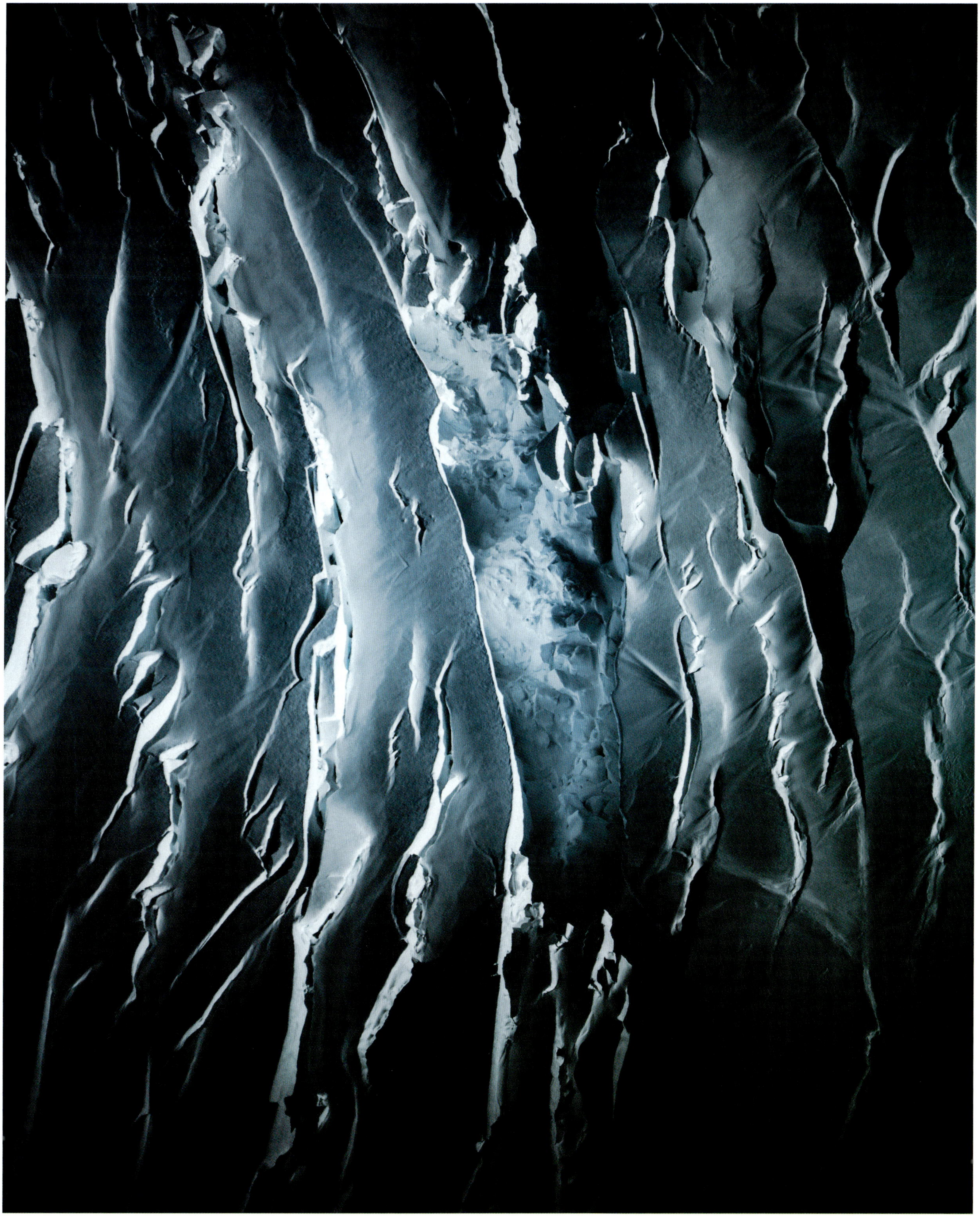

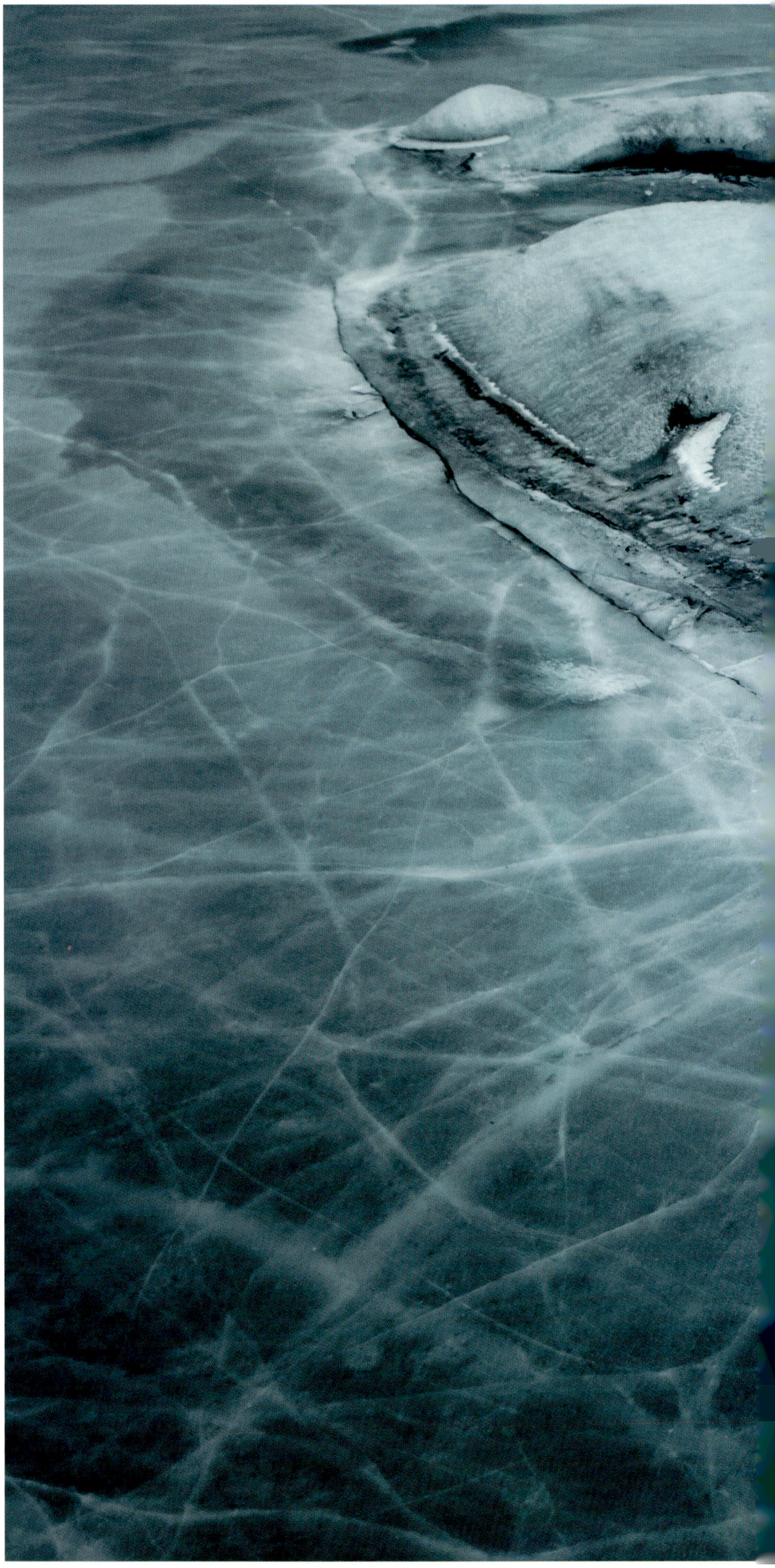

VATNAJÖKULL X

I've spent a lot of my days out here trying to put the glaciers back together piece by piece, but they just seem to keep breaking.

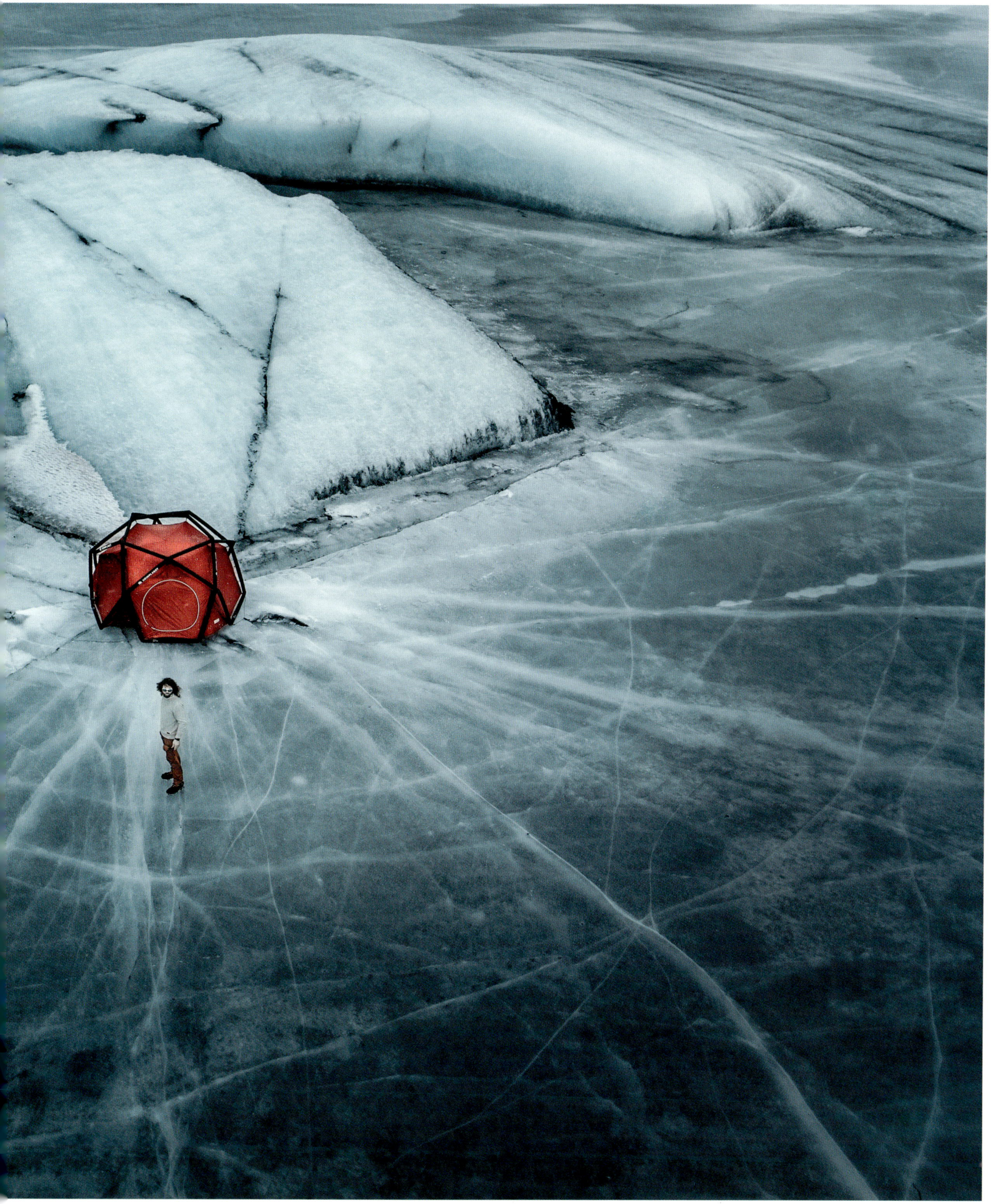

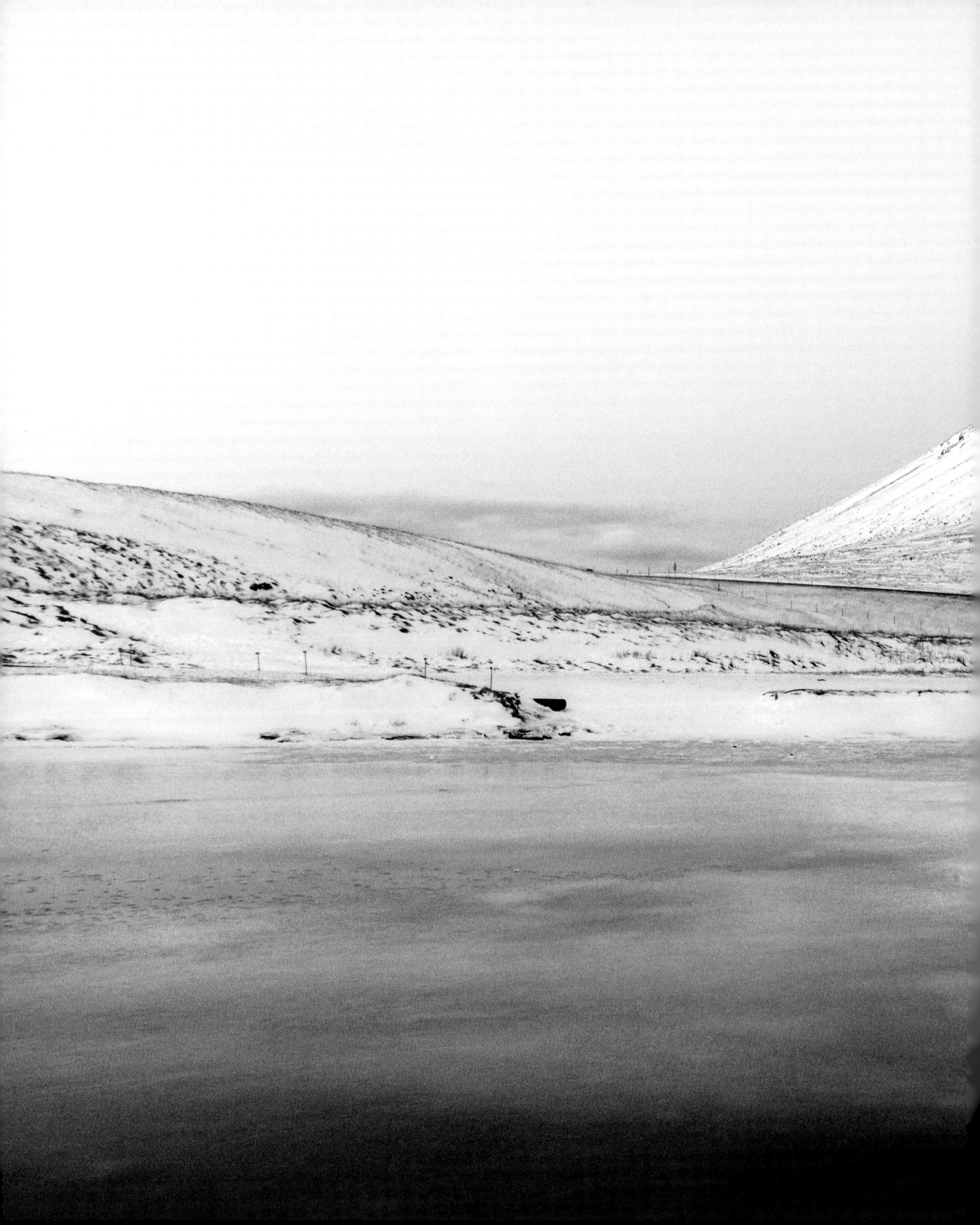

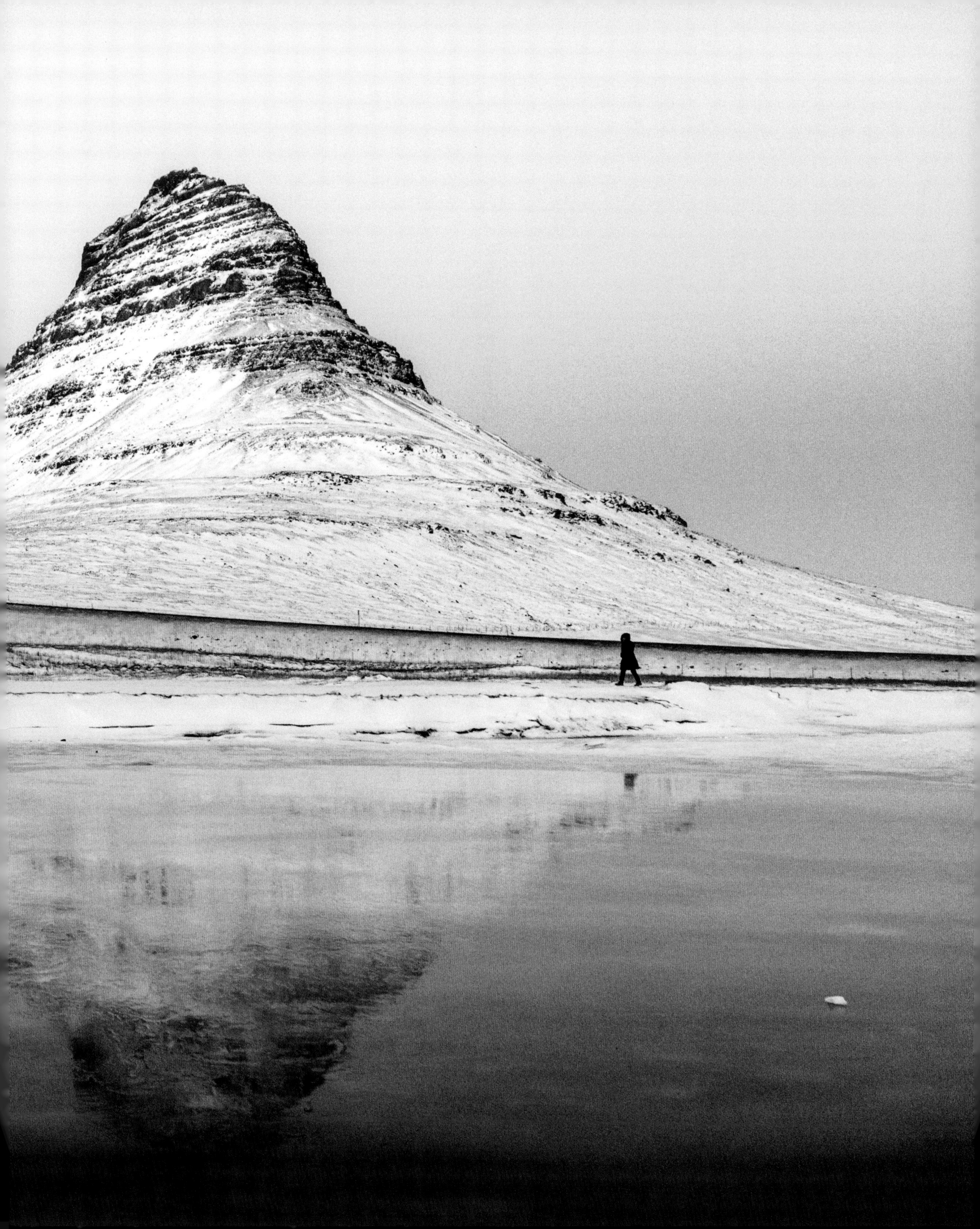

◂◂ KIRKJUFELL II

No photo book is complete without a photo of this mountain.

▸ SÓLHEIMAJÖKULL

Hold on to your camera and try not to get blown away by all these glacial blues.

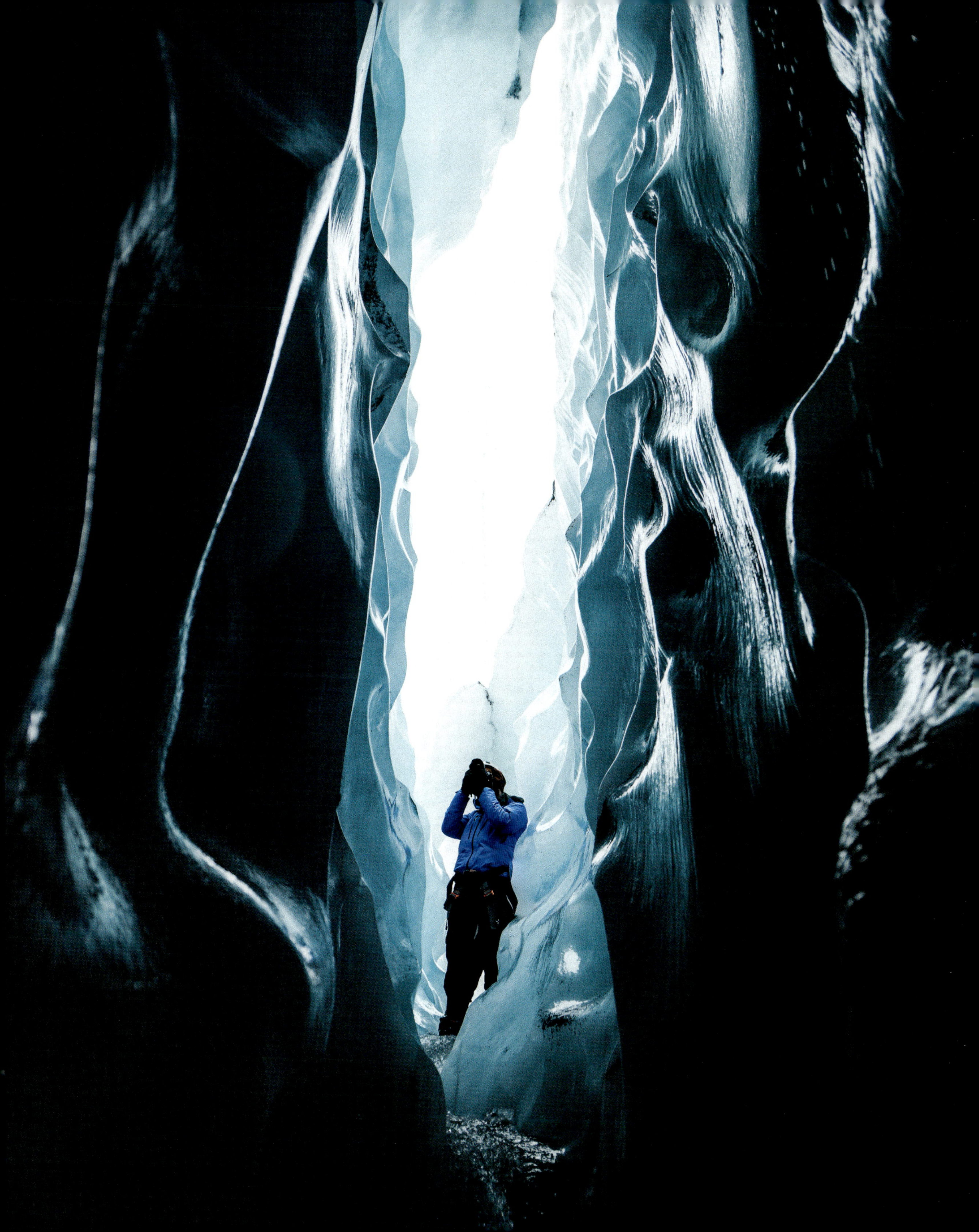

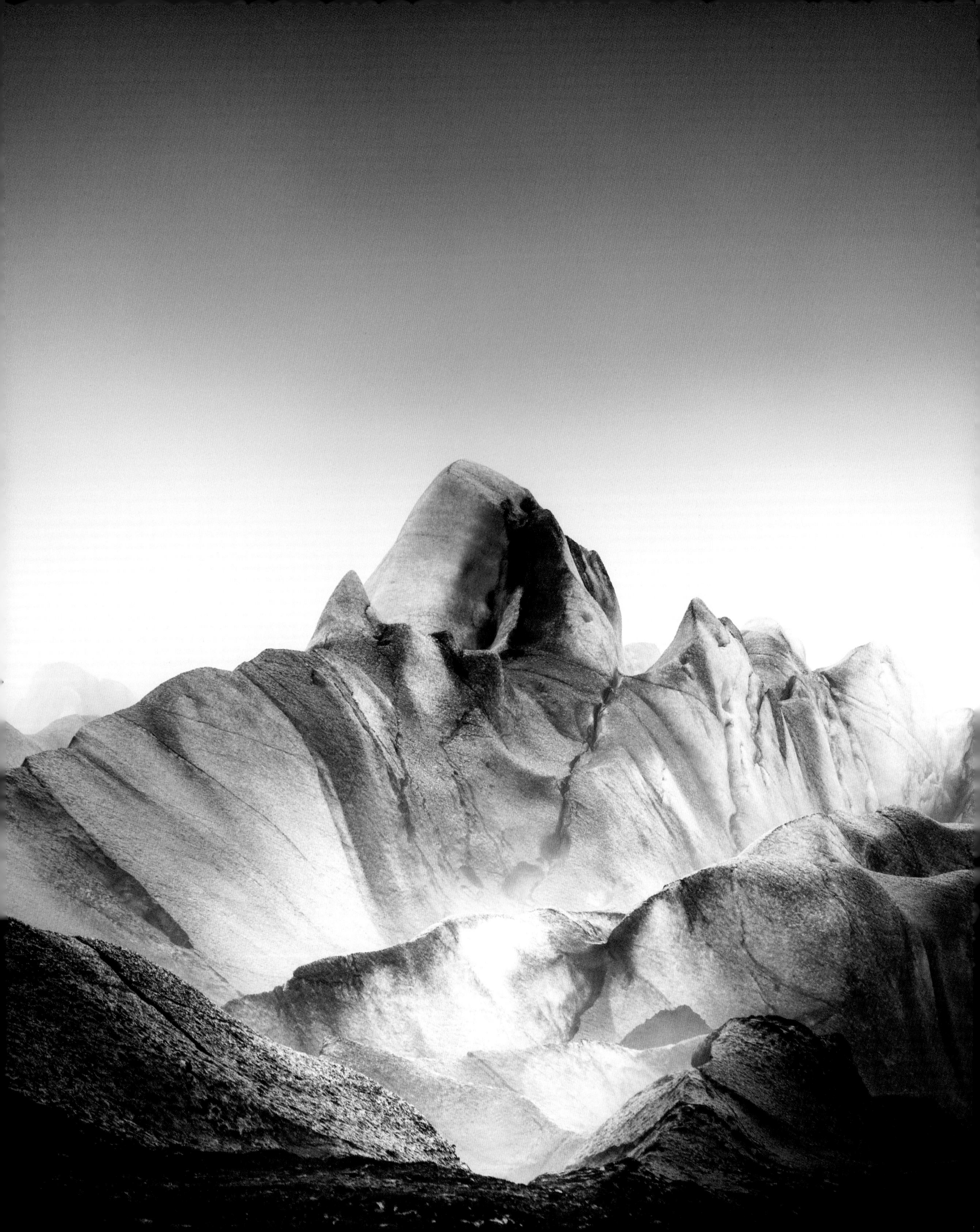

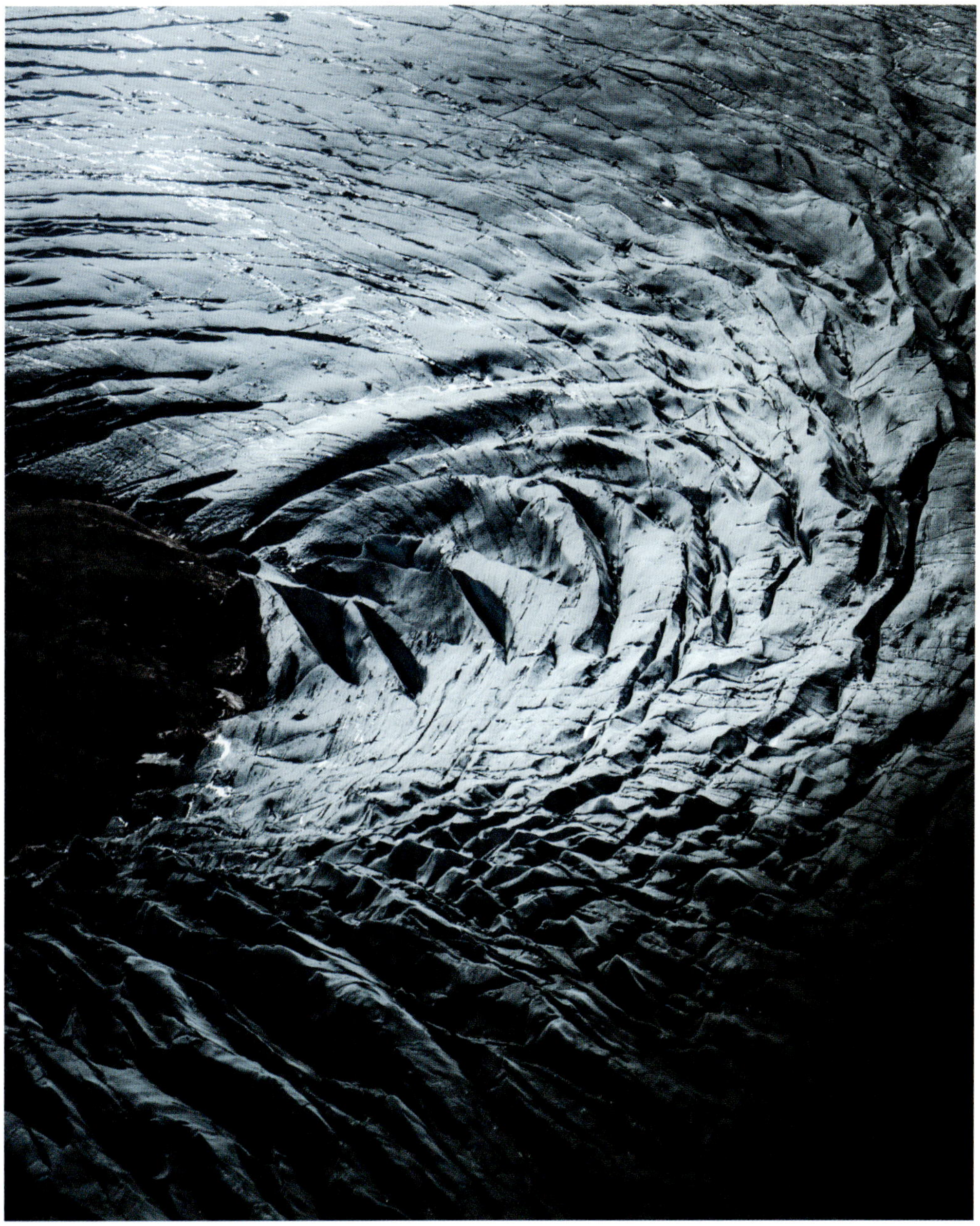

◂ VATNAJÖKULL XI

A glacier expressing its opinion on its survival in this massive nothingness.

▴ VATNAJÖKULL XII

A swirly whirly twirl.

▸▸ MORSÁRJÖKULL II

This is a glacier that doesn't get to see many humans up close. When it heard that we were coming on our three-day mission, it did its hair all nice and put its seracs up.

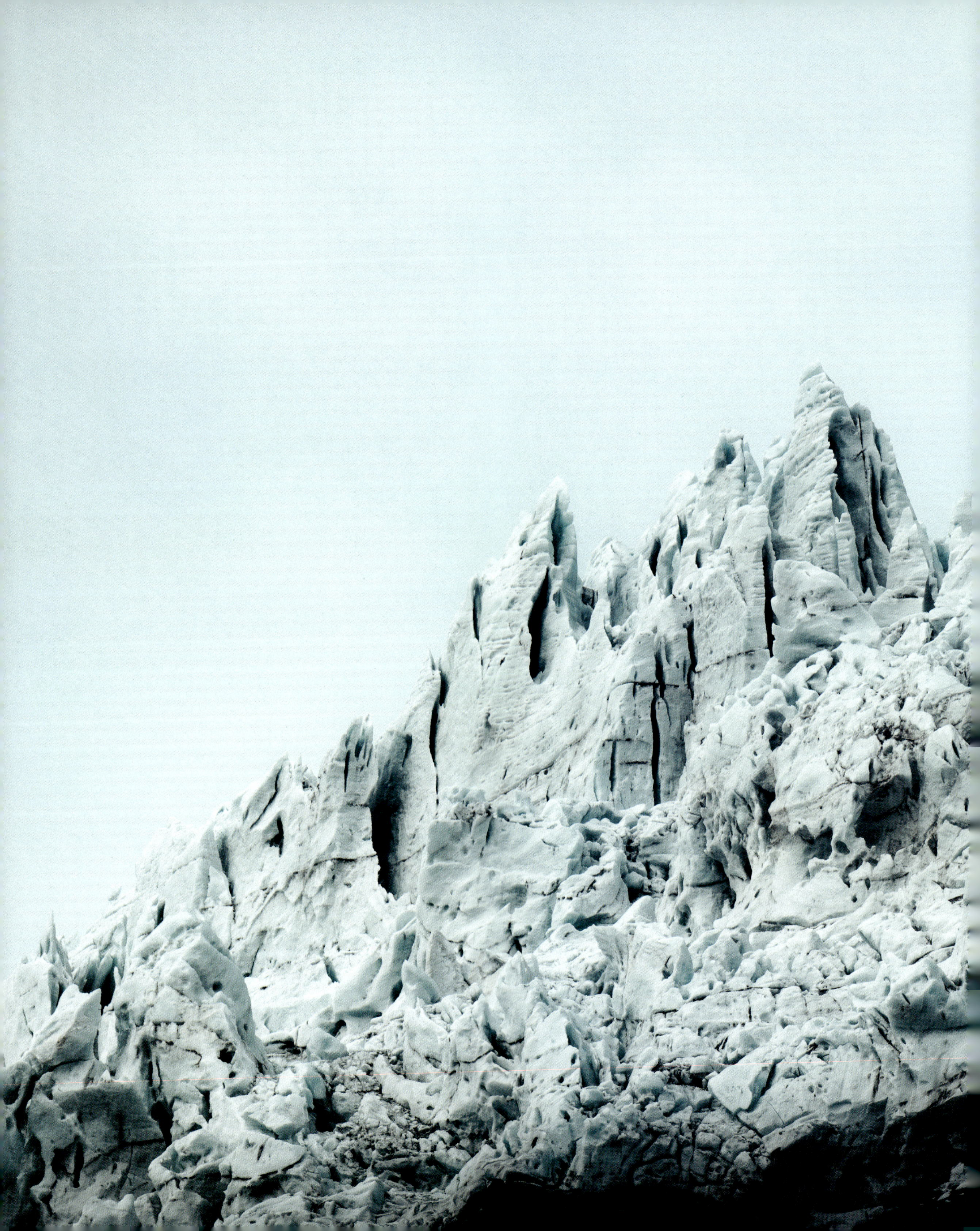

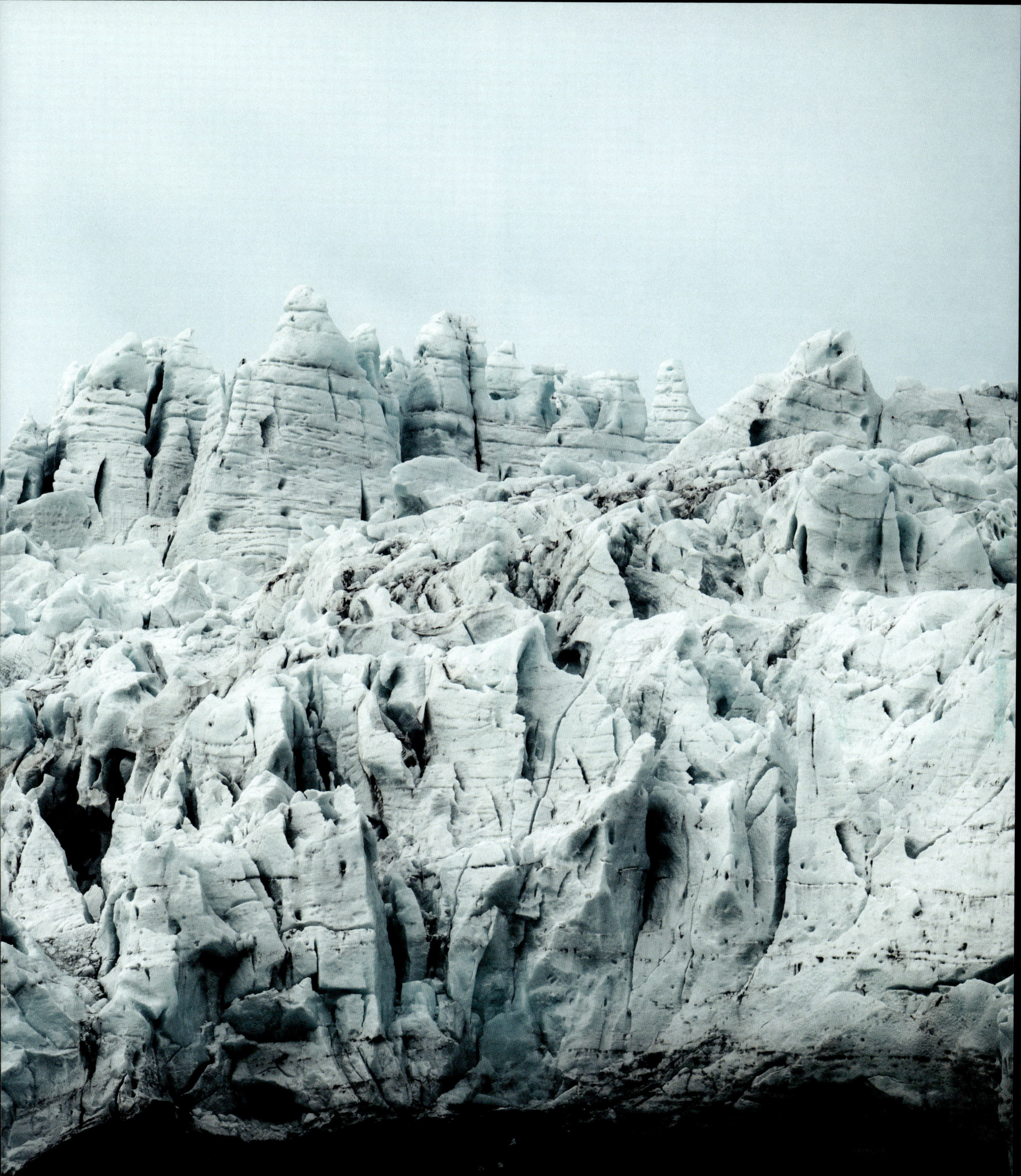

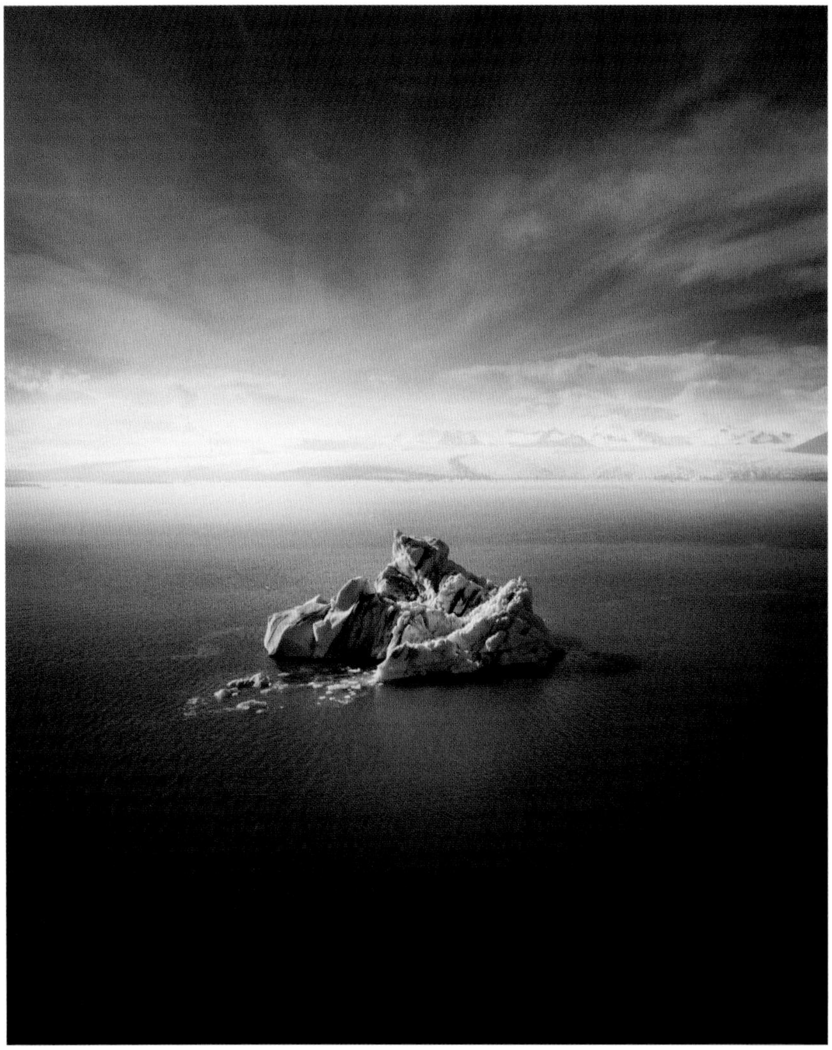

▲ JÖKULSÁRLÓN II

Born high up on the Vatnajökullian ice cap hundreds of years ago, this lone iceberg separated from its glacial family and set out on a journey. Leaving its nest, it headed out into the world to find its purpose—maybe sink a boat somewhere, swim with whales, be towed to the Bahamas for party ice, or find other icebergs to rub against. It doesn't yet know that it will never make it that far in solid form.

▶ SÓLHEIMAJÖKULL II

The two ices—one from above, the other from below—meet to see who is the hardest. One is from this winter while the other one is five hundred years old. So of course, that old one is harder and destroys everything in its path.

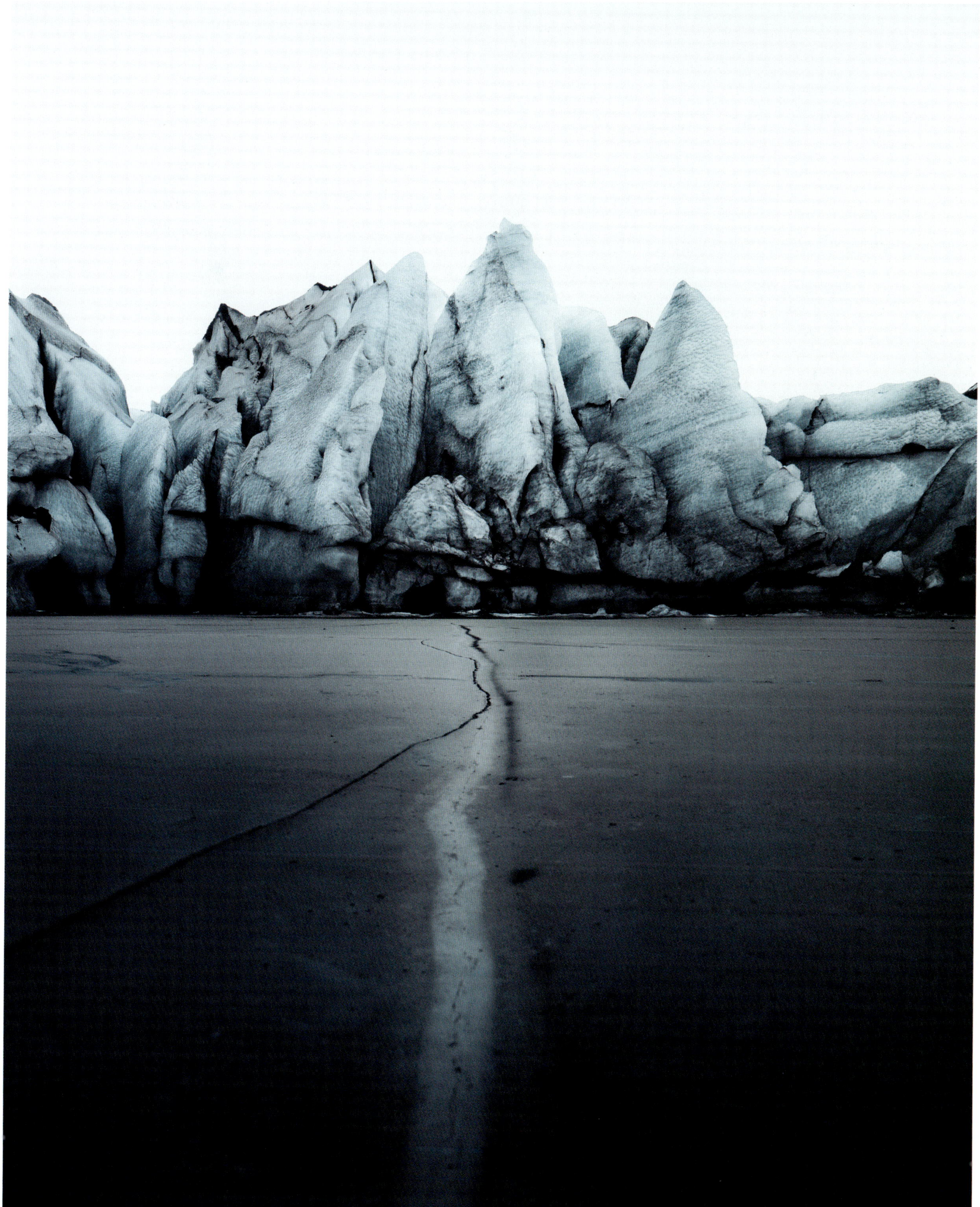

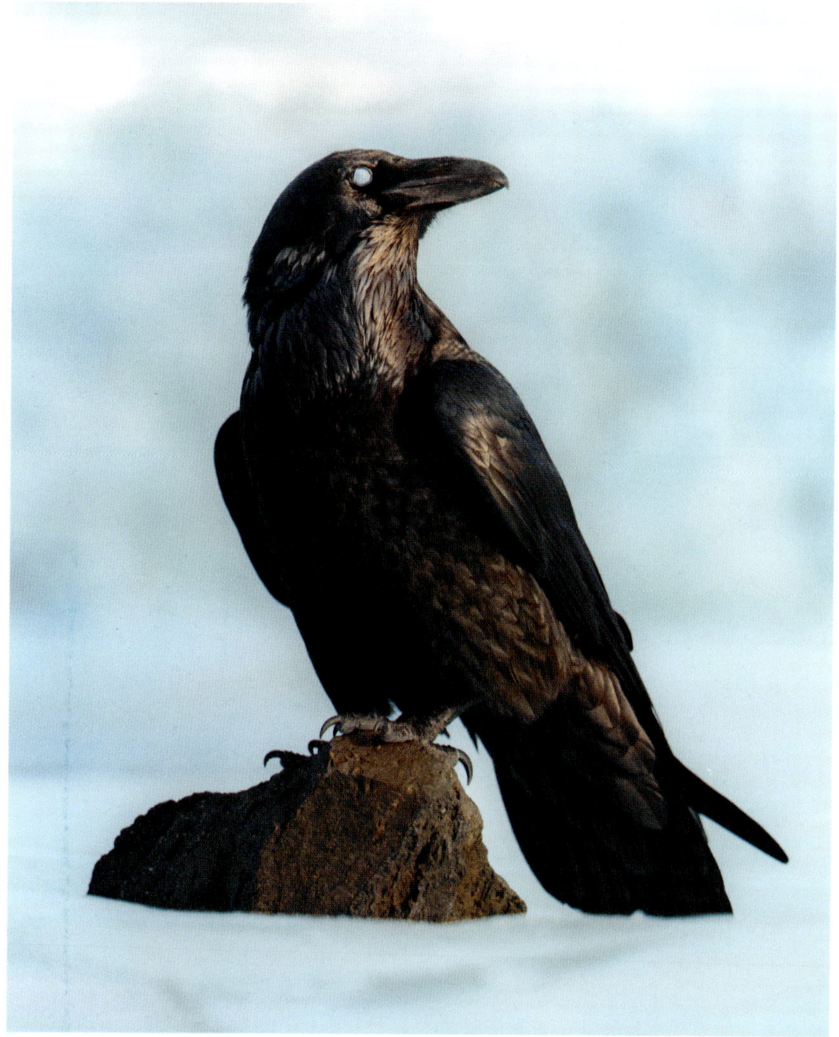

VATNAJÖKULL XIII

Just a bunch of pixels filled with a tiny bit of color, trying to make someone feel something.

FALLJÖKULL IV

Rolling waves freeze into peaks
Following where you have gone
Dusk has passed yet night is pierced
Finding truth in all you seek.

Seeing all, the worlds perceived
All that is now, all that is done
Never hidden, never seen
Windless whispers of all your deeds.

Every grain of ash will fall
Bury roots and crush what's gone
Missing eyes have seen beyond
At the end of the sky awaits the hall.

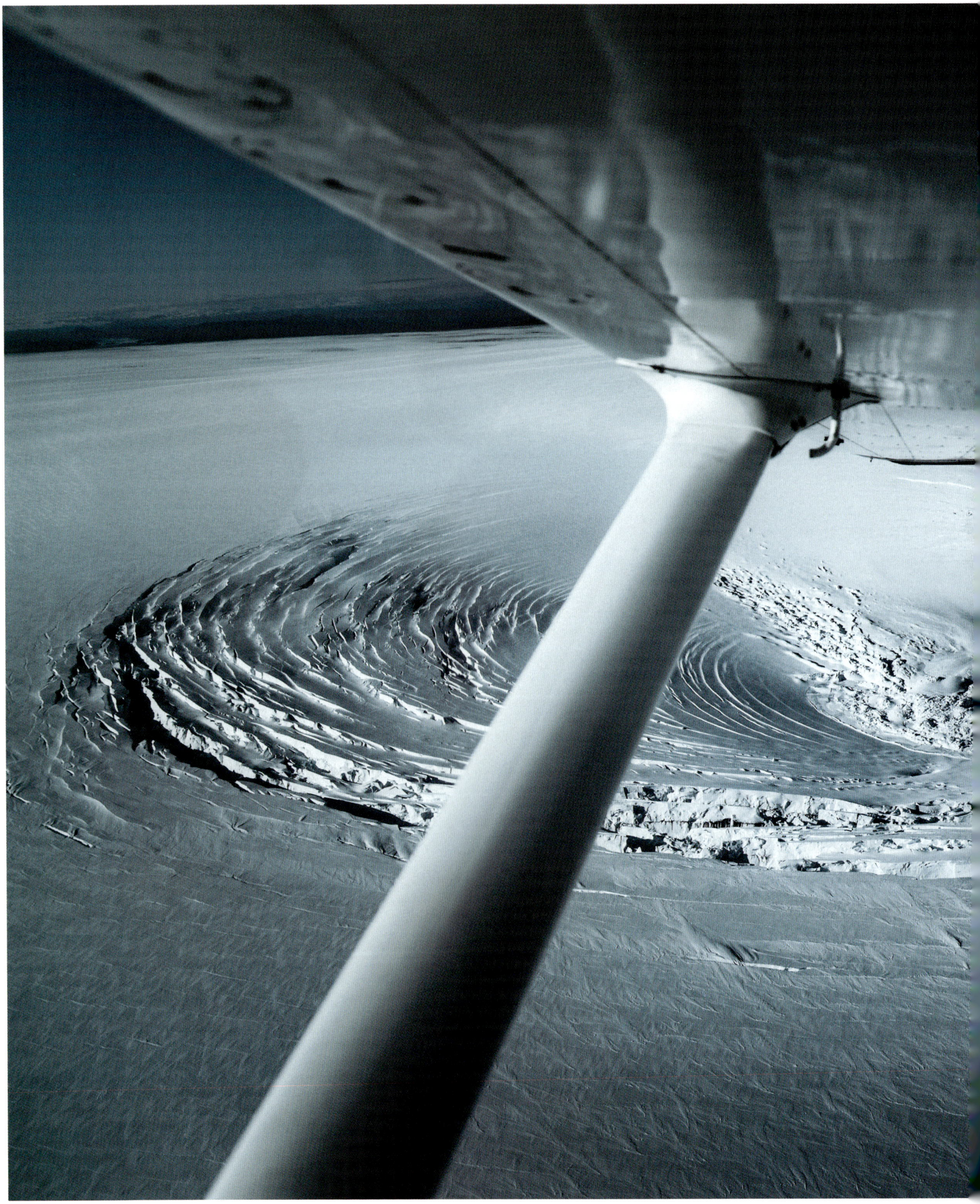

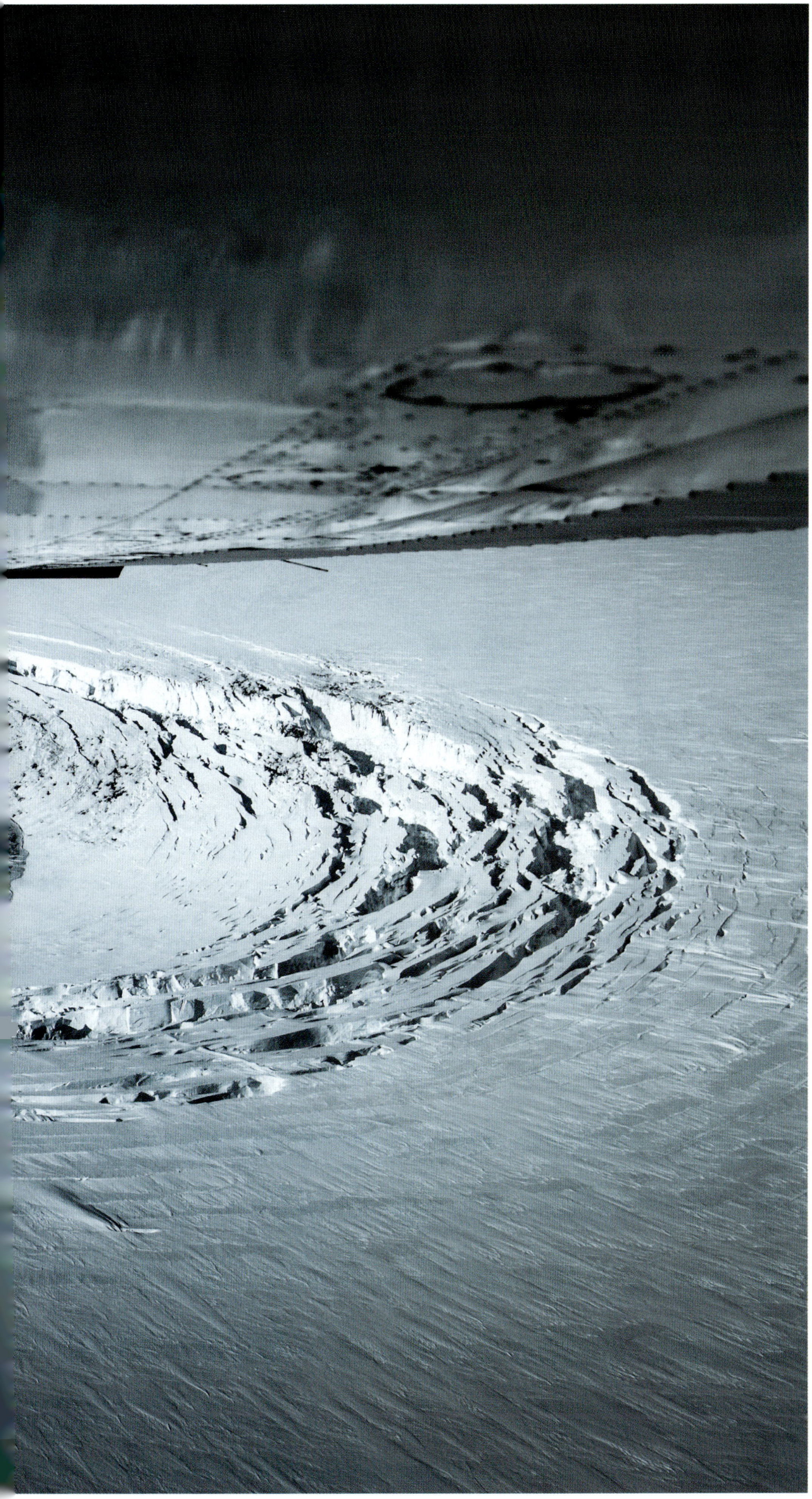

GRÍMSVÖTN III

As the volcano beneath the glacier starts waking up, its geothermal activity melts the ice cap above it, creating some of the most extreme ice formations I have ever witnessed.

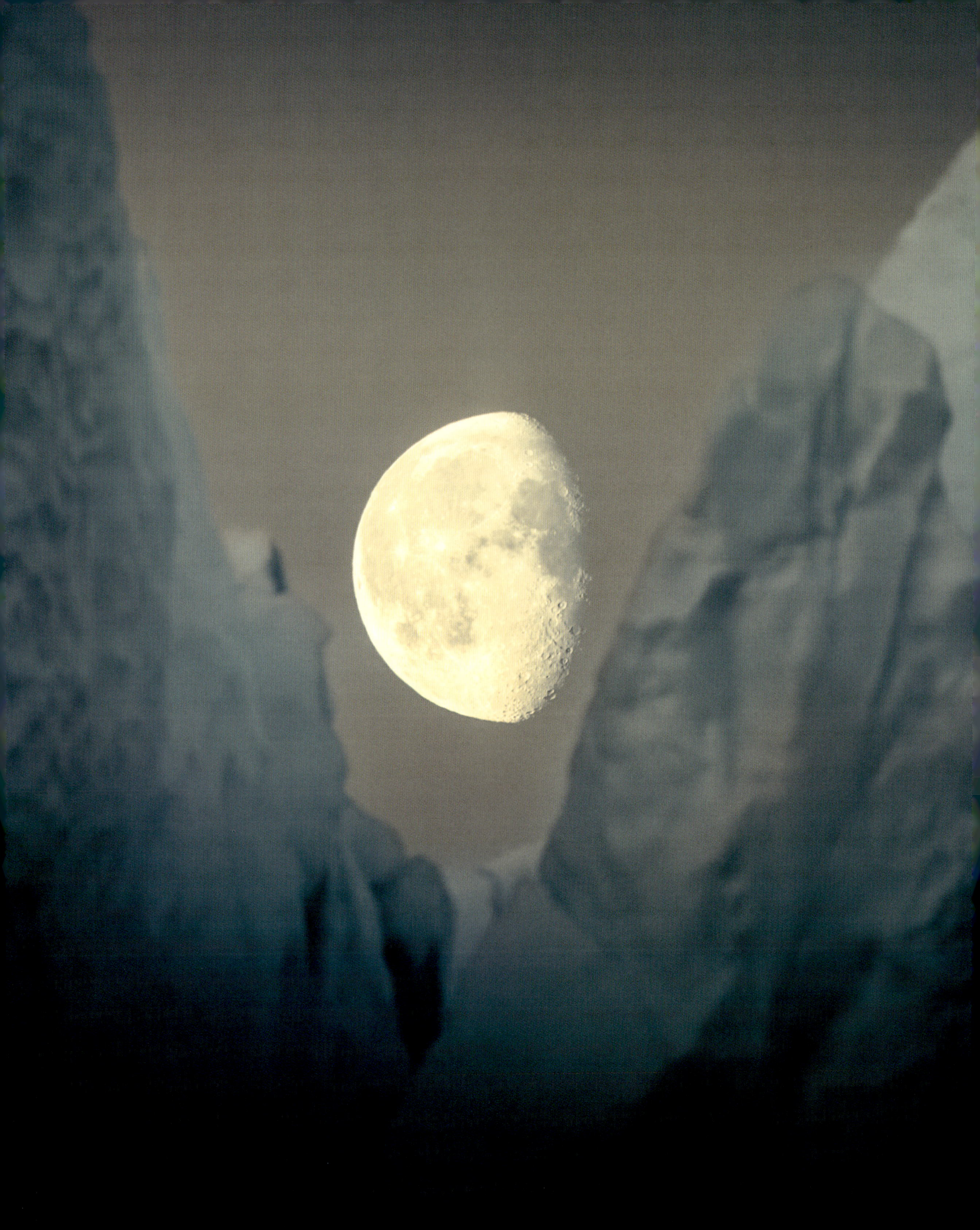

◂ THE MOON

One day, I looked at the moon with my eyes. Then I picked up a tube and looked in the tube and made the moon big inside the tube. Here's the moon, all big inside the tube.

▸▸ JÖKULSÁRLÓN III

Born high up on the Vatnajökullian ice cap hundreds of years ago, this lone iceberg separated from its glacial family and set out on a journey. Leaving its nest, it headed out into the world to find its purpose—maybe sink a boat somewhere, swim with whales, be towed to the Bahamas for party ice, or find other icebergs to rub against. It doesn't yet know that it will never make it that far in solid form.

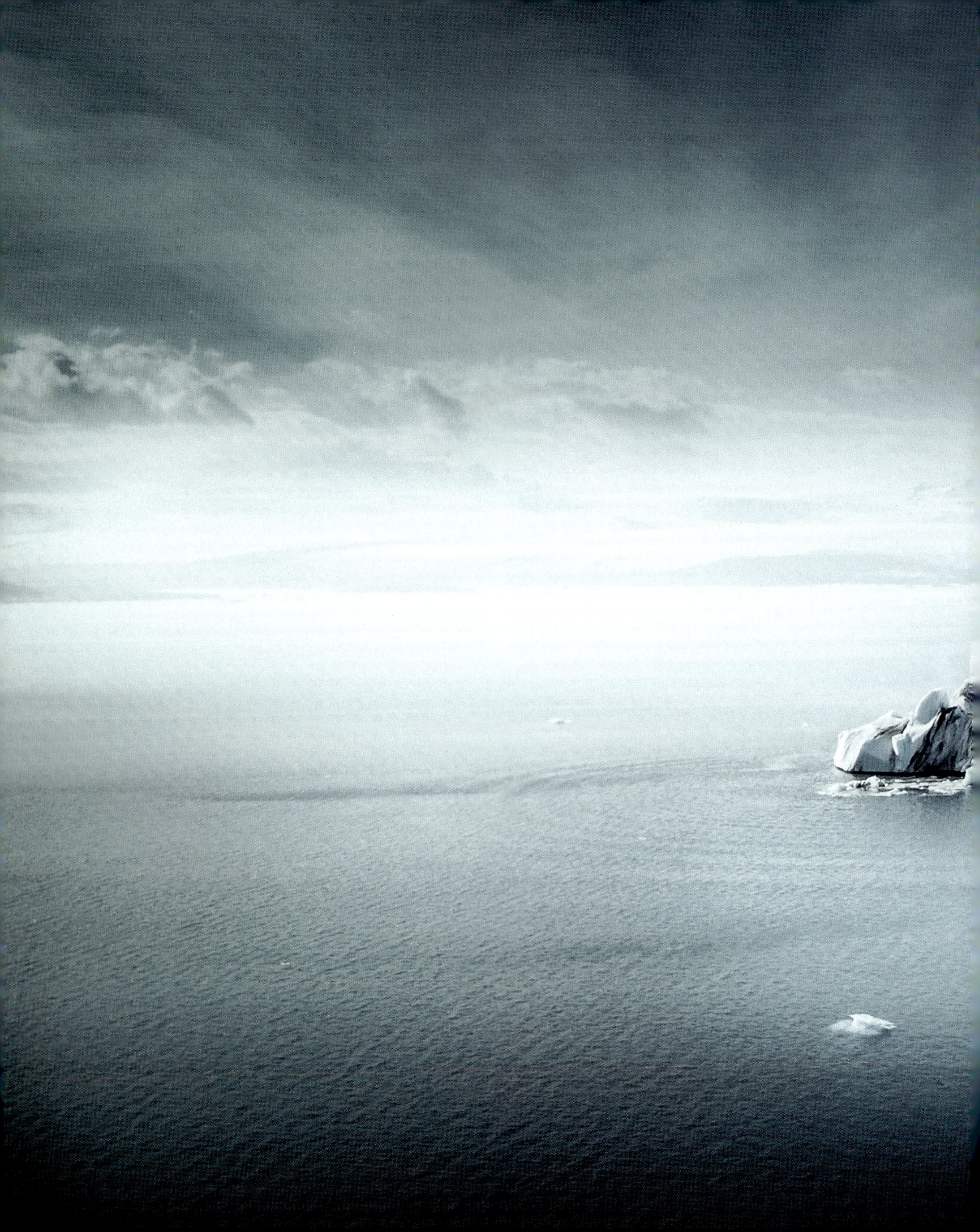

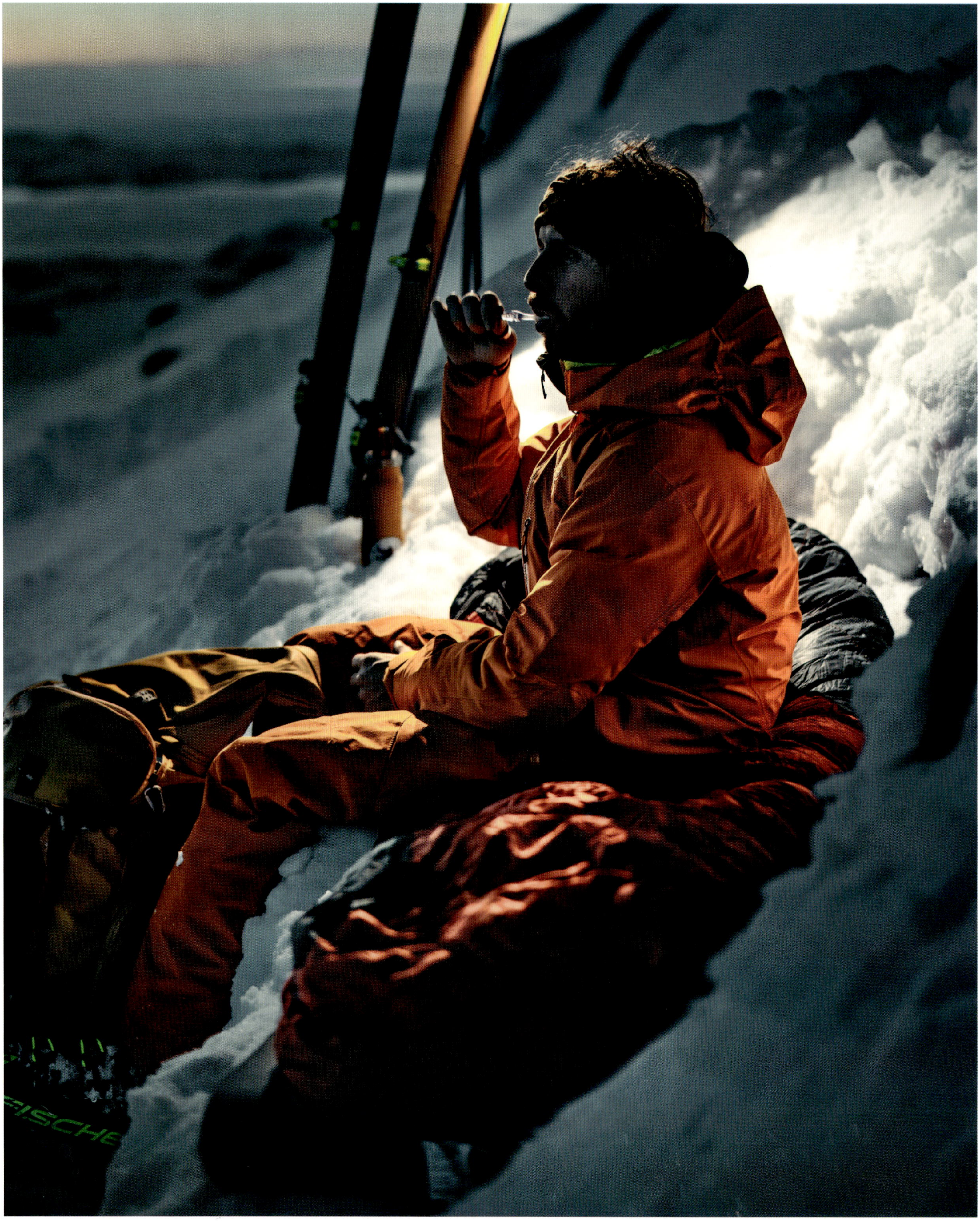

GEAR LIST

In a land where the weather changes every five minutes, usually for the worse, and ten different seasons go by in a day, including Hell and all of its lava, it's important to have the right gear. What I've compiled here isn't really a technical list but more like a survival checklist for what it takes to get these photos out there.

Always bring all your layers. Going away for a few hours should look like leaving for months.

You also need two beers for every mission. One for when you reach the peak, and one for when you're snowed in up there and can't find the way down.

Always have a pair of skis in your back pocket for a quick exit. Or if you run out of snow, maybe get into paragliding. Falling is the fastest way down the glacier.

Crampons, ice axes, rope, and harness are also important—just so you can look like a local if anyone ever doubts you.

A drone, and a backup drone for when the first one tries to fly back to its manufacturer in protest of your choice of a holiday destination.

Three batteries, because the first two usually die from the cold before you even get a chance to use them.

Sunglasses so no one can see you cry when the weather breaks you.

An umbrella, because clinging to one is your ticket to the cheapest possible sightseeing flight around Iceland.

This book, so you can admire these places when the fog doesn't lift for two weeks straight.

ACKNOWLEDGMENTS

A heartfelt thank you to Iceland for not being afraid to be what it is, despite getting a lot of complaints about its weather, its distance from the rest of the world, its prices, and the fact that it stayed undiscovered by almost everyone until its volcano shut down Europe in 2010. I hope you stay original and never change.

Also thank you to GORE-TEX for making clothes that are waterproof for the first fifteen minutes of the horizontal rainstorm that hits every Tuesday, Thursday, Saturday, and every other emotionally unstable Sunday (with a possibility of doubling that time by adding a second layer of GORE-TEX). Their clothes are also lava-proof if you run fast enough over the bubbling glow, as long as you close your eyes while doing it.

A massive thanks to Nikon, who keep sending me cameras despite my best efforts to break them, with assistance from the Icelandic weather. My Nikon cameras are real champs out there in the extremes and have never let me down.

And last of all, I give all my love to the people here in Iceland. Thank you for the space in your hearts, and for staying open and generous in the face of the elements (even if you don't always like to show it).

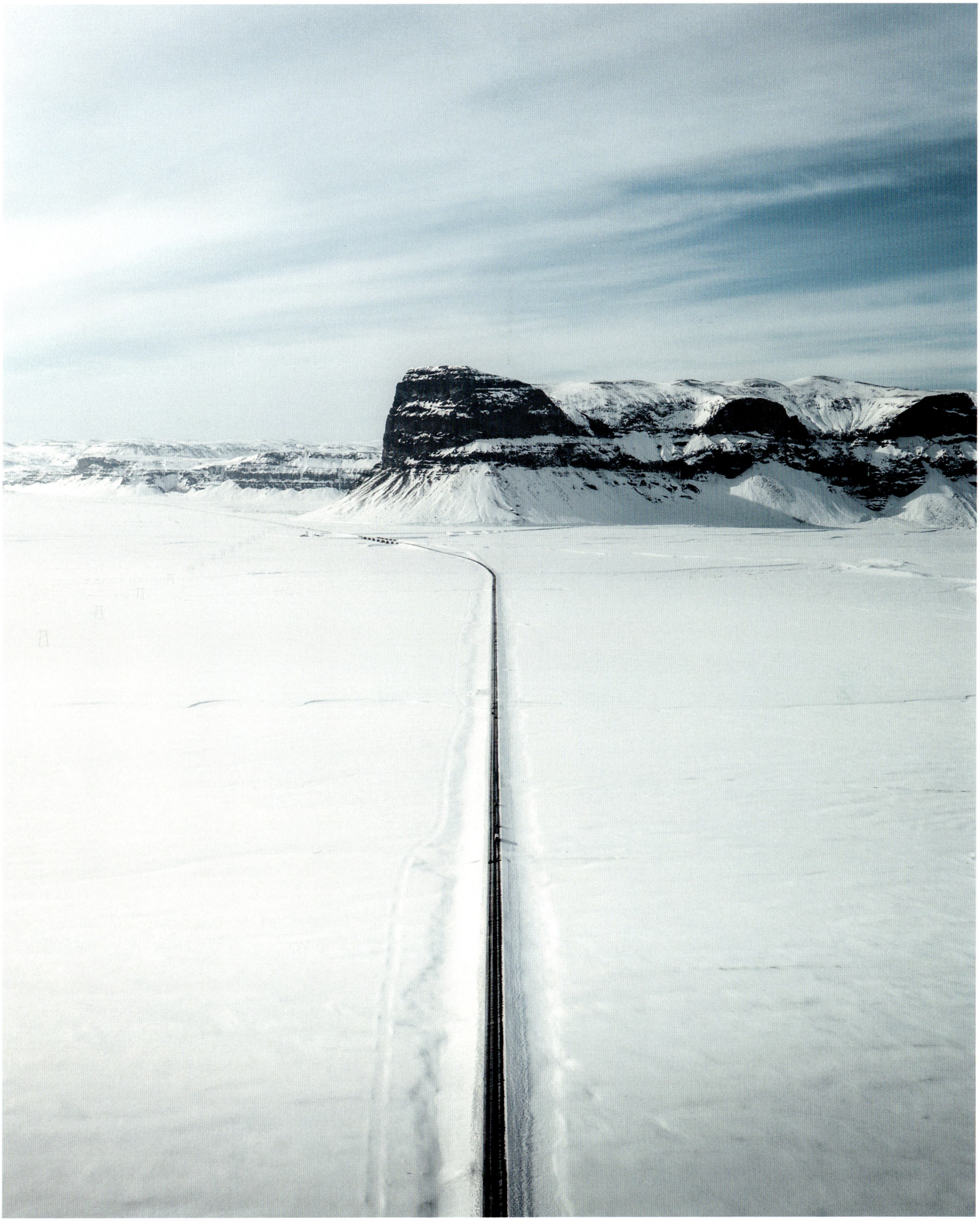

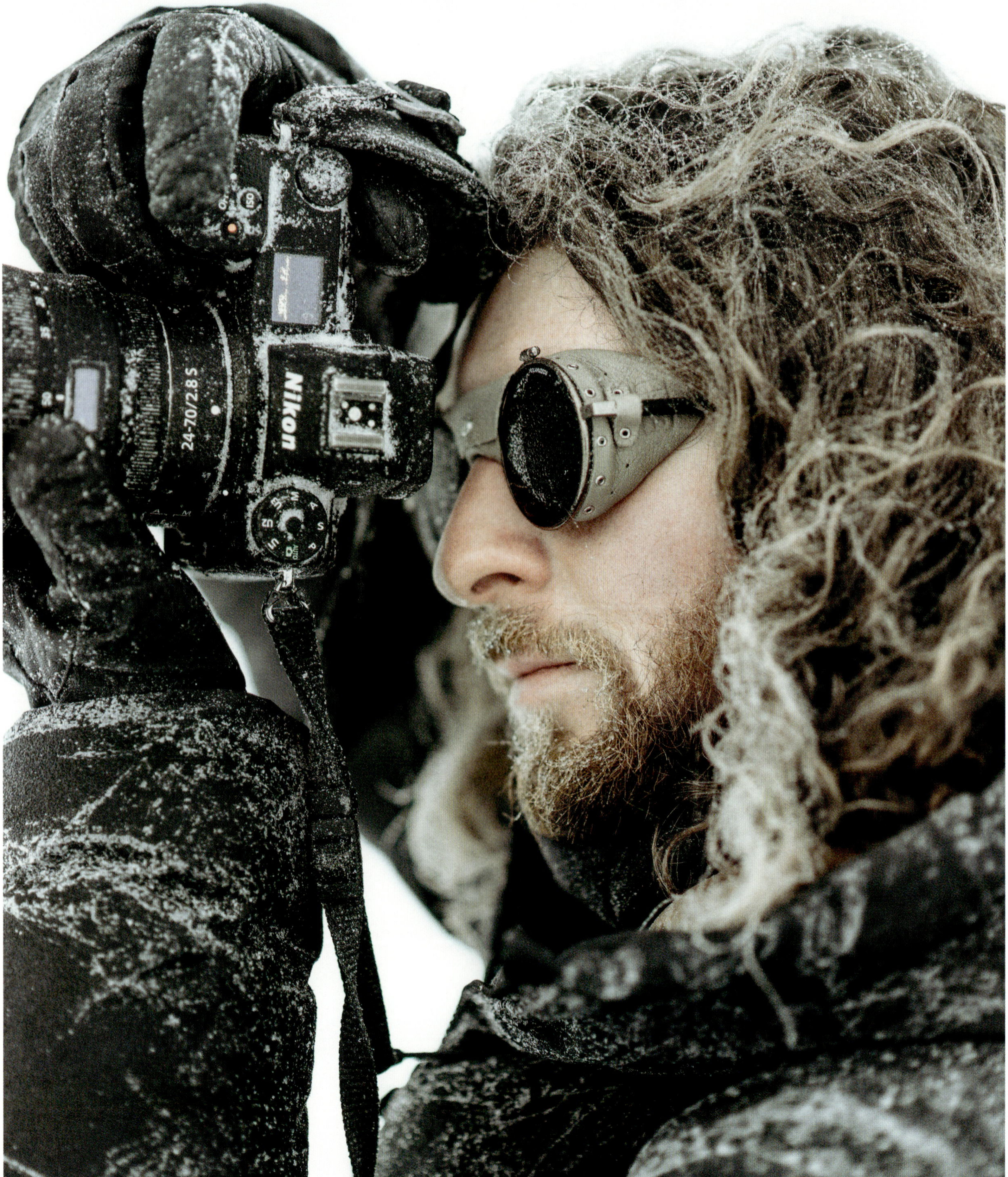
24-70/2.8 S
Nikon

ABOUT THE AUTHOR

Norris Niman's ultimate goal is to capture the remote, untamed parts of the world and share them with you all, bringing you along on grand adventures through the lens, turning wild nature into a massive playground.

Based in the northernmost town in Iceland, Niman has for the past decade forged a path as an award-winning photographer, filmmaker, and adventure guide in the cold climates of the North.

A Nikon Creator who works with brands such as Arc'teryx, DJI, Samsung, Toyota, Kia, Mazda, *Vogue*, and others, Niman's work is built on the excitement of the outdoors, the peace in nature, the harsh arctic climates, and the adventurer's lifestyle. In search of wild, remote destinations and offbeat landscapes, he balances the unreal abstractness of these places with stories of the real people who thrive there.

Hand in hand with Niman's photography and videography comes guiding. Since 2011, Niman has shared the beauty of these fragile landscapes by leading a curated array of specialized adventure tours and photography workshops, with many epic moments shared with thousands of people.

Check out www.norrisniman.com or @norrisniman everywhere else for more photos and fine art prints, as well as tours, workshops, courses, exhibitions, and other good things.

First published in 2026 by Epic Ink,
an imprint of The Quarto Group,
135 West 36th Street, 13th Floor,
New York, NY 10018, USA
(212) 779-4972
www.Quarto.com

EEA Representation, WTS Tax d.o.o.,
Žanova ulica 3, 4000 Kranj, Slovenia.
www.wts-tax.si

10 9 8 7 6 5 4 3 2 1

ISBN: 978-1-57715-959-9

Digital edition published in 2026
eISBN: 978-1-57715-960-5

Library of Congress Cataloging-in-Publication Data

Names: Niman, Norris author photographer
Title: The wild magic of Iceland : a photographic journey through the seasons / Norris Niman.
Description: New York : Epic Ink, 2026. | Summary: "The Wild Magic of Iceland reveals this Arctic wonderland's otherworldly beauty through every season in over one hundred stunning photographs by acclaimed photographer and adventurer Norris Niman"-- Provided by publisher.
Identifiers: LCCN 2026006580 (print) | LCCN 2026006581 (ebook) | ISBN 9781577159599 hardcover | ISBN 9781577159605 ebook
Subjects: LCSH: Iceland--Description and travel | LCGFT: Illustrated works
Classification: LCC DL315 .N56 2026 (print) | LCC DL315 (ebook) | DDC 914.91204--dc23/eng/20260410
LC record available at https://lccn.loc.gov/2026006580
LC ebook record available at https://lccn.loc.gov/2026006581

Publisher: Rage Kindelsperger
Creative Director: Laura Drew
Managing Editor: Cara Donaldson
Senior Acquiring Editor: Nicole James
Editor: Natalie Butterfield
Cover and Interior Design: Annie Marino

Printed in Huizhou City, Guangdong, China TT062026

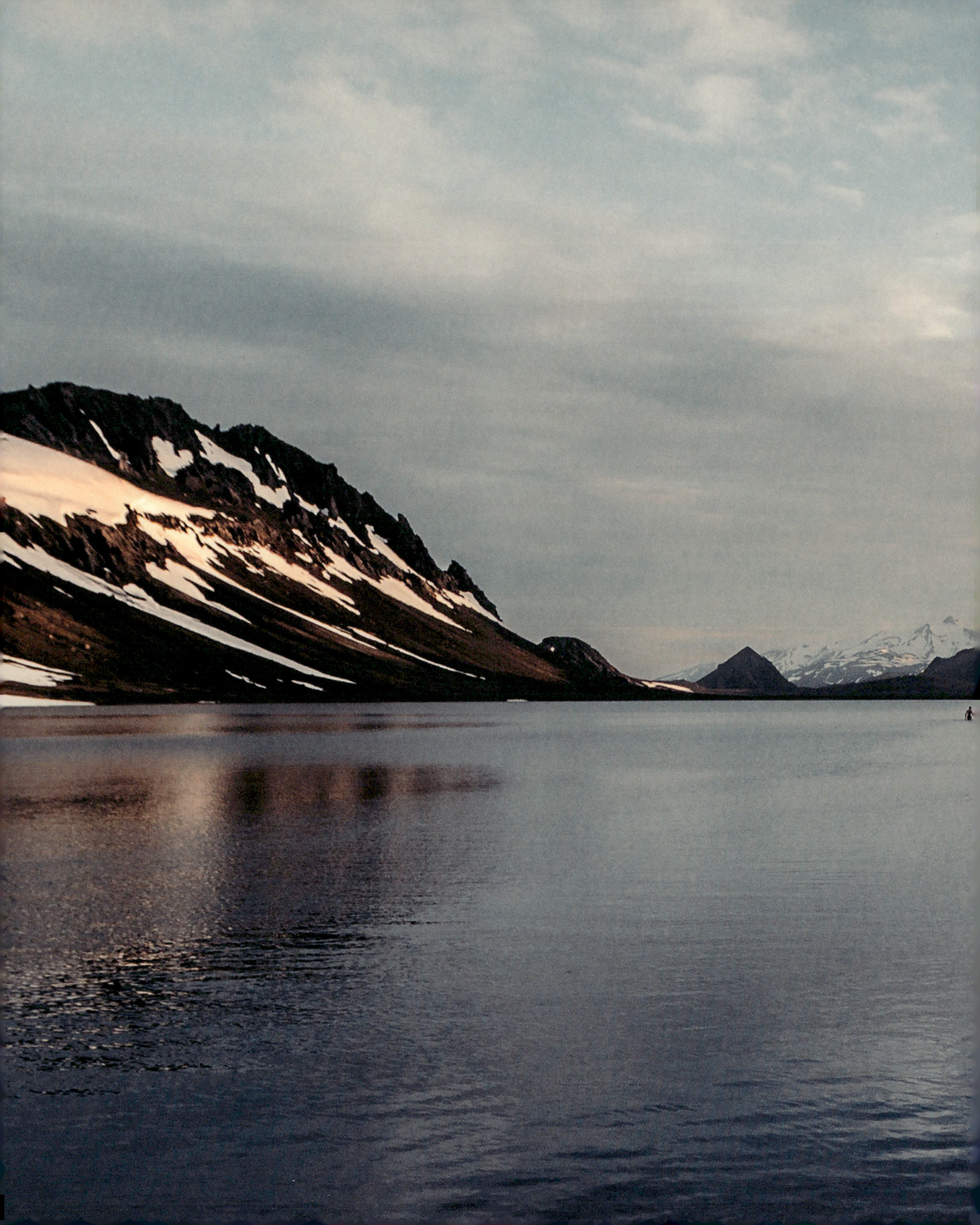